Import/Export Documentation

Books by the same author:

Economics of Shipping Practice and Management, 2nd edition, 1988, Chapman and Hall, London.

Elements of Export Marketing and Management, 1st edition, 1984, Chapman and Hall, London.

Elements of Export Practice, 2nd edition, 1984, Chapman and Hall, London.

Elements of Shipping, 6th edition, 1989, Chapman and Hall, London.

Elements of Port Operation and Management, 1st edition, 1986, Chapman and Hall, London.

Dictionary of Commercial Terms and Abbreviations, 1st edition, 1983, Witherby and Co. Ltd, London.

Dictionary of Shipping International Trade Terms and Abbreviations, 3rd edition, 1987 (9000 entries), Witherby and Co. Ltd, London.

Dictionary of English-Arabic Commercial, International Trade and Shipping Terms, 1st edition, 1988 (2200 entries), Witherby and Co. Ltd, London.

Import/Export Documentation

Alan E. Branch FCIT, FIEx

Senior Lecturer and Chief Examiner in Shipping and Export Practice,
Shipping and Export Consultant, Export Director

CHAPMAN & HALL

London · Glasgow · Weinheim · New York · Tokyo · Melbourne · Madras

Published by Chapman & Hall, 2-6 Boundary Row, London SE1 8HN, UK

Chapman & Hall, 2-6 Boundary Row, London SE1 8HN, UK

Blackie Academic & Professional, Wester Cleddens Road, Bishopbriggs, Glasgow G64 2NZ, UK

Chapman & Hall GmbH, Pappelallee 3, 69469 Weinheim, Germany

Chapman & Hall USA, One Penn Plaza, 41st Floor, New York, NY10119, USA

Chapman & Hall Japan, ITP - Japan, Kyowa Building, 3F, 2-2-1 Hirakawacho, Chiyoda-ku, Tokyo 102, Japan

Chapman & Hall Australia, Thomas Nelson Australia, 102 Dodds Street, South Melbourne, Victoria 3205, Australia

Chapman & Hall India, R. Seshadri, 32 Second Main Road, CIT East, Madras 600 035, India

First edition 1990
Reprinted 1994

© 1990 A. E. Branch

Typeset in 11/13pt Palatino by Mayhew Typesetting, Bristol
Printed in Great Britain at the University Press, Cambridge

ISBN   0 412 27670 4

A Catalogue record for this book is available from the British Library

Library of Congress Cataloging-in-Publication Data available

To
Margaret and David

Contents

Acknowledgements

ABC Company Ltd
Africa Ocean Lines Ltd
Amari Overseas Ltd
Arab-British Chamber of Commerce
Baltic and International Maritime
Conference
Baltic Mercantile and Shipping
Exchange Ltd
Barclays Bank plc
Ben Line Containers Ltd
Bexley London Borough
Borchard Lines Ltd
British Airways
British Overseas Trade Board
China Ocean Shipping Company
Corporation of Lloyd's
Cotecna International Ltd
Formecon Services Ltd
Freight Transport Association
General Council of British Shipping
HM Customs and Excise
International Air Transport
Association
International Maritime Organisation
Islamic Republic of Iran Shipping
Lines

Key Industrial Equipment Ltd
Leapold Walford Shipping Ltd
LEP Transport Ltd
Lloyd's Bank plc
Lloyd's of London
Lloyd's Register of Shipping
London Chamber of Commerce and
Industry
Lufthansa
E.D.F. Mann (Cocoa) Ltd
MAT International Group Ltd
Midland Bank plc
Mitsui OSK Lines Ltd
Morgan Air Freight Ltd
National Westminster Bank plc
P&O Containers Ltd (formerly
OCL, Overseas Containers Ltd)
Port of Singapore Authority
Sea Containers Ltd
SGS Inspection Services Ltd
Simpler of International Trade
Procedures Board (SITPRO)
Stewart Wrightson International
Group Ltd
Swiss Bank Corporation
W.G. Spice and Co. Ltd

Preface

Since the publication of my books *Elements of Shipping, Elements of Export Practice* and *Elements of Export Marketing and Management* – all selling in over 130 countries – I have received numerous requests, both in the UK and overseas for a companion volume on documentation. These requests reflect the growing need for such a publication to serve as an *aide-mémoire* for all those promoting international trade, including the exporter, importer, shipowner, shipbroker, forwarding agent, international bankers and so on.

This book has been written to provide a practical overall understanding of some of the more important documents found in export, import and shipping practice. The opportunity has been taken to provide where appropriate a check list to lessen the risk of the discrepancies or errors when using such documents.

The documents assembled here are intended not only for persons engaged in the day-to-day practice of international trade but also for students attending documentation courses. The book is written both for the UK and overseas markets.

The book will be useful to students taking international trade, shipping, charting, export, transport, import and finance examinations under the aegis of the Institute of Chartered Ship-brokers, the Institute of Freight Forwarders, the Institute of Export, the Institute of Transport Administration, the Institute of Bankers, and the Chartered Institute of Transport. Students attending export, shipping and import documentation courses sponsored by Chambers of Commerce, Colleges, Export Clubs, Trade Associations and so on will find the book essential reading as will those attending the Foundation Course in Overseas Trade International Physical Distribution subjects and Shipbroking. Overall the book will be especially useful in export, import, shipping, forwarding, port, transport or chartering offices. All exporters, importers, freight forwarders, airlines, agents, shipowners, international road hauliers, shipbrokers, etc. will find it essential.

A book containing such a variety of documents cannot be complete without the aid of numerous organizations both at home and overseas who have helped me so enthusiastically in their various contributions. These organizations appear under 'Acknowledgements' and I am grateful for their help.

Finally I would particularly like to acknowledge with grateful thanks the generous secretarial help from my lifelong friends Mr and Mrs Splarn, my friend Maurice Hicks for proof-reading, and as always my dear wife Kathleen for her forbearance, encouragement and help in this task.

19 The Ridings
Emmer Green
Reading
Berkshire

AEB
Course Director of International Trade
Basingstoke College of Technology
Basingstoke, Hampshire

Scope of book

This book is written primarily for the student or businessman/woman (export/import/shipping/port etc. executive) who knows little or virtually nothing of documentation within the practice of international trade.

In particular it covers documentation found in air freight, chartering, commercial documents, customs, dangerous cargo, finance, insurance, road transport, shipping and so on.

Overall it is written in a simple but lucid style. It reflects the author's very wide experience in international trade spanning over 30 years. This embraces work not only in the industry itself, but also as a lecturer and consultant in the subject at home and overseas and as a member of a special four-man subject specialist team brought together to evolve for HM Government a Foundation Course in Overseas Trade sponsored by the British Overseas Trade Board.

Documentation is an area of great importance in international trade. One cannot stress too strongly the need to ensure that individual documents are correctly completed. Successful international trade is only realized through complete professionalism in the use and execution of documentation with a zero error rate, otherwise delays are encountered when processing the goods through Customs, payment etc. which are costly to the shipper. It is a publication which should be found on the office bookshelf of every exporter, importer, shipping and freight forwarder and shipbroker.

1 Air freight: commercial

1.1 INTRODUCTION

Overall some 10 % in value and approximately 1 % in volume of international trade is conveyed by air. The great majority of the merchandise is conveyed on scheduled airline services as distinct from chartered services.

The document accompanying the goods throughout transit is called an Air Waybill. Some 80 % of the goods are conveyed under consolidation/groupage arrangements initiated by the International Air Transport Association (IATA) agent who issues the (house) Air Waybill. The remainder is booked direct with the airline that issues the Air Waybill.

When cargo has arrived at a destination airport, it is the practise for the airline or air freight agent to inform the consignee. However, where the consignee has no agent specified in the Air Waybill and has failed to contact the airline regarding the processing of the imported goods, an (Air) Cargo Arrival Notice may be issued by the airline.

Where the consignment forms part of a groupage or consolidated international consignment a House Air Waybill is issued by a consolidator (usually a freight forwarder) and is a certificate of shipment of a specified consignment for a particular flight.

Information for the preparation of the Air Waybill by the airline or IATA agent is supplied by the shipper in a Shipper's Letter of Instruction.

1.2 AIR WAYBILL

Description

An Air Waybill is the document that accompanies goods conveyed by the airline throughout the transit. It is an air consignment note. It is not a document of title or transferable/negotiable instrument. Overall it is a receipt for the goods for dispatch and is prima facie evidence of the conditions of carriage.

Source of document

Airline, e.g. British Airways.

Purpose/use/function

A single Air Waybill covers carriage over any distance by IATA scheduled services by as many airlines as may be required to complete the transportation. When goods carried by one airline for part of the journey are transferred to another airline, the original Air Waybill is sent forward with the consignment from the point of original departure to the final destination under a through rate. The main functions of the Air Waybill are a contract of carriage, and a receipt for goods; providing a unique reference for handling inventory control and documentation, including description of goods, and full rating information, including special handling requirements, routeing details including interchange airports where the cargo is transferred from one airline to another airline flight, and provides basic details for the aircraft manifest. Post-flight information includes a document source for revenue collection, interlining accounting and proration and cargo statistics. At destination airports the Air Waybill serves as a basic document for verification to consignee, Customs clearance and delivery to consignee. Additionally, it is a source document for clearance and delivery-charges accounting.

Legal context

The conditions of carriage are found on the reverse side of the Air Waybill document and are subject to the Carriage by Air Act 1961. This is based on the Warsaw Convention of 1929 as amended by the Hague Protocol of 1955 and Guadalajara amendments. Overall, it is subject to the supplementary provisions in the Carriage by Air Act 1961.

Ratifying organizations/countries

The IATA Air Waybill is ratified by almost every country throughout the world except certain Comecon countries. This permits interchangeability of the document throughout the transit thereby permitting through cargo transits under one document. A central clearing financial house is situated in Brussels where inter-airline accounts are settled monthly.

Procedure

Instructions for completing the form

Where more than one package is involved, the carrier can require the consignor to make out separate Air Waybills. The air consignment note must be printed in one of the official languages of the country of departure, e.g. French, German, etc. Erasures are not admissible but alterations can be made provided they are authenticated by the consignor's signature or initials. If quantities, weights or values are altered, they must appear in words as well as figures.

Necessary authorization

Goods are either conveyed under consolidation/groupage arrangements initiated by the IATA agent who issues the Air Waybill, or booked direct with the airline that issues the Air Waybill.

Number and allocation of copies

Usually there are 12 copies of each Air Waybill for distribution to the shipper, sales agent, issuing carrier (airline operator), consignee, delivery receipt, airport of destination, third carrier (if applicable), second carrier (if applicable), first carrier, extra copy for carrier (when required), invoice, and airport of departure. Copies 1, 2 and 3 are originals.

Checklist of what should accompany each copy

Documents accompanying each Air Waybill will vary by type of commodity and destination country.

Discrepancies (i.e. likely errors) and their consequences

The cargo description must be identical on all documents accompanying the consignment.

Further information

Under a documentary letter of credit certain specific information or instructions to be shown on the Air Waybill may be requested. This usually includes: names and addresses of the exporter, importer and first carrier/airline; the names of the airports of departure and destination together with details of any special route; the date of the flight; the declared value of the merchandise for Customs purposes; the number of packages with marks, weights, quantity and dimensions; the freight charge per unit of weight/volume; the technical description of the goods and not the commercial description; whether the freight charge has been prepaid or will be paid at the destination; the signature of the exporter (or his agent); the place and date of issue; and finally the signature of the issuing carrier (or his agent).

125 | 1044 4420

CSR/ECI

125-1044 4420

Shipper's Name and Address	Shipper's account Number

Not negotiable
Air Waybill
(Air Consignment note)
Issued by
British Airways London
Member of IATA

British airways

Copies 1, 2 and 3 of this Air Waybill are originals and have the same validity

Consignee's Name and Address	Consignee's account Number

It is agreed that the goods described herein are accepted in apparent good order and condition (except as noted) for carriage SUBJECT TO THE CONDITIONS OF CONTRACT ON THE REVERSE HEREOF. THE SHIPPER'S ATTENTION IS DRAWN TO THE NOTICE CONCERNING CARRIERS' LIMITATION OF LIABILITY. Shipper may increase such limitation of liability by declaring a higher value for carriage and paying a supplemental charge if required.

Issuing Carrier's Agent Name and City	Accounting Information

Agent's IATA Code	Account No.

Airport of Departure (Addr. of first Carrier) and requested Routing

to	By first Carrier	Routing and Destination	to	by	to	by	Currency	CHGS Code	WT/VAL PPD COLL	Other PPD COLL	Declared Value for Carriage	Declared Value for Customs

Airport of Destination	Flight/Date	For Carrier Use only	Flight/Date

Handling Information

No of Pieces RCP	Gross Weight	kg lb	Rate Class / Commodity Item No.	Chargeable Weight	Rate / Charge	Total	Nature and Quantity of Goods (incl. Dimensions or Volume)

Prepaid	Weight Charge	Collect	Other Charges

Valuation Charge

Tax

Total other Charges Due Agent

Total other Charges Due Carrier

Shipper certifies that the particulars on the face hereof are correct and that insofar as any part of the consignment contains dangerous goods, such part is properly described by name and is in proper condition for carriage by air according to the applicable Dangerous Goods Regulations.

....
Signature of Shipper or his Agent

Total prepaid	Total collect

Currency Conversion Rates	cc charges in Dest. Currency

Executed on .... (Date) at .... (Place)

....
Signature of Issuing Carrier or its Agent

For Carrier's Use only at Destination	Charges at Destination	Total collect Charges

125-1044 4420

Original 3 - (For Shipper)

1.3 (AIR) CARGO ARRIVAL NOTICE

Description

An (Air) Cargo Arrival Notice is a letter of advice and request to the consignee, issued only when the client has failed to contact the airline regarding the processing of the imported goods.

Source of document

Airline, e.g. British Airways; or IATA Air Freight agent.

Purpose/use/function

To inform the consignee of the arrival of the goods at the specified airport; and to request the appropriate documents to enable the consignment to be cleared through Customs.

Legal context

The Air Waybill is the contract of carriage between the shipper and airline. The Warsaw convention states that the Air Waybill must have three original copies: one signed by the exporter for the carrier retention; one signed by the exporter and carrier for the consignee, and which accompanies the goods; and thirdly, one signed by the carrier and retained by the exporter.

Ratifying organizations/countries

Most countries except Comecon countries recognize the IATA Air Waybill.

Procedure

Instructions for completing the form

The shipper or his IATA Agent will complete the Air Waybill on date supplied by the shipper found on the export invoice.

Necessary authorization

Forwarding instructions are requested where appropriate, together with confirmation that the consignee wishes the airline to act as the client's agent.

Number and allocation of copies

Up to 12 copies are completed with each consignment.

Checklist of what should accompany each copy

Special attention should be given in the completion of Air Waybill to ensure the correct technical description of the cargo is given and not a commercial description.

Discrepancies

Discrepancies likely to emerge are the cargo valuation relative to insurance provision, wrong routeing, dispute over collection charges at the destination airport debited to the importer and so on.

British Airways

British airways cargo

Urgent cargo arrival notice

Import Customer Services
Cargocentre London (S127)
London (Heathrow) Airport
PO Box 99
Hounslow, Middlesex TW6 2JS
Telephone: 01-759 2351
Telegrams: Cargocentre Heathrow London
Telex: 22707

Arrival date

Air waybill number

Dear Sirs,

We have pleasure in informing you that a consignment as detailed on the enclosed airwaybill has arrived at London (Heathrow) Airport, and awaits Customs clearance.

Will you please complete in full the pro-forma overleaf and return to British Airways together with the airwaybill, forwarding instructions, invoices, packing lists, certificates and any other relevant customs documents.

We will on your request normally arrange to reforward the consignment by a road contractor to final destination. The road contractor's terms and conditions of carriage which have a limited liability will apply.

Alternatively you may complete the Delivery Order attached to this form and send it, together with the airwaybill and relevant documents to your Customs Clearance and Forwarding Agent.

Storage charges are applied to consignments uncollected after a free period of 48 hours, excluding two day weekends and Public Holidays and commencing 0800 hours on the day following the day of arrival. Storage charges terminate on collection or delivery of goods from carrier's premises. Details of storage rates can be obtained from any British Airways Cargo Office.

Note: When an Import consignment is cleared and delivered in split lots, storage charges are applied to each part of this shipment based on the gross weight of each with any appropriate minimum applied.

Yours faithfully

Import Customer Services
K210(5th)

List of enclosures

◯ Invoices ◯ Form C1314
◯ Packing list ◯ Form C3
◯ Form C109A

British Airways can only act as your agent if you fully complete the following questionnaire

Our reference: _____ Telephone Nr: _____

Please arrange Customs clearance of our consignment

The details you require for this purpose are as follows:

Enter details relative to your consignment ▶

Type of goods	Customs tariff heading	Rate of duty
Amount of insurance	Details of Customs Valuation Order	
Our VAT Registration number or TURN number is:		
And you are authorised to enter these goods against these numbers		

We enclose the following:

Indicate enclosure by ticking appropriate boxes ▶

Air waybill	C109A	C1314	C217	C218			
Invoices	Packing lists			Import licence		Cheque for Duty and VAT ax	
Nr	Nr					Amounting to £	

Are you collecting this consignment?
(Tick appropriate box) ▶

Yes	No

If not:—

Enter name and address to which consignment is to be sent *NB ▶

Please arrange delivery to:

NB Delivery not applicable to consignemnts of a high value.

My British Airways account number is: ▶ _____

Importer's signature _____

Enter date, signature and name of Company ▶ Date _____

Company's name _____

1.4 HOUSE AIR WAYBILL

Description

A House Air Waybill is a certificate of shipment of a specified consignment for a particular flight(s); the consignment forms part of a groupage or consolidated international consignment.

Source of document

A consolidator, usually a freight forwarder, e.g. Morgan Air Freight Ltd.

Purpose/use/function

It merely acts as a cargo receipt for the exporter to confirm the goods have been accepted by the airline, but is not recognized by Banks officially as a document to effect payment of the goods. This is found in the Master Air Waybill covering the complete consolidated consignment.

Legal context

It has no legal context but is merely accepted in the trade through 'the custom of the trade' concept reflecting understanding and confidence between the seller and buyer and intermediaries.

Ratifying organizations/countries

No countries have ratified the role of the document.

Procedure

Instructions for completing the form

The IATA Agent completes the House Air Waybill on data supplied by the shipper.

Other aspects

The House Air Waybill has become more common during the past decade as the IATA Air Freight Consolidator Agent has developed his business. It is a document completed by the Agent and discrepancies which arise from its completion usually emerge from incorrect data supplied by the shipper to the Agent. An increasing number of Banks recognize the document as a means of facilitating payment of the goods.

MASTER AWB No		CRN No	HAWB No

Format approved by
The Institute of Freight Forwarders Ltd.
HM Customs & Excise
and SITPRO, London, 1984.
Refer to IATA Recommended Practice 1600j (III)

Consignor/Shipper (Name, Address, A/C No.)

Consignee (Name, Address, A/C No.)

HOUSE AIR WAYBILL (Air Consignment Note)

Issued by

MORGAN
MORGAN AIR FREIGHT LIMITED
Unit 2A, Cathedral Hill Industrial Estate.
Guildford, Surrey GU2 5YB
Telephone: Guildford (0483) 33011-4
Telex: 859542

Copies 1, 2 and 3 of this Air Waybill are originals and have the same validity.

Agent's Name and City

Accounting Information

Place of Departure and requested Routing

to	By first Carrier	Routing and Destination	to	by	to	by	Currency	wt/val PPD COLL	Other PPC COLL		Declared Value for Customs

Place of Destination	Flight/Date	Flight/Date	Amount of Insurance	INSURANCE - If Shipper requests insurance in accordance with issuers conditions indicate amount to be insured in figures in box marked Amount of Insurance.

Handling Information (including Marks or Numbers on packages and method of packing)

No. of packages RCP	Gross Weight	kg/lb	Rate Class / Commodity Item No.	Chargeable Weight	Rate / Charge	Total	Nature and Quantity of Goods (inc. Dimensions or Volume)

Prepaid	Weight Charge	Collect	Other Charges

It is agreed that the goods herein are accepted subject to issuer's conditions of contract. If the carriage involves an ultimate destination or stop in a country other than the country of departure, the Warsaw Convention may be applicable and the Convention governs and in most cases limits the liability of carriers in respect of loss of, damage or delay to cargo. Agreed stopping places are those places (other than the places of departure or destination) detailed under "Routing" herein and/or those places shown in the timetables of any carriers performing carriage hereunder as scheduled stopping places for the route.

Shipper certifies that the particulars on the face hereof are correct

Signature of Shipper or his Agent ....

Total prepaid	Total collect

Currency Conversion Rates	cc charges in Dest. Currency

Executed on   (Date)   at   (Place)   Signature of Issuer

FREIGHT FORMS TTCS LTD. 0908 313656

Original 3-(For the Consignor)

1.5 SHIPPER'S LETTER OF INSTRUCTION

Description

A Shipper's Letter of Instruction is a standardized form prepared by the shipper and submitted to the airline or IATA agent giving clear and complete forwarding instructions.

Source of document

Airline, e.g. Lufthansa.

Purpose/use/function

The Shipper's Letter of Instruction when completed by the shipper is intended to supply accurate information for the preparation of the Air Waybill by the airline or IATA agent. It confirms details of the merchandise to be exported by air provided earlier by telephone from the shipper to the airline/IATA agent.

Legal context

It has no legal context, but the exporter is responsible for the validity of the data relative to the cargo description on the Air Waybill and an indemnity exists to the carrier for any inaccuracies. Misrepresentation of the facts by the Exporter has serious legal implications.

Ratifying organizations/countries

It is recognized by most world Airlines through the IATA umbrella.

Procedure

Instructions for completing the form

The form should be prepared in duplicate by the shipper.

Necessary authorization

The document should be authenticated by an Executive of the Shipper's Company.

Number and allocation of copies

The document (in duplicate) is handed to the vehicle driver at the time the goods are collected. The duplicate copy should be signed upon receipt of goods by the airline or its IATA agent as proof of receipt of goods for shipment and returned to the shipper.

Other aspects

The exporter is required to provide requisite Customs documents and the carrier has an indemnity if the shipper fails to do so. Claims have to be submitted within a prescribed time limit.

Shipper's Letter of Instruction for Dispatch of Goods (SLI)

SHIPPER

⊖ **Lufthansa**

CONSIGNEE

Please prepare this form in duplicate. Duplicate copy of this SLI will be signed upon receipt of goods by Lufthansa or its IATA-CARGO-Agent as proof of receipt of goods for shipment and returned to shipper.

ADDRESS FOR NOTIFICATION

You are hereby requested and authorized upon receipt of the consignment to prepare the air waybill according to the instructions contained herein, sign the air waybill on our behalf and dispatch the consignment in accordance with "Lufthansa Conditions of Contract" as laid down on the reverse of the duplicate copy of this SLI. It is understood that all limitations of liability contained in the said Lufthansa Conditions of Contract shall apply from and after delivery of the goods to Lufthansa, even before the execution of the air waybill.

AIRPORT OF DEPARTURE	AIRPORT OF DESTINATION

REQUESTED ROUTING

REQUESTED BOOKING

We certify that the contents of this consignment is properly identified by name. Insofar as any part of the consignment contains dangerous goods, such part is in proper condition for carriage by air according to IATA's Dangerous Goods Regulation. (This does not replace the Shipper's Declaration for Dangerous Goods.)

MARKS AND NUMBERS	NO. & KIND OF PKGS.	DESCRIPTION OF GOODS	GROSS WEIGHT	MEASUREMENT

AIR FREIGHT CHARGES
(Mark one to apply)

☐ PREPAID

☐ COLLECT (If Service Available)

OTHER CHARGES
At Origin
(Mark one to apply)

☐ PREPAID

☐ COLLECT (If Service Available)

Transport Insurance on Lufthansa Air Waybill
For details please see our brochure "Air Cargo Insurance from Door to Door".
Amount of Insurance: _____
Please check if applicable (subject to premium surcharge) ☒:

☐ The risks of war, hijacking of aircraft, strikes, riots and civil commotions are included.

☐ Storage coverage for further _____ days (initial 30 days free of surcharge)

Please observe the Special Premium for live animals, perishables, personal effects/ household goods.

DECLARED VALUE

For Carriage	For Customs

HANDLING INFORMATION AND REMARKS

RECEIVED IN GOOD ORDER AND CONDITION

DATE   SIGNATURE

Form 1815 N-83 (CGN XC 2) Printed in Germany

2 Chartering: sea transport

2.1 INTRODUCTION

A very large proportion of the world's trade is carried in chartered vessels. The tonnage may be a bulk cargo vessel carrying ore, oil, timber or fertilizer; liner cargo tonnage where a container ship engaged on regular schedules supplements the existing fleet to meet seasonal demands; or a ship carrying an indivisible load requiring special facilities or arrangements.

The contract between the shipowner and the charterer is known as the Charter Party.

The Charter Party can be either demise or non-demise. For a demise charter the shipowner provides only the vessel, and the charterer provides the cargo and crew. For non-demise charter the shipowner provides the vessel and her crew, and the charterer provides only the cargo. For certain commodities in specified trades about 50 different Charter Parties have been approved or recommended by BIMCO/GCBS. Examples are included here of Charter Parties specific to the timber trade in the Baltic and North Sea (code name Nubaltwood), and to the movement of ore (code name Orevoy). A number of Charter Parties have associated Bills of Lading, e.g. Nubaltwood and Orevoy.

For standardizing the presentation of expenses incurred while a vessel is in port, a (Chartering) Standard Disbursements Account form is used as devised/approved by BIMCO. This enables calculations to be made for a demurrage charge on the charterer where the prescribed loading and/or unloading time has been exceeded (Standard Time Sheet), and for dispatch payments to the charterer where loading and/or unloading are ahead of schedule (Standard Statement of Facts).

2.2 CHARTER PARTY

Description

A Charter Party is the document under which a vessel is hired or chartered. There are basically two types of Charter Party: demise, e.g. Barecon 'A'; and non-demise, e.g. Linertime. For particular commodities about 50 specific trade Charter Parties have been approved. See, for example, the Nubaltwood Charter Party (section 2.4).

Source of document

The Baltic and International Maritime Conference (BIMCO), Copenhagen.

Purpose/use/function

The Charter Party serves as a contract whereby a shipowner agrees to place the ship, or part of it, at the disposal of a merchant or other person (known as the charterer), for the carriage of goods from one port to another port on being paid freight, or to let the ship for a specified period, the shipowner's remuneration being known as hire money.

Legal context

In a demise or bareboat charter the charterer is responsible for providing the cargo and crew, while the shipowner provides merely the vessel. In consequence, the charterer appoints the crew, thus taking over full responsibility for the operation of the vessel, and pays all expenses incurred. A demise Charter Party is for a period of time which may vary from a few weeks to several years.

In a non-demise charter the shipowner provides the vessel and her crew, while the charterer supplies merely the cargo for a particular voyage or period of time of specified dates. The shipowners continue to manage their own vessel, both under non-demise voyage and time Charter Parties. With a time charter, it is usual for the charterer to pay port dues and fuel costs, and overtime payments incurred.

The terms, conditions and exceptions under which the goods are carried are set out in the Charter Party. It will be appreciated that the terms and conditions of a Charter Party may vary according to the wishes of the parties to the contract.

Ratifying organizations/countries

The General Council of British Shipping and/or the Baltic and International Maritime Conference have approved or recommended a number of Charter Parties – about 50 – for certain commodities in specified trades.

Barecon 'A'

An example of a bareboat (or demise) Charter Party is Barecon 'A', approved by BIMCO, the Japan Shipping Exchange Inc. and the General Council of British Shipping.

Linertime

An example of a non-demise Charter Party used in the liner cargo trade is the Charter Party code name Linertime, a deep sea charter approved by BIMCO.

Other aspects

It will be appreciated that no statutory terms exist in regard to the terminology found in a Charter Party and both parties are free to insert their own terms. Extensive use is made of the BIMCO/GCBS range of Charter Parties for particular trades which are widely used and recognized. The Shipbroker is responsible for the Charter Party document completion in consultation with the parties to the contract. Some shipowners complete their own Charter Parties.

1. Shipbroker	**THE BALTIC AND INTERNATIONAL MARITIME CONFERENCE** **STANDARD BAREBOAT CHARTER** **CODE NAME: " BARECON 'A' "** PART I
	2. Place and date

3. Owners (Lessors)/Place of business	4. Charterers (Lessees)/Place of business

5. Vessel's name (Cl. 8)	6. Flag & country of registry (Cl. 8)	7. Call sign.

8. Type of Vessel (motor or steam, dry-cargo, tank, reefer or passenger)	9. GRT/NRT	10. When/where built
	11. Total dw. (abt.) in tons of 2,240 lbs. on summer freeboard	

12. Class (Cl. 8)	13. Date of last special survey by the Vessel's classification society

14. Further particulars of Vessel (also indicate minimum of months' validity of class certificates agreed acc. to Cl. 13)

15. Port of delivery (Cl. 1)	16. Time for delivery (Cl. 2)	17. Cancelling date (Cl. 3)	18. Port of re-delivery (Cl. 13)

19. Running days' notice if other than stated in Cl. 2	20. Frequency of dry-docking if other than stated in Cl. 8 (f)

21. Trading limits (Cl. 4)

22. Charter period	23. Charter hire (Cl. 9)

24. Currency and method of payment (Cl. 9)	25. Place of payment; also state beneficiary and bank account (Cl. 9)

26. Bank guarantee/bond (sum and place) (Cl. 21, optional)	27. Mortgage(s), if any (Cl. 10)

28. Insurance (marine and war risks) (state value acc. to Cl. 11 (e) or. if applicable, acc. to Cl. 12 (k)) (also state if Cl. 12 applies)	29. Additional insurance cover for Owners' account limited to (Cl. 11 (b) or, if applicable, Cl. 12 (g))

30. Additional insurance cover for Charterers' account limited to (Cl. 11 (b) or, if applicable, Cl. 12 (g))	31. Brokerage commission and to whom payable (Cl. 24)

32. Latent defects (only to be filled in if period other than stated in Cl.1)	33. Applicable law (Cl. 25)

34. Place of arbitration (Cl. 25)	35. Hire/purchase agreement (state if Part III applies) (optional)

36. Numbers of additional clauses covering special provisions, if agreed

PREAMBLE. – It is mutually agreed that this Contract shall be performed subject to the conditions contained in this Charter which shall include Part I as well as Part II. In the event of a conflict of conditions, the provisions of Part I shall prevail over those of Part II to the extent of such conflict. It is further mutually agreed that Part III shall only apply and shall only form part of this Charter if expressly agreed and stated in Box 35. If Part III applies it is further mutually agreed that in the event of a conflict of conditions, the provisions of Part I and Part II shall prevail over those of Part III to the extent of such conflict.

Signature (Owners (Lessors))	Signature (Charterers (Lessees))

1-0

1. Delivery

The Vessel shall be delivered and taken over by the Charterers at 2
the port indicated in Box 15, in such ready berth as the Charterers 3
may direct. 4
The Owners shall before and at the time of delivery exercise due 5
diligence to make the Vessel seaworthy and in every respect ready 6
in hull, machinery and equipment for service hereunder. The Vessel 7
shall be properly documented at time of delivery. 8
The delivery to the Charterers of the Vessel and the taking over of 9
the Vessel by the Charterers shall constitute a full performance by 10
the Owners of all the Owners' obligations hereunder, and thereafter 11
the Charterers shall not be entitled to make or assert any claim 12
against the Owners on account of any representations or warranties 13
expressed or implied with respect to the Vessel but the Owners 14
shall be responsible for repairs or renewals occasioned by latent 15
defects in the Vessel, her machinery or appurtenances, existing at 16
the time of delivery under the Charter, provided such defects have 17
manifested themselves within 18 months after delivery unless other- 18
wise provided in Box 32. 19

2. Time for Delivery

The Vessel to be delivered not before the date indicated in Box 16 21
unless with Charterers' consent. 22
Unless otherwise agreed in Box 19, the Owners to give the Charterers 23
not less than 30 running days' notice of the date on which the Vessel 24
is expected to be ready for delivery. 25
The Owners to keep the Charterers closely advised of possible 26
changes in the Vessel's position. 27

3. Cancelling

Should the Vessel not be delivered latest by the cancelling date 29
indicated in Box 17, the Charterers to have the option of cancelling 30
this Charter. 31
If it appears that Vessel will be delayed beyond the cancelling date, 32
Owners shall, as soon as they are in a position to state with 33
reasonable certainty the day on which Vessel should be ready, give 34
notice thereof to Charterers asking whether they will exercise their 35
option of cancelling, and the option must then be declared within 36
one hundred and sixty-eight (168) hours of the receipt by Charterers 37
of such notice. If Charterers do not then exercise their option of 38
cancelling, the seventh day after the readiness date stated in 39
Owners' notice shall be regarded as a new cancelling date for the 40
purpose of this Clause. 41

4. Trading Limits

The Vessel shall be employed in lawful trades for the carriage of 43
suitable lawful merchandise within the trading limits indicated in 44
Box 21. 45
Notwithstanding any other provisions contained in this Charter it 46
is agreed that nuclear fuels or radioactive products or waste are 47
specifically excluded from the cargo permitted to be loaded or 48
carried under this Charter. This exclusion does not apply to radio- 49
isotopes used or intended to be used for any industrial, commercial, 50
agricultural, medical or scientific purposes provided the Owners' 51
prior approval has been obtained to loading thereof. 52

5. Surveys

Survey on Delivery and Re-delivery. – The Owners and Charterers 54
shall each appoint surveyors for the purpose of determining and 55
agreeing in writing the condition of the Vessel at the time of delivery 56
and re-delivery hereunder. The Owners shall bear all expenses of 57
the On-Survey including loss of time, if any, and the Charterers 58
shall bear all expenses of the Off-Survey including loss of time, 59
if any, at the rate of hire per day or pro rata, also including in each 60
case the cost of any docking and undocking, if required, in con- 61
nection herewith. 62

6. Inspection

Inspection. – The Owners shall have the right at any time to inspect 64
or survey the Vessel or instruct a duly authorised surveyor to carry 65
out survey on their behalf to ascertain the condition of the 66
Vessel and satisfy themselves that the Vessel is being properly 67
repaired and maintained. Inspection or survey in dry-dock shall be 68
made only when the Vessel shall be in dry-dock for the Charterers' 69
purpose. However, Owners shall have the right to require the Vessel 70
to be dry-docked for inspection if Charterers are not docking her at 71
normal classification intervals. The fees for such inspection or 72
survey shall in the event of the Vessel being found to be in the 73
condition provided in Clause 8 of this Charter be payable by the 74
Owners and shall be paid by the Charterers only in the event of 75
the Vessel being found to require repairs or maintenance in order 76
to achieve the condition so provided. All time taken in respect of 77
inspection, survey or repairs shall count as time on hire and shall 78
form part of the Charter period. 79
The Charterers shall also permit the Owners to inspect the Vessel's 80
log books whenever requested and shall whenever required by the 81
Owners furnish them with full information regarding any casualties 82
or other accidents or damage to the Vessel. If required, the Char- 83
terers shall from time to time keep the Owners advised of the 84
intended employment of the Vessel. 85

7. Inventories and Consumable Oil and Stores

A complete inventory of the Vessel's entire equipment, outfit, ap- 86
pliances and of all consumable stores on board the Vessel shall be 87
made by the Charterers in conjunction with the Owners on delivery 88
and again on re-delivery of the Vessel. The Charterers and the 89
Owners respectively shall at the time of delivery and re-delivery take 90
over and pay for all bunkers, lubricating oil, water and unbroached 91
provisions, paints, oils, ropes and other consumable stores in the 92
said Vessel at their then current market prices at the ports of delivery 93
and re-delivery, respectively. 94
95

8. Maintenance and Operation

(a) The Vessel shall during the Charter period be in the full pos- 96
session and at the absolute disposal for all purposes of the Char- 97
terers and under their complete control in every respect. The Char- 98
terers shall maintain the Vessel, her machinery, boilers, appurtenan- 99
ces and spare parts in a good state of repair, in efficient operating 100
condition and in accordance with good commercial maintenance 102
practice and, except as provided for in Clause 12 (l), they shall keep 103
the Vessel with unexpired classification of the class indicated in 104
Box 12 and with other required certificates in force at all times. 105

The Charterers to take immediate steps to have the necessary 106
repairs done within a reasonable time failing which the Owners 107
shall have the right of withdrawing the Vessel from the service of 108
the Charterers without noting any protest and without prejudice to 109
any claim the Owners may otherwise have on the Charterers under 110
the Charter. 111
Unless otherwise agreed, in the event of any improvement, structural 112
changes or expensive new equipment becoming necessary for the 113
continued operation of the Vessel by reason of new class require- 114
ments or by compulsory legislation costing more than 5 per cent. 115
of the Vessel's marine insurance value as stated in Box 28, then 116
the arbitrators under Clause 25 shall have power to re-negotiate 117
this Contract in a reasonable way having regard, inter alia, to the 118
length of the period remaining under the Charter and may decide 119
the ratio in which the cost of compliance shall be shared between 120
the parties concerned. 121
The Charterers are required to establish and maintain financial 122
security or responsibility in respect of oil or other pollution damage 123
as required by any government, including Federal, state or municipal 124
or other division or authority thereof, to enable the Vessel, without 125
penalty or charge, lawfully to enter, remain at, or leave any port, 126
place, territorial or contiguous waters of any country, state or 127
municipality in performance of this Charter without any delay. This 128
obligation shall apply whether or not such requirements have been 129
lawfully imposed by such government or division or authority thereof. 130
The Charterers shall make and maintain all arrangements by bond 131
or otherwise as may be necessary to satisfy such requirements at 132
the Charterers' sole expense and the Charterers shall indemnify 133
the Owners against all consequences whatsoever (including loss of 134
time) for any failure or inability to do so. 135

TOVALOP SCHEME. *(Applicable to oil tank vessels only).* – The 136
Charterers are required to enter the Vessel under the **TOVALOP** 137
SCHEME or under any similar compulsory scheme upon delivery under 138
this Charter and to maintain her so during the currency of this Charter. 139

(b) The Charterers shall at their own expense and by their own 140
procurement man, victual, navigate, operate, supply, fuel and repair 141
the Vessel whenever required during the Charter period and they 142
shall pay all charges and expenses of every kind and nature what- 143
soever incidental to their use and operation of the Vessel under 144
this Charter, including any foreign government municipality and/or state 145
taxes. The Master, officers and crew of the Vessel shall be the 146
servants of the Charterers for all purposes whatsoever, even if for 147
any reason appointed by the Owners. 148
Charterers shall comply with the regulations regarding officers and 149
crew in force in the country of the Vessel's registry and also with 150
those of their own country. 151

(c) During the currency of this Charter, the Vessel shall retain her 152
present name as indicated in Box 5 and shall remain under and fly 153
the flag as indicated in Box 6. Provided, however, that the Charterers 154
shall have the liberty to paint the Vessel in their own colours, 155
install and display their funnel insignia and fly their own house flag. 156
Painting and re-painting, instalment and re-instalment to be for the 157
Charterers' account and time used thereby to count as time on hire. 158

(d) The Charterers shall make no structural changes in the Vessel 159
or changes in the machinery, boilers, appurtenances or spare parts 160
thereof without in each instance first securing the Owners' approval 161
thereof. If the Owners so agree, the Charterers shall, if the Owners 162
so require, restore the Vessel to its former condition before the 163
termination of the Charter. 164

(e) The Charterers shall have the use of all outfit, equipment, and 165
appliances on board the Vessel at the time of delivery, provided 166
the same or their substantial equivalent shall be returned to the 167
Owners on re-delivery in the same good order and condition as 168
when received, ordinary wear and tear excepted. The Charterers 169
shall from time to time during the Charter period replace such 170
items of equipment as shall be so damaged or worn as to be unfit 171
for use. Charterers are to procure that all repairs to or replacement 172
of any damaged, worn or lost parts or equipment be effected in 173
such manner (both as regards workmanship and quality of materials) 174
as not to diminish the value of the Vessel. The Charterers have the 175
right to fit additional equipment at their expense and risk but the 176
Charterers shall remove such equipment at the end of the period 177
if requested by the Owners. 178
Any equipment including radio equipment on hire on the Vessel 179
at time of delivery shall be kept and maintained by the Charterers 180
and the Charterers shall assume the obligations and liabilities of 181
the Owners under any lease contracts in connection therewith and 182
shall reimburse the Owners for all expenses incurred in connection 183
therewith, also for any new equipment required in order to comply 184
with radio regulations. 185

(f) The Charterers shall dry-dock the Vessel and clean and paint 186
her underwater parts whenever the same may be necessary, but not 187
less than once in every eighteen calendar months after delivery 188
unless otherwise agreed in Box 20. 189

9. Hire

(a) The Charterers shall pay to the Owners for the hire of the Vessel 191
at the lump sum per calendar month as indicated in Box 23 com- 192
mencing on and from the date and hour of her delivery to the 193
Charterers and at and after the agreed lump sum for any part of a 194
month. Hire to continue until the date and hour when the Vessel is 195
re-delivered by the Charterers to her Owners. 196

(b) Payment of Hire, except for the first and last month's Hire, if 197
sub-clause (c) of this Clause is applicable, shall be made in cash 198
without discount every month in advance on the first day of each 199
month in the currency and in the manner indicated in Box 24 and 200
at the place mentioned in Box 25. 201

(c) Payment of Hire for the first and last month's Hire if less than 202
a full month shall be calculated proportionally according to the 203
number of days in the particular calendar month and advance pay- 204
ment be effected accordingly. 205

(d) Should the Vessel be lost or missing, Hire to cease from the 206
date and time when she was lost or last heard of. Any Hire paid in 207
advance to be adjusted accordingly. 208

(e) In default of payment beyond a period of seven running days 209
the Owners to have the right of withdrawing the Vessel from the 210
service of the Charterers, without noting any protest and without 211
interference by any court or any other formality whatsoever and 212

without prejudice to any claim the Owners may otherwise have 213
against the Charterers under the Charter. 214

(f) Any delay in payment of Hire shall entitle the Owners to an 215
interest of 10 per cent. per annum. 216

10. Mortgage 217
Owners warrant that they have not effected any mortgage of the 218
Vessel unless otherwise indicated in Box 27. Owners hereby under- 219
take not to effect any (other) mortgage of the Vessel without Chart- 220
erers' prior approval. Any mortgage approved by Charterers here- 221
under is herein referred to as an "approved mortgage" and any 222
mortgagee under an approved mortgage is herein referred to as an 223
"approved mortgagee". 224

11. Insurance and Repairs 225
(a) During the Charter period the Vessel shall be kept insured by 226
Charterers at their expense against marine, war and Protection and 227
Indemnity risks in such form as Owners shall in writing approve, 228
which approval shall not be unreasonably withheld. Such marine, war 229
and P. and I. insurances shall be arranged by Charterers to protect 230
the interests of both Owners and Charterers and "approved mort- 231
gagees" (if any), and Charterers to be at liberty to protect under 232
such insurances the interests of any managers they may appoint. All 233
insurance policies shall be in the joint names of Owners and Chart- 234
erers as their interests may appear. 235
If the Charterers fail to arrange and keep any of the insurances 236
provided for under the provisions of sub-clause (a) above in the 237
manner described therein, Owners shall notify Charterers whereupon 238
Charterers shall rectify the position within seven running days, 239
failing which Owners shall have the right to withdraw the Vessel 240
from the service of the Charterers without prejudice to any claim 241
the Owners may otherwise have against the Charterers. 242
The Charterers shall, subject to the approval of the Owners and 243
the Underwriters, effect all insured repairs and shall undertake 244
settlement of all costs in connection with such repairs as well as 245
insured charges, expenses and liabilities (reimbursement to be 246
secured by the Charterers from the Underwriters) to the extent of 247
coverage under the insurances herein provided for. 248
The Charterers also to remain responsible for and to effect repairs 249
and settlement of costs and expenses incurred thereby in respect 250
of all other repairs not covered by the insurances and/or not ex- 251
ceeding any possible franchise(s) or deductibles provided for in 252
the insurances. 253
All time used for repairs under the provisions of sub-clause (a) of 254
this Clause and for repairs of latent defects according to Clause 1 255
above including any deviation shall count as time on hire and 256
shall form part of the Charter period. 257

(b) If the conditions of the above insurances permit additional in- 258
surance to be placed by the parties, such cover shall be limited 259
to the amount for each party set out in Box 29 and Box 30, 260
respectively. Owners or Charterers as the case may be shall im- 261
mediately furnish the other party with particulars of any additional 262
insurance effected, including copies of any cover notes or policies 263
and the written consent of the Insurers of any such required in- 264
surance in any case where the consent of such Insurers is necessary. 265

(c) Should the Vessel become an actual or constructive total loss 266
under the insurances required under sub-clause (a) of this Clause, 267
all insurance payments for such loss shall be paid to Owners, who 268
shall distribute the moneys between themselves and Charterers ac- 269
cording to their respective interests. 270

(d) Owners shall upon the request of Charterers, promptly execute 271
such documents as may be required to enable Charterers to abandon 272
the Vessel to Insurers and claim a constructive total loss. 273

(e) For the purpose of insurance coverage against marine and war 274
risks under the provisions of sub-clause (a) of this Clause, the value 275
of the Vessel is the sum indicated in Box 28. 276

12. Insurance, Repairs and Classification 277
(Optional, only to apply if expressly agreed and stated in Box 28, 278
in which event Clause 11 shall be considered deleted). 279

(a) During the Charter period the Vessel shall be kept insured by 280
the Owners at their expense against marine and war risks under 281
the form of policy or policies attached hereto. The Owners and/or 282
Insurers shall not have any right of recovery or subrogation against 283
the Charterers on account of loss of or any damage to the Vessel 284
or her machinery or appurtenances covered by such insurance, or 285
on account of payments made to discharge claims against or 286
liabilities of the Vessel or Owners covered by such insurance. All 287
insurance policies shall be in the joint names of Owners and 288
Charterers as their interests may appear. 289

(b) During the Charter period the Vessel shall be kept insured by 290
the Owners at their expense against Protection and Indemnity 291
risks in such form as Owners shall in writing approve which ap- 292
proval shall not be unreasonably withheld. If the Charterers fail to 293
arrange and keep any of the insurances provided for under the 294
provisions of sub-clause (b) in the manner described therein, Owners 295
shall notify Charterers whereupon Charterers shall rectify the posi- 296
tion within seven running days, failing which Owners shall have 297
the right to withdraw the Vessel from the service of the Charterers 298
without prejudice to any claim the Owners may otherwise have 299
against the Charterers. 300

(c) In the event that any act or negligence of the Charterers shall 301
vitiate any of the insurance herein provided, the Charterers shall 302
pay to the Owners all losses and indemnify the Owners against all 303
claims and demands which would otherwise have been covered by 304
such insurance. 305

(d) The Charterers shall, subject to the approval of the Owners or 306
Owners' Underwriters, effect all insured repairs, and the Charterers 307
shall undertake settlement of all miscellaneous expenses in con- 308
nection with such repairs as well as all insured charges, expenses 309
and liabilities, to the extent of coverage under the insurances 310
provided for under the provisions of sub-clause (a) of this Clause, 311
Charterers to be secured reimbursement through Owners' Under- 312
writers for such expenditures upon presentation of accounts. 313

(e) The Charterers to remain responsible for and to effect repairs 314
and settlement of costs and expenses incurred thereby in respect 315
of all other repairs not covered by the insurances and/or not ex- 316
ceeding any possible franchise(s) or deductibles provided for in 317
the insurances. 318

(f) All time used for repairs under the provisions of sub-clause (d) 319
and (e) of this Clause and for repairs of latent defects according 320
to Clause 1 above, including any deviation, shall count as time on 321
hire and shall form part of the Charter period. 322
The Owners shall not be responsible for any expenses as are in- 323
cident to the use and operation of the Vessel for such time as may 324
be required to make such repairs. 325

(g) If the conditions of the above insurances permit additional in- 326
surance to be placed by the parties such cover shall be limited to 327
the amount for each party set out in Box 29 and Box 30, respectively. 328
Owners or Charterers as the case may be shall immediately furnish 329
the other party with particulars of any additional insurance effected, 330
including copies of any cover notes or policies and the written 331
consent of the Insurers of any such required insurance in any case 332
where the consent of such Insurers is necessary. 333

(h) Should the Vessel become an actual or constructive total loss 334
under the insurances required under sub-clause (a) of this Clause, 335
all insurance payments for such loss shall be paid to Owners, who 336
shall distribute the moneys between themselves and Charterers ac- 337
cording to their respective interests. 338

(i) If the Vessel becomes an actual loss or a constructive total 339
loss under the insurances arranged by Owners in accordance with 340
sub-clause (a) of this Clause, this Charter shall terminate as of the 341
date of the casualty giving rise to such loss. 342

(j) Charterers shall upon the request of Owners, promptly execute 343
such documents as may be required to enable Owners to abandon 344
the Vessel to Insurers and claim a constructive total loss. 345

(k) For the purpose of insurance coverage against marine and war 346
risks under the provisions of sub-clause (a) of this Clause, the value 347
of the Vessel is the sum indicated in Box 28. 348

(l) Notwithstanding anything contained in Clause 8 (a), it is agreed 349
that under the provisions of Clause 12, if applicable, the Owners 350
shall keep the Vessel with unexpired classification in force at all 351
times during the Charter period. 352

13. Re-delivery 353
The Charterers shall at the expiration of the Charter period re- 354
deliver the Vessel at a safe and ice-free port as indicated in Box 18. 355
The Charterers shall give the Owners not less than 30 days' pre- 356
liminary and not less than 14 days' definite notice of expected date, 357
range of ports or port of re-delivery. Any changes thereafter in 358
Vessel's position shall be notified immediately to Owners. 359
Should the Vessel be ordered on a voyage by which the Charter period 360
may be exceeded the Charterers to have the use of the Vessel 361
to enable them to complete the voyage, provided it could be 362
reasonably calculated that the voyage would allow re-delivery about 363
the time fixed for the termination of the Charter. 364
The Vessel to be re-delivered to the Owners in the same or as 365
good structure, state, condition and class as that in which she was 366
delivered, fair wear and tear not affecting class excepted. 367
The Vessel upon re-delivery shall have her survey cycles up to date 368
and class certificates valid for at least the number of months agreed 369
in Box 14. 370

14. Non-Lien 371
Charterers will not suffer, nor permit to be continued, any lien or 372
encumbrance incurred by them or their agents, which might have 373
priority over the title and interest of the Owners in the Vessel. 374
The Charterers further agree to fasten to the Vessel in a conspicuous 375
place and to keep so fastened during the Charter period a notice 376
reading as follows: – 377

"This Vessel is the property of (name of Owners). It is under 378
charter to (name of Charterers) and by the terms of the Charter 379
Party neither the Charterers nor the Master have any right, power 380
or authority to create, incur or permit to be imposed on the 381
Vessel any lien whatsoever." 382

Charterers shall indemnify and hold Owners harmless against any 383
lien of whatsoever nature arising upon the Vessel during the Charter 384
period while she is under the control of Charterers, and against 385
any claims against Owners arising out of the operation of the Vessel 386
by Charterers or out of any neglect of Charterers in relation to the 387
Vessel or the operation thereof. Should the Vessel be arrested by 388
reason of claims or liens arising out of her operation hereunder 389
by Charterers, Charterers shall at their own expense take all 390
reasonable steps to secure that within a reasonable time the Vessel 391
is released and at their own expense put up bail to secure release 392
of the Vessel. 393

15. Lien 394
The Owners to have a lien upon all cargoes and sub-freights be- 395
longing to the Charterers and any Bill of Lading freight for all 396
claims under this Charter, and the Charterers to have a lien on 397
the Vessel for all moneys paid in advance and not earned. 398

16. Salvage 399
All salvage and towage shall be for the Charterers' benefit and the 400
cost of repairing damage occasioned thereby shall be borne by 401
the Charterers. 402

17. Wreck Removal 403
In the event of the Vessel becoming a wreck or obstruction to 404
navigation the Charterers shall indemnify the Owners against any 405
sums whatsoever which the Owners shall become liable to pay 406
and shall pay in consequence of the Vessel becoming a wreck or 407
obstruction to navigation. 408

18. General Average 409
General Average, if any, shall be adjusted according to the York- 410
Antwerp Rules 1974 or any subsequent modification thereof current 411
at the time of the casualty. 412
The Charter Hire not to contribute to General Average. 413

19. Assignment and Sub-Demise 414
The Charterers shall not assign this Charter Party nor sub-demise 415
the Vessel except with the prior consent in writing of the Owners 416
which shall not be unreasonably withheld and subject to such terms 417
and conditions as the Owners shall approve. 418

20. Bills of Lading 419
The Charterers are to procure that all Bills of Lading issued for 420
carriage of goods under this Charter shall contain a Paramount 421
Clause incorporating any legislation relating to Carrier's liability 422
for cargo compulsorily applicable in the trade; if no such legislation 423
exists, the Bills of Lading shall incorporate the British Carriage 424
of Goods by Sea Act. The Bills of Lading shall also contain the 425
amended New Jason Clause and the Both-to-Blame Collision Clause. 426

The Charterers agree to indemnify the Owners against all con- 427
sequences or liabilities arising from the Master, Officers or Agents 428
signing Bills of Lading or other documents. 429

21. Bank Guarantee 430
The Charterers undertake to furnish, before delivery of the Vessel, 431
a first class bank guarantee or bond in the sum and at the place 432
as indicated in Box 26 as guarantee for full performance of their 433
obligations under this Charter. 434
(Optional, only to apply if Box 26 filled in). 435

22. Requisition/Acquisition 436
(a) In the event of the Requisition for Hire of the Vessel by any 437
governmental or other competent authority (hereinafter referred to 438
as "Requisition for Hire") irrespective of the date during the Charter 439
period when "Requisition for Hire" may occur and irrespective of the 440
length thereof and whether or not it be for an indefinite or a limited 441
period of time, and irrespective of whether it may or will remain 442
in force for the remainder of the Charter period, this Charter Party 443
shall not be deemed thereby or thereupon to be frustrated or other- 444
wise terminated and the Charterers shall continue to pay the 445
stipulated hire in the manner provided by this Charter until the 446
time when the Charter Party would have terminated pursuant to 447
any of the provisions hereof always provided however that in the 448
event of "Requisition for Hire" any Requisition Hire or compensation 449
received or receivable by the Owners shall be payable to the 450
Charterers during the remainder of the Charter period or the period 451
of the "Requisition for Hire" whichever be the shorter. 452
The Hire under this Contract shall be payable to the Owners from 453
the same time as the Requisition Hire is payable to the Charterers. 454

(b) In the event of the Owners being deprived of their ownership 455
in the Vessel by any Compulsory Acquisition of the Vessel or re- 456
quisition for title by any governmental or other competent authority 457
(hereinafter referred to as "Compulsory Acquisition"), then, ir- 458
respective of the date during the Charter period when "Compulsory 459
Acquisition" may occur, this Charter shall be deemed terminated 460
as of the date of such "Compulsory Acquisition". In such event 461
Charter Hire to be considered as earned and to be paid up to the 462
date and time of such "Compulsory Acquisition". 463

23. War 464
(a) The Vessel unless the consent of the Owners be first obtained 465
not to be ordered nor continue to any place or on any voyage nor 466
be used on any service which will bring her within a zone which 467
is dangerous as the result of any actual or threatened act of war, 468
war, hostilities, warlike operations, acts of piracy or of hostility or 469
malicious damage against this or any other vessel or its cargo by 470
any person, body or State whatsoever, revolution, civil war, civil 471
commotion or the operation of international law, nor be exposed 472
in any way to any risks or penalties whatsoever consequent upon 473
the imposition of Sanctions, nor carry any goods that may in any 474
way expose her to any risks of seizure, capture, penalties or any 475
other interference of any kind whatsoever by the belligerent or 476
fighting powers or parties or by any Government or Ruler. 477

(b) The Vessel to have liberty to comply with any orders or direc- 478
tions as to departure, arrival, routes, ports of call, stoppages, 479

destination, delivery or in any other wise whatsoever given by the 480
Government of the nation under whose flag the Vessel sails or any 481
other Government or any person (or body) acting or purporting to 482
act with the authority of such Government or by any committee or 483
person having under the terms of the war risks insurance on the 484
Vessel the right to give any such orders or directions. 485

(c) In the event of the outbreak of war (whether there be a declara- 486
tion of war or not) between any two or more of the following 487
countries: the United Kingdom, the United States of America, France, 488
the Union of Soviet Socialist Republics, the People's Republic of 489
China **or** in the event of the nation under whose flag the Vessel sails 490
becoming involved in war (whether there be a declaration of war 491
or not), hostilities, warlike operations, revolution, or civil com- 492
motion preventing Vessel's normal trading either the Owners or 493
the Charterers may cancel this Charter, whereupon the Charterers 494
shall re-deliver the Vessel to the Owners in accordance with Clause 495
13, if she has cargo on board after discharge thereof at destination 496
or if debarred under this Clause from reaching or entering it at a 497
near open and safe port as directed by the Owners, or if she has 498
no cargo on board, at the port at which she then is or if at sea 499
at a near open and safe port as directed by the Owners. In all 500
cases hire shall continue to be paid in accordance with Clause 9 501
and except as aforesaid all other provisions of this Charter shall 502
apply until re-delivery. 503

(d) If in compliance with the provisions of this Clause anything is 504
done or is not done, such not to be deemed a deviation. 505

24. Commission 506
The Owners to pay a commission at the rate indicated in Box 31 507
to the Brokers named in Box 31 on any hire paid under the Charter 508
but in no case less than is necessary to cover the actual expenses 509
of the Brokers and a reasonable fee for their work. If the full hire 510
is not paid owing to breach of Charter by either of the parties the 511
party liable therefor to indemnify the Brokers against their loss of 512
commission. 513
Should the parties agree to cancel the Charter, the Owners to 514
indemnify the Brokers against any loss of commission but in such 515
case the commission not to exceed the brokerage on one year's 516
hire. 517

25. Law and Arbitration 518
This Charter shall be governed by the law of the country agreed 519
in Box 33 (if Box 33 not filled in, English Law shall apply). Any 520
dispute arising out of this Charter shall be referred to arbitration 521
in London or at the place agreed in Box 34, as the case may be, 522
the dispute being settled by a single Arbitrator to be appointed 523
by the parties hereto. If the parties cannot agree upon the appoint- 524
ment of the single Arbitrator the dispute shall be settled by three 525
Arbitrators, each party appointing one Arbitrator, the third being 526
appointed by the Arbitrators of the parties. If the Arbitrators fail 527
to agree on the appointment of the third Arbitrator, such appoint- 528
ment shall be made by The Baltic and International Maritime Con- 529
ference in Copenhagen. If either of the appointed Arbitrators refuses 530
or is incapable of acting, the party who appointed him shall appoint 531
a new Arbitrator in his place. 532
If one party fails to appoint an Arbitrator – either originally or by 533
way of substitution – for two weeks after the other party having 534
appointed his Arbitrator has sent the party making default notice by 535
mail, cable or telex to make the appointment, The Baltic and Inter- 536
national Maritime Conference shall, after application from the party 537
having appointed his Arbitrator, also appoint an Arbitrator on behalf 538
of the party making default. 539
The award rendered by the Arbitration Court shall be final and 540
binding upon the parties and may if necessary be enforced by 541
the Court or any other competent authority in the same manner 542
as a judgement in the Court of Justice. 543

HIRE/PURCHASE AGREEMENT
(Optional, only to apply if expressly agreed and stated in Box 35)

26. On expiration of this Charter and provided Charterers have fulfilled 544
their obligations according to Parts I and II, it is agreed, that on 545
payment of the last month's hire instalment as per Clause 9 the 546
Charterers have purchased the Vessel with everything belonging to 547
her and the Vessel is fully paid for. 548
If the payment of the instalment due is delayed for less than 7 549
running days or for a reason beyond Charterers' control, the right 550
of withdrawal under the terms of Clause 9 (e) of Part II shall not 551
be exercised. However, any delay in payment of the instalment due 552
shall entitle the Owners to an interest of 10 per cent. per annum. 553

27. In the following paragraphs the Owners are referred to as the Sellers 554
and the Charterers as the Buyers. 555

28. The Vessel shall be delivered by the Sellers and taken over by the 556
Buyers on expiration of the Charter. 557

29. The Sellers guarantee that the Vessel, at the time of delivery, is 558
free from all encumbrances and maritime liens or any debts what- 559
soever other than those arising from anything done or not done by 560
the Buyers or any existing mortgage agreed not to be paid off by 561
the time of delivery. Should any claims, which have been incurred 562
prior to the time of delivery be made against the Vessel, the Sellers 563
hereby undertake to indemnify the Buyers against all consequences 564
of such claims to the extent it can be proved that Sellers are 565
responsible for such claims. Any taxes, notarial, consular and other 566
charges and expenses connected with the purchase and registration 567
under Buyers' flag, shall be for Buyers' account. Any taxes, consular 568
and other charges and expenses connected with closing of the 569
Sellers' register, shall be for Sellers' account. 570
In exchange for payment of the last month's hire instalment the 571
Sellers shall furnish the Buyers with a Bill of Sale duly attested 572
and legalized, together with a certificate setting out the registered 573
encumbrances, if any. On delivery of the Vessel the Sellers shall 574
provide for deletion of the Vessel from the Ship's Register and 575
deliver a certificate of deletion to the Buyers. 576
The Sellers shall, at the time of delivery, hand to the Buyers all 577
classification certificates (for hull, engines, anchors, chains, etc.), 578
as well as all plans which may be in Sellers' possession. 579

30. The Wireless Installation and Nautical Instruments, unless on hire, 580
shall be included in the sale without any extra payment. 581

31. The Vessel with everything belonging to her shall be at Sellers' risk 582
and expense until she is delivered to the Buyers, subject to the 583
conditions of this Contract and the Vessel with everything belonging 584
to her shall be delivered and taken over as she is at the time of 585
delivery, after which the Sellers shall have no responsibility for 586
possible faults or deficiencies of any description. 587

32. The Buyers undertake to pay for the repatriation of the Captain, 588
Officers and other personnel if appointed by the Sellers to the port 589
where the Vessel entered the Bareboat Charter as per Clause 1 590
(Part II) or to pay the equivalent cost for their journey to any other 591
place. 592

Issued September 1st, 1968

THE BALTIC AND INTERNATIONAL MARITIME CONFERENCE
DEEP SEA TIME CHARTER

Code Name:
"LINERTIME"

19 ....

	IT IS THIS DAY MUTUALLY AGREED between 1
Description of Vessel.	.... Owners of the Vessel called 2
	.... of ———————— tons gross / tons net Register, 3
	classed .... of .... indicated horse power, carrying 4
	about .... tons deadweight on summer freeboard inclusive of bunkers, as well as stores, provisions 5
	and fresh water not exceeding .... tons having .... cubic-feet grain / bale 6
	capacity available for cargo, exclusive of permanent bunkers, which contain about .... tons, and fully 7
	loaded capable of steaming about .... knots in good weather and smooth water on a consumption of 8
	about .... tons .... per 24 hours now 9
	 10
	 11
Charterers.	and 12
	of .... Charterers, as follows: 13
Period.	1. The Owners let, and the Charterers hire the Vessel for a period of 14
	 15
	 16
	 17
	 18
Port of Delivery.	calendar months from the time (not a Sunday or a legal Holiday unless taken over) the Vessel is delivered and placed 19
	at the disposal of the Charterers between 7 a.m. and 10 p.m., or between 7 a.m. and noon if on Saturday, at 20
	 21
Note: Delete alternative not applicable.	in such ready berth where she can safely lie 22
	always afloat 23
	always afloat or safely aground where it is customary for vessels of similar size and draught to be safe aground 24
	as the Charterers may direct, she being in every way fitted for ordinary dry cargo service with cargo holds well swept, 25
	cleaned and ready to receive cargo before delivery under this Charter. 26
	 27
	 28
Time for Delivery.	The Vessel to be delivered not before 29
	The Owners to give the Charterers not less than .... days' notice of the date on which the 30
	Vessel is expected to be ready for delivery. 31
	The Owners to keep the Charterers closely advised of possible changes in Vessel's position. 32
Cancelling.	2. Should the Vessel not be delivered by the .... day of .... 19.......... 33
	the Charterers to have the option of cancelling. 34
	If the Vessel cannot be delivered by the cancelling date, the Charterers, if required, to declare within 48 hours (Sun- 35
	days and Holidays excluded) after receiving notice thereof whether they cancel or will take delivery of the Vessel. 36
Trade.	3. The Vessel to be employed in lawful trades for the carriage of lawful merchandise only between good and safe 37
	ports or places where she can safely lie 38
Note: Delete alternative not applicable.	always afloat 39
	always afloat or safely aground where it is customary for vessels of similar size and draught to be safe aground 40
	within the following limits: 41
	 42
	 43
	 44
	 45
	 46
	 47
	 48
	No live stock, sulphur and pitch in bulk to be shipped. Injurious, inflammable or dangerous goods (such as acids, ex- 49
	plosives, calcium carbide, ferro silicon, naphta, motor spirit, tar, or any of their products) to be limited to 50
	tons and same to be packed, loaded, stowed and discharged in accordance with the regulations of the local authorities 51
	and Board of Trade 52
	and if any special measures have to be taken by reason of having this cargo aboard including cost of erection and dis- 53
	mantling magazines, etc., same to be at Charterers' expense and in Charterers' time. 54
Nuclear Fuel.	Notwithstanding any other provisions contained in this Charter it is agreed that nuclear fuels or radioactive products 55
	or waste are specifically excluded from the cargo permitted to be loaded or carried under this Charter. This exclusion 56
	does not apply to radioisotopes used or intended to be used for any industrial, commercial, agricultural, medical or 57
	scientific purposes provided the Owners' prior approval has been obtained to loading thereof. 58
Owners to Provide.	4. The Owners to provide and pay for all provisions and wages, for insurance of the Vessel, for all deck and en- 59
	gine-room stores and maintain her in a thoroughly efficient state in hull and machinery during service. 60
	The Owners to provide one winchman per working hatch. In lieu of winchmen the Charterers are entitled to ask 61
	for two watchmen. If further winchmen or watchmen are required, or if the stevedores refuse or are not permitted to 62
	work with the Crew, the Charterers to provide and pay qualified men. The gangway watchman to be provided by the 63
	Owners but where compulsory to employ gangway watchmen from shore, the expenses to be for the Charterers' account. 64

Charterers to Provide.

5. The Charterers to pay all dock, harbour, light and tonnage dues at the ports of delivery and re-delivery (unless in- 65
curred through cargo carried before delivery or after re-delivery). 66

Whilst on hire the Charterers to provide and pay for all fuel, water for boilers, port charges, pilotages (whether 67
compulsory or not), canal steersmen, boatage, lights, tug-assistance, consular charges (except those payable to the con- 68
sulates of the country of the Vessel's flag) canal, dock and other dues and charges, including any foreign general mu- 69
nicipality or state taxes, agencies, commissions, also to arrange and pay for loading, trimming, stowing (including dun- 70
nage and shifting boards, excepting any already on board), unloading, weighing, tallying and delivery of cargoes, sur- 71
veys on hatches, any other survey on cargo, meals supplied to officials and men in their service at the rate per man 72
per meal indicated in Clause 28 and all other charges and expenses whatsoever. 73

All ropes, slings and special runners actually used for loading and discharging and any special gear, including special 74
ropes, hawsers and chains required by the custom of the port for mooring to be for the Charterers' account unless al- 75

Cargo Gear.

ready on board. The Vessel is fitted with the following cargo handling gear: 76

.... 77

.... 78

This gear is to be kept in full working order for immediate use, the Charterers however to give sufficient notice of 79
their intention to use heavy lift gear. 80

Cargo Gear Certificate.

The Owners guarantee the Vessel possesses cargo gear register and certificates in compliance with requirement of 81

International Labour Organization Convention No. 32. 82

.... 83

.... 84

.... 85

Fuel Consumption in Port.

The Vessel's normal fuel consumption whilst in port working all cargo gear is about .... tons 86

.... per 24 hours. 87

Bunkers.

6. The Charterers at port of delivery and the Owners at port of re-delivery to take over and pay for all fuel re- 88
maining in the Vessel's bunkers at 89

Note:
Delete alternative not applicable.

current price, at the respective ports. 90

a fixed price of .... per ton. 91

The Vessel to be delivered with not less than .... tons and not exceeding .... tons 92

.... in the Vessel's bunkers. 93

The Vessel to be re-delivered with not less than .... tons and not exceeding .... tons 94

.... in the Vessel's bunkers. 95

Hire.

7. The Charterers to pay as hire: 96

Note:
Delete alternative not applicable.

per 30 days

per day , commencing in accordance with Clause 1 until her re-delivery to the Owners. 97

Payment.

Payment of hire to be made in cash, in 98
without discount, every 30 days, in advance. 99

.... 100

.... 101

.... 102

In default of payment the Owners to have the right of withdrawing the Vessel from the service of the Charterers, 103
without noting any protest and without interference by any court or any other formality whatsoever and without pre- 104
judice to any claim the Owners may otherwise have on the Charterers under the Charter. 105

Last Hire Payment.

Should the Vessel be on her voyage towards port of re-delivery at time a payment of hire is due, said payment to 106
be made for such length of time as the Owners or their Agents and the Charterers or their Agents may agree upon as 107
estimated time necessary to complete the voyage, taking into account bunkers to be taken over by the Vessel and estim- 108
ated disbursements for the Owners' account before re-delivery and when the Vessel is re-delivered any difference to be 109
refunded by the Owners or paid by the Charterers, as the case may require. 110

Re-delivery.

8. The Vessel to be re-delivered on the expiration of the Charter in the same good order as when delivered to the 111

Charterers (fair wear and tear excepted) at a safe and ice-free port in the Charterers' option in 112

.... 113

.... 114

between 7 a.m. and 10 p.m., and 7 a.m. and noon on Saturday, but the day of re-delivery shall not be a Sunday or 115
legal Holiday. 116

Repairs for the Charterers' account as far as possible to be effected simultaneously with dry-docking or annual re- 117
pairs, respectively; if any further repairs are required, for time occupied in effecting such repairs the Owners to receive 118
compensation at the hire agreed in this Charter. The Charterers always to be properly notified of the time and place 119
when and where repairs for their account will be performed. 120

Notice.

The Charterers to give the Owners not less than .... days' preliminary and .... days' 121
final notice of the port of re-delivery and the date on which the Vessel is expected to be ready for re-delivery. The Char- 122
terers to keep the Owners closely advised of possible changes in the Vessel's position. 123

Should the Vessel be ordered on a voyage by which the Charter period may be exceeded the Charterers to have the 124
use of the Vessel to enable them to complete the voyage, provided it could be reasonably calculated that the voyage 125
would allow re-delivery about the time fixed for the termination of the Charter, but for any time exceeding the termin- 126
ation date the Charterers to pay the market rate if higher than the rate stipulated herein. 127

Cargo Space.

9. The whole reach and burden of the Vessel, including lawful deck-capacity to be at the Charterers' disposal, re- 128
serving proper and sufficient space for the Vessel's Master, Officers, Crew, tackle, apparel, furniture, provisions and 129
stores. 130

Master.

10. The Charterers to give the necessary sailing instructions, subject to the limits of the Charter. 131

The Master to be under the orders of the Charterers as regards employment, agency, or other arrangements. The 132
Master to prosecute all voyages with the utmost despatch and render customary assistance with the Vessel's Crew. 133

The Master and Engineer to keep full and correct logs including scrap logs accessible to the Charterers or their 134
Agents. 135

If the Charterers have reason to be dissatisfied with the conduct of the Master, Officers, or Engineers, the Owners on 136
receiving particulars of the complaint, promptly to investigate the matter, and, if necessary and practicable, to make a 137
change in the appointments. 138

Bills of Lading.

11. The Charterers to have the option of using their own regular Bill of Lading form. The Bill of Lading to con- 139
tain Paramount Clause incorporating Hague Rules legislation, the Amended Jason Clause and the Both-to-Blame Colli- 140
sion Clause. 141

Responsibility.

12. The Charterers shall keep and care for the cargo at loading and discharging ports, arrange for any tranship- 142
ment, and deliver the cargo at destination. 143

The Charterers shall load, stow, trim and discharge the cargo at their expense under supervision of the Master who 144
shall sign Bills of Lading as presented, in conformity with Mate's or tally clerk's receipts. The Charterers shall be res- 145
ponsible for the accuracy of all statements of fact in such Bills of Lading. 146

The Owners shall be liable for claims in respect of cargo arising or resulting from: 147

a) Failure on their part properly and carefully to carry, keep and care for the cargo while on board.   148

b) Unreasonable deviation from the voyage described in the Bills of Lading unless such deviation is ordered or ap- 149
proved by the Charterers.   150

c) Lack of due diligence on their part before and at the beginning of each voyage to make the Vessel seaworthy but 151
claims arising or resulting from faulty preparation of the holds and/or tanks of the Vessel or from bad stowage 152
of the cargo not affecting the trim or stability of the Vessel on sailing shall be the Charterers' liability.   153

Except as aforesaid the Charterers shall be liable for all cargo claims.   154

If the cargo is the property of the Charterers, the Owners shall have the same responsibility as they would have had 155
under this Clause had the cargo been the property of a third party and carried under a Bill of Lading incorporating 156
the Hague Rules.   157

The Charterers shall be liable for Customs or other fines or penalties, whether or not lawfully levied or imposed, 158
relating to the cargo or other property or persons carried with Charterers' approval or to the acts or omissions of the 159
owners of the cargo.   160

Claims for death and personal injury shall be borne by the Owners unless caused by the act, neglect or default of 161
the Charterers, their servants or agents including stevedores and all others for whom Charterers are responsible under 162
this Charter.   163

If for any reason the Owners or the Charterers are obliged to pay any claims, Customs or other fines or penalties, 164
for which the other party has assumed liability as above, that other party hereby agrees to indemnify the Owners or 165
Charterers as the case may be against all loss, damage or expenses arising or resulting from such claims. However, the 166
Owners' indemnity to the Charterers under this clause shall be restricted in that amount to which the Owners' liability 167
would have been limited had they been sued directly.   168

Exceptions.   13. As between the Charterers and the Owners, the responsibility for any loss, damage, delay or failure in per- 169
formance of this Charter, not dealt with in Clause 12, to be subject to the following mutual exceptions: 170

Act of God, act of war, civil commotions, strikes, lock-outs, restraint of princes and rulers, quarantine restric- 171
tions.   172

Further, such responsibility upon the Owners to be subject to the following exceptions: 173

Any act or neglect by the Master, pilots or other servants of the Owners in the navigation or management of the 174
Vessel, fire or explosion not due to the personal fault of the Owners or their Manager, collision or stranding, 175
unforeseeable breakdown or any latent defect in the Vessel's hull, equipment or machinery.   176

The above provisions in no way to affect the provisions as to suspension of hire in this Charter.   177

Suspension of Hire, etc.   14. (A) In the event of dry-docking or other necessary measures to maintain the efficiency of the Vessel, defi- 178
ciency of men or Owners' stores, strike of Master, Officers and Crew, breakdown of machinery, damage to hull or other 179
accident, either hindering or preventing the working of the Vessel and continuing for more than 180
consecutive hours, no hire to be paid in respect of any time lost thereby during the period in which the Vessel is 181
unable to perform the service immediately required.   182

Should the Vessel deviate or put back during a voyage, contrary to the orders or directions of the Charterers, for any 183
reason other than accident to the Cargo, the hire to be suspended from the time of her deviating or putting back until 184
she is again in the same or equidistant position from the destination and the voyage resumed therefrom.   185

Winch Breakdown.   In the event of a breakdown of a winch or winches, not caused by carelessness of shore labourers, the time lost to 186
be calculated pro rata for the period of such inefficiency in relation to the number of winches required for work. If the 187
Charterers elect to continue work, the Owners are to pay for shore appliances in lieu of the winches, but in such cases 188
the Charterers to pay full hire.   189

Any hire paid in advance to be adjusted accordingly.   190

Detention for Charterers' Account.   (B) In the event of the Vessel being driven into port or to anchorage through stress of weather, trading to shallow 191
harbours or to rivers or ports with bars or suffering an accident to her cargo, any detention of the Vessel and/or ex- 192
penses resulting from such detention to be for the Charterers' account even if such detention and/or expenses, or the 193
cause by reason of which either is incurred, be due to, or be contributed to by, the negligence of the Owners' servants. 194

Dry-docking.   Owners to give the Charterers at least four weeks notice of their intention of dry-docking the ship for bottom painting 195
and normal maintenance work and actual time and place for such dry-docking to be mutually agreed.   196

Cleaning Boilers, etc.   15. Cleaning of boilers or opening of pistons whenever possible to be done during service, but if impossible the 197
Charterers to give the Owners necessary time for such work at an interval of not less than three months for this pur- 198
pose. Should the Vessel be detained beyond .... hours the hire to cease until she again ready. The Owners or the 199
Master to give the Charterers reasonable notice of their intention to clean boilers or open pistons.   200

Advances.   16. The Charterers or their Agents to advance to the Master, if required, necessary funds for ordinary disburse- 201
ments for the Vessel's account at any port charging only one per cent. commission, such advances to be deducted from 202
hire.   203

.... 204

.... 205

Excluded Ports.   17. The Vessel not to be ordered to nor bound to enter: 206

a) any place where fever or epidemics are prevalent or to which the Master, Officers and Crew by law are not bound 207
to follow the Vessel;   208

Ice.   b) any ice-bound place or any place where lights, lightships, marks and buoys are or are likely to be withdrawn by 209
reason of ice on the Vessel's arrival or where there is risk that ordinarily the Vessel will not be able on account of ice 210
to reach the place or to get out after having completed loading or discharging. The Vessel not to be obliged to 211
force ice, nor to follow ice-breakers when inwards bound. If on account of ice the Master considers it dangerous to 212
remain at the loading or discharging place for fear of the Vessel being frozen in and/or damaged, he has liberty to 213
sail to a convenient open place and await the Charterers' fresh instructions.   214

Detention through any of above causes to be for the Charterers' account.   215

Loss of Vessel.   18. Should the Vessel be lost or missing, hire to cease from the date when she was lost. If the date of loss cannot 216
be ascertained half hire to be paid from the date the Vessel was last reported until the calculated date of arrival at 217
the destination. Any hire paid in advance to be adjusted accordingly.   218

Overtime.   19. The Vessel to work day and night if required. The Charterers to pay Owners a lumpsum of 219

.... per 30 days or pro rata for any overtime to Officers and Crew. 220

.... 221

.... 222

Lien.   20. The Owners to have a lien upon all cargoes and sub-freights belonging to the Time-Charterers and any Bill 223
of Lading freight for all claims under this Charter, and the Charterers to have a lien on the Vessel for all moneys paid 224
in advance and not earned.   225

The Charterers will not suffer, nor permit to be continued any lien or encumbrance incurred by them or their Agents, 226
which might have priority over the title and interest of the Owners in the Vessel.   227

Salvage.   21. All salvage and assistance to other vessels to be for the Owners' and the Charterers' equal benefit after de- 228
ducting the Master's and Crew's proportion and all legal and other expenses including hire paid under the Charter for 229
time lost in the salvage, also repairs of damage and fuel consumed. The Charterers to be bound by all measures taken 230
by the Owners in order to secure payment of salvage and to fix its amount.   231

Sublet.   22. The Charterers to have the option of subletting the Vessel, giving due notice to the Owners, but the original 232
Charterers always to remain responsible to the Owners for due performance of the Charter.   233

War.

23. (A) The Vessel unless the consent of the Owners be first obtained not to be ordered nor continue to any 234
place or on any voyage nor be used on any service which will bring her within a zone which is dangerous as the result 235
of any actual or threatened act of war, war, hostilities, warlike operations, acts of piracy or of hostility or malicious 236
damage against this or any other vessel or its cargo by any person, body or State whatsoever, revolution, civil war, civil 237
commotion or the operation of international law, nor be exposed in any way to any risks or penalties whatsoever conse- 238
quent upon the imposition of Sanctions, nor carry any goods that may in any way expose her to any risks of seizure, 239
capture, penalties or any other interference of any kind whatsoever by the belligerent or fighting powers or parties or 240
by any Government or Ruler. 241

(B) Should the Vessel approach or be brought or ordered within such zone, or be exposed in any way to the said 242
risks, 243

1) the Owners to be entitled from time to time to insure their interests in the Vessel and/or hire against any of the risks 244
likely to be involved thereby on such terms as they shall think fit, the Charterers to make a refund to the Owners 245
of the premium on demand; and 246

2) notwithstanding the terms of Clause 14 hire to be paid for all time lost including any lost owing to loss of or 247
injury to the Master, Officers or Crew or to the action of the Crew in refusing to proceed to such zone or to be 248
exposed to such risks. 249

(C) In the event of the wages and/or war bonus of the Master, Officers and/or Crew or the cost of provisions and/ 250
or stores for deck and/or engine room and/or insurance and/or war risk insurance premiums being increased by reason 251
of or during the existence of any of the matters mentioned in Section (A) the amount of any increase to be added to 252
the hire and paid by the Charterers on production of the Owners' account therefor, such account being rendered monthly. 253

(D) The Vessel to have liberty to comply with any orders or directions as to departure, arrival, routes, ports of 254
call, stoppages, destination, delivery or in any other wise whatsoever given by the Government of the nation under 255
whose flag the Vessel sails or any other Government or any person (or body) acting or purporting to act with the 256
authority of such Government or by any committee or person having under the terms of the war risks insurance on 257
the Vessel the right to give any such orders or directions. 258

(E) In the event of the outbreak of war (whether there be a declaration of war or not) between any two or more 259
of the following countries: the United Kingdom, the United States of America, France, the Union of Soviet Socialist 260
Republics, the People's Republic of China 261
or 262
in the event of the nation under whose flag the vessel sails becoming involved in war (whether there be a declaration 263
of war or not) 264
either the Owners or the Charterers may cancel this Charter, whereupon the Charterers shall re-deliver the Vessel 265
to the Owners in accordance with Clause 8, if she has cargo on board after discharge thereof at destination or if 266
debarred under this clause from reaching or entering it at a near open and safe port as directed by the Owners, or if 267
she has no cargo on board, at the port at which she then is or if at sea at a near open and safe port as directed by the 268
Owners. In all cases hire shall continue to be paid in accordance with Clause 7 and except as aforesaid all other 269
provisions of this Charter shall apply until re-delivery. 270

(F) If in compliance with the provisions of this clause anything is done or is not done, such not to be deemed a 271
deviation. 272

General Average.

24. General Average to be settled in 273
according to York/Antwerp Rules, 1974. Hire not to contribute to General Average. 274

Fumigation.

25. Expenses in connection with fumigations and/or quarantine ordered because of cargoes carried or ports visited 275
while the Vessel is employed under this Charter to be for the Charterers' account. Expenses in connection with all 276
other fumigations and/or quarantine to be for the Owners' account. 277

Funnel Mark.

26. The Charterers to have the option of painting the Vessel's funnel in their own colours, but the Vessel to be 278
re-delivered with the Owners' colours. Painting and repainting to be for the Charterers' account and time to count. The 279
Charterers also to have the option of flying their house flag during the currency of this Charter. 280

Supercargo.

27. The Charterers to have the option of placing a Supercargo on board, they paying 281
per day for lodging and victualling at the Master's table. 282

Meals.

28. The Owners to victual pilots and Customs officers and also, when authorised by Charterers or their Agents, 283
to victual tally clerks, stevedores' foremen, Charterers' guests, etc., the Charterers paying .... per man per 284
meal, for all such victualling. 285

Light.

29. The Owners to supply light on deck and in holds, as on board at all times, free of expense to the Charterers, 286
unless electrical clusters from shore are compulsory, in which case same to be for the Charterers' account. 287

Stevedoring Damage.

30. The Owners to instruct the Master to report in writing to the Supercargo, if on board, and to the Charterers 288
and/or their Agents at the port involved, about any stevedoring damage caused to the Vessel. Such reports to be made 289
immediately after the damage is done unless the damage could not be detected at once in spite of close supervision of 290
the stevedoring. 291

Ballast.

31. If any ballast is required, all expenses for same, including time used in loading and discharging, to be for the 292
Owners' account. 293

Arbitration.

32. Any dispute arising under the Charter to be referred to arbitration in London, one Arbitrator to be nominated 294
by the Owners and the other by the Charterers, and in case the Arbitrators shall not agree then to the decision of an 295
Umpire to be appointed by them, the award of the Arbitrators or the Umpire to be final and binding upon both par- 296
ties. 297
If either of the appointed Arbitrators refuses to act, or is incapable of acting, or dies, the party who appointed him 298
may appoint a new Arbitrator in his place. 299
If one party fails to appoint an Arbitrator, either originally, or by way of substitution as aforesaid, for seven clear days 300
after the other party, having appointed his Arbitrator, has served the party making default with notice to make the 301
appointment, the party who has appointed an Arbitrator may appoint that Arbitrator to act as sole Arbitrator in the 302
reference and his award shall be binding on both parties as if he had been appointed by consent. 303

Commission.

33. The Owners to pay a commission of .... to 304
.... on 305
any hire paid under the Charter but in no case less than is necessary to cover the actual expenses of the Brokers and a 306
reasonable fee for their work. If the full hire is not paid owing to breach of Charter by either of the parties the party 307
liable therefor to indemnify the Brokers against their loss of commission. 308
Should the parties agree to cancel the Charter, the Owners to indemnify the Brokers against any loss of commis- 309
sion but in such case the commission not to exceed the brokerage on one year's hire. 310

Printed and sold
by Fr. G. Knudtzon, Ltd., 55, Toldbodgade, Copenhagen,
by authority of The Baltic and International Maritime Conference.
(BIMCO), Copenhagen.

46-0

2.3 (CHARTERING) DISBURSEMENTS ACCOUNT

Description

A (Chartering) Disbursements Account is a standardized form for collating expenses incurred while a vessel is in port.

Source of document

The Baltic and International Maritime Conference (BIMCO), Copenhagen.

Purpose/use/function

During the period when a vessel is in port specific expenses are incurred according to circumstances. The vessel may arrive and/or depart to load/discharge cargo or be in ballast. It is necessary to collate such expenses and the (Chartering) Disbursements Account has been devised for this purpose.

Legal context

It has no statutory legal enforcement but is merely a document engaged in the chartering business of disbursements accounts. It is subject to the usual litigation procedure in regard to fraud and deliberate misrepresentation.

Ratifying organizations/countries

The form is the result of the work of a committee formed by BIMCO and the Federation of National Associations of Ship Brokers and Agents (FONASBA).

Procedure

Instructions for completing the form

The form is usually compiled by the shipowner or ship agent.

Other aspects

The (Chartering) Disbursements Account document is widely used in the chartering business as the recognized document/layout for its role. The BIMCO Documentation Committee review the layout and its contents when market and legislative circumstances warrant a change.

STANDARD DISBURSEMENTS ACCOUNT

RECOMMENDED BY
THE BALTIC AND INTERNATIONAL MARITIME CONFERENCE (BIMCO)
AND THE FEDERATION OF NATIONAL ASSOCIATIONS
OF SHIP BROKERS AND AGENTS (FONASBA)

Shipagent		Owners/Chartered Owners/Disponent Owners	

Port:		Date:		Vessel:	Voy. No.
Arrived from:		Date/Hour:		NRT	GRT
Sailed for:		Date/Hour:		TDW	LOA
Cargo loaded:		Cargo discharged:		☐ Repairs ☐ Other	☐ Bunkers

Voucher No.				
	PORT CHARGES	Harbour Dues		
		Light Dues		
		Pilotage		
		Towage		
		Mooring/Unmooring		
		Shifting		
		Customs Charges		
		Launch/Car Hire		
		Agency Remuneration		
		Telex, Postage, Telegrams		
			Total	
	CARGO CHARGES	Stevedoring Expenses		
		Winchmen/Cranage		
		Tally		
		Overtime		
			Total	
	SHIP CHARGES	Cash to Master		
		Water		
		Stores/Provisions		
		Crew Expenses		
		Repairs		
			Total	
			TOTAL	
	STATEMENT	Credit to Owners' Account		
		Balance due us/you		

Printed and sold by Fr. G. Knudtzon Ltd., 55 Toldbodgade, Copenhagen, by authority of BIMCO
89-0

The Standard Disbursements Account printed overleaf is the result of the work of a committee formed by BIMCO and FONASBA and it is hoped that it will prove useful to shipowners and shipagents.

A main object in preparing the form has been to standardise the format as well as the contents and this has naturally put a certain limit to the number of items appearing in the printed text.

Apart from the Preamble the form has been divided into four sections and it is hoped that the empty spaces provided in each section will suffice for the listing of additional items and further details of charges, as necessary.

2.4 NUBALTWOOD CHARTER PARTY AND BILL OF LADING

Description

The Nubaltwood Charter Party is the document under which a vessel is hired or chartered specifically for the Scandinavian timber trade market operating in the Baltic and North Sea seaboards. An associated Bill of Lading is provided to reflect the terms found in the Nubaltwood Charter Party.

Source of document

The Chamber of Shipping of the United Kingdom.

Purpose/use/function

The Charter Party serves as a contract whereby a shipowner agrees to place the ship, or part of it, at the disposal of a merchant or other person (known as the charterer), for the carriage of goods from one port to another on being paid freight, or to let the ship for a specified period, the shipowner's remuneration being known as hire money.

Legal context

The terms, conditions and exceptions under which the goods are carried out are set out in the Charter Party. It will be appreciated that the terms and conditions of a Charter Party will vary according to the wishes of the parties to the contract.

Ratifying organizations/countries

The Nubaltwood Charter Party and Bill of Lading has been agreed by the Baltic and International Maritime Conference (BIMCO), Copenhagen, the Timber Trade Federation of the United Kingdom, the Finnish Sawmill Owners' Association and the Swedish Wood Exporters' Association.

Other aspects

The Nubaltwood Charter Party is well recognized in the Scandinavian timber trade and its content is reviewed in the light of changing market and legislative conditions. The Bill of Lading associated with it reflects the Charter Party terms and is the document used by the shipper forwarding the timber cargo. It is subservient to the Nubaltwood Charter Party. The cargo description must conform to the commercial invoice and insurance cover provisions.

CHAMBER OF SHIPPING BALTIC WOOD CHARTER PARTY 1973
(Baltic and Norway to the United Kingdom and to the
Republic of Ireland)
CODE NAME: " NUBALTWOOD "

1. Shipbroker	2. Place and date
3. Owners/Disponent Owners (see below)—Delete whichever is inappropriate	4. Charterers (see below)
5. Ship's Manager/Chartering Agent—Delete whichever is inappropriate	6. Name and Telegraphic Address of Shipper (Cl. 2)
7. Vessel's Name (see below)	8. Present Position (see below)

9. Date of Build (see below)	10. Net Register Tons (see below)	11. Carrying Cap. in cbm. (see below)	12. Max. Sets of B/L (Cl. 11)
13. No. of Hatches and their Dimensions (see below)		14. Previous Discharging Port if agreed (Cl. 1)	
		15. Laydays (see below and Cl. 3b)	16. Cancel. Date if Cl. 3(b) Applies

17. Port of Loading (Cl. 1)	18. Port of Discharge (Cl. 1)
Ship's Agent (Cl. 27)	Ship's Agent (Cl. 27)

19. Cargo (Cl. 1)—Delete A or B whichever is inappropriate
A (Cl. 1A)—State Description of Cargo. Margin if Cargo greater than 2500 cbm. (see below), and Quantity Packaged/Truck Bundled/Pre-Slung*

B (Cl. 1B)—Lumpsum Basis—State Description of Cargo, and Margin if Cargo greater than 2500 cbm. (see below).

20. Freight (Cl. 1)—Delete A or B whichever is inappropriate	£p per delivered cubic metre		£p per delivered cubic metre
A For DEALS and BATTENS*		For SCANTLINGS	
„ SAWN BOARDS		„ SLATINGS*	
„ „ „ under 25 millimetres thick		„ LATHS	
„ PLANED BOARDS		„ STAVES	
„ PACKAGED GOODS*			
TRUCK BUNDLED GOODS*			

B Lumpsum Freight—Type Sum in Figures Letters Stating Currency

21. Method of Discharge—State Alternative of Cl. 15. If not completed 15 (a) applies	22. State Fixed Price Agreed if Cl. 15 (c) applies. If not completed Clause 15 (c) is void and 15 (a) applies.

23. Brokerage Rate (Cl. 26)	24. Brokerage to be Paid to (Cl. 26)

THE AGREEMENT

It is this day agreed between the Owners (Disponents) named in Box 3 (hereinafter referred to as Owners) of the vessel named in Box 7 and with net registered tonnage indicated in Box 10, having the number of cargo hatches of the dimensions as indicated in Box 13 each with at least one workable winch, and of the carrying capacity inclusive of deck load expressed in cubic metres as indicated in Box 11, the Owners having a margin of 10 per cent, more or less up to a maximum of 250 cubic metres (a greater margin may be agreed in Box 19 for cargoes beyond 2,500 cubic metres), now in position as indicated in Box 8 and expected ready to load about the date indicated in Box 15, but latest on the cancelling date indicated in Box 16 (if Clause 3(b) applicable) and the Charterers named in Box 4 that the said vessel will perform a voyage on the terms of this Charterparty (Charter) which consists of this page and of the ' Nubaltwood General Terms and Conditions and Warranties 1973 ' to which the clauses referred to above relate. In the event of any conflict between any typewritten provisions on this page and the printed terms of the ' Nubaltwood General Terms and Conditions and Warranties 1973 ' the typewritten provisions on this page shall prevail.

For the Owners	For the Charterers

* FOR DEFINITIONS SEE OVERLEAF

DEFINITIONS—BOXES 19 and 20

(a) Battens to be considered 44 mm. x 100 mm. and up to 75 mm. x 175 mm.

(b) Slatings to be considered 25 mm. and under in thickness and 75 mm. and under in width.

(c) Packaged Goods: Packaged Goods shall mean goods which have a single length and size in each package, except that where the residue is insufficient for a complete package lengths may be combined provided that one end of each package is squared off.

(d) Truck Bundled Goods: Truck Bundled Goods shall mean goods bundled in mixed lengths of one size provided that one end of each bundle is squared off.

(e) Pre-slung goods: To pre-sling is to have a sling or slings provided by the owner, unless otherwise agreed, placed around the cargo before loading into vessel and for these to remain during the voyage until after the cargo has been discharged.

1. Loading/Discharging Ports and Cargo

That the said Vessel being tight, staunch and strong, and in every way fitted for the Voyage shall, with all convenient speed (having liberty to take cargo for Owners' benefit, to any port or ports in the Baltic or North Sea, or to the port indicated in Box 14 and after discharging the same) sail and proceed to the Port of Loading indicated in Box 17 or so near thereunto as she may safely get, and there load, always afloat, from the Charterers or their Agents.

A. Ordinary Specified Sawn Wood Cargo.
A full and complete cargo, described in the purchase contract as properly seasoned for shipment to the U.K., of Mill-sawn Red and/or White Softwood Deals and/or Battens and/or Boards and/or Scantlings and/or Slatings in Bundles and/or Laths in Bundles and/or Staves in Bundles and/or Planed Boards and/or Floorings (the approximate quantities of Sawn Boards over and under 25 millimetres thick respectively, of Scantlings ; of Slatings ; of Laths ; of Staves ; of Planed Boards and/or Floorings, if any to be shipped shall be as indicated in Box 19, the word "approximate" within this bracketed clause being read as meaning 10 per cent. more or less).

The Vessel shall be provided with a deck load, at full freight as under, at Charterers' risk, not exceeding what she can reasonably stow and carry over and above her Tackle, Apparel, Provisions and Furniture.

B. Cargo of Sawn Wood and/or Round Wood and/or Telegraph Poles on Lumpsum Basis.
A cargo as described in Box 19, the Charterers having at their disposal the full reach of the Vessel's holds and deck and other available spaces where wood is usually stowed such as spare bunkers, etc. Deck cargo shall be carried at Charterers' risk and shall not exceed what the Vessel can reasonably stow and carry over and above her Tackle, Apparel, Provisions and Furniture.

Memo **(A or B are alternatives, the one applicable being indicated in Box 19. The Owners may agree any other description of cargo, such description to be indicated in Box 19.)**

Being so loaded the Vessel shall proceed therewith to the Port of Discharge indicated in Box 18 or so near thereunto as she may safely get, and deliver the cargo always afloat, upon being paid freight as indicated in Box 20 together with charges, if any, as in the last paragraph of this Clause or under Clause 15.

If the Consignees select one of the alternatives mentioned in Clause 15, other than discharge on to the quay (which includes rough stacking thereon if and where customary and not usually done by the Consignees), any additional expense, plus 15 per cent. thereon, of such delivery beyond the expense of delivery on to the quay as aforesaid, shall be paid by the Consignees to the Shipowner, in addition to the amount(s) above mentioned. If the port of discharge is included in the Schedule of Apportionment agreed between the Chamber of Shipping of the United Kingdom and the Timber Trade Federation of the United Kingdom, such additional expenses shall be limited to the sum ascertained in accordance with the said Schedule current at the date discharging commences under this Charter. Memo **(The Owners may agree to delete the words "always afloat" at loading and/or discharging ports, or agree a special lighterage clause for shallow ports or places, such special agreement being laid down in Boxes 17 and/or 18.)**

2. Notice of Probable Arrival at the Loading Ports

The Master or Owners shall telegraph the Shipper or Shippers of the cargo (telegraphic address(es) as per Box 6) stating the Vessel's and the Charterers' names, and giving at least nine consecutive days' (except the following days: New Year Day, Epiphany, Good Friday, Easter Eve, Easter Monday, May Day, Ascension Day, Whit Monday (not Finland), Whitsun Eve (Finland only), Mid Summer Eve, Mid Summer Day, All Saints' Day, Independence Day (Finland only), Christmas Eve, Christmas Day, Second Christmas Day (Boxing Day), and Sunday immediately preceding or following the aforementioned days) notice of the probable date of Vessel's arrival at loading port or ports. Owners also to inform shippers by telegram when vessel is leaving her last outward port for her first port of loading. If it be found that the vessel cannot arrive at that probable date notified, the Master or Owners shall immediately inform the shipper or shippers thereof by telegram or by radiogram and state as early as practicable when the vessel will probably arrive. Default under this clause shall not be considered a breach of charter, but the Owners shall be responsible to the Charterers and/or Shippers for demurrage on lighters or trucks due to non-arrival by the stated date or dates if due care has not been exercised in the giving of notice of the probable date of Vessel's arrival. In the event of the Owners or Master failing to give notice as required by this clause, then lay-days shall be extended by the period of nine consecutive days (those Sundays and holidays as above excepted) from the date of arrival of the Vessel where no notice has been given or by the number of days by which the notice falls short of nine consecutive days, holidays as above excepted, in cases where short notice has been given. In either case if Charterers or Shippers should commence loading before the expiration of such extended period then lay-days shall count as from the commencement of such loading.

3. Cancelling Date (Delete a or b whichever is inappropriate)

a) In the event of the vessel being chartered for "first open water," if the Vessel be not ready to load within four weeks of the official opening for navigation of the port where the Vessel is to commence loading, the Charterers shall have the option of cancelling the Charter.

(b) Lay-days shall not commence before the date indicated in Box 15 unless loading be commenced sooner, and the Charterers shall have the option of cancelling the Charter if the Vessel be not ready, at the (first) loading port, to load on or before the date indicated in Box 16.

(c) If, when the Vessel is ready to leave her last outward port for the (first) port of loading, the Owners inform the Charterers by telegram that she cannot reach the (first) loading port before the cancelling date named in the Charter, the Charterers shall declare by telegram within twelve business hours from their receipt of such notice whether or not they cancel the Charter.

4. Fire

If the goods intended for shipment under this Charter by the Shippers mentioned in Box 6 of the Charter are destroyed by fire or if fire prevents their being provided, the Charterers shall have the right of cancelling this Charter, immediate notice thereof being given by telegram to the Owners or their Brokers. If at any time before or after loading begins any part of the goods intended for shipment is destroyed by fire, or if fire prevents part of the goods being provided, Charterers shall notify Owners immediately the quantity available for shipment is known and their liability to ship shall be limited to such goods. If the quantity stated in such notice is not more than 50 per cent. of the quantity which the charterers but for the fire would have been required to ship and provided no cargo has been loaded the Owners shall have the option of cancelling this charter, but otherwise or in the event that such option is not exercised, the vessel shall proceed with such remainder having liberty to fill up for Owners' benefit at the same or at any other port or ports either for the same destination or for any other port or ports whether any of such ports are in the course of the chartered voyage or not.

If floods and/or ice conditions prevent the manufacture of the goods or their transit to the port of shipment then the Charterers, provided they give notice of such prevention to the Owners or their Brokers before the Vessel leaves her last outward port for the (first) port of loading, shall have the right to cancel this Charter without liability for damages.

5. Ballast

The Master shall be at liberty to bring iron or other deadweight as ballast from the loading or any port.

6. Loading

On arrival at loading port the Master shall give to the Shippers or their Agents written notice of the approximate quantity of cargo required. The Master shall exercise due care in giving such notice and in adjusting the said approximate quantity required as soon as the loading of the holds is completed.

The cargo shall be brought alongside the Vessel in the customary manner at Charterer's risk and expense, and shall be loaded at the average rate as provided by Clause 20 hereof. Laytime shall be calculated as provided by Clause 20 hereof. Saturdays afternoon, Sundays, general and local holidays excepted, unless used, in which event actual time used to count.

Subject to the provisions of Clauses 3 (b) and 8 (e) time for loading shall commence at 14.00 if the Vessel be ready to load (whether in berth or not) and written notice of readiness has been given to the Shippers or their Agents before 10.00 and the commencement of the next working day if notice be given after 10.00 within ordinary office hours, but if the work be commenced earlier time shall count from such commencement.

If the Vessel arrives at the loading port earlier than the date notified, the Shippers are not compelled to give cargo before 14.00 of the notified day of arrival if not otherwise agreed upon between Shippers and the Master of the Vessel.

Subject to the provisions of Clause 9, should the Vessel be prevented from entering port, harbour or dock, or from arriving at or off loading place by any reason other than weather or inefficiency of the Vessel the Vessel shall be regarded as if ready in berth on arrival at or off the port, or so near thereunto as she may be permitted to approach, and time shall count as above. The time occupied in moving to loading berth shall not count.

The Shippers shall present the Bills of Lading to the Master for signature and pay the Export Duty (if any) on the cargo in time to enable the Vessel to sail without delay upon completion of the loading.

Subject to the provisions of Clause 18, any dispute arising at the port of loading shall be settled before signing Bills of Lading, otherwise claims shall be endorsed upon the Bills of Lading, and if for any reason the Master is prevented from so doing he shall telegraph notice of the claim and the amount thereof to the Charterers. If the claim be not so endorsed or the Master does not telegraph before the Vessel sails, or radiograph prior to the Vessel's arrival at the discharging port, the Vessel shall have liberty to deviate to any port after sailing for the purpose of enabling the Master to telegraph. If such claim be not so endorsed or such telegram be not sent either from loading port or some port after sailing, or by radiogram before arrival at discharging port, the Shipowner shall not be entitled to exercise any lien on the cargo in respect of such claim of the Shipowner arising at the loading port.

7. Advance Freight

Cash for Vessel's ordinary disbursements only at port of loading, and not in excess of one-third of the total freight, shall be advanced by the Shipper, if required by the Master, at the closing rate of exchange at the port of shipment on the day the advance is taken, subject to a charge of 2 per cent. to be deducted by Shippers. The amount of the advance shall be endorsed upon the Bill of Lading in British sterling.

8. Ice

a) Where the Charter provides for one loading port only, if when the Vessel is ready to proceed from her last port of call (whether a discharging port or not) or at any time during the voyage to the loading port the Owners be informed by the Shippers, whose name first appears in Box 6 of this Charter, and the Owners' agents at port of loading that in their opinion the port is not accessible and/or the shipment of the goods is not practicable by reason of ice, the Charter shall be cancelled forthwith and the Owners shall advise the Charterers by telegram.

(b) Where the Charter provides for one loading port only, if upon Vessel's arrival off the port or so near thereunto as she can get, ice, in the opinion of the Master, prevents the Vessel reaching or entering the port of loading, the Charter shall be cancelled forthwith and the Owners shall advise the Charterers by telegram.

If after arrival, the Master, for fear of the Vessel being frozen in, deems it advisable to sail, he shall be at liberty to leave either without cargo, in which case the Charter shall be cancelled forthwith and the Master shall notify the Charterers by telegram accordingly, or with part cargo and to fill up for the Vessel's benefit at any port for any port or ports whether such ports be in the course of the chartered voyage or not; but in case of leaving with part cargo the Vessel shall deliver such part cargo at its port of delivery or shall, without undue delay, forward it thereto and there deliver it in accordance with this Charter.

c) Where the Charter provides for more than one loading port, if, in the opinion of the Master, the first loading port be inaccessible, or, if after arrival at any loading port the Master, for fear of the Vessel being frozen in, deems it advisable to sail without cargo or with a part cargo, the Vessel shall proceed in rotation to the next loading port named in Box 17 which in the opinion of the Master is accessible. On arrival at such loading port the Charterers shall declare forthwith, in writing, to the Master or Owners' Agents at such port, either to cancel the Charter to the extent to which it is unfulfilled or to load a full and complete cargo at the loading ports named in Box 17 which, in the opinion of the Master, are accessible, completing, if necessary, at any other safe open port on the same coast and in the same country. In the event of the Charterers declaring to cancel the Charter to the extent to which it is unfulfilled the Vessel shall nevertheless have the right to fill up for Vessel's benefit at any port for any port or ports, whether in the course of the Chartered voyage or not, but shall without undue delay deliver any part cargo which had previously been loaded under this Charter at its port of delivery or forward it thereto and there deliver it in accordance with this Charter. If all ports be in the opinion of the Master inaccessible the Charter shall forthwith be cancelled and the Owners shall advise the Charterers by telegram.

(d) Clauses 8 (a), (b) and (c) shall not apply in the Spring.

(e) The Charterers' liability to supply cargo and to load shall not commence earlier than 48 hours after the navigation of lighters between the Shipper's wharf and/or quay and the Vessel is unimpeded by ice.

9. Strikes, etc.

(a) If the cargo cannot be loaded and/or discharged by reason of a strike or lock-out of any class of workmen essential to the loading and/or discharge of the cargo, or by reason of epidemics, the time for loading and/or discharge shall not count during the continuance of such strike or lock-out or epidemic, and in case of any delay by reason of the before-mentioned causes, no claim for damages shall be made by the Shipper, the Consignees of the cargo, the Owners of the Vessel or by any other party under this Charter.

(b) If within seven days of the Vessel's expected readiness to load there is a strike or lock-out interfering with the loading of cargo at the loading port or ports and the Vessel is ready to proceed to the first loading port from her last outward port of discharge or from her bunkering port if in ballast the Owners shall, after the Vessel has waited three consecutive calendar days, have the option, which shall be declared by telegram to the Charterers, of sending the Vessel to the loading port or cancelling the Charter forthwith.

c) If before any cargo has been loaded the Vessel be delayed at the loading port by a strike for six consecutive calendar days either the Owners or Charterers shall thereafter be entitled by notice in writing to cancel this Charter.

(d) If a strike or lock-out occurs at the loading port after part cargo has been loaded and continues for six consecutive calendar days, the Vessel may proceed with the cargo then on board, having liberty to fill up for the Vessel's benefit at any other port or ports either for the same destination

or for any other port or ports whether any of such ports be in the course 252
of the chartered voyage or not, and the Owners shall advise the 253
Charterers by telegram that the Vessel has left the port. In case of 254
lerving with part cargo the Vessel shall deliver such part cargo at its 255
port of delivery or shall, without undue delay, forward it thereto and 256
there deliver it in accordance with this Charter. 257

10. Bills of Lading 258

(a) The Bill of Lading shall be prepared on the " Nubaltwood " Bill of 259
Lading form and shall be signed by the Master, quality, condition and 260
measure unknown, freight and all terms, conditions, clauses (including 261
Clause 30) and exceptions as per this Charter. The Owners shall be 262
responsible for the number of pieces signed for by the Master or his 263
duly authorised Agents, but the Owners shall not be responsible for 264
any cargo which is lost or destroyed while lying alongside the Vessel in 265
lighters or on quay waiting shipment even if receipted for by Master or 266
Owners' Agents. In case of any such loss or destruction the Master 267
shall furnish proof thereof. The Owners shall not be responsible for 268
broken bundles unless due care is not taken either in loading and/or dis- 269
charging. 270
In the event of there being only one Consignee all cargo on board 271
shall be delivered to him. 272

(b) If the Owners and the Receivers of all parcels to be discharged at any one 273
port so agree, and if it is practicable to do so, the cargo for that port 274
shall not be tallied ex ship. In lieu of tallying the Owners shall pay to 275
the Receivers an allowance per cubic metre as agreed between them 276
and no liability for shortage of pieces shall attach to the Owners based 277
on a tally taken elsewhere after discharge. 278

(c) If there is no agreement between owners and receivers under Clause 10 279
(b), or any such agreement is found impracticable, the cargo for that 280
port shall be tallied ex ship by all or any of the interested parties, but 281
notwithstanding the provisions of the Hague Rules, no liability for 282
shortage of pieces on ex ship tally shall attach to the Owners unless due 283
notice be given to the Owners or their Agents within eight days of 284
completion of discharge. 285

11. Sets of Bills of Lading 286

The Master shall not be obliged to sign more than one set of Bills of 287
Lading, unless due written notice be given him before commencing to 288
load. Not more than the number of sets indicated in Box 12 shall be 289
required. Further, the cargo shall be sent alongside in such a manner as 290
to enable the Master to keep separate the cargo under each Bill of 291
Lading. Parcels of 250 cubic metres or less for which a separate Bill of 292
Lading is required shall be delivered to the Vessel at one and the same 293
time so as to enable the Master to make one stowage of that parcel in 294
the Vessel except such part thereof as may be stowed on deck. For the 295
Master's information but without obligation upon the Owners, 296
Charterers shall supply the Owners or their Agents with a copy of their 297
" loading instructions to the Shippers " as soon as issued. 298

12. Exceptions 299

The Owners shall not be liable for loss or damage arising or resulting 300
from unseaworthiness unless caused by want of due diligence on the 301
part of the Owners to make the Vessel seaworthy, and to secure that 302
the Vessel be properly manned, equipped and supplied, and to make 303
the holds and all other parts of the Vessel in which goods are carried 304
fit and safe for their reception, carriage and preservation. The Owners 305
shall not be responsible for loss or damage arising or resulting from: 306
Act, neglect, or default of the Master, mariner, pilot, or the servants of 307
the Owners in the navigation or in the management of the Vessel: Fire, 308
unless caused by the actual fault or privity of the Owners: Perils, 309
dangers and accidents of the sea or other navigable waters: Act of 310
God: Act of war: Act of public enemies: Arrest or restraint of princes, 311
rulers or people, or seizure under legal process: Quarantine restrictions: 312
Act or omission of the Shippers or owners of the goods, their Agents or 313
representatives: Strikes or lockouts or stoppage or restraint of labour 314
from whatever cause, whether partial or general: Riots and civil com- 315
motion: Saving or attempting to save life or property at sea: Wastage 316
in bulk or weight or any other loss or damage arising from inherent 317
defect, quality, or vice of the goods: Insufficiency of packing: In- 318
sufficiency or inadequacy of marks: Latent defects not discoverable by 319
due diligence: Any other cause arising without the actual fault or 320
privity of the Owners, or without the fault or neglect of the Agents or 321
servants of the Owners. 322

13. Contractual Voyage 323

The Vessel shall have liberty to sail without pilots, to proceed via any 324
route, to proceed to and stay at any port or ports whatsoever in any 325
order in or out of the route or in a contrary direction to or beyond the 326
port of destination once or oftener for bunkering or loading or dis- 327
charging cargo or embarking or disembarking passengers or any other 328
purposes whatsoever, and to carry the within cargo into and then 329
beyond the port of discharge named in box 18 and to return to and dis- 330
charge the said cargo at such port, to tow or be towed, to make trial 331
trips with or without notice, to adjust or calibrate compasses, or to 332
repair or drydock with or without cargo on board, all as part of the 333
contract voyage. 334

14. War 335

(a) If the nation under whose flag the Vessel sails shall be at war, whereby 336
the free navigation of the Vessel is endangered, or if prohibition of 337
export or blockade prevent the loading or completion of cargo, this 338
Charter shall be cancelled forthwith at the last outward port or at any 339
subsequent period when the difficulty may arise. 340

(b) The Vessel shall have liberty to comply with any orders or directions as 341
to departure, arrival, routes, ports of call. stoppages, destination or 342
otherwise howsoever given by the Government of the nation under 343
whose flag the Vessel sails or any department thereof, or any person 344
acting or purporting to act with the authority of such Government or of 345
any department thereof, or by any Committee or person having, under 346
the terms of the War Risks' Insurance on the Vessel, the right to give 347
such orders or directions and if by reason of and in compliance with 348
any such orders or directions anything is done or is not done, the same 349
shall not be deemed a deviation and delivery in accordance with such 350
orders or directions shall be a fulfilment of the contract voyage and 351
the freight shall be payable accordingly. 352

Memo

15. Discharging (Method of discharge as shown in Box 21 to 353
apply. If Box 21 is not completed or if a fixed price is not 354
inserted in Box 22, Clause 15 (a) is to apply.) 355

(a) The Owner's liability shall cease at the port of discharge when the cargo 356
is discharged at the ship's rail if discharged by hand or within reach of 357
the ship's tackle or shore crane tackle if thereby discharged (the Owners 358
having the option of using the ship's tackle or shore crane where per- 359
missible by local regulations). The cargo shall, however, be discharged 360
by the vessel by any method approved for the port of discharge by the 361
Chamber of Shipping of the United Kingdom and by the Timber Trade 362
Federation of the United Kingdom current at the time discharging 363
commences. Receivers shall have the right to select any one or more of 364
the approved methods of discharge if available at the time of discharge. 365
For any work done by the Vessel at the port of discharge beyond 366
delivering cargo at the ship's rail if discharged by hand, or within reach 367
of the ship's tackle or of the shore crane tackle if thereby discharged, 368
the Receiver shall pay to the Owners the cost thereof, plus 15 per cent. 369
If the port of discharge is included in the Schedule of Apportionment 370

agreed between the Chamber of Shipping of the United Kingdom and 371
the Timber Trade Federation of the United Kingdom the charge for 372
such work shall be limited to the sum ascertained in accordance with 373
the said Schedule current at the date discharging commences under this 374
Charter. 375
In the execution of any work done beyond discharging cargo at the 376
ship's rail or within reach of the ship's tackle or shore crane tackle, as 377
the case may be, the Owners shall act as stevedores with the liabilities 378
only of such and not further or otherwise, but the Owners shall not be 379
liable for damage by fire, even though caused by the act or neglect of 380
the Owners or their servants or of any person for whom they are 381
responsible, or 382

(b) The Receivers shall effect the discharging free of any risk and expense 383
whatsoever to the Vessel. The Owners shall provide winches, motive 384
power and winchmen from the crew, if requested and permitted; if not 385
so requested and/or permitted the Receivers shall provide and pay for 386
winchmen from shore and/or for shore cranes, if any. The stevedores 387
shall be appointed by, and shall be the servants of, the Receivers but 388
shall follow the reasonable instructions of the Master in connection 389
with the discharging which shall be to his reasonable satisfaction. 390
Incentive money shall be payable to the Receivers on laytime saved 391
at 50 per cent. of the demurrage rate laid down in the Schedule referred 392
to in Clause 20, or 393

c) The Receivers shall effect the discharge free of any risk and expense 394
whatsoever to the Vessel, save that the Owners shall pay to the Receivers 395
the fixed price indicated in Box 22 per cubic metre of cargo discharged. 396
The Owners shall provide winches, motive power and winchmen from 397
the crew, if requested and permitted; if not so requested and permitted 398
the Receivers shall provide and pay for winchmen from shore and/or 3⁰⁰
for shore cranes if any. The stevedores shall be appointed by, and shall 400
be the servants of, the Receivers but shall follow the reasonable in- 401
structions of the Master in connection with the discharging which shall 402
be to his reasonable satisfaction. 403
Incentive money shall be payable to the Receivers on laytime saved 404
at 50 per cent. of the demurrage rate laid down in the Schedule referred 405
to in Clause 20, or 406

(d) The Owner's liability shall cease at the port of discharge when the cargo 407
is discharged at the ship's rail if discharged by hand or within reach of 408
the ship's tackle or shore crane tackle if thereby discharged (the Owner 409
having the option of using the ship's tackle or shore crane where per- 410
missible by local regulations). The cargo shall, however, be discharged 411
by the vessel by any method approved for the port of discharge by the 412
Chamber of Shipping of the United Kingdom and by the Timber Trade 413
Federation of the United Kingdom current at the time discharging 414
commences. Receivers shall have the right to select any one or more of 415
the approved methods of discharge if available at the time of discharge. 416
Discharging Costs shall be borne by Owners and Receivers as 417
shown in the Schedule agreed between the Chamber of Shipping of the 418
United Kingdom and the Timber Trade Federation of the United 419
Kingdom current at the date discharging commences. If the actual cost 420
per cubic metre of the discharge of the goods exceeds the average cost 421
per cubic metre shown in such Schedule for the Port concerned half the 422
total of such excess shall be payable to the Owners by the Receivers. If 423
the actual cost per cubic metre be less than the average cost per cubic 424
metre so ascertained half the total of such difference shall be paid to 425
the Receivers by the Owners. For the purpose of this Clause the actual 426
cost shall comprise such items of expenditure as are included in the 427
assessment of the average cost of discharging as contained in the 428
Schedule. 429
Incentive money shall be payable to the Receivers on laytime 4??
saved at 25 per cent. of the demurrage rate laid down in the Schedule
referred to in Clause 20. '
In the execution of any work done beyond discharging cargo at the 433
ship's rail or within reach of the ship's tackle or shore crane tackle, as the 434
case may be, the Owners shall act as stevedores with the liabilities only 435
of such and not further or otherwise, but the Owners shall not be liable 436
for damage by fire, even though caused by the act or neglect of the 437
Owners or their servants or any person for whom they are responsible. 438

(e) Laytime shall be calculated in accordance with Clause 20 hereof. 439
Saturdays, Sundays and general and local holidays are excepted, unless 440
used, in which event time shall count in accordance with Clause 20. and 441
The time for discharging shall commence at 14.00 if the 442
Vessel be ready to discharge (whether in berth or not) and written or 443
telegraphic notice of readiness has been given to the Receivers or their 444
Agents before noon, and at the commencement of the next working 445
day if notice be given after noon within ordinary office hours. Subject 446
to the provisions of Clause 9, should the Vessel be prevented from 447
entering port, harbour or dock, or from arriving at or off discharging 448
place by any reason other than weather, tidal conditions or inefficiency 449
of the Vessel, the Vessel shall be regarded as if ready in berth from the 450
first high water after arrival at or off the port, or so near thereunto as she 451
may be permitted to approach, and the time shall count as above. The
time occupied in moving to discharging berth shall not count.
The Receivers have liberty to work on excepted days and outside 4...
ordinary working hours, they paying extra expenses in accordance with 455
Clause 29. 456

16. London Dock Dues 457

If discharged in a dock in London the Consignees shall pay two thirds 458
of the dock dues. 459

17 UK Timber Trade Shipowners' Mutual Association 460

The Owners undertake to become Members of the United Kingdom 461

(a) Timber Trade Shipowners' Mutual Association Limited (hereinafter 462
referred to as " The Association ") if not already Members and for the 463
purpose of this Charter shall be deemed to be Members. On signing 464
this Charter the Owners and Charterers shall ensure that the Association 465
is notified of the date hereof, the name of the Owners and of the Vessel 466
or if no Vessel is named or there be a substitution under Clause 28 467
thereof or if the Charter be cancelled, then the Owners and Charterers 468
shall in due course notify the Association of the Vessel nominated or 469
substituted or of the cancellation of the Charter. 470

(b) The Owners also undertake to pay the voyage subscription required by 471
the Association at the rate current at the time of signing this Charter. 472
The said subscription shall be based on the Bill of Lading quantity. 473
The said voyage subscription shall be remitted to the Association by 474
the Owner's Agent at discharging port together with the payment due 475

(c) from the Bill of Lading holder under Clause 19 hereof, when the first 476
instalment of freight is received. 477
In the event of clauses 15 (b), 15 (c) or 15 (d) applying the Owners shall pay 478
to the Association, at the rate prescribed in Clause 17 (b), a Timber Dis- 479
charging Equalisation Charge as provided under Clause 20. In con- 480
sideration of such payment the Association shall pay to the Receivers 481
any incentive money due on receipt of a claim from the said receivers. 482

(d) No demurrage shall be payable under this Charter unless Rules 12 and 13 483
of the Association have been complied with. 485

18. Demurrage at Loading Port 486

(a) Should the Vessel not be loaded at the rate provided in Clause 20 whereby 487
the Vessel is detained the Owners shall be entitled to claim demurrage 488
from the Association. Subject to the Rules and Conditions of the 489
Association, such demurrage shall be payable by the Association to the 4⁰⁰
Owners at the rate provided by Clause 20 hereof. 491

(b) The Owners expressly waive any right to claim demurrage in respect of 493
the loading port otherwise than is provided for in the preceding para- 494
graph of this clause and undertake that neither they nor the Master will 495
endorse or clause any Bill of Lading with a claim for loading port 495
demurrage. 496

19. Demurrage at Discharging Port 497
(a) Should the Vessel not be discharged at the rate provided in Clause 20 whereby the Vessel is detained, demurrage shall be payable at the rate as provided by Clause 20 hereof per running day and *pro rata* for any part of a day. 498–501

(b) In consideration of the Owners waiving any rights they may have to claim demurrage under the preceding paragraph of this clause the holder of each Bill of Lading shall severally pay to the Association or for its account, whether the Vessel has been detained beyond her lay-days at discharging port(s) or not, the sum as provided by Clause 20 hereof per cubic metre on the total number of cubic metres delivered. The said payment shall be made by each Bill of Lading holder to the Owners, Agents or Brokers with the first instalment of freight by cheque in favour of the Association, such payment shall be based on the Bill of Lading quantity but shall be subject to adjustment when final out-turn is ascertained on the same basis as the final instalment for freight is payable under Clause 21 hereof. 502–513

(c) Should it appear to the Owner or his Agent at the port of discharge that for reasons within the control of any Receiver the Vessel may not be discharged within the laydays, the agents shall forthwith send to such Receiver Notice of Warning to the effect that the Agent considers that demurrage may be incurred because of his conduct and the Agent shall send a copy of such Notice of Warning to the Association. Failure by the Owner's Agents to send a Notice of Warning shall not in any way prejudice the Owner's right or affect the Receiver's liabilities under this Charter. Where bill of lading holders, through any reason within their control, cause demurrage in excess of the total contribution payable by them under (b) of this Clause they shall also pay to the Association half the cost of such excess demurrage. 514–525

20. Loading/Discharge Rates, etc. 526
The Schedule of the Association current at the time of signing this charter shall apply to: 527–528
   (i) Rates for loading under Clause 6 and for discharging under Clause 15 at the appropriate port(s) of loading and discharge. 529–530
   (ii) Calculation of laytime under Clauses 6 and 15. 531
   (iii) Voyage subscription under Clause 17 (b). 532
   (iv) The timber discharging equalisation charge under Clause 17 (c). 533
   (v) Demurrage rates under Clauses 18 (a) and 19 (a). 534
   (vi) Contribution under Clause 19 (b). 535

21. Payment of Freight 536
The freight (as indicated in Box 20) and charges (if any) payable by the Consignees under Clause 15 shall be paid in cash less advance freight (if any) as follows 537–539
90 per cent. (as calculated upon the quantity of cargo on board the vessel upon arrival at destination) shall be paid upon vessel's commencing discharge and the remainder upon final out-turn being ascertained or 60 days from completion of discharge, whichever is the earlier, without prejudice to the owner's right to exercise his lien under Clause 24. Where balance of freight is paid before final out-turn is ascertained it shall be on the basis of Bill of Lading quantity less allowances for pieces short delivered provided that the consignees may within six months of completion of discharge claim refund of any over-payment on the basis of final out-turn. 540–549

22. General Average 550
General Average shall be payable according to the York-Antwerp Rules 1974, but where the adjustment is made in accordance with the law and practice of the United States of America, the following Clause shall apply: 551–554

New Jason Clause 555

In the event of accident, danger, damage or disaster, before or after the commencement of the voyage, resulting from any cause whatsoever, whether due to negligence or not, for which, or for the consequence of which, the carrier is not responsible by statute, contract or otherwise, the goods, shippers, consignees or owners of the goods shall contribute with the carrier in general average to the payment of any sacrifices, losses or expenses of a general average nature that may be made or incurred and shall pay salvage and special charges incurred in respect of the goods. 556–564

If a salving ship is owned or operated by the carrier, salvage shall be paid for as fully as if the said salving ship or ships belonged to strangers. Such deposit as the carrier or his agents may deem sufficient to cover the estimated contribution of the goods and any salvage and special charges thereon shall, if required, be made by the goods, shippers, consignees or owners of the goods to the carrier before delivery. 565–570

23. Both to Blame Collision Clause 571
If the liability for any collision in which the Vessel is involved while 572

performing this Charter falls to be determined in accordance with the laws of the United States of America, the following Clause shall apply: 573–574

If the ship comes into collision with another ship as a result of the negligence of the other ship and any act, neglect or default of the Master, Mariner, Pilot or the servants of the carrier in the navigation or in the management of the ship, the owners of the goods carried hereunder will indemnify the carrier against all loss or liability to the other or non-carrying ship or her owners in so far as such loss or liability represents loss of, or damage to, or any claim whatsoever of the owners of said goods, paid or payable by the other or non-carrying ship or her owners to the owners of said goods and set off, recouped or recovered by the other or non-carrying ship or her owners as part of their claim against the carrying ship or carrier. 575–585

The foregoing provisions shall also apply where the Owners, Operators or those in charge of any ship or ships or objects other than, or in addition to, the colliding ships or objects are at fault in respect to a collision or contact. 586–589

24. Lien 590
The Master or Owners shall have an absolute lien upon the cargo for all freight, deadfreight, demurrage contribution payable under Clause 19 (b), average and charges under Clause 15. 591–593

25. Telegrams 594
A letter may be substituted for a telegram wherever required herein if it be sent so as to arrive as speedily. 595–596

26. Brokerage 597
A brokerage as indicated in Box 23 calculated upon the amount of the freight and/or deadfreight is due by the Owners upon shipment of cargo to the party mentioned in Box 24. 598–600

27. Agency 601
The Owners shall appoint their own Brokers or Agents at both loading and discharging ports. 602–603

28. Substitution 604
The Owners have liberty to substitute a Vessel of similar size, draught, class and position and on the same terms of Charter provided they give telegraphic notice to Charterers not less than 14 days prior to the probable date of Vessel's arrival at the (first) port of loading. 605–608

29. Overtime 609
If work is done outside ordinary working hours or on excepted days (a) at the request or on the orders of the owners all extra expenses incurred, including any extra sums paid by the Charterers/Receivers to lightermen, tally clerks and cargo superintendents and others and demurrage on lighters, trucks and bogies, shall be borne and paid by the owner of the Vessel; (b) if at the request or on the orders of Charterers/Receivers all extra expenses shall be for their account; (c) if on the orders of the Port Authority or any person empowered to order the Vessel to work after ordinary working hours or on excepted days then the Owners and Charterers/Receivers shall bear and pay such extra expenses incurred by them respectively in complying with any such orders or directions. 610–620

30. Arbitration 621
Any dispute arising out of this Charter or any Bill of Lading issued hereunder shall be referred to arbitration in accordance with the provisions of the Arbitration Act, 1950, or any statutory modification or re-enactment thereof for the time being in force except in cases where the Charterer or Receiver is resident or carries on business in Scotland, then such disputes shall be referred to arbitration in accordance with the provisions of the Scottish Arbitration Act, 1894, or any statutory modification or re-enactment thereof for the time being in force and Arbitrators shall have power to assess and award damages. All arbitrations, except those to which the Scottish Arbitration Act, applies shall in default of agreement between the parties to the contrary, be held in London and arbitrations to which the Scottish Arbitration Act, 1894, applies shall in default of agreement between the parties to the contrary be held in Glasgow. 622–635

The dispute shall be referred to a sole arbitrator to be agreed between the parties or failing such agreement to two arbitrators one to be appointed by each of the parties with power to appoint an Umpire. The Arbitrators and Umpire shall be commercial men. 636–639

All claims must be made in writing and the Claimant's Arbitrator must be appointed within twelve months of the date of final discharge or of the date when the goods should have been so discharged otherwise the claim shall be deemed waived and absolutely barred. 640–643

31. Telex 644
Wherever the word telegram appears in the Charter or General Conditions it shall be deemed to include Telex. 645–646

The attention of Owners is drawn to the necessity of reporting this fixture by sending a copy of The Agreement Sheet to the United Kingdom Timber Trade Shipowners' Mutual Association Limited.

Agreed and Published by:
CHAMBER OF SHIPPING OF THE UNITED KINGDOM (Copyright).
Agreed and Adopted by:
THE BALTIC AND INTERNATIONAL MARITIME CONFERENCE

Agreed with:
THE TIMBER TRADE FEDERATION OF THE UNITED KINGDOM
THE FINNISH SAWMILL OWNERS' ASSOCIATION
THE SWEDISH WOOD EXPORTERS' ASSOCIATION

Authorised Printer:
S. Straker & Sons Ltd.,
49 Fenchurch Street, London

Shipper

Consignee

Reference No.

Master for this present voyage

Date of Charter party

Notify address

'NUBALTWOOD' BILL OF LADING

(The Vessel has liberty to sail without pilots, to proceed via any route, to proceed to and stay at any port or ports whatsoever in any order in or out of the route or in a contrary direction to or beyond the port of destination once or oftener for bunkering or loading or discharging cargo or embarking or disembarking passengers or any other purposes whatsoever, and to carry the within cargo into and then beyond the port of discharge named herein and to return to and discharge the said cargo at such port, to tow or to be towed, to make trial trips with or without notice, to adjust or calibrate compasses or to repair or drydock with or without cargo on board, all as part of the contract vorage)

Vessel   Port of loading

Port of discharge

Specification

of which   pieces on deck at Charterers' risk

All the terms, conditions, clauses and exceptions including Clause 30, contained in the said Charter party apply to this Bill of Lading and are deemed to be incorporated herein. Further, notwithstanding anything to the contrary contained in the said Charter party and notwithstanding the transfer, indorsement or negotiation of this Bill of Lading to any person, the Shippers but no other person shall pay any demurrage at loading port calculated in accordance with the terms of the Agreement concerning Loading Port Conditions agreed between The United Kingdom Timber Trade Shipowners' Mutual Association Ltd., and the Finnish Sawmill Owners Association and the Swedish Wood Exporters' Association. In the case of other than Finnish or Swedish Shippers the Loading Port Conditions shall be those agreed between The United Kingdom Timber Trade Shipowners' Mutual Association Ltd. and the Shippers' organisation of the country concerned recognised by The Timber Trade Federation of the United Kingdom, or failing such agreement the Loading Port Conditions set out in the schedule of The United Kingdom Timber Trade Shipowners' Mutual Association Ltd. In all cases the rates shall be those current at the date of the said Charter party.

GENERAL PARAMOUNT CLAUSE

This Bill of Lading shall have effect subject to the provisions of any legislation relating to the carriage of goods by sea which incorporates the rules relating to Bills of Lading contained in the International Convention, dated Brussels 25th August, 1924, and which is compulsorily applicable to the contract of carriage herein contained. Such legislation shall be deemed to be incorporated herein, but nothing herein contained shall be deemed a surrender by the Carrier of any of its rights or immunities or an increase of any of its responsibilities or liabilities thereunder. If any term of this Bill of Lading be repugnant to any extent to any legislation by this clause incorporated, such term shall be void to that extent but no further. Nothing in this Bill of Lading shall operate to limit or deprive the Carrier of any statutory protection or exemption from, or limitation of liability.

The goods described above have been shipped on the above-mentioned vessel in good order and condition and are to be delivered at the above-named port of discharge in the like good order and condition to the consignees and/or his or their assigns subject to the terms and conditions set out in this Bill of Lading.

In WITNESS whereof the Master or Agent of the said ship hath signed

Bills of Lading all of this tenor and date, any one of which being accomplished the others shall be void.

Received upon account of freight ....

Pounds and...Pence

from which a charge of 2% has been deducted.

£ ....

Freight payable at   Place and date of issue

Number of original B/L.   Signature

QUALITY, CONDITION and MEASURE UNKNOWN

2.5 OREVOY CHARTER PARTY AND BILL OF LADING

Description

The Orevoy Charter Party is the document under which a vessel is chartered specifically for the movement of ore under voyage charter conditions. An associated Bill of Lading is code named Orevoybill.

Source of document

The Baltic and International Maritime Conference (BIMCO), Copenhagen.

Purpose/use/function

The Charter Party serves as a contract whereby a shipowner agrees to place the ship, or part of it, at the disposal of a merchant or other person (known as the charterer), for the carriage of goods from one port to another on being paid freight, or to let the ship for a specified period, the shipowner's remuneration being known as hire money.

Legal context

The terms, conditions and exceptions under which the goods are carried are set out in the Charter Party. It will be appreciated that the terms and conditions of a Charter Party will vary according to the wishes of the parties to the contract.

Ratifying organizations/countries

The Orevoy Charter Party has been adopted by BIMCO, by the Documents Committee of the General Council of British Shipping and by the Federation of National Associations of Ship Brokers and Agents (FONASBA). It has been agreed with Malmexport AB, Stockholm and Rohstoffhandel GmbH, Düsseldorf.

Other aspects

The Orevoy Charter Party is well recognized in the ore chartering market worldwide. Its content is reviewed in the light of changing market and legislative conditions. The Bill of Lading associated with it reflects the Charter Party terms and is the document used by the shipper forwarding the ore. It is subservient to the Orevoy Charter Party. The cargo description must conform to the commercial invoice and insurance cover provisions.

1. Shipbroker	THE BALTIC AND INTERNATIONAL MARITIME CONFERENCE STANDARD ORE CHARTER PARTY CODE NAME: "OREVOY" PART I
	2. Place and date of Charter Party
3. Owners/Disponent Owners/Time-Chartered Owners (indicate name, address & telex number)	4. Charterers (indicate name, address & telex number)
5. Vessel's name and flag	6. Rate in tons per hour (load.) (Cl. 1.4.)
7. Vessel's particulars, if required (Cl. 1)	8. Present position and prior commitments, if known (Cl. 2.2.)
9. Laydays date (Cl. 2.1.)	10. Expected readiness to load (Cl. 2.2.)
11. Cancelling date (also state if other period of declaration of cancelling agreed) (Cl. 2.3.)	12. Substitution (state "no" if not agreed) (Cl. 4)
13. Cargo (5 per cent. more or less in Owners' option unless other margin agreed) in tons of 1000 kilos (if full and complete cargo not agreed indicate "part cargo") (Cl. 5.1.)	
14. Advance notices (load. and disch.) (State number of running days' notice to be given and to whom) (Cl. 6)	
15. Loading port(s)/berth(s) (Cl. 7.1.)	16. Discharging port(s)/berth(s) (Cl. 7.2.)
17. Reduced voyage speed (state "no" if not agreed) (Cl. 7.2.)	18. Notice time in running hours (load. and disch.) (only to be filled in if agreed) (Cl. 8.2.1.)
19. Laytime (if separate laytime for load. and disch. is agreed, fill in a) and b); If total laytime for load. and disch., fill in c) only) (Cl. 8.2.5. & 8.2.6.) a) Laytime for loading b) Laytime for discharging c) Total laytime for loading and discharging	20. Laytime exceptions (loading) (Cl. 8.3.1.) 21. Laytime exceptions (discharging) (Cl. 8.3.1.)
22. Demurrage rate (loading) (Cl. 8.5.2.)	23. Demurrage rate (discharging) (Cl. 8.5.2.)
24. Despatch money (load. &/or disch.) (Optional; if agreed indicate rate of despatch money) (Cl. 8.5.3.)	25. Freight tax (state whether for Owners' or Charterers' account) (Cl. 11.3.)
26. Agents at loading port(s) (Cl. 12)	27. Agents at discharging port(s) (Cl. 12)
28. Freight rate per metric ton (state whether fully or partly prepaid) (Cl. 13)	29. Freight payment (currency and when/where payable; also state beneficiary and bank account) (Cl. 13)
30. General average shall be adjusted/settled at (Cl. 20)	31. Law and Arbitration (state 23.1., 23.2. or 23.3. of Cl. 23, as agreed; if 23.3. agreed state place of arbitration) (if not filled in 23.1. shall apply) (Cl. 23)
32. Brokerage commission and to whom payable (Cl. 24)	
	33. Numbers of additional clauses covering special provisions, if agreed

It is mutually agreed that this Contract shall be performed subject to the conditions contained in the Charter consisting of PART I including additional clauses, if any agreed and stated in Box 33 and PART II. In the event of a conflict of conditions, the provisions of PART I shall prevail over those of PART II to the extent of such conflict but no further.

Signature (Owners)	Signature (Charterers)

1. Vessel 1

The Owners shall 2

1.1. before and at the beginning of the loaded voyage exercise due 3
diligence to make the Vessel seaworthy and in every way fit for the 4
voyage, with a full complement of Master, officers and crew for a 5
vessel of her type, tonnage and flag; 6

1.2. ensure that the Vessel and her Master and crew will comply with 7
all safety and health regulations and other statutory rules or regu- 8
lations and internationally recognized requirements necessary to 9
secure safe and unhindered loading of the cargo, performance of 10
the voyage and discharge of the cargo. 11

The Vessel shall 12

1.3. be classed Lloyd's 100 A1 or equivalent unless otherwise agreed 13
in Box 7, the Owners exercising due diligence to maintain that class 14
during the currency of this Charter Party; 15

1.4. be suitable for mechanical loading of the cargo and capable of 16
receiving the cargo at the rate (if any) specified in Box 6 and be 17
suitable for grab discharge, failing which Clause 8.3.3. shall apply 18
and the Owners shall reimburse the Charterers any actual extra dis- 19
charge costs; 20

1.5. be equipped to meet the technical requirements if and as 21
specified in Box 7. 22

2. Laydays Date, Expected Time of Arrival (E.T.A.) and Cancelling 23

2.1. Laydays shall not commence before 00.00 hours on the date 24
stated in Box 9. However, notice of readiness may be given before 25
that date and notice time, if provided for in Box 18, shall run forth- 26
with. 27

2.2. Present position of Vessel as per Box 8. 28
Commitments prior to commencement of this Charter as per Box 8. 29
Expected readiness to load as per Box 10. 30

2.3. The Charterers shall have the option of cancelling the Charter 31
Party if the Vessel be not ready to load on or before twelve midnight 32
(24.00 hours) on the cancelling date stated in Box 11. 33
If it appears that the Vessel will be delayed beyond the cancelling 34
date stated in Box 11 the Owners shall, as soon as they are in a 35
position to state with reasonable certainty the day on which the 36
Vessel should be ready, give notice thereof to the Charterers asking 37
whether they will exercise their option of cancelling the Charter 38
Party. The option must then be declared within five (5) running days 39
(unless otherwise agreed in Box 11) of the receipt by the Charterers 40
of such notice, but not earlier than twenty (20) running days before 41
the revised date stated in the Owners' notice shall be regarded as a 42
exercise their option of cancelling, the seventh (7th) day after the 43
readiness date stated in the Owners' notice shall be regarded as a 44
new cancelling date. This provision shall operate only once, and 45
should the Vessel not be ready to load on the new cancelling date 46
the Charterers shall have the option of cancelling the Charter Party. 47
The Charterers shall in any event declare whether they exercise their 48
option of cancelling under sub-clause 2.3. no later than the time of 49
the Vessel's readiness to load. 50

3. Subletting, Assigning 51

The Charterers shall have the liberty of subletting or assigning this 52
Charter Party to any individual or company, but the Charterers shall 53
always remain responsible for the due fulfilment of all the terms and 54
conditions of this Charter Party and shall warrant that any such sublet 55
or assignment will not result in the Vessel being restricted in her 56
future trading. 57

4. Substitution 58

The Owners shall have liberty to substitute a Vessel, provided that 59
such substitute Vessel's main particulars and position shall be sub- 60
ject to the Charterers' prior approval, which is not to be unreason- 61
ably withheld, but the Owners under this Charter Party shall remain 62
responsible to the Charterers for the due fulfilment of this Charter 63
Party. 64
This Clause shall not apply if "No" inserted in Box 12. 65

5. Cargo 66

5.1. The Charterers warrant that unless otherwise specified in Part I, 67
the cargo referred to in Box 13 is non-hazardous and non-dangerous 68
for carriage according to applicable safety regulations including 69
IMCO Code(s). 70

5.2. The Charterers shall have the right to ship parcels of different 71
qualities and/or for different receivers in separate holds within the 72
Vessel's natural segregation and suitable for her trim provided that 73
such parcels can be loaded, carried and discharged in accordance 74
with the Vessel's seaworthiness. Other means of separation of dif- 75
ferent parcels may be specified in Part I. 76

5.3. Unless otherwise agreed in Part I, all quantities shall be expres- 77
sed in tons of 1,000 kilograms. 78

6. Advance Notices 79

The Owners or the Master shall give notices of expected readiness 80
to load/discharge as specified in Box 14 to the parties named therein 81
and shall keep those parties advised of any alteration in expected 82
readiness. 83

7. Port of Loading, Voyage, Port of Discharge 84

7.1. After completion of prior commitments as may be stated in Box 85
8, the Vessel shall proceed to the loading port(s)/berth(s) as stated 86
in Box 15. 87

7.2. The Vessel shall carry the cargo with all possible despatch to 88
the port(s)/berth(s) of discharge stated in Box 16. However, unless 89
"No" is inserted in Box 17, the Owners may order the Vessel to pro- 90
ceed at reduced speed solely to conserve fuel. 91
If the Charterers have the right to order the Vessel to discharge at 92
one or more ports out of several ports named or within a specific 93
range, the Charterers shall declare the actual port(s) of discharge 94
to be inserted in the Bills of Lading prior to the arrival of the Vessel 95
at the port of loading. 96

7.3. Only when the loading/discharging port(s)/berth(s) are not spe- 97
cifically mentioned herein, the Charterers warrant the safety of port(s)/ 98
berth(s) nominated and that the Vessel will be loaded and discharged 99
always afloat. 100

7.4. The Vessel shall be left in seaworthy trim for shifting between 101
berths and ports. 102

7.5. Unless otherwise agreed, loading and/or discharging at two or 103
more ports shall be effected in geographical rotation. 104

8. Notices of Readiness, Laytime, Demurrage/Despatch Money 105

8.1. *Notice of Readiness* 106

8.1.1. At each port of loading and discharging notice of readiness 107
shall be given to the Charterers or their Agents when the Vessel is 108
in all respects ready to load/discharge at the loading/discharging 109
berth. 110

8.1.2. If a loading/discharging berth is not designated or if such 111
designated berth is not available upon the Vessel's arrival at or off 112
the port, notice of readiness may be given upon arrival at the 113
waiting place at or off the port. 114
However, if the Vessel is at that time prevented from proceeding to 115
the loading/discharging berth due to her inefficiency, weather, tidal 116
conditions, strikes of tugs or pilots or mandatory regulations, notice 117
of readiness may be given only when such hindrance(s) has (have) 118
ceased. 119

8.1.3. Notice of readiness may be given on any day at any time. 120

8.2. *Laytime* 121

8.2.1. The laytime shall commence when notice of readiness has 122
been given and after expiration of notice time, if any, provided for 123
in Box 18. 124
Should the Vessel arrive at the (first) loading port and be ready to 125
load before the date stated in Box 9, the Charterers shall have the 126
right to start loading. The Charterers shall also have the right to 127
load/discharge before the expiration of notice time. In either event, 128
during such periods only time actually used shall count as laytime 129
or as time on demurrage. 130

8.2.2. The notice time shall run continuously. 131

8.2.3. The notice time, if any, shall only apply at first or sole loading 132
and discharging port, respectively. 133

8.2.4. If total time for loading and discharging has been agreed in 134
Box 19 notice time, if any, at port of discharge shall be applied 135
whether the Vessel be on demurrage or not on sailing from the last 136
loading port. 137

8.2.5. *Separate laytime.* – The cargo shall be loaded within the number 138
of hours/days or at the average loading rate 139
per day of 24 consecutive hours as stated in Box 19a). 140
The cargo shall be discharged within the number of hours/days of 141
24 consecutive hours or at the average discharging rate per day of 142
24 consecutive hours as stated in Box 19b). 143

8.2.6. *Total laytime.* – The cargo shall be loaded and discharged within 144
the number of hours/days of 24 consecutive hours stated in Box 19c). 145

8.2.7. In the case of loading and/or discharging at more than one 146
berth, laytime shall run continuously as if loading/discharging has been 147
effected at one berth only but without prejudice to sub-clause 8.3. 148

8.3. *Suspension of Laytime* 149

8.3.1. Unless the Vessel is on demurrage, laytime shall not count 150

(i) during periods excepted as per Boxes 20 and 21, unless used, 151
in which case only time actually used shall count; 152

(ii) for the duration of bad weather or sea conditions which actually 153
prevent the Vessel's loading, discharging or the shifting between 154
loading/discharging berths of the Vessel; 155

(iii) if so provided for in Clause 14. 156

8.3.2. Time shall not count as laytime or as time on demurrage whilst 157
Vessel actually moving from waiting place whether at or off the port 158
or from a lightening place off the port, until the Vessel is securely 159
moored at the designated loading/discharging berth. 160

8.3.3. Time lost due to inefficiency or any other cause attributable 161
to the Vessel, her Master, her crew or the Owners shall not count 162
as notice time or as laytime or as time on demurrage to the extent 163
that loading or discharging or the matters covered by sub-clause 164
8.4.1. are thereby affected. 165

8.3.4. If pursuant to Clause 9.13. the Vessel has to vacate the loading/ 166
discharging berth, notice time or laytime or time on demurrage 167
shall not count from that time until she be in all respects ready to 168
load/discharge and notification has been given to the Charterers 169
accordingly. 170

8.3.5. If due to the matters referred to in sub-clauses 8.3.3. or 8.3.4., 171
the Vessel loses her turn, time shall count again only as from 24 172
hours after notification of the Vessel's new readiness has been given 173
to the Charterers or when loading/discharging resumes whichever 174
may be the sooner. 175

8.4. *Termination of Laytime* 176

8.4.1. Laytime/Demurrage shall stop counting on completion of: 177
(a) loading/discharging at the relevant port, (b) cargo documentation 178
and/or draft survey for determination of cargo weight, (c) repairs to 179
stevedore damage under Clause 10.2, whichever may be the later. 180

8.4.2. If required, the Vessel shall leave the berth as soon as pos- 181
sible within her control on completion of loading/discharging, failing 182
which the Charterers shall be entitled to proved damages provided 183
that if she then has to wait for reasons (b) and/or (c) above, there 184
must be a place available at which she can safely wait, and any 185
extra expenses shall be for the Charterers' account. 186

8.5. *Demurrage/Despatch Money* 187

8.5.1. Demurrage accrued under this Charter Party shall be con- 188
sidered as constituting liquidated damages for exceeding the laytime 189
provided for herein. However, if the Vessel has been on demurrage 190
for 15 days or more and no cargo has been loaded, the Owners shall 191
have the option of cancelling this Charter Party. No claim which the 192
Owners may otherwise have against the Charterers shall be pre- 193
judiced by the Owners exercising their option of cancelling. 194

8.5.2. Demurrage shall be due and payable by the Charterers day by 195
day at the rate specified in Boxes 22 and 23 and in the manner pro- 196
vided for in Box 29. 197

8.5.3. Despatch money, if agreed upon in Box 24, shall be paid 198
promptly by the Owners to the Charterers at half the demurrage rate 199
or as otherwise agreed upon in Box 24 for laytime saved in loading 200
and/or discharging. 201

9. Loading and Discharging 202

9.1. The Vessel shall be loaded and discharged as and where ordered 203
by the Charterers. 204

9.2. If the Charterers have not nominated a suitable loading or dis- 205
charging berth on the Vessel's arrival off the port, or if such berth 206
should not be available, the Vessel is to wait at a suitable place 207
at or off the port. 208
The Charterers shall have the right to designate a safe waiting 209
place, otherwise the Master shall choose a waiting place using due 210
diligence to minimize extra shifting costs provided for in sub- 211
clause 9.4. 212

9.3. The Charterers shall have the right to load and/or discharge at 213
two berths at each port or place subject to sub-clause 9.4. 214

9.4. *Shifting.* – Costs of moving the Vessel, including bunkers, in 215
excess of those which would have been incurred if the Charterers 216
had nominated a free loading or discharging berth on arrival, pro- 217
vided the Vessel arrives on or after the date stated in Box 9, and/or 218
if all cargo had been loaded or discharged during one operation at 219
the first berth only other than a lightening place off the port, shall be 220
for the Charterers' account unless caused by the Vessel's default. 221
Other costs on board the Vessel including wages and officers' and 222
crew's overtime charges to be for the Owners' account. 223

9.5. The Owners or the Master shall in due time prior to commence- 224
ment of loading submit to the Charterers (or their nominees) at the 225
loading port a loading plan which shall be based on a reasonable 226
number of shiftings between hatches and also meet applicable rules 227
and regulations, including IMCO Code(s). The Charterers shall inform 228
the Owners/Master of any special composition of cargo required in 229
sufficient time to permit the Owners/Master to work out and submit 230
such loading plan. 231

9.6. Prior to loading, the Vessel's holds shall be adequately cleaned 232
for loading the contracted cargo. 233

9.7. The Charterers shall, always within the capacity of the loading 234
installations, load and trim the cargo as per the loading plan, free 235
of any risk, liability and expense to the Vessel. Any extra trimming 236
and/or levelling required by the Master or Owners shall be per- 237
formed at the Owners' expense and any time lost thereby shall not 238
count as laytime/demurrage. Discharging, including shovel cleaning, 239
shall be effected by the Charterers free of any risk, liability and 240
expense to the Vessel. 241

9.8. The Vessel shall move along any one berth, as reasonably 242
required by the Charterers, solely for the purpose of making any 243
hatch or hatches available to the loading/discharging appliances at 244
that berth, and costs on board the Vessel including bunkers, wages 245
and officers' and crew's overtime charges shall be for the Owners' 246
account. However, the costs of any necessary outside services shall 247
be for the Charterers' account. Laytime or time on demurrage shall 248
not be interrupted thereby. 249

9.9. The Vessel shall work day and night and during any time as may 250
be excepted as per Box 20 and Box 21, as required by the Charterers. 251

9.10. The Vessel shall, at her own risk and expense, open and close 252
hatches prior to and after loading/discharging and also during load- 253
ing/discharging as may be required by the Charterers to protect the 254
cargo, provided local shore regulations permit. If same, however, is 255
not permitted by local shore regulations, shore labour is to be 256
employed by the Charterers at their risk, liability and expense. 257
The Vessel shall furnish and give free use of sufficient light for deck 258
and holds, as on board. 259

9.11. The Charterers shall have the right to order the Vessel to leave 260
without having loaded a full cargo, always provided that the Vessel 261
be in seaworthy condition and that the Charterers pay deadfreight 262
according to Clause 13.7. 263

9.12. Overtime for loading and discharging to be for the account of 264
the party ordering the same. If overtime be ordered by Port Author- 265
ities or any other Governmental Agencies, the Charterers to pay any 266
extra expenses incurred. Officers' and crew's overtime charges 267
always to be paid by the Owners. 268

9.13. In the event of loading/discharging being impossible due to 269
inefficiency or any other cause attributable to the Vessel, her Master, 270
her crew or the Owners and such impossibility continuing for more 271
than three consecutive hours, the Charterers shall have the right to 272
order the Vessel to vacate the berth and shifting from and back to 273
berth shall be at the Owners' expense and time. 274

10. Stevedore Damage 275

10.1. The Charterers shall be responsible for damage (beyond ordi- 276
nary wear and tear) to any part of the Vessel caused by Stevedores 277
at both ends. Such damage, as soon as apparent, shall be notified 278
immediately by the Master to the Charterers or their port agents 279
and to their Stevedores. The Owners/Master shall endeavour to 280
obtain the Stevedores' written acknowledgment of liability and to 281
settle stevedore damage claims direct with the Stevedores. 282

10.2. The Charterers have the right to perform any repairs of steve- 283
dore damage at any moment prior to or before the completion of 284
the voyage, but must repair stevedore damage affecting the Vessel's 285
seaworthiness before the Vessel sails from the port where such 286
damage was caused. 287

11. Dues, Taxes and Charges, Extra Insurance 288

11.1. *On the Vessel.* – The Owners shall pay all dues, duties, taxes 289
and other charges customarily levied on the Vessel, howsoever the 290
amount thereof may be assessed. 291

11.2. *On the cargo.* – The Charterers shall pay all dues, duties, taxes 292
and charges levied on the cargo at the port of loading/discharging, 293
howsoever the amount thereof may be assessed. 294

11.3. *On the freight.* – Taxes levied on the freight shall be paid by the 295
Owners or the Charterers as agreed in Box 25. 296

11.4. *Extra Insurance.* – Any extra insurance on cargo actually paid 297
by the Charterers owing to Vessel's age, class, flag or ownership 298
shall be for the Owners' account and may be deducted from the 299
freight. The Charterers shall furnish evidence of payment supporting 300
any such deduction. Unless a maximum amount has been agreed in 301
Part I, such extra insurance shall not exceed the lowest extra pre- 302
mium which would be charged for the Vessel and voyage in the 303
London insurance market. 304

12. Agents 305

At the port(s) of loading the Vessel shall be consigned to the Agents 306
as stated in Box 26 and at the port(s) of discharge to the Agents as 307
stipulated in Box 27, the Owners always paying the customary fees. 308

13. Freight 309

The freight at the rate stated in Box 28 shall be calculated on 310
intaken quantity. 311

13.1. *Prepaid.* – If according to Boxes 28 or 29 freight is to be paid on 312
shipment, it shall be deemed earned and non-returnable Vessel and/or 313
cargo lost or not lost. 314
Bills of Lading showing "Freight prepaid" or the like shall not be 315
released until the freight has been duly paid. 316

13.2. *After shipment.* – If according to Box 29 freight shall be payable 317
within a number of days after shipment, the freight shall be deemed 318
earned as per sub-clause 13.1. 319
In such case Bills of Lading shall not be endorsed "Freight prepaid" 320
or the like, unless the freight has been paid. 321

13.3. *Partly on Delivery.* – If according to Boxes 28 or 29 a percentage 322
of the freight shall be payable as per sub-clauses 13.1. or 13.2. the 323
balance shall be paid as per sub-clause 13.4. However, in such case 324
the total freight shall be deemed earned as per sub-clause 13.1. and 325
the Charterers shall not have the option referred to in sub-clause 326
13.4.1. 327

13.4. *On Delivery.* – If according to Boxes 28 or 29 freight is payable 328
at destination or on right and true delivery of the cargo, it shall 329
not be deemed earned until the cargo is thus delivered. 330

13.4.1. *On Delivered Weight.* – When the freight is payable on delivery 331
of cargo the Charterers shall have the option of paying freight on 332
delivered weight, provided such option be declared in writing before 333
breaking bulk and the weight be ascertained by official weighing ma- 334
chine, otherwise by joint draught survey. The Charterers shall pay 335
all costs incurred in connection with weighing or draught survey. 336
The Owners shall be at liberty to appoint check clerks at their own 337
expense. 338

13.5. *Deductions.* – The freight shall be paid in cash without discount 339
in the manner described in Box 29. The Charterers shall only be 340
entitled to deduct from the freight any freight advances made as per 341
sub-clause 13.6., despatch money and extra insurance, provided 342
properly documented, as per Clause 11.4. 343

13.6. *Freight Advances.* – The Owners shall put the Agents at the load- 344
ing port(s) in funds to cover the Vessel's ordinary disbursements 345
for Owners' account, prior to the Vessel's sailing from the port(s) 346
of loading. Otherwise the amount shall be advanced by Charterers 347
and be endorsed upon Bills of Lading as advance freight, with the 348
addition of 3 per cent. to cover interest, commission and the cost 349
of insurance. 350

13.7. *Deadfreight.* – If the Charterers fail to supply a cargo as speci- 351
fied in Box 13, deadfreight shall be payable but the Charterers shall 352
not be bound to supply cargo in excess of any quantity stated by 353
the Owners as the Vessel's capacity made available to the Charterers. 354
The laytime shall be calculated on that quantity. 355
The Owners/Master shall be entitled to clause Bills of Lading for 356
any deadfreight due. 357
If the Shippers/Suppliers state in writing that no more cargo will be 358
shipped, the Owners shall not need to have any such statement con- 359
firmed by the Charterers. 360

14. Strikes and Other Hindrances 361

In the event of any of the causes referred to in Clause 21.2. either 362
preventing or delaying or, being already in existence, threatening to 363
prevent or delay the loading of the cargo intended for the Vessel, 364
or its discharging, the following provisions shall apply: 365

14.1. *Loading Port.* – When the Vessel is ready to proceed from her 366
last port or at any time during the voyage to the port or ports of 367
loading or after her arrival there, the Owners may ask the Charterers 368
to declare that they agree to count the laytime as if there were 369
no such hindrance. Unless the Charterers have given such de- 370
claration in writing (by telegram or telex if necessary) on the second 371
business day after receipt of the request, the Owners shall have the 372
option of cancelling this Charter Party. If part cargo has already 373
been loaded the Vessel must carry it to the port of discharge 374
(freight payable on loaded quantity only) having liberty to complete 375
with other cargo on the way for the Owners' own account, but the 376
Owners are entitled to keep the Vessel waiting at the loading port 377

without time counting. In case of more than one loading port and 378
if the causes referred to above do not prevent the loading in all 379
ports, the Charterers are entitled to order the Vessel to proceed to 380
the second or subsequent port and there to load a full cargo; in 381
such event, the Owners are not entitled to cancel the Charter Party 382
as hereabove stipulated. 383

14.2. *Discharging Port.* – On or after the Vessel's arrival at or off the 384
port of discharge, the Vessel shall wait until any such hindrance is 385
at an end, the Charterers paying half demurrage after expiration of 386
the laytime (unless the Vessel is already on demurrage in which 387
event full demurrage remains payable) full demurrage being payable 388
from the moment when the hindrance is at an end. 389
The Charterers shall have the option at any time of ordering the 390
Vessel to another safe port within 600 nautical miles' distance where 391
she can safely discharge without being detained by any cause 392
enumerated above. Shifting time shall count as laytime or as full 393
demurrage time as the case may be. 394
The Charterers shall reimburse the Owners additional port charges 395
including pilotage and canal dues, if any, incurred thereby; however, 396
the Owners shall bear the costs of bunkers consumed. All conditions 397
of this Charter Party and/or of the Bills of Lading issued hereunder 398
shall apply to the delivery of the cargo at the substituted port and 399
the Owners shall receive the same freight as if the cargo had been 400
discharged at the original destination. 401

15. Ice 402

Loading Port 403

15.1. If the Vessel cannot reach the loading port by reason of ice 404
when she is ready to proceed from her last port, or at any time during 405
the voyage, or on her arrival, or if frost sets in after her arrival, the 406
Master – for fear of the Vessel being frozen in – is at liberty to leave 407
without cargo; in such cases this Charter Party shall become null 408
and void. 409

15.2. If during the loading the Master, for fear of the Vessel being 410
frozen in, deems it advisable to leave, he has liberty to do so with 411
what cargo he has on board and to proceed to any other port with 412
option of completing with cargo for the Owners' own account to any 413
port or ports including the port of discharge. Any part cargo thus 414
loaded under this Charter Party is to be forwarded to destination 415
at the Vessel's expense against payment of the agreed freight, pro- 416
vided that no extra expenses be thereby caused to the Charterers, 417
freight being paid on the quantity delivered (in proportion if lump 418
sum), all other conditions as per Charter Party. 419

15.3. In the case of more than one loading port, and if one or more 420
of the ports are closed by ice, the Master or Owners are to be at 421
liberty either to load the part cargo at the open port and fill up else- 422
where for the Owners' account under sub-clause 15.2. or to 423
declare the Charter Party null and void, unless the Charterers 424
agree to load full cargo at the open port. 425

Voyage and Discharging Port 426

15.4. Should ice prevent the Vessel from reaching the port of dis- 427
charge, the Charterers shall have the option of keeping the Vessel 428
waiting until the re-opening of navigation and paying demurrage, or 429
of ordering the Vessel to a safe and immediately accessible port 430
where she can safely discharge without risk of detention by ice. Such 431
orders are to be given within 48 hours after the Owners or Master 432
have given notice to the Charterers of the impossibility of reaching 433
the port of destination. 434

15.5. If during discharging the Master, for fear of the Vessel being 435
frozen in, deems it advisable to leave, he has liberty to do so with 436
what cargo he has on board and to proceed to the nearest safe and 437
accessible port. Such port to be nominated by the Charterers as 438
soon as possible, but not later than 24 running hours, Sundays 439
and holidays excluded, of receipt of the Owners' request for nomi- 440
nation of a substitute discharging port, failing which the Master will 441
himself choose such port. 442

15.6. On delivery of the cargo at such port, all conditions of the Bill 443
of Lading shall apply and the Owners shall receive the same freight 444
as if the Vessel had discharged at the original port of destination 445
except that if the distance to the substitute port exceeds 100 nautical 446
miles, the freight on the cargo delivered at that port is to be in- 447
creased in proportion. 448

16. War Risks ("Voywar 1950") 449

16.1. In these Clauses "war risks" shall include any blockade or any 450
action which is announced as a blockade by any Government or by 451
any belligerent or by any organized body, sabotage, piracy, and any 452
actual or threatened war, hostilities, warlike operations, civil war, 453
civil commotion, or revolution. 454

16.2. If at any time before the Vessel commences loading, it appears 455
that performance of the contract will subject the Vessel or her Master 456
and crew or her cargo to war risks at any stage of the adventure, 457
the Owners shall be entitled by letter or telegram despatched to the 458
Charterers, to cancel this Charter Party. 459

16.3. The Master shall not be required to load cargo or to continue 460
loading or to proceed on or to sign Bill(s) of Lading for any adventure 461
on which or any port at which it appears that the Vessel, her Master 462
and crew or her cargo will be subjected to war risks. In the event of 463
the exercise by the Master of his right under this Clause after part 464
or full cargo has been loaded, the Master shall be at liberty either 465
to discharge such cargo at the loading port or to proceed therewith. 466
In the latter case the Vessel shall have liberty to carry other cargo 467
for Owners' benefit and accordingly to proceed to and load or 468
discharge such other cargo at any other port or ports whatsoever, 469
backwards or forwards, although in a contrary direction to or out of 470
or beyond the ordinary route. In the event of the Master electing to 471
proceed with part cargo under this Clause freight shall in any case 472
be payable on the quantity delivered. 473

16.4. If at the time the Master elects to proceed with part or full 474
cargo under Clause 16.3. or after the Vessel has left the loading port, 475
or the last of the loading ports if more than one, it appears that 476
further performance of the Charter Party will subject the Vessel, 477

her Master and crew or her cargo, to war risks, the cargo shall be 478
discharged, or if the discharge has been commenced shall be com- 479
pleted, at any safe port in vicinity of the port of discharge as may 480
be ordered by the Charterers. If no such orders shall be received 481
from the Charterers within 48 hours after the Owners have despatched 482
a request by telegram or telex to the Charterers for the nomination 483
of a substitute discharging port, the Owners shall be at liberty to 484
discharge the cargo at any safe port which they may, in their discre- 485
tion, decide on and such discharge shall be deemed to be due ful- 486
filment of the Charter Party. In the event of cargo being discharged 487
at any such other port, the Owners shall be entitled to freight as if 488
the discharge had been effected at the port or ports named in the 489
Bill(s) of Lading, or to which the Vessel may have been ordered 490
pursuant thereto. 491

16.5. (a) The Vessel shall have liberty to comply with any directions 492
or recommendations as to loading, departure, arrival, routes, ports 493
of call, stoppages, destination, zones, waters, discharges, delivery or 494
in any other wise whatsoever (including any direction or recommen- 495
dation not to go to the port of destination or to delay proceeding 496
thereto or to proceed to some other port) given by any Government 497
or by any belligerent or by any organized body engaged in civil war, 498
hostilities or warlike operations or by any person or body acting or 499
purporting to act as or with the authority of any Government or bel- 500
ligerent or of any such organized body or by any committee or person 501
having under the terms of the war risks insurance on the Vessel, the 502
right to give any such directions or recommendations. If, by reason 503
of or in compliance with any such direction or recommendation, any- 504
thing is done or is not done, such shall not be deemed a deviation. 505

(b) If, by reason of or in compliance with any such directions or 506
recommendations, the Vessel does not proceed to the port or ports 507
named in the Bill(s) of Lading or to which she may have been 508
ordered pursuant thereto, the Vessel may proceed to any port as 509
directed or recommended or to any safe port which the Owners in 510
their discretion may decide on and there discharge the cargo. Such 511
discharge shall be deemed to be due fulfilment of the Charter Party 512
and the Owners shall be entitled to freight as if discharge had been 513
effected at the port or ports named in the Bill(s) of Lading or to 514
which the Vessel may have been ordered pursuant thereto. 515

16.6. All extra expenses (including insurance costs) involved in dis- 516
charging cargo at the loading port or in reaching or discharging the 517
cargo at any port as provided in Clauses 16.4. and 16.5.(b) hereof 518
shall be paid by the Charterers and/or cargo owners, and the Owners 519
shall have a lien on the cargo for all moneys due under these 520
Clauses. 521

17. Lien 522

The Owners shall have a lien on the cargo for freight, deadfreight, 523
demurrage and damages for detention. The Charterers shall remain 524
responsible for deadfreight and demurrage (including damages for 525
detention), incurred at port of loading. The Charterers shall also 526
remain responsible for freight and demurrage (including damages 527
for detention) incurred at port of discharge, but only to such extent 528
as the Owners have been unable to obtain payment thereof by exer- 529
cising the lien on the cargo. 530

18. Liberty 531

The Vessel shall have liberty to sail with or without pilots, to tow or 532
go to the assistance of vessels in distress, to call at any port or 533
place for oil fuel supplies, and to deviate for the purpose of saving 534
life or property, or for any other reasonable purpose whatsoever. 535

19. Both-to-Blame Collision Clause 536

If the Vessel comes into collision with another vessel as a result of 537
the negligence of the other vessel and any act, neglect or default of 538
the Master, mariner, pilot or the servants of the Owners in the navi- 539
gation or in the management of the Vessel, the owners of the cargo 540
carried hereunder will indemnify Owners against all loss or liability 541
to the other or non-carrying vessel or her Owners in so far as such 542
loss or liability represents loss of, or damage to, or any claim what- 543
soever of the owners of said cargo, paid or payable by the other or 544
non-carrying vessel or her Owners to the owners of said cargo and 545
set-off, recouped or recovered by the other or non-carrying vessel 546
or her Owners as part of their claim against the carrying vessel or 547
Owners. 548
The foregoing provisions shall also apply where the owners, ope- 549
rators or those in charge of any vessel or vessels or objects other 550
than, or in addition to, the colliding vessels or objects are at fault 551
in respect of a collision or contact. 552

20. General Average and New Jason Clause 553

General Average shall be adjusted and settled at the place indicated 554
in Box 30 according to the York/Antwerp Rules, 1974, or any modi- 555
fication thereof, but if, notwithstanding the provisions specified in 556
Box 30, the adjustment is made in accordance with the law and 557
practice of the United States of America, the following clause shall 558
apply: 559
"In the event of accident, danger, damage or disaster before or after- 560
the commencement of the voyage, resulting from any cause what- 561
soever, whether due to negligence or not, for which, or for the con- 562
sequence of which, Owners are not responsible, by statute, contract 563
or otherwise, the goods, shippers, consignees or owners of the goods 564
shall contribute with Owners in general average to the payment of 565
any sacrifices, losses or expenses of a general average nature that 566
may be made or incurred and shall pay salvage and special charges 567
incurred in respect of the goods. If a salving Vessel is owned or 568
operated by Owners, salvage shall be paid for as fully as if the said 569
salving Vessel or vessels belonged to strangers. Such deposit as 570
Owners, or their agents, may deem sufficient to cover the estimated 571
contribution of the goods and any salvage and special charges 572
thereon shall, if required, be made by the goods, shippers, con- 573
signees or owners of the goods to Owners before delivery". 574

PART II
"OREVOY" Charter Party

21. Responsibilities and Immunities 575

21.1.1. The Hague Rules contained in the International Convention 576 for the Unification of certain rules relating to Bills of Lading, dated 577 Brussels the 25th August 1924 as enacted in the country of shipment 578 shall apply to this Contract and to any Bill of Lading issued here- 579 under. 580
When no such enactment is in force in the country of shipment, the 581 corresponding legislation of the country of destination shall apply, 582 but in respect of shipments to which no such enactments are com- 583 pulsorily applicable, the terms of the said Convention shall apply. 584
21.1.2. In trades where the International Brussels Convention 1924 as 585 amended by the Protocol signed at Brussels on February 23rd, 1968 586 – The Hague-Visby Rules – apply compulsorily, the provisions of the 587 respective legislation shall apply. 588
21.1.3. The Owners shall in no case be responsible for loss of or 589 damage to cargo howsoever arising prior to loading into and after 590 discharge from the Vessel or while the goods are in the charge of 591 another owner nor in respect of deck cargo and live animals. This 592 sub-clause shall not detract from the Owners' obligations under 593 Clause 4. 594

21.2. Save to the extent otherwise in this Charter Party expressly 595 provided, neither party shall be responsible for any loss or damage 596 or delay or failure in performance hereunder resulting from Act of 597 God, war, civil commotion, quarantine, strikes, lockouts, arrest or 598 restraint of princes, rulers and peoples or any other event what- 599 soever which cannot be avoided or guarded against. 600

22. Bills of Lading 601

22.1. Bills of Lading are to be signed as per the "Orevoybill" Bill of 602 Lading without prejudice to this Charter Party, and the Charterers 603 hereby indemnify the Owners against all liabilities that may arise 604 from the signing of Bills of Lading as presented to the extent that 605 the terms of such Bills of Lading impose more onerous liabilities 606 upon the Owners than those assumed by the Owners under the terms 607 of this Charter Party. 608
Neither the Owners nor their Servants shall be required to sign or 609 endorse Bills of Lading showing freight prepaid unless and until the 610 freight due to the Owners has actually been paid. 611

22.2. The Master may be required to sign separate Bills of Lading 612 for cargo in different holds or for parcels properly separated upon 613 shipment by the Charterers or their Agents, the Owners not being 614 answerable for separate delivery, nor for the cost of cargo short- 615 delivered (if any) provided all the cargo taken on board is delivered. 616

23. Law and Arbitration 617

23.1. Unless otherwise agreed in Box 31, this Charter Party shall be 618 governed by English Law and any dispute arising out of this Charter 619 Party or any Bill of Lading issued thereunder shall be referred to 620 arbitration in London, one arbitrator being appointed by each party, 621 in accordance with the Arbitration Acts 1950 and 1979 or any statutory 622 modification or re-enactment thereof for the time being in force. 623 On the receipt by one party of the notification in writing of the 624 appointment of the other party's arbitrator, that party shall appoint 625 their arbitrator within fourteen days failing which the decision of the 626 single arbitrator appointed shall apply. If two arbitrators properly 627 appointed shall not agree they shall appoint an umpire whose de- 628 cision shall be final. 629

23.2. If agreed and stated in Box 31, this Charter Party shall be 630 governed by U.S. Law and all disputes arising out of this Charter 631 Party or any Bill of Lading issued thereunder shall be arbitrated at 632 New York in the following manner: 633
One arbitrator is to be appointed by each of the parties hereto and 634 a third by the two so chosen. Their decision or that of any two of 635 them shall be final, and for the purpose of enforcing any award, this 636 agreement may be made a rule of the court. The arbitrators shall be 637 commercial men. Such arbitration is to be conducted in accordance 638 with the rules of the Society of Maritime Arbitrators, Inc. 639
For disputes where the total amount claimed by either party does 640 not exceed U.S. $ 3,500.00, or an amount as mutually agreed, the 641 arbitration may be conducted in accordance with the Simplified Arbi- 642 tration Procedure of the Society of Maritime Arbitrators Inc. if so 643 desired by both parties. 644

23.3. If agreed and stated in Box 31, any disputes arising out of this 645 Charter Party or any Bill of Lading issued thereunder shall be re- 646 ferred to arbitration at the place or before the arbitration tribunal 647 indicated in Box 31, subject to the law and procedures applicable 648 there. 649

24. Brokerage 650

24.1. The brokerage as stated in Box 32 on freight and deadfreight 651 shall be paid by the Owners and is deemed to be earned by the 652 Brokers upon shipment of cargo. 653

24.2. In case of cancellation pursuant to Clause 2.3., at least one 654 third of the brokerage on the estimated amount of freight shall be 655 paid by the Owners as indemnity to the Brokers. 656

CODE NAME: "OREVOYBILL"

BILL OF LADING

Shipper

B/L No.

Reference No.

Consignee

Notify address

| Vessel | Port of loading |

Port of discharge

Shipper's description of cargo   Gross weight

Issued pursuant to
CHARTER-PARTY dated ....

Freight payable in accordance therewith.

FREIGHT ADVANCE.
Received on account of freight:

....

SHIPPED at the Port of Loading in apparent good order and condition on board the Vessel for carriage to the Port of Discharge or so near thereto as she may safely get the goods specified above.

Weight, measure, quality, quantity, condition, contents and value unknown.

IN WITNESS whereof the Master or Agent of the said Vessel has signed the number of Bills of Lading indicated below all of this tenor and date, any of which being accomplished the others shall be void.

FOR CONDITIONS OF CARRIAGE SEE OVERLEAF

Freight payable at	Place and date of issue
Number of original Bs/L	Signature

Printed and sold
by Fr. G. Knudtzon Ltd., 55, Toldbodgade, Copenhagen,
by authority of The Baltic and International Maritime Conference
(BIMCO), Copenhagen.

BILL OF LADING

TO BE USED FOR SHIPMENTS UNDER THE "OREVOY" CHARTER
CODE NAME: "OREVOYBILL"
EDITION 1980

Conditions of Carriage.

(1) All terms and conditions, liberties and exceptions of the Charter Party, dated as overleaf, including the War Risks Clause (Clause 16) and the Law and Arbitration Clause (Clause 23) are hereby expressly incorporated. If this Bill of Lading covers a transport for which no Charter Party has been agreed, the terms of the "Orevoy" Charter shall be deemed to be incorporated in this Bill of Lading.

(2) General Paramount Clause.

(a) The Hague Rules contained in the International Convention for the Unification of certain rules relating to Bills of Lading, dated Brussels the 25th August 1924 as enacted in the country of shipment shall apply to this contract. When no such enactment is in force in the country of shipment, the corresponding legislation of the country of destination shall apply, but in respect of shipments to which no such enactments are compulsorily applicable, the terms of the said Convention shall apply.

(b) *Trades where Hague-Visby Rules apply.*

In trades where the International Brussels Convention 1924 as amended by the Protocol signed at Brussels on February 23rd 1968 – the Hague-Visby Rules – apply compulsorily, the provisions of the respective legislation shall be considered incorporated in this Bill of Lading.

(c) The Carrier shall in no case be responsible for loss of or damage to cargo howsoever arising prior to loading into and after discharge from the Vessel or while the goods are in the charge of another Carrier nor in respect of deck cargo and live animals.

(3) General Average.

General Average shall be adjusted, stated and settled according to York-Antwerp Rules 1974 or any modification thereof.
Cargo's contribution to General Average shall be paid to the Carrier even when such average is the result of a fault, neglect or error of the Master, Pilot or Crew. The Charterers, Shippers and Consignees expressly renounce the Netherlands Commercial Code, Art. 700, and the Belgium Commercial Code, Part II, Art. 148.

(4) New Jason Clause.

In the event of accident, danger, damage or disaster before or after the commencement of the voyage, resulting from any cause whatsoever, whether due to negligence or not, for which, or for the consequence of which, the Carrier is not responsible, by Statute, contract or otherwise, the cargo, shippers, consignees or owners of the cargo shall contribute with the Carrier in general average to the payment of any sacrifices, losses or expenses of a general average nature that may be made or incurred and shall pay salvage and special charges incurred in respect of the cargo.
If a salving vessel is owned or operated by the Carrier, salvage shall be paid for as fully as if the said salving vessel or vessels belonged to strangers. Such deposit as the Carrier, or his agent, may deem sufficient to cover the estimated contribution of the cargo and any salvage and special charges thereon shall, if required, be made by the cargo, shippers, consignees or owners of the cargo to the Carrier before delivery.

(5) Both-to-Blame Collision Clause.

If the Vessel comes into collision with another vessel as a result of the negligence of the other vessel and any act, neglect or default of the Master, Mariner, Pilot or the Servants of the Carrier in the navigation or in the management of the Vessel, the owners of the cargo carried hereunder will indemnify the Carrier against all loss or liability to the other or non-carrying vessel or her owners in so far as such loss or liability represents loss of, or damage to, or any claim whatsoever of the owners of the said cargo, paid or payable by the other or non-carrying vessel or her owners to the owners of the said cargo and set-off, recouped or recovered by the other or non-carrying vessel or her owners as part of their claim against the carrying vessel or the Carrier.
The foregoing provisions shall also apply where the owners, operators or those in charge of any vessel or vessels or objects other than, or in addition to, the colliding vessels or objects are at fault in respect of a collision or contact.

For particulars of cargo, freight,
destination, etc., see overleaf.

2.6 STANDARD TIME SHEET (SHORT FORM) (VOYAGE CHARTER PARTY)

Description

A time sheet for the calculation of laytime.

Source of document

The Baltic and International Maritime Conference (BIMCO), Copenhagen.

Purpose/use/function

To enable calculations to be made under the terms of a voyage Charter Party the period agreed to load and discharge the cargo is called laytime. This will depend on the quantity of cargo, method of transhipment, nature of cargo and so on. Provided the laytime is not exceeded no demurrage will be raised by the shipowner.

The Standard Time Sheet features the laytime calculation. The Standard Statement of Facts (for example, oil and chemical tank vessels) (section 2.7) is more comprehensive and gives details of the daily working of the ship while in port.

Legal context

Circumstances do arise where the vessel exceeds her laytime – prescribed loading and/or unloading time – and such a situation places the vessel on demurrage. This is a form of penalty charge raised by the shipowner on the charterer as compensation for the delayed departure of the vessel from the destination port. Conversely, in the event of the vessel loading and/or unloading earlier than scheduled, dispatch will arise. This is a form of bonus payment payable by the shipowner to the charterer (section 2.7).

Ratifying organizations/countries

BIMCO and the Federation of National Associations of Ship Brokers and Agents (FONASBA) recommend the form.

Other aspects

The laytime period reflects the agreement reached between the charterer and the shipowner for a Voyage Charter Party. It will specify the period of loading and unloading, and indicate periods of holiday and the working periods during which cargo transhipment can take place. Much case law exists regarding the interpretation of laytime application in various circumstances. When the laytime period is exceeded demurrage arises. Conversely, when the cargo transhipment is completed earlier than planned in the laytime period, the charterer is entitled to dispatch money. The Ship's Agent usually handles the Standard Time Sheet (short form) Voyage Charter Party documentation which contains up to three signatures embracing the Master, Ship Agent etc.

1. Agents		STANDARD TIME SHEET (SHORT FORM) RECOMMENDED BY THE BALTIC AND INTERNATIONAL MARITIME CONFERENCE (BIMCO) AND THE FEDERATION OF NATIONAL ASSOCIATIONS OF SHIP BROKERS AND AGENTS (FONASBA)	

2. Vessel's name	3. Port	
4. Owners/Disponent Owners	5. Vessel berthed	
	6. Loading commenced	7. Loading completed
8. Cargo	9. Discharging commenced	10. Discharging completed
	11. Cargo documents on board	12. Vessel sailed
13. Charter Party *	14. Working hours/meal hours of the port *	
15. Bill of Lading weight/quantity / 16. Outturn weight/quantity		
17. Vessel arrived on roads	18. Time to count from	
19. Notice of readiness tendered	20. Rate of demurrage	21. Rate of despatch money
22. Next tide available	23.	
24. Laytime allowed for loading / 25. Laytime allowed for discharging	26.	

LAYTIME COMPUTATION *

Date	Day	Time worked		Laytime used			Time saved/on demurrage			Remarks *
		From	to	days	hours	minutes	days	hours	minutes	

General remarks *

Place and date	Signature *
Signature *	Signature *

* See Explanatory Notes overleaf for filling in the boxes

Printed and sold by Fr. G. Knudtzon Ltd., 55 Toldbodgade, Copenhagen, by authority of BIMCO

85-0

Published by The Baltic and International Maritime Conference (BIMCO), Copenhagen

INSTRUCTIONS FOR FILLING IN THE BOXES

General

It is recommended to fill in the boxes with a short text. When it is a matter of figures to be inserted as is the case in most of the boxes, this should be done as follows:

7. Loading commenced
1975-03-15-0800

the figures being mentioned in the following order: year—month—date—time.

Boxes Calling for Special Attention

Charter Party*:

Insert name and date of charter, for instance, "Intertankvoy" dated 1975-03-01.

Vessel Sailed*:

Insert date and hour of departure.

Vessel Sailed to*:

State destination.

Details of Daily Working*:

Insert day-by-day figures and indicate in the vertical column marked "Remarks*" all relevant details as to reasons for stoppages such as breakdown of pumps, strikes, shortage of cargo, etc. Moreover, in this box should be stated reasons and duration of delays before berthing, during berthing, between moored and commenced loading, during loading, between completed loading and leaving berth and after leaving berth. Same applies to discharging.

General Remarks*:

This box should be used for insertion of such general observations which are not covered in any of the boxes provided for in the first main group of boxes, for instance, delays on account of slow pumping, excess back pressure, or other general observations.

Signatures*:

It is of importance that the boxes provided for signatures are duly signed by the parties concerned.

2.7 STANDARD STATEMENT OF FACTS (OIL AND CHEMICAL TANK VESSELS) (SHORT FORM) (VOYAGE CHARTER PARTY)

Description

A form for entering details of the daily working hours of a ship while in port.

Source of document

The Baltic and International Maritime Conference (BIMCO), Copenhagen.

Purpose/use/function

To enable laytime calculations to be undertaken under the terms of a voyage Charter Party the period agreed to load and discharge the cargo is called laytime. This will depend on the quantity of cargo, method of transhipment, nature of cargo and so on. Provided the laytime is not exceeded no charge will be raised by the shipowner, as the vessel is enabled to leave the destination port in accord with the original schedule.

The Standard Time Sheet (section 2.6) features the laytime calculation. The Standard Statement of Facts (for example, oil and chemical tank vessels) is more comprehensive and gives details of the daily working of the ship in port and thereby provides data on which laytime can be determined.

Legal context

Circumstances do arise where the vessel exceeds her laytime – prescribed loading and/or unloading time – and such a situation places the vessel on demurrage. This is a form of penalty charge raised by the shipowner on the charterer as compensation for the delayed departure of the vessel from the destination port. Conversely, in the event of the vessel loading and/or unloading earlier than scheduled, dispatch will arise. This is a form of bonus payment payable by the shipowner to the charterer for earlier release of the vessel.

Ratifying organizations/countries

BIMCO and the Federation of National Associations of Ship Brokers and Agents (FONASBA) recommend the form.

Other aspects

This document merely records the fullest details of the progress of the vessel from the time it approached the seaport until the ship's departure. It gives special emphasis to the cargo working arrangements and performance. It is specially designed for oil and chemical cargoes. The document is completed by the Master/Ship's Agent, both of whose signatures feature on it. Legally it is subject to the usual legislative procedure in regard to fraud and misrepresentation.

1. Agents		STANDARD STATEMENT OF FACTS (OIL AND CHEMICAL TANK VESSELS) (SHORT FORM) RECOMMENDED BY THE BALTIC AND INTERNATIONAL MARITIME CONFERENCE (BIMCO) AND THE FEDERATION OF NATIONAL ASSOCIATIONS OF SHIP BROKERS AND AGENTS (FONASBA)		
2. Vessel's name		3. Port or Place		
4. Owners/Disponent Owners		5. Vessel moored		
		6. Hoses connected (load.)	7. Loading commenced	
8. Cargo (also indicate possible details as to slops)		9. Loading completed	10. Hoses disconnected (load.)	
		11. Hoses connected (disch.)	12. Discharging commenced	
13. Charter Party *		14. Discharging completed	15. Hoses disconnected (disch.)	
16. Bill of Lading quantity	17. Outturn quantity	18. Cargo documents on board	19. Vessel sailed *	
20. Vessel arrived at anchorage	21. Pilot on board	22. Draft on arrival (fore and aft)	23. Draft on sailing (fore and aft)	
24. Notice of readiness tendered		25. Vessel arrived from	26. Vessel sailed to *	
27. Next tide available	28. Weighed anchor	29.		
30. Free Pratique given		31.		
32. Deballasting commenced	33. Deballasting completed	34.		
35. Ballasting commenced	36. Ballasting completed	37.		
38. Tanks inspected	39. Tanks passed	40.		

DETAILS OF DAILY WORKING *

Date	Day	Hours worked		Hours stopped		Quantity load./disch.	Remarks *
		From	to	From	to		

General remarks (state reasons and duration of delays, such as slow pumping, excess back pressure, etc.) *

Place and date	Name and signature (Master) *
Name and signature (Agents) *	Name and signature (for the Charterers/Shippers/Receivers) *

* See Explanatory Notes overleaf for filling in the boxes

Printed and sold by Fr. G. Knudtzon Ltd., 55 Toldbodgade, Copenhagen, by authority of BIMCO

Published by The Baltic and International Maritime Conference (BIMCO), Copenhagen

87-0

INSTRUCTIONS FOR FILLING IN THE BOXES

General

It is recommended to fill in the boxes with a short text. When it is a matter of figures to be inserted as is the case in most of the boxes, this should be done as follows:

6. Loading commenced
1975-03-15-0800

the figures being mentioned in the following order: year—month—date—time.

Boxes Calling for Special Attention

Charter Party*:

Insert name and date of charter, for instance, "Gencon" dated 1975-03-01.

Working hours/meal hours of the port*:

Indicate normal working hours/meal hours of the port and not the actual hours worked on board the vessel which may be longer or shorter than the hours normally worked in the port. Such day-by-day figures should be indicated in the box provided for under "Laytime Computation".

Some empty boxes are made available in which other relevant information applying to the particular port or vessel could be inserted, such as, time of granting free pratique, if applicable, etc.

Laytime Computation*:

Insert day-by-day figures and indicate in the vertical column marked "Remarks*" all relevant details as to reasons for stoppages such as bad weather, strikes, breakdown of winches/cranes, shortage of cargo, etc.

General Remarks*:

This box should be used for insertion of such general observations which are not covered in any of the boxes provided for in the first main group of boxes, for instance, reasons for berthing delay or other general observations.

Signatures*:

It is of importance that the boxes provided for signatures are duly signed by the parties concerned.

3 Commercial documents: international trade

3.1 INTRODUCTION

It is the practice in a number of countries to permit preferential import duties subject to the condition that a Certificate of Origin accompanies the goods in question when presented to Customs.

To serve as the basis for an international trade transaction entered into by a seller and buyer, an Export Invoice showing the price of a particular consignment of goods is issued by the seller (exporter).

To certify for example, that agricultural products due for export to the buyer are in good condition prior to shipment, some overseas territories require a Health Certificate to be issued in the exporter's country.

A form known as a Master Document has been developed to serve as a one-run export documentation system ('aligned' documentation).

Preshipment inspection of goods is a requirement of some 30 countries, mostly underdeveloped countries. The use of the Preshipment Inspection Certificate aims to ensure goods are shipped in a quality condition and in accordance with the terms of the export sales contract.

For export licence or Letter of Credit purposes, where an invoice is required in advance of dispatch of goods, a Proforma Invoice may be prepared by the exporter.

To confirm the quality/specification of a particular consignment of goods, a Quality Certificate may be required by the importer.

To confirm the weight of a particular consignment of goods, a Weight Certificate may be required by the importer.

For the purpose of allowing the temporary importation of goods, free of Customs duties, taxes, etc., international Customs documents known as ATA Carnets are issued by Chambers of Commerce in most major countries.

To replace the various member States' export and import declarations and the Community transit document, the European Commission has introduced its Single Administrative Document to serve as export declaration; dispatch/transportation and Community/procedures document; and import declaration in the destination country.

For the movement of goods between member States of the EEC, plus Austria and Switzerland, Form T2L is used.

3.2 CERTIFICATE OF ORIGIN

Description

A Certificate of Origin is a document confirming the nature, quantity, value etc. of goods shipped and their place of manufacture, and includes a declaration stating the country of origin of the goods.

Source of document

Chamber of Commerce issued document or exporters' commercial invoice certified by the Chamber of Commerce or Trade Association.

Purpose/use/function

When goods are presented to Customs for clearance purposes at the time of importation, the Certificate of Origin accompanies the goods and empowers the authorities to permit preferential import duties where appropriate. Such an arrangement usually reflects a bilateral trade agreement between two nations.

Legal context

The declaration may be authenticated by a Chamber of Commerce such as the Arab–British Chamber of Commerce, the Dorset Chamber of Commerce and Industry, or a Consulate. For example, in order that goods from the UK may enjoy the lower schedule of duties, the Customs authorities of the importing country must be satisfied as to the value of the goods and that they substantially represent British labour and British material.

Ratifying organizations/countries

A Certificate of Origin has been adopted for use in the European Community and many other countries worldwide exercising control over the level and origins of their imports.

Other aspects

The Certificate of Origin is a long established document and is required as one of the support documents at the time of importation. No particular format exists internationally but it enables the buyer not only to process the importation of the goods, but also permits a lower level of import duty to be applied. Basically, there are two types of Certificate of Origin in the UK: the one issued by the Arab–British Chamber of Commerce, and the one used by the European Community.

The EEC Certificate of Origin is a three-part document embracing the original (orange), copy (buff) and application copy (pink). It is completed by the Exporter or his Agent. The Chambers of Commerce issue the Certificate of Origin by 'certifying it', i.e. signing it and appending its stamp. The applicant/exporter must submit documentary evidence of the goods to the Chamber usually in the form of a commercial invoice.

The Arab–British Chamber of Commerce Certificate of Origin is a documentary requirement of the Arab League States. It is a three-part document comprising original (green), application copy (blue) and central copy (green). The certificate and application must not contain erasures or superimposed corrections. Any alteration must be authenticated by the person making it and endorsed by the competent authorities. The application procedure involves the following: the exporter submits the Certificate of Origin to an authorized agent, local Chamber of Commerce or direct to the Arab–British Chamber of Commerce. Documentary proof of origin must also be submitted, usually the manufacturers' invoices with appropriate origin declarations. Ultimately, the Arab–British Chamber of Commerce certifies it by adding its signature and stamp. Where legislation is required, the Certificate of Origin plus additional supporting documentation is submitted to the Embassy of the importing country which adds its own stamp and returns it to the applicant.

An alternative to the two foregoing Certificates of Origin is the process of the commercial invoice being certified and legalized to fulfil any requirements of the importing country and consignee. It is treated in the same manner as a Certificate of Origin.

Consignor: ⟨المرسل⟩ 1 ABC Company Ltd, Verwood Wimborne, Dorset England.	**F/ 622063** Consignor's ref.: 4 EXP222 STN6265/85

شهـــادة منشـــأ

CERTIFICATE OF ORIGIN

Consignee: ⟨المرسل اليه⟩ 2 General Establishment of Bakeries & Ovens, Baghdad IRAQ	تشهد السلطة الموقعة بأن البضائع الوارد بيانها أدناه The undersigned authority certifies that the goods shown below originated in: ⟨منشأها⟩ 5 "UNITED KINGDOM EUROPEAN COMMUNITY"

Method of Transport: ⟨مرسلة بواسطة⟩ 3 By Road. From England ro C&F Baghdad Via Turkey By Trucks.	

Marks and Numbers: الأرقام والعلامات	Quantity and Kind of Packages: كمية ونوع الطرود	Description of Goods: مواصفات البضاعة	Weight (gross & net): الوزن (الصافي والاجمالي) 6
(EASHA) Order No 143 General Establishment of Bakeries & Ovens, Baghdad. L/C 31 Rafidian Bank, Baghdad. Rafidian Bank, London. D/C 6042/HO I/L No 145	7 Packages One Shipment of: All Items of conveyor + All Items of spare parts for Loaders as per Supp Tlx 85/6587 of 10th Oct 1985 I/L No 145 1985 Dated 15th Oct 1985 L/C 31 of Rafidian Bank, Baghdad Rafidian Bank, London D/C 6042/HO English Origin.		Nett Wt 2760 KGS Gross Wt 2760KGS

We hereby certify that the goods are of English Origin.
We certify that the goods are wholly produced in the United Kingdom and
do not comprise any raw parts, raw materials, labour or capital of Israeli
origin
ABC Company Ltd is not a branch or mother company of firms
included in the Arab Boycott.

Manufacturer:- ABC Company Ltd, Tamworth, Staffordshire.

Date   10 Oct 1985
Place   Verwood Dorset

مكـان وتاريخ الاصـدار
Place and Date of Issue

غُرْفَة التِّجَارَة العَرَبِيَّة البَريطَانِيَة
ARAB-BRITISH CHAMBER OF COMMERCE

Issuing Authority   سلطة الاصـدار

1 Consignor		No. **PP 591363**	ORIGINAL
ABC Company Limited Verwood Wimborne Dorset England			

EUROPEAN COMMUNITY	
CERTIFICATE OF ORIGIN	

2 Consignee	3 Country of Origin
General Precision Eng Ltd Alexandria Egypt	"EUROPEAN COMMUNITY UNITED KINGDOM"

4 Transport details (Optional)	5 Remarks
Seafreight	

6 Item number; marks, numbers, number and kind of packages; description of goods	7 Quantity
001 1 W/C 100X150X100CMS GPE Nett WGT 700KGS Gross 950KGS O/N 123 Coveyor Sparesfor Loaders EGYPT	ONE CASE

8 THE UNDERSIGNED AUTHORITY CERTIFIES THAT THE GOODS DESCRIBED ABOVE ORIGINATE IN THE COUNTRY SHOWN IN BOX 3

THE DORSET CHAMBER OF COMMERCE AND INDUSTRY

Place and date of issue; name, signature and stamp of competent authority

Poole

...........................19......

....

The Dorset Chamber of Commerce and Industry

DTI/XP/1302.

H. E. Warne Ltd, London and St. Austell

3.3 EXPORT INVOICE

Description

The document contains details of invoice number, the date, seller's/buyer's references, consignee country of origin and destination; terms of delivery and payment; vessel/flight details; port/airport of loading; port/airport of discharge; place of delivery; and fullest details of the merchandise, including unit price.

An Export Invoice usually bears the exporter's own headed invoice form stationery and contractual address.

Source of document

The Export Invoice is issued by the seller (exporter).

Purpose/use/function

The Export Invoice forms the basis of the transaction between the seller and buyer. It can also be used as a basis for combined invoices termed Certificates of Value and Origin (CVO).

Legal context

The invoice can be certified by the appropriate authority to confirm the authenticity of the value and origin of the goods. In such circumstances it would be termed a Certificate of Value and Origin. Some countries merely accept the exporter's signature as the required certification, but others require the Export Invoice to be legalized by the buying nation's Consulate in the exporter's/ seller's country before the goods can enter the importer's/buyer's country.

Ratifying organizations/countries

It is used worldwide by countries exercising some degree of regulation/control over their level of imports, especially in particular commodity areas.

Procedure

Instructions for completing the form

The Export Invoice is prepared by the shipper, exporter or agent.

Necessary authorization

Exporter's signature accepted as required certification in some countries. Other countries require clearance from the buying nation's Consulate in the exporter's country.

Number and allocation of copies

The document is required by the buyer/Bank/Customs to process the cargo through Customs and the Bank to effect payment of the goods.

Checklist of what should accompany each copy

The document is required/specified under the export contract terms as specified, for example, under a Letter of Credit and custom importer arrangements as requested by the importer to the exporter.

Discrepancies (i.e. likely errors) and their consequences

The following discrepancies relating to processing invoices under Letters of Credit do arise and should be avoided:

1 value exceeds credit amount;
2 amount differs from that of Bill of Exchange;
3 price of goods not as indicated in credit;
4 omission of the price basis and shipment terms, for example, CIF, FOB, C&F, etc.;
5 inclusion of charges not specified in the credit;
6 invoice not certified, notarized or signed as required by the credit;
7 buyer's name differs from that mentioned in the credit;
8 invoice not issued by the exporter;
9 invoice does not contain declaration required under the credit;
10 description of goods differs from that in the credit.

The following items must be borne in mind when the shipper/exporter/agent prepares the invoice and presents them to the bank under a documentary Letter of Credit:

1 the invoice description of the goods agrees exactly with the documentary Letter of Credit;
2 the invoice is addressed to the importer;
3 the invoice includes the exact licence and/or certificate numbers required by the credit;
4 the invoice shows the terms of shipment mentioned in the credit.

Further information

Banks will provide on request, for specific countries, details of the data discrepancy areas and terms under which the document is used.

INVOICE	FACTURE FACTURA	RECHNUNG FACTUUR

	Invoice number
United Kingdom Seller Limited	91011

United Kingdom Seller Limited
Baltic House
27 Leadenhall Street
LONDON E.C.3.

Invoice date (tax point)	Seller's reference
14 May 1987	91011

Buyer's reference	Other reference
CONTRACT 1234	

Consignee
TO ORDER

Buyer (if not consignee)
Japan Buyer Corporation
c/o NYK Line
3-2 Marunouchi 2-Chome
Chiyoda-Ku
TOKYO 100, Japan

Country of origin of goods	Country of destination
UNITED KINGDOM	JAPAN

Terms of delivery and payment

1 CIF TOKYO, JAPAN. payment at sight against presentation of documents through National Westminster Bank PLC under a Documentary Letter of Credit

Vessel/flight no. and date	Port/airport of loading
2 NIPPON MARU	SOUTHAMPTON

Port/airport of discharge	Place of delivery
2 TOKYO	

Shipping marks, container number	No. and kind of packages, description of goods	Commodity code	Total gross wt (kg)	Total cube (m³)
2 JAPAN BUYER CORPORATION ◇ J.B.C. ◇ TOKYO 1-9	9 P'KGS OF MECHANICAL SPARE PARTS		18,500	25.5
			Total net wt (kg)	

Item/packages	Gross/net/cube	Description	Quantity	Unit price	Amount
9		MECHANICAL SPARE PARTS IN ACCORDANCE WITH CONTRACT NUMBER 1234 DATED 10 APRIL 1987			

	Invoice total
	£100,000

We certify the mechanical spare parts are in accordance with Contract No. 1234 dated 10 April 1987 between United Kingdom Seller Limited and Japan Buyer Corporation

Name of Signatory
C.DOVER

Place and Date
London   14 May 1987

Signature
C. Dover

It is hereby certified that this invoice shows the actual price of the goods described, that no other invoice has been or will be issued, and that all particulars are true and correct.

380-1

© SITPRO OVERLAYS 1983 V1

1 Terms of delivery (CIF) and payment.

2 Shipping details and marks should be consistent with the other documents. The description of the goods must be identical with that stipulated in the credit terms.

3.4 HEALTH CERTIFICATE

Description

A Health Certificate is the document issued when agricultural products are being exported to certify that they comply with the relevant legislation in the exporter's country.

Source of document

The document is issued by the appropriate health authority in the exporter's country, e.g. Environmental Health Department, London Borough of Bexley.

Purpose/use/function

To comply with the buyer's request, it is necessary in some overseas territories to provide a Health Certificate. It certifies that the product was in good condition at the time of inspection – prior to shipment– and fit for human consumption.

Legal context

The Health Certificate issued in the UK certifies that all relevant legislation is complied with and that the requirements of the Food Hygiene Regulations of the United Kingdom are satisfied.

Other aspects

The Health Certificate document is used worldwide in the conduct of international trade. No special format exists. It confirms the goods are fit for human consumption and basically is an approval certificate to import the cargo. It is supplied by the Governmental department responsible for environmental health and is required by Customs.

DIRECTORATE OF HOUSING AND PERSONAL SERVICES
Bexley Civic Offices Broadway Bexleyheath Kent DA6 7LB 01-303 7777
DX 31807 Bexleyheath   Fax 01 301 4937

Bexley

m/r   extn
y/r   date

The person dealing with this matter is

HEALTH CERTIFICATE

Certificat de salubrite/Genusstauglichkeitsbescheinigung
Certificato Sanitario

BOLDLY AND RIGHTLY

Product:

Brand:

Manufacturer:

Production Date:

DETAILS OF CONSIGNMENT

Quantity:

Batch No:

Container No:

Credit No:

Invoice No:

Name and Address of
Consignor:

Consignee:

I hereby certify that to the best of my knowledge and belief
the product described above is wholesome and fit for human
consumption.

The product complies with all relevant legislation in the
United Kingdom and has been packed in premises which were
clean and satisfactory as required by the Food Hygiene
Regulations in this country.

                        Signed _____
                               Environmental Health Officer
                               (Inspecteur de la Sante Publique
Seal (cachet, siegel,   Gesundheitaufsichtsbeamte
timbro)   Ispettore Sanitario Ufficiale)

CERT2.1

Director of Social Services and Housing Services Nick Johnson
Chief Social Services Officer Roger Hampson
Chief Housing Officer Peter M Taunton MA BSc(Econ) MIH
Chief Environmental Health Officer
Chief Consumer Services Officer R E Pett MITSA
Housing and Personal Services Secretary Mrs Jill F Tombs BA(Hons) MBIM

3.5 MASTER DOCUMENT

Description

A Master Document is a form where as much information as possible is entered so that all or part of the information can be reproduced mechanically or electronically (by computer) on to individual forms of similar design ('aligned' documentation), relative to an export sale.

Purpose/use/function

The form is intended to serve as a one-run export documentation system. Advantages include improved accuracy and complete elimination of variations in detailed information shown on documents relating to any one consignment; quicker and cheaper production of paperwork; elimination of repetitive typing of information on to numerous end-documents and related checking; uniform presentation of information and easier document filing and reference; a reference for all paperwork run off is provided, thus eliminating the need to produce separate copies of individual documents for future reference, often with substantial reduction in filing.

Legal context

It has no legal role other than it contains the basic information of the export sales contract commodity and thereby is called the Master Document.

Ratifying organizations/countries

Overall such documents broadly conform to the United Nations Economic Commission for Europe (ECE) layout key with whom SITPRO closely work.

Procedure

Instructions for completing the form

It is completed by the seller in the Export Office as soon as the export sale is completed and production/delivery/payment data established.

Other aspects

The Master Document is essentially an in-house document completed in the Export Office and from which other documents are derived insofar as an extract of data or the export sales contract and the commodity/delivery/payment time-scale are concerned. It is ideal for the computerized documentation procedures.

SITPRO has pioneered a system intended to suit all exporters, from simple manual systems using office copiers, through semi-automatic systems to computer-based systems depending on the exporter's requirements. A simple one-typing set for postal exports has also been developed. The system saves about 50 % in document preparation cost – about £40 per consignment at 1988 prices. Further details from SITPRO.

MASTER DOCUMENT

Exporter	No.		Invoice no.		Customs reference/status
			Invoice date	Carrier's bkg. no.	Exporter's reference
			Buyer's reference		Forwarder's reference

Consignee	Buyer

Freight forwarder	Country of despatch	Carrier	Country of destination code
	Country of origin	Country of final destination	

Other UK transport details	Terms of delivery and payment

Vessel/flight no. and date	Port/airport of loading	
Port/airport of discharge	Place of delivery	Insured value	EUR 1 or C. of O. remarks

Shipping marks; container number	Number and kind of packages; description of goods *	Item no.	Commodity code		
			Quantity 2	Gross weight (kg)	Cube (m³)
			Procedure	Net weight (kg)	FOB value (£)
			Summary declaration/previous document		
			Commodity code		
			Quantity 2	Gross weight (kg)	Cube (m³)
			Procedure	Net weight (kg)	FOB value (£)
			Summary declaration/previous document		
			Commodity code		
			Quantity 2	Gross weight (kg)	Cube (m³)
			Procedure	Net weight (kg)	FOB value (£)
			Summary declaration/previous document		

Identification of warehouse	FREE DISPOSAL	Invoice total (state currency)	
		Total gross wt (kg)	Total cube (m³)

Freight payable at	Signatory's company and telephone number
Number of bills of lading Original Copy	Name of signatory
	Place and date
	Signature

3.6 PRESHIPMENT INSPECTION CERTIFICATES

Description

Preshipment Certificates can comprise a six-part Export Declaration document, a five-part Inspection Report, and a two-part Inspection Report and Clean Report of Findings. In preshipment inspection procedures both Letters of Credit and contracts relevant to the import of goods contain a condition that a Clean Report of Findings covering quality, quantity and price must be presented along with other documents required to negotiate payment.

Source of document

An inspection company, e.g. SGS Inspection Services Ltd (Export Declaration and Inspection Report) or Cotecna International Ltd (Inspection Report and Clean Report of Findings).

Purpose/use/function

Implementation of a control system imposed by government regulation in certain countries where the buyer's country requires preshipment inspection to be carried out by an inspection company in the seller's country at the port of departure or other convenient place. Its prime function is to ensure goods at time of dispatch are in a good condition and in requisite quantity.

Legal context

Preshipment inspection has to satisfy the requirements of the buyer's country exchange control regulations but has no legal role by convention in international trade documentation.

Ratifying organizations/countries

Preshipment inspection is a requirement in some 30 countries and its administration in regard to preshipment inspection code is conducted by the International Federation of Inspection Agencies (IFIA).

Procedure

The Code of Practice for Government Mandated Preshipment Inspection is as follows:

1 Activities of preshipment inspection companies (hereinafter 'PIC') in the country of export may be undertaken on behalf of a foreign government, government agency, central bank, or other appropriate governmental authority and may include:
   (a) physical inspection for quantity and quality of goods;
   (b) verification of export prices, including financial terms of the export transaction and currency exchange rates where appropriate;
   (c) support services to the customs authorities of the country of importation.
2 The general procedures for physical inspection of goods and the examination

of the price of exports out of any particular country will be the same in all exporting countries and the specific requirements established by the importing country will be administered by the PIC in a consistent and objective manner.

3 The PIC will provide assistance to exporters by furnishing information and guidelines necessary to enable exporters to comply with the preshipment inspection regulations of the importing country. This assistance on the part of the PIC is not intended to relieve exporters from the responsibility for compliance with the import regulations of the importing country.

4 Quantity and quality inspections will be performed in accordance with accepted national/international standards.

5 The conduct of preshipment activities should facilitate legitimate foreign trade and assist bona fide exporters by providing independent evidence of compliance with the laws and regulations of the importing country.

6 Preshipment activities will be conducted and the Clean Report of Findings, or notice of non-issuance thereof, will be sent to the exporter in a timely and convenient manner.

7 Confidential business information will not be shared by the PICs with any third party other than the appropriate government authority for which the inspection in question is being performed.

8 Adequate procedures to safeguard all information submitted by exporters will be maintained by the PIC, together with proper security for any information provided in confidence to them.

9 The PIC will not request from exporters information regarding manufacturing data related to patents (issued or pending) or licensing agreements. Nor will the PIC attempt to identify the cost of manufacture, level of profit or, except in the case of exports made through a buying agent or a confirming house, the terms of contracts between exporters and their suppliers.

10 The PIC will avoid conflicts of interest between the PIC, any related entities of the PIC or entities in which the PIC has a financial interest, and companies whose shipments the PIC is inspecting.

11 The PIC will state in writing the reason for any decision declining issuance of a Clean Report of Findings.

12 If a rejection occurs at the stage of physical inspection the PIC will, if requested by the exporter, arrange the earliest date for reinspection.

13 Whenever so requested by the exporter, and provided no contrary instruction has been issued by the government authority, the PIC will undertake a preliminary price verification prior to receipt of the import licence on the basis of the binding contractual documents, proforma invoice and application for import approval. An invoice price and/or currency exchange rate that has been accepted by the PIC on the basis of such preliminary price verification will not be withdrawn, provided the goods and the previously submitted documentation conform with the information contained in the import licence. The Clean Report of Findings, however, will not be issued until appropriate final documents have been received by the PIC.

14 Price verification will be undertaken on the basis of the terms of the sales contract and it will take into consideration any generally applicable and allowable adjusting factors pertaining to the transaction.

15 Commissions due to an agent in the country of destination will be treated in strict confidence by the PIC, and will only be reported to the appropriate government authority when so requested.

16 Exporters or importers who are unable to resolve differences with the PIC may appeal in writing, stating facts of the specific transaction and the nature of the complaint, directly to a designated appeals official of the PIC. Exporters wishing to appeal the results of a preshipment inspection may

also seek review of the decision of the PIC in the importing country.

In cases where a PIC is considered not to have observed any article of this Code of Practice, this may be reported to the Director General of IFIA.

Other aspects

The code of practice for the Government mandated preshipment inspection system is outlined precisely under 3.6(c) and overall it conforms to the buyer's country exchange control regulations. It yields the following benefits:

1 it minimizes losses of foreign exchange through over invoicing, concealed commission payments and illegal money transfers;
2 it minimizes losses of revenue and duty payments through under-invoicing;
3 it reduces evasion of import controls and helps combat smuggling;
4 it helps control landed prices and therefore helps control local inflation.

To understand the main reasons for the expanding use of preshipment inspection one must bear in mind the following aspects:

1 effective protection can only be taken as a preventative measure before goods are shipped and it must cover contractual aspects as well as the physical aspects;
2 preshipment inspection is intended to prevent losses due to the normal commercial risks. The examination of both goods and documents is conducted on the basis of natural standards and normal customs and practices of the trades concerned.

The inspection companies are required to provide an independent opinion as to whether the price on the proforma invoice represents the normal price charged for those goods to overseas buyers. Many factors can cause prices to vary over time and between different orders. If the evaluation of price, description and/or customs classification differs from that given in the order, then it is assumed that some sort of adjusting factor has been overlooked. The exporter is always invited to discuss this and supply additional justification before a final opinion is given. What the inspection authority has to ensure is that any differences can be explained and justified against normal commercial considerations and the normal custom of that trade.

The inspection company is not asked to give advice on sources of supply, contractual conditions, cost effectiveness or user benefits. These are decisions for the appropriate government or free market to determine.

The Preshipment Certificate is a document of some controversy in certain expert markets, particularly in the area of price verification. Sellers take the view that the price is fixed contractually at the time of negotiation and should not be varied at the time of shipment.

S.G.S. Inspection Services Limited — Request For Information
C.I.S.S.

- 24 -

Description of goods per licence/proforma

IT IS ESSENTIAL TO QUOTE THESE REFERENCE
NUMBERS IN ALL COMMUNICATIONS WITH SGS

SGS REF.

RFI No.

Telephone   Telex
Importer
Seller's Ref.

EXPORT TO

DECLARATION

(This information is required by SGS's Principals, but SGS undertakes not to disclose the information to any
other party unless authorised.)

EITHER:

The price(s) invoiced for the above
referenced goods is/are nett of all
rebates/discounts/other financial contributions and no such payments will
be remitted to our importer, agent or
any other third party.

OR:

A commission/rebate/other financial contribution

of ....%

based on (e.g. FOB) ....

amounting to...

is granted to:

Name ....

Company..

Address ....

....

....

....

	for SGS use only						

Signed... Date...
(This must be signed by an authorised employee)

Name and Title (Please print) ....

**THE ABOVE DECLARATION MUST BE
FULLY COMPLETED AND RETURNED
TO SGS BEFORE A REPORT
OF FINDINGS CAN BE ISSUED.**

Member of the SGS Group (Société Générale de Surveillance)

R 361400

S.G.S. Inspection Services Limited — Request For Information
C.I.S.S.

– 24 –

SELLER'S
COPY

PAGE
A

Description of goods per licence/proforma

1

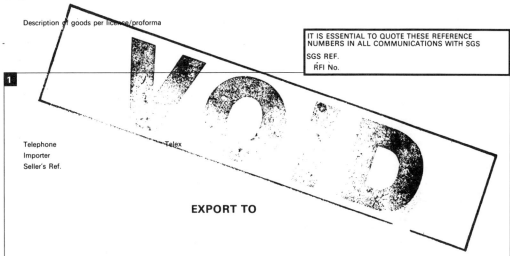

IT IS ESSENTIAL TO QUOTE THESE REFERENCE NUMBERS IN ALL COMMUNICATIONS WITH SGS
SGS REF.
RFI No.

Telephone   Telex
Importer
Seller's Ref.

EXPORT TO

PLEASE READ CAREFULLY

In accordance with the regulations established by the Authorities of the importing country, we are instructed to carry out our inspection and price comparison before shipment of the goods described above. If this can be satisfactorily completed, SGS will issue a report of findings which is necessary to negotiate payment for these goods and/or to effect import Customs clearance.

INSTRUCTIONS

To request pre-shipment inspection, **please use this formset.**

1. Detach and retain this page.

2. Complete unshaded areas of formset i.e. Sellers' contact and boxes 2, 3, 4, 5 and 6 (please type if possible). In Section 5 please quote **a date** from which goods will be available for inspection—"NOW", "A.S.A.P.", etc. are not sufficient. (See A.2 and C.3 Guidance Notes printed on the back of this page.)

3. Return the completed formset and the completed confidential declaration **with 2 copies of your proforma and specification** (for each inspection requested). This declaration must always be completed before a report of findings can be issued.

   In addition, the following documents should be enclosed where applicable:

   1 copy of Letter of Credit
   1 copy of supplier's/manufacturer's invoice
   1 copy of your/manufacturer's (i) export price list
                                  (ii) UK trade price list
   1 copy of list itemising goods (for each inspection requested)
   1 copy of test certificate/certificate of analysis (also to be made available to our Inspector)
   1 copy of the importer's indent/order

4. We recommend that you do not ship without an inspection report stating **'satisfactory'** for quantity and quality.

5. You should note that the importation of goods which are second hand, reconditioned or not new is governed by special regulations in some countries. You must ensure that your customer has complied with these regulations and obtained the necessary authority to import them.

6. GUIDANCE NOTES ARE PRINTED ON BACK OF THIS PAGE—**PLEASE READ THEM.**

VERY IMPORTANT

We require   **working days notice (minimum) to execute inspection from receipt of inspection request or date goods available (whichever is the later) together with documentation. Please allow for manufacturing visits/tests or N.D.T. to be included—see Guidance Note C.3 over.**

R 361400

A. INFORMATION ABOUT PRE-SHIPMENT INSPECTION

1. The following guidelines apply where Société Générale de Surveillance S.A. (SGS) has been appointed by the Authorities of various countries to carry out pre-shipment inspection on quality, quantity and price comparison.

2. SGS normally receives a copy of the Import Document from their Principal upon receipt of which they forward a Request for Information and Inspection Form (RFI) to the Seller requesting basic information regarding the shipment. Initial documents as specified in RFI must be supplied to SGS by the Seller. Speedy and accurate response to this form by the Seller has a direct bearing on the ability of SGS to carry out the inspection promptly and ascertain the facts necessary to issue a Report of Findings (ROF).

3. Since price is related to quality/quantity, a physical examination is necessary to ensure that the goods comply with the Buyer's contractual requirements and/or conform to accepted trade standards and norms. This examination is, however, not intended to relieve Buyers or Sellers from their contractual obligations.

4. Within the context of regulations laid down by Principals SGS carries out its mandate on the basis of national and international standards and practices and the custom of the trade as applicable to each country of export.

5. On receipt of the basic information and documentation requested in the form, SGS makes arrangements to inspect the goods. A minimum notice period required to arrange inspection is shown on the form.

6. Upon satisfactory inspection and price comparison SGS will issue a negotiable clean report of findings which you can present to your commercial bank with other prescribed documents to secure payment.

B. COMPLETING THIS FORMSET

1. The formset should be completed with either a ballpoint pen or typewriter. If you have several Suppliers and/or places of inspection for each shipment against this SGS reference, an estimate of the numbers involved should be given in Box 3 so that we may send you further separate formsets for each place of inspection.

C. INSPECTION

1. The cost of SGS inspection is paid for by the Authorities, although the costs of adequately presenting the goods for inspection (including unpacking and repacking), providing samples, weighing facilities or any tests you undertake at our request are for **your** account. Repeat, supplementary or abortive inspection visits necessitated by the fault of the Seller (or Supplier) in not presenting the goods satisfactorily will be charged to you, as the Seller of Record, at the rate of £60 + VAT per inspection visit.

2. To enable our Inspectors to verify that suitable quality control procedures have been applied, inspection will only be carried out at Manufacturers' or Suppliers' premises unless previously agreed with SGS Inspection Control. It will not normally be carried out at Warehouses or Packing Depots. Functional equipment should not be presented for inspection unless adequate facilities are provided, such that equipment can be fully operated to verify specification. A representative of the Seller/Supplier should be in attendance. PLEASE NOTE that Manufacturers' test certificates and/or test certificates issued by statutory inspecting authorities may not be accepted in place of a functional test by our Inspector.

3. If manufacture is not yet completed, please return RFI formset immediately, advising us of the situation, as we may wish to conduct stage inspections. Under such circumstances we will endeavour to fit in with your own inspection programme.

4. It is the responsibility of the Seller or his agent to provide SGS with the opportunity to inspect or re-inspect the goods at time of loading into containers or on the ocean going vessel. Therefore you should advise the SGS Field Inspector, or send details, to confirm the loading schedule at the earliest possible stage. In accordance with the Exchange Control Regulations, all costs in connection with the such (re-) inspection will be for the account of the Seller.

5. Please note that, in order to make an efficient allocation of our Inspector's time and to offer the best possible service to everyone, we are unable to accept requests for specific dates and times. However, every effort will be made to inspect at a convenient time—our Inspector will contact the place of inspection before visiting.

6. After inspection you will receive an authorised copy of an inspection report. (N.B. The inspection report is not a negotiable document.) If this is marked "Satisfactory" you may then send us copies of your final documents comprising:

1. A copy of the 'Inspection Report'.
2. 3 copies of your final invoice signed in ink and dated, showing separately the FOB value, freight, insurance, and discount or commission, interest charges and the payment terms (notably period of credit, settlement discounts).
3. 1 copy of your Supplier's final invoice.
4. 1 copy of your Manufacturer's final invoice.
   N.B. All invoices must show the FOB, freight, commission, etc., amounts separately.
5. 1 non-negotiable, dated, numbered copy of the shipped-on-board ocean Bill of Lading (B/L) (if applicable).
   or 6. 1 copy of the Air Way Bill (AWB) endorsed to show actual flight number and date.

7. A satisfactory inspection report is normally valid for a period of three months, however, the inspector may indicate a shorter validity period. Goods not shipped during this time may be subject to re-inspection at the Seller's cost.

8. If goods are shipped without SGS inspection confirming satisfactory condition, SGS issue a non-negotiable Report of Findings.

D. FINAL PRICE COMPARISON

1. This is completed after quality and quantity inspection and as soon as we have received the final invoices. Where evidence of shipment is required a non-negotiable copy of the Bill of Lading/Airway Bill must be submitted before a Report of Findings can be issued. In this case final invoices may be sent earlier, since this may assist in the prompt issuance of the Report of Findings.

E. THE REPORT OF FINDINGS

1. This is issued to the Seller at the address shown on the foreign exchange licence after: (a) satisfactory inspection report has been issued, (b) final documents have been received, (c) the SGS opinion confirms that the price invoiced by Sellers corresponds with the export or other applicable price generally prevailing in the country of supply/origin, (d) any required evidence of shipment has been received, (e) Sellers and/or Importers have complied with any special regulations, or obtained approvals for the import of second hand goods. The Report of Findings incorporates an opinion expressed by SGS and is usually required with other commercial documents to obtain payment through a commercial bank. In some cases it is also required for import customs clearance. The opinion expressed by SGS is made after consideration of all factors made known to them by the Seller and is made in good faith but without any liability whatsoever to the Seller for any loss, damage or expense howsoever arising from the issue of any report of findings.

2. In the absence of an original Licence/Inspection Order, no Report of Findings can be issued.

F. COMMUNICATIONS WITH SGS

1. Please use the address/telephone number shown overleaf. In all communications (particularly those with documents) it is important to quote the SGS reference numbers.

S.G.S. Inspection Services Limited — Request For Inspection
C.I.S.S.

RETURN TO SGS

Description of goods per licence/proforma

IT IS ESSENTIAL TO QUOTE THESE REFERENCE
NUMBERS IN ALL COMMUNICATIONS WITH SGS

SGS REF.

RFI No.

1

for SGS use only | V623

Place of insp.:

RFI received/
goods available:

Telephone | Telex

Importer

Seller's Ref.

Mandate expires:

Contact

Earliest insp.:

2 Please provide more complete description/specification of goods to be presented
for this inspection. Continue on referenced attachment if necessary.

Planned insp.:

Office

Inspector

Company

OP ID

State whether goods are new and unused | YES | NO

Seller's Ref. No. (if different from Box 1).

Date

3 If you will be presenting goods for inspection in several parts or at more
than one place of inspection PLEASE REQUEST MORE RFI's HERE:
Quantity:

V66O

4
SUPPLIER/MANUFACTURER

Special instructions for Inspector

Contact

Company

Address

Telephone

Ref./Works Order No.

5
PLACE OF INSPECTION

6 Special requests from Seller

Contact

Company

Address

Telephone

Ref./Works Order No.

Despatch Sea/Air/Container/Post   (indicate)

Week goods available

VERY IMPORTANT

We require **working days notice (minimum) to execute inspection from receipt of inspection request or
date goods available (whichever is the later) together with documentation. Please allow for
manufacturing visits/tests or N.D.T. to be included—see Guidance Note C.3 on reverse of Page A.**

Member of the SGS Group (Société Générale de Surveillance)

R 361490

S.G.S. Inspection Services Limited – Request For Inspection
C.I.S.S.

Description of goods per licence/proforma

IT IS ESSENTIAL TO QUOTE THESE REFERENCE
NUMBERS IN ALL COMMUNICATIONS WITH SGS

SGS REF.

RFI No.

1

Telephone   Telex
Importer
Seller's Ref.

Contact

RFI received/
goods available:

Mandate expires:

2 Please provide more complete description/specification of goods to be presented
for this inspection. Continue on referenced attachment if necessary.

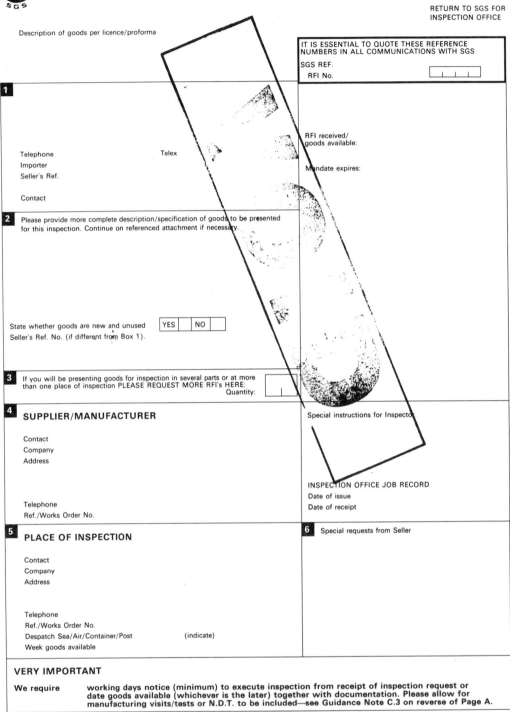

State whether goods are new and unused | YES | NO |
Seller's Ref. No. (if different from Box 1).

3 If you will be presenting goods for inspection in several parts or at more
than one place of inspection PLEASE REQUEST MORE RFI's HERE:
                                                    Quantity:

4
SUPPLIER/MANUFACTURER

Contact
Company
Address

Telephone
Ref./Works Order No.

Special instructions for Inspector

INSPECTION OFFICE JOB RECORD
Date of issue
Date of receipt

5
PLACE OF INSPECTION

Contact
Company
Address

Telephone
Ref./Works Order No.
Despatch Sea/Air/Container/Post   (indicate)
Week goods available

6 Special requests from Seller

VERY IMPORTANT

We require   working days notice (minimum) to execute inspection from receipt of inspection request or
date goods available (whichever is the later) together with documentation. Please allow for
manufacturing visits/tests or N.D.T. to be included—see Guidance Note C.3 on reverse of Page A.

Member of the SGS Group (Société Générale de Surveillance)

R   3 1 0

S.G.S. Inspection Services Limited
C.I.S.S.

PRICE COMPARISON RECORD

Description of goods per licence/proforma

IT IS ESSENTIAL TO QUOTE THESE REFERENCE NUMBERS IN ALL COMMUNICATIONS WITH SGS
SGS REF.
RFI No.

1

F.O.B. VALUE
TOTAL VALUE
E.R.   DECLARED/UNDECLARED
P.P.C. BASIS

Telephone   Telex

Importer

Seller's Ref.

SUPPLIER/MANUFACTURER

Contact   Title

CONTACT   TITLE
TEL.   TELEX

DISCOUNTS: TRADE/QUANTITY/CASH/SPECIAL/.../........................%

ITEM	FOB PRICE/UNIT			FREIGHT			ANCILLARIES		
	P.F.	NORMAL	ACCEPTED	P.F.	NORMAL	ACCEPTED	P.F.	NORMAL	ACCEPTED
ADJUSTMENTS									

DATE	ACTION TAKEN	by

Date of Issue: Shipment Date: Licence Requirement:

R 391470

SGS SGS Inspection Services Ltd.
PVI

Orchard Lea, Winkfield, Windsor SL4 4RT
Member of the SGS Group (Société Générale de Surveillance)
TELEPHONE: 0344-884131 FAX No: 0344 884223 TELEX: 848529/848520

1 FOR SELLER

1.

EXPORT TO

IT IS ESSENTIAL TO QUOTE THESE NUMBERS IN ALL COMMUNICATIONS

2. Specify DOCUMENT against which inspection performed (doc. type; ref(s); general description of goods on doc. – incl. quantity).

5.
SGS REF

RFI

INSPECTION No.

6.

(Specify GOODS ACTUALLY SEEN in "Summary" below.)

3. P.O.I. Contact:
Company:
Town:
Works Ref:

4. Packing/Marking

7.
To: SELLER/EXPORTER

Seller's reference no.

8-10.
Physical inspection result

Date of inspection   Stamp

Inspection valid until

Date of report

Inspector's signature

I 350023

11. Summary of conclusions and any special instructions (address for Test/Analysis Certs. etc. (Cont. sheet? YES ☐ NO ☐)

VOID

A RESULT OF "NON-CONFORMANCE" DOES NOT AUTOMATICALLY MEAN REJECTION OF THE GOODS.
IN CASE OF FURTHER ENQUIRY PLEASE CONTACT THE TELEPHONE NUMBER SHOWN AT TOP OF PAGE.

INSPECTION REPORT (NOT NEGOTIABLE)

This is the summary of the physical inspection report for quality and quantity only. It is NOT a clean report of findings and in NO WAY implies acceptance of price or contractual conditions.
SGS RESERVES THE RIGHT TO RE-EXAMINE THESE GOODS AT ANY TIME AS REQUESTED BY OUR PRINCIPALS (PLEASE READ NOTES OVERLEAF).

IF THE RESULT SHOWN ABOVE IS SATISFACTORY, PLEASE SEND THE DOCUMENTS LISTED BELOW TO THE ADDRESS SHOWN AT THE TOP OF PAGE.

1. 1 copy of this page.
2. 3 copies of your final invoice(s) signed and dated in ink on every copy.
3. 1 copy of your supplier's final invoice—if applicable.
4. 1 copy of your manufacturer's final invoice—if applicable.
   NB - All invoices must show the FOB, freight, commission etc. amounts separately.
5. 1 non-negotiable, dated, numbered copy of the shipped-on-board, ocean B/L—if applicable.
6. 1 copy Air Way Bill (AWB) endorsed to show flight number and date—if applicable.

If no documents have been received within six weeks of the date of inspection, SGS may automatically issue a Non-Negotiable Report of Findings. This may be converted by SGS to a Clean Report of Findings if documents are submitted later in compliance with regulations.

In the absence of an original Licence/Inspection Order no Report of Findings can be issued by SGS.

SGS Inspection Services Ltd.
PVI

Orchard Lea, Winkfield, Windsor SL4 4RT
Member of the SGS Group (Société Générale de Surveillance)
TELEPHONE: 0344-884131 FAX No: 0344 884223 TELEX: 848529/848520

2 FOR C.I.S.S. OFFICE

1.

EXPORT TO

IT IS ESSENTIAL TO QUOTE THESE NUMBERS IN ALL COMMUNICATIONS

2. Specify DOCUMENT against which inspection performed (doc. type; ref(s); general description of goods on doc. – incl. quantity).

5. SGS REF

RFI

INSPECTION No.

6.

7. To: SELLER/EXPORTER

(Specify GOODS ACTUALLY SEEN in "Summary" below.)

3. P.O.I. Contact:
    Company:
    Town:
    Works Ref:

Seller's reference no.

8-10.

Physical inspection result

4. Packing/Marking

Date of inspection   Stamp

Inspection valid until

Date of report

Inspector's signature

I 350023

11. Summary of conclusions and any special instructions e.g. address for Test/Analysis Certs. etc. (Cont. sheet? YES ☐ NO ☐)

VOID

12. 1. Authority for inspection received by: RFI ☐; Telex ☐; Verbal ☐.
          If verbal, by whom and when?_____

13. 2. Are goods presented complete against reference document? Yes ☐; No ☐.
    3. Shipping route: Sea ☐; Air ☐; Land ☐; Container ☐; Not stated ☐.
       Was packing seen? ☐.   Is packing adequate? Yes ☐; No ☐.
    4. Was visual examination/identification of goods satisfactory? Yes ☐; No ☐.
    5. Were storage conditions satisfactory for product? Yes ☐; No ☐.

QUANTITY/CONDITION

14. 6. If inspecting more than one item, how many items were checked?_____ out of _____
      What sampling techniques were used? 100% ☐; spot check ☐; sampling plan ☐.
      Basis of quantity check: tally ☐; checkweigh ☐; volume ☐; draft ☐; other ☐.

15. 7. If inspecting more than one item, how many items were checked?_____ out of _____
      What sampling techniques were used? 100% ☐; spot check ☐; sampling plan ☐.
      Were samples taken? Yes ☐; No ☐. Date to laboratory _____.
      Basis of quality check: visual ☐; test witnessed ☐; QA records ☐; certificates ☐;
                               independent analysis ☐; other ☐.
      What standard was used to compare quality? NCP/TC ☐; Manufacturer's ☐; National ☐.
      Does quality conform to referenced document? Yes ☐; No ☐; Not specified ☐.
    8. Are goods of standard manufacture? Yes ☐; No ☐.
    9. Is age/shelf life satisfactory? Yes ☐; No ☐.

QUALITY

16. 10. Documents attached: Reference Document ☐; Inspection Notes ☐; Discrepancy Report ☐;
       Technical Report (3H goods etc.) ☐; Test Certificate(s) ☐; other ☐ | Date to Co-ord (MBR only):

SGS Inspection Services Ltd.
PVI

Orchard Lea, Winkfield, Windsor SL4 4RT
Member of the SGS Group (Société Générale de Surveillance)
TELEPHONE: 0344-884131 FAX No: 0344 884223 TELEX: 848529/848520

3 FOR INSPECTOR

I 350023

1. **EXPORT TO**	**IT IS ESSENTIAL TO QUOTE THESE NUMBERS IN ALL COMMUNICATIONS**

2. Specify DOCUMENT against which inspection performed (doc. type; ref(s); general description of goods on doc. – incl. quantity).

5. SGS REF

RFI

INSPECTION No.

6.

(Specify GOODS ACTUALLY SEEN in "Summary" below.)

7. To: SELLER/EXPORTER

3. P.O.I. Contact:
　　　Company:
　　　　Town:
　　Works Ref:

Seller's reference no.

8-10.

Physical inspection result

4. Packing/Marking

Date of inspection　　　　　　　Stamp

Inspection valid until

Date of report

Inspector's signature

11. Summary of conclusions and any special instructions, incl. address for Test/Analysis Certs. etc. (Continuation sheet? YES ☐ NO ☐)

VOID

12. 1. Authority for inspection received by: RFI ☐; Telex ☐; Verbal ☐.
　　　　　If verbal, by whom and when?_____

13. **QUANTITY/CONDITION**

2. Are goods presented complete against reference document? Yes ☐; No ☐.
3. Shipping route: Sea ☐; Air ☐; Land ☐; Container ☐; Not stated ☐.
　 Was packing seen? ☐.　　　　Is packing adequate? Yes ☐; No ☐.
4. Was visual examination/identification of goods satisfactory? Yes ☐; No ☐.
5. Were storage conditions satisfactory for product? Yes ☐; No ☐.

14.

6. If inspecting more than one item, how many items were checked?_____ out of _____
　 What sampling techniques were used? 100% ☐; spot check ☐; sampling plan ☐.
　 Basis of quantity check: tally ☐; checkweigh ☐; volume ☐; draft ☐; other ☐.

15. **QUALITY**

7. If inspecting more than one item, how many items were checked?_____ out of _____
　 What sampling techniques were used? 100% ☐; spot check ☐; sampling plan ☐.
　 Were samples taken? Yes ☐; No ☐. Date to laboratory _____.
　 Basis of quality check: visual ☐; test witnessed ☐; QA records ☐; certificates ☐;
　　　　　　　　　　　　　　　independent analysis ☐; other ☐.
　 What standard was used to compare quality? NCP/TC ☐; Manufacturer's ☐; National ☐.
　 Does quality conform to referenced document? Yes ☐; No ☐; Not specified ☐.
8. Are goods of standard manufacture? Yes ☐; No ☐.
9. Is age/shelf life satisfactory? Yes ☐; No ☐.

16.

10. Documents attached: Reference Document ☐; Inspection Notes ☐; Discrepancy Report ☐;
　　 Technical Report (SH goods etc.) ☐; Test Certificate(s) ☐; other ☐. | Date to Co-ord (MBR only):

SGS Inspection Services Ltd.
PVI

Orchard Lea, Winkfield, Windsor SL4 4RT
Member of the SGS Group (Société Générale de Surveillance)
TELEPHONE: 0344-884131 FAX No: 0344 884223 TELEX: 848529/848520

4 FOR INSPECTION OFFICE

I350023

1. **EXPORT TO**	IT IS ESSENTIAL TO QUOTE THESE NUMBERS IN ALL COMMUNICATIONS

2. Specify DOCUMENT against which inspection performed (doc. type; ref(s); general description of goods on doc. – incl. quantity).

5. SGS REF   INSPECTION No.

RFI   6.

7. To: SELLER/EXPORTER

(Specify GOODS ACTUALLY SEEN in "Summary" below.)

3. P.O.I. Contact:
   Company:
   Town:
   Works Ref:

Seller's reference no.

8-10.
Physical inspection result

4. Packing/Marking

Date of inspection   Stamp

Inspection valid until

Date of report

Inspector's signature

11. Summary of conclusions and any special instructions, incl. names for Test/Analysis Certs. etc. (Cont. Sheet YES ☐ NO ☐)

12.   1.   Authority for inspection received by: RFI ☐ ;   Telex ☐ ;   Verbal ☐ .
      If verbal, by whom and when?_____

13. QUANTITY/CONDITION
   2.   Are goods presented complete against reference document?   Yes ☐ ;   No ☐ .
   3.   Shipping route: Sea ☐ ;   Air ☐ ;   Land ☐ ;   Container ☐ ;   Not stated ☐ .
        Was packing seen? ☐ .   Is packing adequate?   Yes ☐ ;   No ☐ .
   4.   Was visual examination/identification of goods satisfactory?   Yes ☐ ;   No ☐ .
   5.   Were storage conditions satisfactory for product?   Yes ☐ ;   No ☐ .

14.   6.   If inspecting more than one item, how many items were checked?_____ out of _____
        What sampling techniques were used?   100% ☐ ;   spot check ☐ ;   sampling plan ☐ .
        Basis of quantity check: tally ☐ ;   checkweigh ☐ ;   volume ☐ ;   draft ☐ ;   other ☐ .

15. QUALITY
   7.   If inspecting more than one item, how many items were checked?_____ out of _____
        What sampling techniques were used?   100% ☐ ;   spot check ☐ ;   sampling plan ☐ .
        Were samples taken?   Yes ☐ ;   No ☐ .   Date to laboratory _____ .
        Basis of quality check: visual ☐ ;   test witnessed ☐ ;   QA records ☐ ;   certificates ☐ ;
                                         independent analysis ☐ ;   other ☐ .
        What standard was used to compare quality?   NCP/TC ☐ ;   Manufacturer's ☐ ;   National ☐ .
        Does quality conform to referenced document?   Yes ☐ ;   No ☐ ;   Not specified ☐ .
   8.   Are goods of standard manufacture?   Yes ☐ ;   No ☐ .
   9.   Is age/shelf life satisfactory?   Yes ☐ ;   No ☐ .

16.   10.   Documents attached: Reference Document ☐ ;   Inspection Notes ☐ ;   Discrepancy Report ☐ ;
        Technical Report (eII goods etc.) ☐ ;   Test Certificate(s) ☐ ;   other ☐ | Date to Co-ord (MBR only):

SGS SGS Inspection Services Ltd.
PVI

Orchard Lea, Winkfield, Windsor SL4 4RT
Member of the SGS Group (Société Générale de Surveillance)
TELEPHONE: 0344-884131 FAX No: 0344 884223 TELEX: 848529/848520

5 FOR FINDIV

EXPORT TO	IT IS ESSENTIAL TO QUOTE THESE NUMBERS IN ALL COMMUNICATIONS

1.

EXPORT TO

2. Specify DOCUMENT against which inspection performed (doc. type; ref(s); general description of goods on doc. – incl. quantity).

5.

SGS REF   INSPECTION No.

RFI

6.

7.

To: SELLER/EXPORTER

(Specify GOODS ACTUALLY SEEN in "Summary" below.)

3. P.O.I. Contact:
    Company:
    Town:
    Works Ref:

Seller's reference no.

8-10.

Physical inspection result

4. Packing/Marking

Date of inspection   Stamp

Inspection valid until

Date of report

Inspector's signature

I 350023

11. Summary of conclusions and any special instructions, incl. address for Test/Analysis Certs. etc. (Cont. Sheet? YES ☐ NO ☐)

TO BE COMPLETED BY OPERATIONAL INSPECTION CONTROL

18. INSPECTION RESULT:	Tick as approp.	**19.** OTHER ACCOUNTING INFORMATION:
SATISFACTORY		
REJECTED		
NON CONFORMANCE		
CONDITIONAL		
ABORTIVE		Hours: _____ Miles: _____
STAGE INSPECTION		**20.** Delete as appropriate: CHARGEABLE/NON CHARGEABLE

COTECNA INTERNATIONAL LIMITED

2 Perry Road, Witham, Essex, CM8 3TU, England
Telephone: Witham (0376) 520505   Telex: 987902/3 COINUK G

1 FOR SELLER

EXPORT TO NIGERIA	IT IS ESSENTIAL TO QUOTE THESE NUMBERS IN ALL COMMUNICATIONS

Specify DOCUMENT against which inspection performed (doc. type; ref(s); general description of goods on doc. - incl. quantity).

Bankers safe parts as per
Pro-forma Invoice No. 84/916

Form M .020/003121/03	INSPECTION No.
IR No. C.004000	2

(Specify GOODS ACTUALLY SEEN in "Summary" below.)

To: SELLER/EXPORTER

TERRY SECURITY,
4, Mill Road,
Mayland,
Chelmsford,
Essex.

P.O.I. Contact:	R.K. Terry.
Company:	Terry Security.
Town:	Mayland, Essex.
Works Ref:	-

Mr. R.K. Terry.

Seller's reference no.   -

Packing/Marking *

6 Reconditioned Bankers Safes
strapped on separate wood pallets.

Packed in 20ft. Container
No. INTU 234603-2
Seal No. 42653.

Vessel 'Zenit Clipper'
E.T.S. Harwich 22-2-85.

Physical inspection result
Conditional
                         1-2-85)
Date of inspection 11-2-85)

Inspection valid until

Date of report   11-2-85

Inspector's name G.B. Albury   No. 80

Signed *[signature]*

Stamp: COTECNA INTERNATIONAL LTD. 80

Summary of conclusions and any special instructions, incl. address for Test/Analysis Certs. etc. (Cont. Sheet? YES ☒ NO ☐)

Second-hand goods - reconditioned.
Subject to satisfactory price comparison.

* Scan African (Nigeria) Ltd. Asogun Village,
   K.M.15 Badagry Road, P.O. Box 1792, LAGOS, NIGERIA via APAPA.

INSPECTION REPORT (NOT NEGOTIABLE)

This is the summary of the physical inspection report for quality and quantity only. It is NOT a clean report of findings and in NO WAY implies acceptance of price or contractual conditions.
COTECNA INTERNATIONAL RESERVES THE RIGHT TO RE-EXAMINE THESE GOODS AT ANY TIME AS REQUESTED BY OUR PRINCIPALS.

IF THE RESULT SHOWN ABOVE IS SATISFACTORY, PLEASE SEND THE DOCUMENTS LISTED BELOW TO THE ADDRESS SHOWN AT THE TOP OF THE PAGE.

1. 1 copy of this page.

2. 3 copies of your final invoice.

3. 1 copy of your supplier's final invoice - if applicable.

4. 1 copy of your manufacturer's final invoice - if applicable.

    NB - All invoices must show the FOB, freight, commission etc. amounts separately.

5. 1 non-negotiable, dated, numbered copy of the shipped-on-board, ocean B/L or AWB if applicable.

If no documents have been received within six weeks of the date of inspection, Cotecna International may automatically issue a Non-Negotiable Report of Findings. This may be converted by Cotecna International to a Clean Report of Findings if documents are submitted later in compliance with regulations.

In the absence of an original Licence/Inspection Order no Report of Findings can be issued.

COTECNA INTERNATIONAL LIMITED
(COTECNA — D.C. GRIFFITH — OMIC INT.)

2,PERRY ROAD,WITHAM,ESSEX,CM8 3TU,ENGLAND

CLEAN REPORT OF FINDINGS

(according to import regulations
of the Federal Republic of Nigeria) No. 004683

REF. OF CIL ISSUING UNIT: COC4000	Date: **7.3.85**	**COPY A** TO EXPORTER / SELLER
FORM M APPOINTED AGENT'S No: 020/003121		IMPORT LICENCE No: 84P005399
TOTAL VALUE OF IMPORT LICENCE: N1,000,000.00		VALIDITY 30.4.85

AS PER INSPECTION ORDER
Description of goods: BANKERS SAFE - FULLY RECONDITIONED

FOB value: STG 15,600.00
C&F CIF value: STG 18,760.00
Country of Origin: U.K.

Seller: R.K. TERRY, CHELMSFORD.
Importer: SCAN AFRICAN NIGERIA LIMITED, LAGOS.
Code: ------

SUBMITTED TO INSPECTION
Goods/Commodity: BANKERS SAFE - FULLY RECONDITIONED

Delivery No: 1ST FINAL
FOB value: STG 15,600.00
C&F CIF value: STG 18,760.00
SITC code: NOT STATED

Quantity	Packing	Weight	Marks
6	TO BE ONE	Gross: 20800	CONT. NOS ....
OFF	CONTAINER	KGS	SEAL NOS ....
		Net: -------	

FINDINGS

1 - Quality : The quality of goods submitted to us for inspection is found to comply with the documents presented to the extent that their examination is within our mandate.

2 - Quantity : The quantity of goods presented to us is as indicated above in § Submitted to Inspection.

3 - Price : Seller's Final Invoice No 3042 dated 25.02.85 showing a
C&F CIF value of STG 18,760.00 in words ONE/EIGHT/SEVEN/SIX/ZERO POUNDS STERLING
ZERO PENCE has been submitted to us and we have compared and found acceptable the
FOB value of STG 15,600.00 in words ONE/FIVE/SIX/ZERO/ZERO POUNDS STERLING
ZERO PENCE

4 - Loading : Scheduled to be shipped at HARWICH on board ZENIT CLIPPER
as per B/L, AWB No .... date 21.02.85

5 - Shipment : This consignment represents part/all of the goods covered by the above mentioned Form M which is /is not fully utilised.

6 - Remarks : This document is valid only if signed by an authorised Representative of the Inspection Company and accompanied by the following documents:
- negotiable bill of lading or equivalent evidence of shipment to Nigeria.
- copy of Seller's Final Invoice certified by Cotecna International Limited's authorised Representative.

FINAL DOCUMENTS RECEIVED 26.02.85

at WITHAM date 7.3.85
COTECNA INTERNATIONAL LIMITED REPRESENTATIVE
Signature and stamp

Enclosures to original report
☐ one copy of Seller's Final Invoice
This Report of Findings does not relieve Sellers from their legal and contractual obligations to Importers

3.7 PROFORMA INVOICE

Description

A Proforma Invoice includes details of the date, name of consignee, quantity and description of the goods, marks and measurement of packages, cost of the goods, packing carriage and freight, postage, insurance premium, terms of sale, terms of payment etc.

Source of document

The Proforma Invoice is issued by the exporter.

Purpose/use/function

This type of invoice may be required in advance of dispatch of goods for an import licence or Letter of Credit purposes.

Legal context

It has no legal status other than a means of facilitating the buyer's bank providing the necessary fund provision to buy the importer's product.

Ratifying organizations/countries

It is a recognized document in international trade but has no convention status other than it is mentioned as one of many documents required under the cargo delivery terms' arrangements found in INCO TERMS 1980.

Procedure

Instructions for completing the form

The Proforma Invoice is prepared by the shipper, exporter or agent who shall bear the following points in mind:

1 the invoice description of the goods should agree exactly with the documentary Letter of Credit;
2 the invoice should be addressed to the importer;
3 the invoice should include the exact licence and/or certificate numbers required by the credit;
4 the invoice should show the terms of shipment mentioned in the credit.

Necessary authorization

It is provided by the exporter and certified by a senior executive.

Number and allocation of copies

The shipper, exporter or agent presents the Proforma Invoice to the bank under a documentary Letter of Credit.

Checklist of what should accompany each copy

The documents required to process the consignment and the time-scale will be recorded on the Letter of Credit.

Discrepancies (i.e. likely errors) and their consequences

The following discrepancies relating to the processing of invoices under Letters of Credit do arise and should be avoided:

1 value exceeds credit amount;
2 amount differs from that of Bill of Exchange;
3 price of goods not as indicated in credit;
4 omission of the price basis and shipment terms, e.g. FOB, CIF, C&F, etc.;
5 inclusion of charges not specified in the credit;
6 invoice not issued by the exporter;
7 invoice does not contain declaration required under the credit;
8 description of goods differs from that in the credit.

Further information

The Proforma Invoice is widely used in international trade and enables the exporter to have subsequent confirmation through a Letter of Credit that the buyer has funds to make the purchase as authorized/permitted by the buyer exchange control/import regulations.

PROFORMA INVOICE

No.

Amari Overseas Limited
Suite 2, Smith Bradbeer House,
41 High Street, Eastleigh,
Hampshire SO5 5LG
Telephone: 0703 629449
Telex: 47398 Amari G
Facsimile: 0703 629301

INVOICE TO		

DELIVER TO		CUSTOMER ORDER No.	DATE
		OUR ORDER No.	DESPATCH DATE
SHIPPING MARKS	SPECIAL INSTRUCTIONS	ADVICE NOTE No.	CUSTOMS FORMS ATTACHED
		METHOD OF SHIPMENT	

QUANTITY ORDERED	DESCRIPTION & SPECIFICATIONS	UNIT PRICE State Currency	

NETT WEIGHT	SIGNED	NETT TOTAL	
GROSS WEIGHT		VAT @ %	
SIZE	AMARI OVERSEAS LIMITED	**TOTAL DUE**	

E&OE

A member of the **AMARI** Group   VAT No. 411 7029 90

Registered Office: Amari House, 52 High Street
Kingston Upon Thames, Surrey KT1 1HN
Registered Number: 1805847 England

3.8 QUALITY CERTIFICATE

Description

A Quality Certificate confirms that the description/specification of the cargo is as found on the Bill of Lading/Certificate of Insurance/Export Invoice and so on.

Source of document

The Quality Certificate is issued by the exporter, e.g. W.G. Spice and shipper.

Purpose/use/function

To confirm for the importer that the quality/specification of a particular consignment of goods is in accord with the export sales contract at the time of shipment.

Other aspects

The Quality Certificate document is usually required under Letter of Credit terms to accord with the terms of sale. A copy is required by the Bank for financial settlement purposes and copies are distributed to the agent and buyer/importer. It is essential that cargo description conforms to its terms found in the Bill of Lading/Export Invoice/Insurance Certificate.

W. G. Spice and Company Ltd.

Court Mills,
Hook, Nr. Basingstoke,
Hampshire, RG27 9JD.

Tel: Hook (025 672) 2206
Cables: Wigespice, Hook.
Telex: 858505

QUALITY CERTIFICATE

400 Cartons (10,000 Kilos Nett)
Pure Ghana Cocoa Liquor "TAKSI" Brand,
for shipment per m.v. "CITY OF MANCHESTER"
from Ellesmere Port to Lisbon

We certify above to be:-

Pure Ghana Cocoa Liquor, "TAKSI" Brand

for
W. G. SPICE & COMPANY LTD

A member of the Guinness Peat Group (est. about 1780).
Registered in England number: 632893. Registered Office: 32 St. Mary at Hill, London EC3R 8DH

3.9 WEIGHT CERTIFICATE

Description

A Weight Certificate confirms that the goods in question accord with the weight specified on the Bill of Lading/Invoice/Certificate of Insurance or other specified document and in so doing confirms for the buyer/seller/Insurance Company or other specified party that the goods were at a specified weight at the time of shipment.

Source of document

The Weight Certificate is issued by the exporter, e.g. W.G. Spice and shipper.

Purpose/use/function

Usually the Weight Certificate is requested by the importer to confirm that the weight of the goods is in accord with the export sales contract at the time of shipment.

Other aspects

The Weight Certificate document is usually required under Letter of Credit though often under exporter forwarding arrangements involving a bulk cargo shipment. The cargo weight must accord with the details found in the Charter Party and its subservient Bill of Lading.

W.G. Spice and Company Ltd.

Court Mills,
Hook, Nr. Basingstoke,
Hampshire, RG27 9JD.

Tel: Hook (025 672) 2206
Cables: Wigespice, Hook.
Telex: 858505

WEIGHT CERTIFICATE

```
    400 Cartons (10,000 Kilos Nett)
    Pure Ghana Cocoa Liquor "TAKSI" Brand,
for shipment per m.v. "CITY OF MANCHESTER"
      from Ellesmere Port to Lisbon
```
_____

PACKED IN 400 CARTONS

EACH: 25,657 KILOS GROSS

               25,000 KILOS NETT

TOTAL GROSS: 10,270 KILOS

TOTAL NETT: 10,000 KILOS

for
W. G. SPICE & COMPANY LTD

....

A member of the Guinness Peat Group (est. about 1780).
Registered in England number: 632893. Registered Office: 32 St. Mary at Hill, London EC3R 8DH

3.10 ATA CARNET

Description

An ATA Carnet is a nine-copy international Customs document that allows the temporary importation of goods, whether accompanied or not, free of Customs duties, taxes etc. and without the necessity to raise bonds or deposit amounts for duty, or complete Customs documentation in foreign countries. It may be used for practically all kinds of goods and can provide for a simple entry and exit to and from a single country, or for numerous multi-destination journeys during the validity of the Carnet. This validity can never exceed one year.

The ATA Carnet is issued after completion of the associated official Application Form (Section 3.11) and ATA Bank or Insurance Company guarantee (Section 3.12) where applicable.

Source of document

A Chamber of Commerce, e.g. the London Chamber of Commerce and Industry. The procedure for obtaining an ATA Carnet is as follows:

1 completion of the official Application Form (Section 3.11) and payment of the issuing fee;
2 lodging of adequate security to cover duty etc. (Section 3.12);
3 completion of the ATA Carnet forms.

Purpose/use/function

ATA Carnets are now commonly used by business travellers carrying (or dispatching in advance) samples when making sales or demonstration tours, and by professional people – educationalists, engineers or entertainers fulfilling overseas engagements and taking equipment with them. Goods for showing at overseas fairs and exhibitions are specifically covered by ATA Carnets, often allowing for the goods to be finally examined at the exhibition site rather than at the frontier post.

Legal context

The system is governed by International Convention under which Carnets can be issued for the following categories of goods:

1 commercial samples and advertising film (16 mm);
2 goods for international exhibition;
3 professional equipment.

Ratifying organizations/countries

Most major countries throughout the world.

Procedure

Instructions for completing the form

The Carnet will contain a green front cover; a series of yellow, white and in certain circumstances blue counterfoil/vouchers. These forms are completed by the applicant, but when the Carnet is finally issued by the Chamber of Commerce, it will also contain a green back cover which does not require completion by the applicant.

Necessary authorization

The Carnet is not valid without the green back cover, the official serial number, validity date, and the date and signature of the issuing authority.

Number of copies

Top copy (green), copy 2 (yellow), copy 3 (white), copy 4 (white), copy 5 (blue), copy 9 (yellow) only are reproduced here in monochrome.

Discrepancy aspects of the ATA Carnet

It is important the document be completed adequately and the following items specified on the Carnet may not be amended subsequently:

1 the countries for which the Carnet is valid;
2 name of Carnet user;
3 intended use of the goods;
4 period of validity – may not exceed one year;
5 holder's name and address;
6 a detailed list of the goods covered including their identification marks and numbers as displayed on the packaging.

Goods intended for sale while temporarily imported should not use an ATA Carnet but follow the normal method of exportation.

THE LONDON CHAMBER OF COMMERCE & INDUSTRY

INTERNATIONAL GUARANTEE CHAIN
CHAINE DE GARANTIE INTERNATIONALE

A.T.A. CARNET No.
CARNET A.T.A. No.

ATA/GB/LO

CARNET DE PASSAGES EN DOUANE FOR TEMPORARY ADMISSION
CARNET DE PASSAGES EN DOUANE POUR L'ADMISSION TEMPORAIRE

CUSTOMS CONVENTION ON THE A.T.A. CARNET FOR THE TEMPORARY ADMISSION OF GOODS
CONVENTION DOUANIERE SUR LE CARNET A.T.A. POUR L'ADMISSION TEMPORAIRE DE MARCHANDISES

(Before completing the carnet, please read notes on page 3 of the cover)
(Avant de remplir le carnet, lire la notice page 3 de la couverture)

CARNET VALID UNTIL
CARNET VALABLE JUSQU'AU

INCLUSIVE
INCLUS

ISSUED BY
DELIVRE PAR LONDON CHAMBER OF COMMERCE & INDUSTRY, 69-75, CANNON STREET, LONDON EC4N 5AB

HOLDER
TITULAIRE

REPRESENTED BY*)
REPRESENTE PAR)*

Intended use of goods / *Utilisation prévue des marchandises*

This carnet may be used in the following countries under the guarantee of the following associations. / *Ce carnet est valable dans les pays ci-après, sous la garantie des associations suivantes:*

AUSTRALIA The Melbourne Chamber of Commerce, Melbourne.

AUSTRIA Bundeskammer der Gewerblichen Wirtschaft, Vienna.

BELGIUM & LUXEMBURG Federation Nationale des Chambres de Commerce et d'Industrie de Belgique, Brussels.

BULGARIA Bulgaria Chamber of Commerce, Sofia.

CANADA The Canadian Chamber of Commerce, Montreal 128, Quebec.

CYPRUS Cyprus Chamber of Commerce, Nicosia.

CZECHOSLOVAKIA Ceskoslovenska Obchodni Komora, Prague.

DENMARK Kobenhavns Handelskammer, Copenhagen.

FINLAND The Central Chamber of Commerce of Finland, Helsinki.

FRANCE Chambre de Commerce et d'industrie de Paris. Paris.

GERMANY Deutscher Industrie-und Handelstag Bonn.

GIBRALTAR Gibraltar Chamber of Commerce, Gibraltar.

GREECE The Athens Chamber of Commerce and Industry, Athens.

HONG KONG The Hong Kong General Chamber of Commerce.

HUNGARY Magyar Kereskadelmi Kamara, Budapest.

ICELAND Iceland Chamber of Commerce (Verzlunarrad Islands) Reykjavik.

IRAN Iran Chamber of Commerce, Industries & Mines, Teheran.

IRELAND The Dublin Chamber of Commerce, Dublin.

ISRAEL Tel-Aviv-Yaffo Chamber of Commerce, Tel-Aviv.

ITALY Unione Italiana delle Camere di Commercio Industria e Agricoltura Rome.

IVORY COAST The Ivory Coast Chamber of Commerce, Inc. Abidjan.

JAPAN Japan Chamber of Commerce, Tokyo.

KOREA The Korea Chamber of Commerce and Industry, Seoul.

MAURITIUS Mauritius Chamber of Commerce & Industry. Port Louis.

NETHERLANDS Kamer van Koophandel en Fabrieken voor 'S-Gravenhage 'S-Gravenhage.

NEW ZEALAND The Wellington Chamber of Commerce, Wellington.

NORWAY Oslo Chamber of Commerce, Oslo.

POLAND Polish Chamber of Foreign Trade, Warsaw.

PORTUGAL Associacao Comercial de Lisboa, Lisbon.

ROMANIA Camera di Comert & Republich Socialiste Romania, Bucarest.

SENEGAL Chambre de Commerce d'Industrie et d'Artisanat de la region du Cap Vert-Dakar.

SINGAPORE The Singapore International Chamber of Commerce, Singapore.

SOUTH AFRICA The Association of Chambers of Commerce of South Africa, Johannesburg.

SPAIN Consejo Superior de las Cameras Oficiales de Comercio Industria y Navegacion de Espana, Madrid.

SRI LANKA National Council of the International Chamber of Commerce. Colombo.

SWEDEN The Stockholm Chamber of Commerce, Stockholm.

SWITZERLAND Alliance des Chambres de Commerce Suisses, Geneva.

TURKEY Union of Chambers of Commerce of Produce Exchanges in Turkey, Ankara.

UNITED KINGDOM The London Chamber of Commerce and Industry London.

UNITED STATES OF AMERICA U.S. Council of the International Chamber of Commerce Inc. New York.

YUGOSLAVIA The Yugoslav Federal Economic Chamber, Belgrade.

The holder of this carnet and his representative will be held responsible for compliance with the laws and regulations of the country of departure and the countries of importation. / *A charge pour le titulaire et son représentant de se conformer aux lois et règlements du pays de départ et des pays d'importation.*

Issued at/*Emis à* .... **London**

Date

(Holders signature/Signature du titulaire)

(Signature of authorised Official of the Issuing Association
(Signature du Délégué de l'Association émettrice)

TO BE RETURNED TO THE LONDON CHAMBER OF COMMERCE AFTER USE

CERTIFICATE BY CUSTOMS AUTHORITIES/*ATTESTATION DES AUTORITES DOUANIERES*

1. Identification marks have been affixed as indicated in column 7 against the following item No(s) of the General List.
   Marques d'identification mentionées dans la colonne 7 apposées en regard du(des) numéro(s) d'ordre suivant(s) de la liste generale.

2. Goods examined.*)/*Verifié les marchandises.*)*

3. Registered under reference No.*)/ *Enregistré sous le no.*)*

| (Customs office) | (Place/*Lieu*) | (Date/*Date*) | (Signature and stamp) |
| (Bureau de douane) | | | (Signature et Timbre) |

*) Delete if inapplicable./*Biffer s'il y a lieu.*

F1A

EXPORTATION COUNTERFOIL No. ....

SOUCHE DESORTIE No.

A.T.A. CARNET No.

CARNET A.T.A. No.

F3

1. The goods described in the General List under item No(s)
   Les Marchandises énumérées à la liste générale sous le(s) no(s)

   have been exported.
   ont été exportées.

2. Final date for duty-free re-importation*) /*Date limite pour la réimportation en franchise*)* ....

3. Other remarks*) /*Autres mentions*)* ....

(Customs office)	(Place/*Lieu*)	(Date/*Date*)	(Signature and stamp)
(*Bureau de douane*)			(*Signature et Timbre*)

*)*Delete if inapplicable/Biffer s'il y a lieu.*

EXPORTATION VOUCHER No. ....

VOLET DE SORTIE No.

GB/LO

A.T.A. CARNET No.

CARNET A.T.A. No.

A) This carnet is valid until/*Le carnet est valable jusqu'au* .... inclusive./*inclus*

Issued by/*Délivré par* .... LONDON CHAMBER OF COMMERCE AND INDUSTRY, 69 CANNON ST. EC4N 5AB.

Holder/*Titulaire* ....

Represented by*)/*Représenté par*)* ....

B) Temporary exportation declaration/*Déclaration d'exportation temporaire*

I,/*Je soussigné,* .... **)

duly authorised by*) /*dûment autorisé par*)* .... **)

a) declare that I am temporarily exporting the goods enumerated in the list overleaf and described in the General List under
   déclare exporter temporairement les marchandises énumérées à la liste figurant au verso et reprises à la liste générale

   item No(s) ....
   sous le(s) no(s).

b) declare that the purpose for which the goods are being temporarily exported is ....
   déclare que les marchandises sont destinées à être utilisées pour

c) undertake to re-import the goods within the period stipulated by the Customs office.*)
   m'engage à réimporter ces marchandises dans le délai fixé par le bureau de douane.)*

2. Identifying particulars concerning:/*Indications concernant:*

a) packages (number, kind, marks, etc.) *)
   *Nombre, nature, marques, etc., des colis *)*

b) means of transport*)/*Moyen de transport*)* ....

(Place/*Lieu*)	(Date/*Date*)	(Signature/*Signature*)

C) Clearance on exportation/*Dédouanement à la sortie*

1. The goods referred to in the above declaration have been exported.
   Les marchandises faisant l'objet de la déclaration ci-dessus ont été exportées.

2. Final date for duty-free re-importation*) *Date limite pour la réimportation en franchise*)* ....

3. Other remarks*)/*Autres mentions*)* ....

4. This voucher must be forwarded to the Customs office of*) ....
   Le présent volet devra être transmis au bureau de douane de)*

(Customs office)	(Place/*Lieu*)	(Date/*Date*)	(Signature and stamp)
(*Bureau de douane*)			(*Signature et Timbre*)

*) Delete if inapplicable/ *Biffer s'il y a lieu.* — **) Name and address in block letters./ *Nom et adresse en majuacules d'imprimerie.*

D) For official use/*Réservé à la douane*

F3

F3

Identification marks have been affixed as indicated in column 7 or 8 against the following items No(s) of the General List. *Apposé les marques d'identification mentionnées, dans la colonne 7 ou 8, en regard du(des) numéro(s) d'ordre suivant(s) de la liste generale*

(Customs office)/   (Place/*Lieu*)   (Date/*Date*)   (Signature and stamp)
(Bureau de Douane)   (Signature et Timbre)

Identification marks have been affixed as indicated in column 7 or 8 against the following item No(s) of the General List/*Apposé les marques d'identification mentionnées, dans la colonne 7 ou 8 en regard du(des) numéro(s) d'ordre suivant(s) de la liste générale*

(Customs office)/   (Place/*Lieu*)   (Date/*Date*)   (Signature and stamp)
(Bureau de douane)   (Signature et Timbre)

GENERAL LIST/*Liste Générale*

Item No. No. d'ordre	Trade description of goods and marks and numbers, if any *Désignation commerciale des marchandises et, le cas échéant, marques et numéros*	Number *Nombre*	Weight or Quantity *Poids ou quantité*	Value *Valeur* *)	Country of origin *Pays d'origine* **)	Identification marks affixed by Customs *Marques d'identification apposées par la douane*	
1	2	3	4	5	6	7	8
—	Total carried over/*A reporter*						

*) Commercial value in country of issue of the carnet./*Valeur commerciale dans le pays d'émission du carnet.*

**) If different from country of issue of the carnet./*S'il est différent du pays d'émission du carnet.*

B1A

3.11 ATA APPLICATION FORM

Description

An ATA Application Form is the official form which needs to be completed when application is made for an ATA Carnet (Section 3.10).

Source of document

A Chamber of Commerce, e.g. the London Chamber of Commerce and Industry.

Purpose/use/function

To allow the Chamber of Commerce to process the applicant's ATA Carnet (Section 3.10).

Legal context

It is a document required by Customs and is mandatory.

Ratifying organizations/countries

It is a document used worldwide.

Other aspects

The London Chamber of Commerce and Industry is the guarantor for the ATA Carnet. When issuing an ATA Carnet it requires the holder to indemnify it against any claim for duties and taxes payable as a result of importation or loss of the goods while temporarily imported under an ATA Agent. The level of indemnity varies by country.

PLEASE READ THE ENCLOSED BOOKLET CAREFULLY

PLEASE NOTE IT TAKES A MINIMUM OF 24 HRS
TO PROCESS YOUR CARNET. IF YOU REQUIRE
THIS CARNET TO BE POSTED BACK PLEASE
ENCLOSE A STAMPED ADDRESSED ENVELOPE.

ATA Carnet No.

APPLICATION FORM & UNDERTAKING

(This form must be typed)

To: The .... Chamber of Commerce and Industry

I, ... for and on behalf of

(name and address of firm) ....

....

Telephone No. .... Ext. ....

I am a member of the .... Chamber of Commerce, and my membership No. is ....

apply for a Carnet in the name(s) of ....
(give name(s) of accredited person(s) who will use the Carnet)

....

for use in the Following countries (please indicate the number of VISITS being made to each country and those countries
being crossed in TRANSIT). Number of EXITS from the UK. [   ]   (Yellow)

Visits (White)

Country	No of visits	Country	No of visits	Country	No of visits	Country	No of visits

Transits (Blue)

Country	No. of transits	Country	No. of transits	Country	No. of transits	Country	No. of transits

PLEASE NOTE:
YOU MAY NEED BLUE TRANSIT FORMS FOR FRANCE, ITALY & GREECE SO PLEASE
ENSURE THAT YOU HAVE AT LEAST 2 PAIRS FOR EACH VISIT.

the Carnet is required for:

	(a)	Commercial Samples
delete as appropriate	✱ (b)	International Trade Fair/Exhibition (please give name and place) ....
	(c)	Professional Equipment ....

✱ Ensure that you have sufficient pairs of blue/transit vouchers as per fair/exhibition
literature e.g. Switzerland & France require 3 pairs of blues as well as 1 pair of whites.

IMPORTANT: The reverse side of this form MUST also be completed

3.12 ATA BANK OR INSURANCE COMPANY GUARANTEE

Description

An official form for a guarantee given by a bank or an approved insurance company as required in the procedure for obtaining an ATA Carnet (Section 3.10).

Source of document

A Chamber of Commerce, e.g. the London Chamber of Commerce and Industry.

Purpose/use/function

Since the primary purpose of the ATA Carnet (Section 3.10) is to guarantee to the Customs of a foreign country into which all the goods in question are temporarily imported that all duties, taxes, etc. will be paid to them if the conditions under which they allow these goods into the country are breached, and since the Chambers of Commerce participating in the Carnet scheme provide this guarantee to the Customs authorities, it follows that the issuing Chamber must in turn receive equivalent security from the Carnet user.

This security must be for an amount equal to the highest rate of duty and taxes applicable to the goods in any country of destination and transit if applicable. It may be cash, or banker's draft, or in the form of a guarantee given by a bank or an approved insurance company. Such a guarantee will only be accepted when given on an official form, such as the ATA Bank or Insurance Company Guarantee form.

Other aspects

Usually the shipper's Bank will provide the requisite guarantee. It is important the cargo description and valuation conforms to the data found on the ATA application form.

 # LONDON
CHAMBER of COMMERCE

69 CANNON STREET LONDON EC4N 5AB TEL: 01-248 4444 TELEX: 888 941 LCCI G FACSIMILE: 01-489 0391.

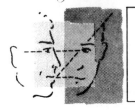

A.T.A. CARNET

BANK OR INSURANCE COMPANY GUARANTEE (Specific)
(It is imperative that the Carnet Number is referred to in all future communications.
This is obtainable from your client).

To:—

(A) London Chamber of Commerce and Industry, 69 Cannon Street, London EC4N 5AB.

In consideration of your issuing an A.T.A. Carnet to (insert name of firm) . . . .

. . . . in accordance with
arrangements made under the Customs Convention regarding E.C.S. Carnets for Commercial Samples
done at Brussels on the 1st March, 1956, or the Customs Convention regarding A.T.A. Carnets for
temporary admission of goods done at Brussels on the 6th December, 1961, or any subsequent
amendments or alterations thereto, we guarantee payment to you on demand of all or any such sum or
sums of money as you may have paid or are called upon to pay in respect of customs duties and other
charges relating to goods imported into any country concerned under cover of the Carnet (as well as
any fee therefore) to which this guarantee applies and such demand shall constitute evidence that the
moneys demanded by you are due and payable by us without further enquiry. This guarantee shall
remain in force for a period of not less than thirty-one calendar months from the date of signature
provided that:—

(1) our liability hereunder shall be limited to a payment or payments not exceeding

£ . . . . in aggregate and any demand must be received at our office at
the address shown in the box below within that period of 31 months from the date of
signature to this guarantee.

(2) this guarantee shall be delivered up by you to us when no longer required.

Date . . . . 19 . . . .

Signed . . . .

An official stamp showing name and address of
Bank or Insurance Company giving this guarantee
to be placed here.

NOTES:

(i) Any alteration or insertion in the text of this guarantee to be authenticated by the full signature of the
signatories to the guarantee.

(ii) THE GUARANTEE PERIOD OF 31 MONTHS IS THE MINIMUM ACCEPTABLE BEING THE
PERIOD OF CONTINGENT LIABILITY OF THE LONDON CHAMBER UNDER ANY ONE
CARNET.

(iii) The London Chamber reserves the right — (a) to refuse to cancel this guarantee, or (b) to invoke it —
in the event of non-payment of any fee or other charges in connection with any carnet secured by
this guarantee.

Undertaking

I, the undersigned .... of

....

attach the list of goods to be entered in the Carnet and undertake to repatriate the goods in question. Further that the goods will be re-exported from any country into which they have been temporarily imported WITHIN SUCH PERIOD AS STIPULATED BY ANY CUSTOMS*

If the goods are not re-exported within such period, I accept responsibility for any negotiations or proceedings with any Customs direct or indirect, and to pay all duties, taxes and charges which may result from non-re-export or failure to observe Customs regulations and requirements both in the United Kingdom and abroad.

I enclose:-   Cheque/Cash for   £ .... in payment of the issuing fee†

      (1)   Bank Draft/Cash for £ .... as deposit of security (to nearest £1)

or

      (2)   A Guarantee for   £ .... from the following Bank or
               Insurance Company

              ....

              ....

              ....

(name address and telephone No.)

I agree that the Draft/cash on deposit or Guarantee may be used to reimburse the Chamber for any duty, taxes or charges as above should these be incurred and for any fees charged by the Chamber for the issue or regularisation of the Carnet.

I further agree to pay the Chamber immediately upon receipt of its demand in writing all or any such sum or sums of money which it may have paid or be called upon to pay in respect of any professional or other fees, costs, liabilities and expenses of any nature whatsoever incurred by the Chamber as a result of, or in connection with, the issue of the Carnet.

I further agree that the Chamber may at its discretion, effect a conditional Discharge subject to the Chamber not receiving any further claims etc, within the 31 month period.

I have read and understood the conditions of the guarantee, and declare that the above particulars and those in the list of goods attached are true and correct and I undertake to return the Carnet to the Chamber after use.

The use of a Carnet does not absolve the holder from observing the Customs regulations of the countries operating the scheme. For example, in certain circumstances a U.K. export licence or an import/export licence for countries to be visited or crossed in transit may be required. For U.K. information please contact D.O.T., Export Licensing Branch, (01-211 6611).

Date ....   Signed **X** .... **X**

for and on behalf of ....
Director, Secretary, Proprietor, Partner or duly authorised person.

NOTES:

The guarantee/deposit should be for a sum (Calculated to the nearest pound sterling only) equivalent to the highest total amount of customs duty, taxes and additional charges to which the goods listed would become liable on importation into any one of the countries for which the carnet is valid, plus, a further 10 per cent of that amount.

If the amount of duty payable is not readily assessable, the Chamber reserves the right to fix the amount of the guarantee/deposit in the light of individual cases.

Any guarantee/ deposit will be returned when the Carnet is surrendered to the Chamber and found to be correctly discharged.

For imported goods the Chamber may require sight of either a duty paid invoice or customs entry.

*   For commercial samples carnets the period may be up to 12 months; for "exhibitions" and "professional equipment" carnets the period may be limited to 6 months; for imports covered by a blue transit voucher, the period of transit may be one of days.

†   Fees:—   Standard Fee = £63.00   Special Fee = £38.00   (applicable to members of the Chamber or ABCC affiliated Chambers).

The Chamber reserves the right to refuse to issue a Carnet to any applicant at anytime without indicating any reason.

Item No. No. d'ordre	Trade description of goods and marks and numbers, if any Désignation commerciale des marchandises et, le cas échéant, marques et numéros	Number Nombre	Weight or Quantity Poids ou quantité	Value Valeur •)	Country of origin Pays d'origine ••)	Identification marks affixed by Customs Marques d'identification apposées par la douane	
1	2	3	4	5	6	7	8
▬	Total carried over/A reporter		▬		▬	▬	▬

*) Commercial value in country of issue of the carnet./Valeur commerciale dans le pays d'émission du carnet.

**) If different from country of issue of the carnet./S'il est différent du pays d'émission du carnet.

3.13 SINGLE ADMINISTRATIVE DOCUMENT (SAD)

Description

The Single Administrative Document was introduced on 1 January 1988 by the European Commission to replace the various member States' export declarations, import declarations and the Community transit document. The document has up to 8 copies and involves a data input for 54 boxes. This includes consignor and consignee (including addresses), cargo description, gross weight, net weight, calculation of taxes, and many statistical data.

Source of document

Customs authority, e.g. HM Customs and Excise, UK.

Purpose/use/function

The concept of the single administrative document is that it will be raised by the exporter and used as an export declaration; carried by the transport operator and used as a transit document; and completed by the importer and used as an import declaration. Hence it will have three basic functions: an export declaration; dispatch/transportation and Community transit/procedures document, and import declaration in the destination country.

The full SAD set consists of the 8 copy Customs form C88 (1–8) (copies 1, 3 and 8 only are reproduced here). The function of each copy is as follows:

1 copy 1 (copy for the country of dispatch/export) remains at the office of departure for the purposes of Community transit control and may also be used for other export control purposes;

2 copy 2 (statistical copy – country of dispatch/export) is the copy of the export declaration for statistical purposes;

3 copy 3 (copy for the consignor/exporter) is the exporter's or agent's copy or may be retained by the Community transit principal;

4 copy 4 (copy for the office of destination) is for Customs in the member State of destination to act as evidence that the goods are (or are not) in free circulation (i.e. to indicate whether Customs duty is payable);

5 copy 5 (copy for return – Community Transport) is returned from the Office of Destination to Customs in the member State of dispatch to provide evidence that the goods reached their destination intact;

6 copy 6 (copy for the Country of Destination) is used in the member State of destination as the Customs import declaration on arrival;

7 copy 7 (statistical copy – country of Destination) is the copy of the import declaration for statistical purposes;

8 copy 8 (copy for consignee) is for retention by the importer or the importer's agent and, in the UK, will serve as the VAT copy for goods cleared at locations which are not served by the Customs computerized entry processing system (DEPS).

The copies for statistical use are edged in green at the right-hand margin to facilitate recognition. Certain boxes are also shaded in the same colour to indicate that they are used for Community transit.

Copies 1–3, therefore, remain in the member State of dispatch, while copies 4–8 travel forward with the goods.

Each set is printed on self-copying paper which is treated so that certain items of information do not copy through to those sheets on which they are not required. On arrival, because certain information cannot copy through to the destination copies of the set, any missing information must be added before the document is signed by the importer or the importer's authorized agent and presented to Customs.

It is important to understand that signing the form at this stage commits the signatory to all the information, including that which was completed at export. If any of this information is incorrect it must be amended and the amendments must be drawn to Customs' attention.

Traders using computers to prepare full SAD sets may find that their printers are incapable of printing through all 8 copies of the full set. A 4-copy alternative set exists to meet this situation. Each set in this set has a dual function, as under Customs Form C88A:

1 copy 1 and copy 6 are combined
2 copy 2 and copy 7 are combined
3 copy 3 and copy 8 are combined
4 copy 4 and copy 5 are combined

Legal context

It is mandatory throughout the European Commission.

Ratifying organizations/countries

The European Commission.

Procedure

Instructions for completing the form

Two sets have to be printed for each consignment and each set must be printed in a way that indicates the use to which it is being put, i.e. the numbers and titles relating to copies 6, 7, 8 and 5 must be deleted on the first set and for 1, 2, 3 and 4 on the second set.

The 8 and 4-copy sets cater for the declaration of single item consignments. Where consignments consist of several items continuation sheets may be used to declare additional items. Each continuation sheet provides for the declaration of three further items. Up to 32 continuation sheets may be used for 1 consignment.

The full 8 copy set [or 2 sets of the 4 copy alternative Customs form C88 (1–4)] must be completed when the same set is used for:

1 dispatch (transportation), Community transit and destination purposes, or
2 dispatch (transportation) and Community transit purposes only.

This applies both when the export declaration is being presented in full and when a preshipment advice under the Simplified Clearance Procedure (SCP) (see HM Customs Notice 275) is being provided but not on a commercial document. The full set should also be used when the Community transit procedure is used on its own, unless the 'transit' element of the procedure is confined to the need to provide evidence that the goods are in free circulation and the set is not to be used as the import declaration.

Where the full set is to be used as the import declaration and there are several consignees for different items in a consignment, a full set will have to be provided for each consignee. If, on the other hand, the set is only being used for dispatch and transit purposes one set will normally suffice, irrespective of the number of consignees involved.

When a full set arriving with the goods is to be used to complete destination formalities in the UK, the self-copying properties of the set will no longer function and carbon paper will have to be inserted.

For importations from non-Community countries the 4-copy alternative will be used. The copy numbers and titles relating to exports should be deleted and copy 4/5 should be detached.

Although the SAD is designed to serve the three functions of export, Community transit and import declaration for goods in trade between EC member States, there are a variety of situations in which it may not be convenient to use it in this way. For this reason the option exists to 'split' the SAD into its constituent elements and use separate sets of copies for each element or any combination of them.

For example, exporters may wish to complete their own export declarations but prefer to employ an agent to deal with Community transit formalities. Although in this situation exporters can forward a partly completed SAD to their agent to add the transit details (there is provision for each party to sign the declarant separately), this may not be convenient in practice. In those circumstances separate SADs can be produced for each function.

In addition, the Simplified Clearance Procedure (SCP) for exports which are not subject to special controls (see HM Customs Notice 275) allows goods to be cleared for export using convenient documents, but where Community transit declarations are still needed a SAD has to be used for that purpose.

The 'split-use' sets available are as follows:

1 SCP preshipment advice (when commercial documents are not used) and post-shipment declaration (when computerized or other scheduling facilities are not used) – Customs form C88 (2+3);
2 full pre-entry of exports where Community transit is not involved – Customs form C88 (2+3);
3 evidence of the free circulation status of the goods only – Customs form C88 (1+4);
4 SCP preshipment advice combined with a status declaration – Customs form C88 (1–4);
5 full pre-entry of exports combined with a status declaration – Customs form C88 (1–4);
6 import where Customs clearance is computerized and entry is not made on plain paper (Customs only require a single copy of the entry) – Customs form C88 (6) (CONT);
7 Period Entry (Imports) simplified entry Customs form 88 (6) (CONT).

Traders who do not wish to use these special sets and prefer, for example, to use the dual-function four-part set for all their consignments may do so but must remove those copies which are not required before presentation to Customs.

Other aspects of SAD

It is important the SAD Boxes are correctly completed and traders/shippers seeking guidance should contact their local Customs and Excise Officer.

EUROPEAN COMMUNITY

A OFFICE OF DISPATCH EXPORT

| 1 | **1 DECLARATION** | | |

2 Consignor/*Exporter*   No

3 Forms

4 Loading lists

5 Items

6 Total packages

7 Reference number

8 Consignee   No

9 Person responsible for financial settlement   No

10 *Country first destin.*

11 *Trading country*

13 *CAP*

14 Declarant/Representative   No

15 Country of dispatch/*export*

15 C disp./*exp.* Code a| b|

17 Country destin. Code a| b|

16 Country of origin

17 Country of destination

18 Identity and nationality of means of transport at departure

19 Ctr.

20 Delivery terms

21 Identity and nationality of active means of transport crossing the border

22 Currency and total amount invoiced

23 Exchange rate

24 Nature of transaction

25 Mode of transport at the border

26 Inland mode of transport

27 Place of loading

28 Financial and banking data

29 Office of exit

30 Location of goods

31 Packages and description of goods   Marks and numbers — Container No(s) — Number and kind

32 Item No

33 Commodity Code

34 Country origin Code a| b|

35 Gross mass (kg)

37 PROCEDURE

38 Net mass (kg)

39 *Quota*

40 Summary declaration/Previous document

41 Supplementary units

44 Additional information/ Documents produced/ Certificates and authorisations

A.I. Code

46 Statistical value

47 Calculation of taxes

Type	Tax base	Rate	Amount	MP
		Total:		

48 Deferred payment

49 Identification of warehouse

B ACCOUNTING DETAILS

50 Principal   No

Signature:

C OFFICE OF DEPARTURE

51 Intended offices of transit (and country)

represented by

Place and date:

52 Guarantee not valid for

Code

53 Office of destination (and country)

D CONTROL BY OFFICE OF DEPARTURE

Result:

Seals affixed: Number:

identity:

Time limit (date):

Signature:

Stamp:

54 Place and date:

Signature and name of declarant/representative:

C88 (1-8)   Printed in the UK for HMSO 8979692 12/86 Multiform Printing

Copy for the country of dispatch/export

EUROPEAN COMMUNITY

3

1 DECLARATION

A OFFICE OF DISPATCH/EXPORT

2 Consignor/*Exporter*   No

3 Forms	4 Loading lists
5 Items	6 Total packages	7 Reference number

8 Consignee   No

9 Person responsible for financial settlement   No

10 *Country first destin*	11 *Trading country*		13 *CAP*

14 Declarant/Representative   No

15 Country of dispatch/*export*

15 C disp./exp. Code		17 Country destin Code	
a|	b|	a|	b|

16 Country of origin

17 Country of destination

18 Identity and nationality of means of transport at departure

19 Ctr

20 Delivery terms

21 Identity and nationality of active means of transport crossing the border

22 Currency and total amount invoiced

23 Exchange rate

24 Nature of transaction

25 Mode of transport at the border	26 Inland mode of transport	27 Place of loading	28 Financial and banking data

3

29 Office of exit

30 Location of goods

31 Packages and description of goods

Marks and numbers — Container No(s) — Number and kind

32 Item No	33 Commodity Code			

34 Country origin Code	35 Gross mass (kg)
a| b|	

37 PROCEDURE	38 Net mass (kg)	39 *Quota*

40 Summary declaration/Previous document

41 Supplementary units

A I Code

44 Additional information/ Documents produced/ Certificates and authorisations

46 Statistical value

47 Calculation of taxes	Type	Tax base	Rate	Amount	MP

48 Deferred payment

49 Identification of warehouse

B ACCOUNTING DETAILS

Total:

50 Principal   No

Signature

C OFFICE OF DEPARTURE

51 Intended offices of transit (and country)

represented by

Place and date

52 Guarantee not valid for

Code

53 Office of destination (and country)

D CONTROL BY OFFICE OF DEPARTURE

Stamp

54 Place and date

Result

Seals affixed Number:

identity

Signature and name of declarant/representative

Time limit (date)

Signature

Copy for the consignor/exporter

C88 (1-8)   Printed in the UK for HMSO 8055017 8 87 G B R F5877 (SEPT 1987)

EUROPEAN COMMUNITY

8

1 DECLARATION

A OFFICE OF DESTINATION

2 Consignor/*Exporter*　　　　No

3 Forms

4 Loading lists

5 Items

6 Total packages

7 Reference number

8 Consignee　　　　No

9 Person responsible for financial settlement　No

Copy for the consignee

10 *Country last con-signed*

11 *Trad./Prod. country*

12 *Value details*

13 *CAP*

14 Declarant/Representative　　　　No

15 Country of dispatch/*export*

15 C disp./*exp.* Code　a|　b|

17 Country destin. Code　a|　b|

16 Country of origin

17 Country of destination

18 Identity and nationality of means of transport on arrival

19 Ctr

20 Delivery terms

21 Identity and nationality of active means of transport crossing the border

22 Currency and total amount invoiced

23 Exchange rate

24 Nature of transaction

25 Mode of transport at the border

26 Inland mode of transport

27 Place of unloading

28 Financial and banking data

8

29 Office of entry

30 Location of goods

31 Packages and description of goods

Marks and numbers — Container No(s) — Number and kind

32 Item No

33 Commodity Code

34 Country origin Code　a|　b|

35 Gross mass (kg)

36 *Preference*

37 PROCEDURE

38 Net mass (kg)

39 *Quota*

40 Summary declaration/Previous document

41 Supplementary units

42 *Item price*

43 *VM Code*

44 Additional information/ Documents produced/ Certificates and authori-sations

A I Code

45 *Adjustment*

46 Statistical value

47 Calculation of taxes

Type	Tax base	Rate	Amount	MP
	Total:			

48 Deferred payment

49 Identification of warehouse

B ACCOUNTING DETAILS

50 Principal　　　　No

Signature

C OFFICE OF DEPARTURE

51 Intended offices of transit (and country)

represented by

Place and date:

52 Guarantee not valid for

Code

53 Office of destination (and country)

J CONTROL BY OFFICE OF DESTINATION

54 Place and date:

Signature and name of declarant/representative

C88 (1-8)　Printed in the UK for HMSO 8055017 8/87 G.B.R. F5877 (SEPT. 1987)

4 Dangerous cargo

4.1 INTRODUCTION

The carriage of dangerous classified cargo by sea transport requires special precautions/procedures/facilities concerning its shipment. A Dangerous Goods Note is completed by the shipper and serves as a multi-purpose document valid for the whole journey using any combination of surface modes of transport.

A form entitled the Export Cargo Shipping Instruction (Special Cargo and Dangerous Goods) provides confirmation for the shipowner or agent of information previously telephoned by the shipper regarding the dangerous or special goods to be shipped, and is intended to speed the completion of the Bill of Lading/Sea Waybill and associated documentation.

4.2 DANGEROUS GOODS NOTE

Description

A Dangerous Goods Note is a multi-purpose document used for any combination of surface modes of transport valid for the whole journey involving a dangerous classified cargo transit. It is a seven-part document.

Source of document

The document is available from the shipowner or Forwarding Agent.

Purpose/use/function

The Dangerous Goods Note combines the function of application for stowage space on the transport unit(s); the dangerous goods declaration completed by the shipper; the special stowage order in the transport unit as allocated by the carrier; the container/vehicle packing certificate; the standard shipping note; and finally the 'back up' document for the forwarder/haulier.

Other aspects

The document must be completed by the shipper dispatching the goods and must feature the technical name of the substance, the class of substance of which there are nine, and the United Nations' number.

The SOLAS (Safety of Life at Sea) divides dangerous cargo into nine classifications as detailed below:

- ☐ Class 1 Explosives
- ☐ Class 2 Gases
- ☐ Class 3 Flammable liquids
- ☐ Class 4 Flammable solids and substances liable to spontaneous combustion or which emit flammable gases in contact with water (the class is subdivided into three sub-classes)
- ☐ Class 5 Oxidizing substances and organic peroxides (subdivided into two sub-classes)
- ☐ Class 6 Toxic substances and infectious substances (subdivided into two sub-classes)
- ☐ Class 7 Radio-active products
- ☐ Class 8 Corrosive products
- ☐ Class 9 Other miscellaneous hazardous products

The cargo must be correctly labelled/marked and display a label featuring its class. Packing requirements are also mandatory and depend on the cargo classification. Overall there are three groups:

- ☐ Class 1 maximum hazard
- ☐ Class 2 intermediate hazard
- ☐ Class 3 low level hazard

Shippers are advised to contact the carrier with adequate notice prior to date of intended shipment to determine cargo acceptance, stowage/sailing reference details, nature of packaging, documentation requirements, quantity limitations, and so on.

The shipper is subject to severe penalties if the goods are incorrectly described.

By 1989 a major revision was underway relative to Class 1 explosives; Class 3 inflammable liquids; Class 7 radioactive materials and segregation of radio-active cargoes.

DANGEROUS GOODS NOTE

DG

DANGEROUS GOODS DECLARATION, SHIPPING NOTE & CONTAINER/VEHICLE PACKING CERTIFICATE
© SITPRO 1981

Special Information is required for (a) Dangerous Goods in Limited Quantities (b) Radioactive Substances (class 7) (c) Tank Containers and (d) In certain circumstances a weathering certificate is required

SHADED AREAS NEED NOT BE SHIPPER COMPLETED FOR SHORT SEA, RO. RO./RAIL

IDEM is a trade mark of Wiggins Teape Limited, Papermakers to the World.

MUST BE COMPLETED FOR FULL CONTAINER/VEHICLE LOADS:—

Exporter	1	Veh. Bkg. Ref.	2	Customs Reference/Status	3

Exporter's Reference | 4

| | Exporter Freight Forwarder | Port Charges Payable by* | 5 | Fwdr's Ref. | 6 | SS Co Bkg No. | 7 |

| Consignee | 8A | Other (Name & Address) | |

Name of Shipping Line or CTO | 8 | Port Account No.

| Freight Forwarder | 9 | For Use of Receiving Authority Only |

| Receiving Date(s) | Berth/Dock/Containerbase etc | 10 |

Consecutive no. or DG reference allocated by shipping line or C.T.O. (if any) | 10A

| Vessel | Port of Loading | 11 | TO THE RECEIVING AUTHORITY
Please receive for shipment the goods described below subject to your published regulations & conditions (including those as to liability) |

| Port of Discharge | Destination Depot | 12 | Name of Receiving Authority | 13 |

Marks & Numbers; No. & Kind of Packages; Description of goods.†
INDICATE: HAZARD CLASS, UN NUMBER, FLASHPOINT °C. | 14 | Receiving Authority Use | Gross Wt(kg) of goods 15 | Cube (m³) of goods 16 |

Net Wt(kg) of goods | 16A

†CORRECT TECHNICAL NAME, PROPRIETARY NAMES ALONE ARE NOT SUFFICIENT.

CONTAINER/VEHICLE PACKING CERTIFICATE | 17
It is declared that the packing of the container has been carried out in accordance with the provisions shown overleaf:—

Name of Company   *FCL*

Signature   Date
of person responsible for packing container

DANGEROUS GOODS DECLARATION
I hereby declare that the contents of this consignment are fully and accurately described above by the correct technical name(s) (proper shipping name(s)), that the shipment is packaged in such a manner as to withstand the ordinary risks of handling and transport by sea, having regard to the properties of the goods to be carried, and that the goods are classified, packaged, marked and labelled in accordance with the requirements of the Merchant Shipping (Dangerous Goods) Rules 1978 as currently amended. I further declare that if appropriate the goods are classified, packaged and marked to comply with the requirements of the European Agreement concerning the International Carriage of Dangerous Goods by Road (ADR) and of Annex 1 (RID) to the International Convention concerning the Carriage of Goods by Rail (CIM) or special arrangements made between the contracting parties to these Agreements.

The shipper must complete and sign box 19.

Total Gross weight of goods | Total Cube of goods

| Prefix & Container/Vehicle Number | 18 | Seal Number(s) | 18A | Container/Vehicle Size & Type | 18B | Tare wt (kg) as marked on container | 18C | Weight of container and goods (kg) | 18D |

Received the above number of packages/containers/trailers in apparent good order and condition unless stated hereon.
RECEIVING AUTHORITY REMARKS

Haulier's Name

Vehicle Reg No.

DRIVER'S SIGNATURE | SIGNATURE & DATE

Name of Shipper preparing this note & tel. no. | 19

NAME/STATUS OF DECLARANT

DATE

Signature of Declarant

890

LONSDALE BUSINESS FORMS LTD 0933 223456

* Mark 'X' as appropriate. If box 5 is not completed the company preparing this note may be held liable for payment of port charges.

4.3 EXPORT CARGO SHIPPING INSTRUCTION (SPECIAL CARGO AND DANGEROUS GOODS)

Description

The Export Cargo Shipping Instruction serves as confirmation of the information regarding the goods to be shipped provided earlier on the telephone by the shipper to the shipowner/agent.

Source of document

Freight carrier, shipowner, e.g. P&O Containers Ltd (previously OCL).

Purpose/use/function

The document is intended to facilitate accurate completion of the Bill of Lading/Sea Waybill and associated documentation. It can only be used for dangerous classified cargo, and special cargo such as livestock, obnoxious cargo, merchandise requiring controlled temperature (refrigerated cargo), and so on.

Other aspects

The document is completed by the shipper and misrepresentation of the cargo description can result in serious legal penalties. The shipowner processes the document including confirming the stowage order number and checking the cargo classification and associated packaging and marking/labelling needs have been provided.

EXPORT CARGO SHIPPING INSTRUCTIONS (SPECIAL CARGO AND DANGEROUS GOODS.)

PLEASE QUOTE REFERENCE ON ALL COMMUNICATIONS

SEE NOTES ON REVERSE OF SHIPPER'S COPY

(left margin, vertical) OCL RESERVE THE RIGHT TO REFUSE CARGO WHICH IN THEIR OPINION IS NOT IN A FIT CONDITION FOR CARRIAGE.

S Shipper (Name and Address)

REBATE

OCL
Overseas Containers Limited.

C.A.N./Pre-entry No./Other Customs Ref

Exporter's Ref.

OCL Booking Ref No.

C Consignee (if Order, state "Order" and give Name and Address of Notify Party)

N Notify Party

F Forwarding Agent (Name and Address)

A Place of Receipt

U.K. Containerbase

D Place of Delivery

Intended Ship & Voyage | Port of Loading

O Other Freight Payer

Destination Port | Destination Containerbase

Marks and Numbers:	Number and type of Packages, Correct Technical Name and Description of Goods. (Please List Different Commodities Separately).	DTI/IMCO Class U.N. No. Flash Point °(c) or Refrig. Temp.	Freight Class and SITC code	Gross Weight (Kg)	Cube (M³)
				Net Weight	FOB Value for U.K. Customs (£)

Total Number of Packages =

Number of Containers =

OCL
USE ONLY

Serial No.	PD No.	Commodity Code	Ind.	Declared Value	Container No.

Container Seal No.	Type	Size	Quar	Temp	Haz	Reb

	Computer	Payer	Ch.Cd	Basis	Frt. Rate	Frt. Amount	Curr.
O.L.							
O.C.							
S.F.							
D.C.							
D.L.							
EXTRA CHARGES							
				TOTAL			

Continuation of Header Data

Pay	PCf	Curr

Narrative (applies to last extra charge)

OM 271A (2/80)

GOODS ARE ACCEPTED FOR TRANSPORTATION ON THE TERMS OF CARRIER'S TARIFF RULES AND CONDITIONS. OTHER SERVICES ARE RENDERED SUBJECT TO OCL'S APPLICABLE TRADING CONDITIONS.

OM 271A (9/83)

EXPORT CARGO SHIPPING INSTRUCTIONS (SPECIAL CARGO AND DANGEROUS GOODS.)

OCL
Overseas Containers Limited.

OCL RESERVE THE RIGHT TO REFUSE CARGO WHICH IN THEIR OPINION IS NOT IN A FIT CONDITION FOR CARRIAGE.

(S) Shipper (Name and Address)

Customs Ref./Status

Exporter's Ref.

OCL Booking Ref No.

(C) Consignee (if Order, state "Order" and give Name and Address of Notify Party)

(N) Notify Party

(F) Forwarding Agent (Name and Address)

(A) Place of Receipt

U.K. Containerbase

(D) Place of Delivery

Intended Ship & Voyage | Port of Loading

(O) Other Freight Payer

Destination Port | Destination Containerbase

Marks and Numbers:	Number and type of Packages, Correct Technical Name and Description of Goods. (Please List Different Commodities Separately).	DTI/IMCO Class U.N. No. Flash Point °(c) or Refrig. Temp.	Tariff/Trade Code No.	Gross Weight (Kg)	Cube (M³)
			Quantity 2 for U.K. Customs	Net Weight	FOB Value for U.K. Customs (£)
			Quantity 3 for U.K. Customs		

TYPE OF SERVICE ('X' BOX)	Container Packed	LCL (Carrier)	
		FCL (Shipper)	
	Container Unpacked	LCL (Carrier)	
		FCL (Consignee)	

Total Number of Packages =
Number of Containers =

CUSTOMS STATUS ('x' Box or Boxes if more than one status applies)	Non-Restricted	CAP	
	Non-Stat.	IPR	
	Low Value	LEC	
		Licenced	
		Under Bond	
		Drawback	

FREIGHT & CHARGES (Specify payers using appropriate letter code) — Payer

- UK/Europe Inland Transport Charge
- UK/Europe LCL Service Charge/Terminal Handling
- Ocean Freight
- Destination LCL Service Charge/Terminal Handling
- Destination Inland Transport Charge

SUPPLEMENTARY SERVICE CHARGES

SHIPPER'S DECLARATION (REQUIRED FOR ALL DANGEROUS GOODS)

It is certified that the goods are packed in a manner adequate to withstand the ordinary risks of handling and transport by sea having regard to the nature of the goods, and the packages durably labelled or stencilled on the outside to indicate with the correct technical name, the identity of the goods and the nature of the danger to which the goods give rise the foregoing in accordance with the requirements of the Merchant Shipping (Dangerous Goods) Regulations 1981, and any re-enactment, amendment, or revision thereof and The Blue Book and any amendment or any revision thereof; and the IMDG Code 1977 and any applicable revision thereof, (and with Chapter VII (Carriage of Dangerous Goods) of the Convention for the Safety of Life at Sea 1960 and any applicable revision or replacement thereof).

Note: As for the purpose of the M.S. (Dangerous Goods) Regulations 1981, the Department of Transport consider a container loaded Dangerous Cargo as a single dangerous package. Shippers are reminded of their responsibility in ensuring that when loading a container it is properly packed and secured under the supervision of a competent person, as recommended in the IMDG Code and that inter alia:—

1. The container is clean, dry and fit to receive the goods.
2. No goods known to be incompatable are stowed therein.
3. All packages are inspected for damage and only dry, sound packages loaded.
4. All packages are properly stowed and secured and suitable securing methods used.
5. The container is labelled with the proper IMCO label(s) and a label stating the correct technical name(s) of the dangerous substance(s) it contains.

A certificate to this effect must be completed after the container has been packed and must accompany the goods.

FAILURE TO MAKE DECLARATION CAN RESULT IN DELAY AND EXTRA EXPENSE TO CARGO

We require Overseas Containers Ltd. to arrange transport of the goods detailed above between the Place of Receipt and the Place of Delivery shown above. We warrant that the details of goods declared are correct as known to us. We undertake to advise OCL of any subsequent alterations.

QUARANTINE REGULATIONS * MUST be completed for all Australian and New Zealand FCLs. See conditions on reverse	('X' BOX) USED TREATED	USED NOT TREATED	NOT USED
Wooden crates, cases			
Wooden pallets, Dunnage			
Packing: straw, rice hulls and/or similar			
Wooden contents excl. Packing material			
Alternative Packing Material			

OCL to Prepare and Lodge Customs Entry in UK

Forward Documents: To: (S) (C) (F) (N) (O)→

Number of B/Ls required — Orig — Copies

* Non-Negotiable Waybill Required ('x' Box)

* 'Concise' – Cargo Insurance
Cover Required ('x' Box) — Institute Clauses 'A'
" 'B'
Declared Value: £ — " 'C'

* Disbursements: Total Net Value £

Shipper's Name:

Tel No.: — Ext No. or Dept.

Date:

SIGNATURE

4.4 SHIPPER'S DECLARATION FOR DANGEROUS GOODS BY AIR

Description

A Shipper's Declaration for Dangerous Goods, together with an Air Waybill, must accompany a consignment of dangerous classified cargo on each occasion when it is dispatched by air.

Sources of document

The International Air Transport Association (IATA).

Purpose/use/function

To identify the nature and quantity of a consignment of dangerous goods according to sub-Section 8.1 of the IATA Dangerous Goods Regulations. The technical instructions for the conveyance of goods by air transport are produced by the International Civil Aviation Authority.

Legal context

The Shipper's Declaration for Dangerous Goods must comply with the regulations governing the movement of dangerous classified cargo by air laid down by IATA. The document carries a warning that failure to comply in all respects with the applicable Dangerous Goods Regulations may be in breach of the applicable law, subject to legal penalties. Under no circumstances 'shall it be signed by an IATA cargo agent, consolidator or forwarder'.

Other aspects

The document must be completed by the shipper and presented in duplicate to the carrier at the time the goods are dispatched. Overall there are nine classifications of dangerous cargo and they broadly conform to those applicable to sea transport. Different labelling featuring the cargo classification applies and marking of the consignment.

The technical packaging instructions as defined by the International Civil Aviation Authority embrace: the goods must be packaged in properly constructed and sound condition materials; the packaging must be capable of preventing any spillage from occurring during normal transit; ventilation must be tightly controlled, and any interior surface of the packaging must not deteriorate in contact with the substance being carried.

The cargo description reflected on the document must reflect the technical name of the substance, the class of substance and the United Nations' number.

The regulations and documentation needs are broadly similar for international consignments dispatched by rail RID – Regulations concerning the International Carriage of Dangerous Goods by rail, and by road ADR – the European Agreement concerning the International Carriage of Dangerous Goods by Road. The latter involves the TREM CARDS (Transport Emergency

Cards) which outline the instructions to the driver for the particular substance in the event of an emergency arising during transit.

SHIPPERS DECLARATION FOR DANGEROUS GOODS

Shipper	Air Waybill No.
	Page of Pages
	Shipper's Reference Number
	(Optional)

Consignee	
	IATA

Two completed and signed copies of this Declaration must be handed to the operator

TRANSPORT DETAILS

This shipment is within the limitations prescribed for *(delete non applicable)*	Airport of Departure
PASSENGER AND CARGO AIRCRAFT / CARGO AIRCRAFT ONLY	

Airport of Destination

WARNING

Failure to comply in all respects with the applicable Dangerous Goods Regulations may be in breach of the applicable law, subject to legal penalties. This Declaration must not, in any circumstances, be completed and/or signed by a consolidator, a forwarder or an IATA cargo agent.

Shipment type *(delete non-applicable)*
NON-RADIOACTIVE | RADIOACTIVE

NATURE AND QUANTITY OF DANGEROUS GOODS *(see sub-Section 8.1 of IATA Dangerous Goods Regulations)*

Dangerous Goods identification						
Proper Shipping Name	Class or Division	UN or ID No.	Subsidiary Risk	Quantity and type of packing	Packing inst.	Authorization

Additional Handling Information

I hereby declare that the contents of this consignment are fully and accurately described above by proper shipping name and are classified, packed, marked and labelled, and are in all respects in the proper condition for transport by air according to the applicable international and National Government Regulations.	Name/Title of Signatory
	Place and Date
	Signature *(see warning above)*

PRINTED IN ENGLAND BY I.A.L.

5 Finance: international trade

5.1 INTRODUCTION

Basically the type of payment chosen by an exporter and reflected in the contract of sale varies according to circumstances as given below:

1 currency situation;
2 exchange control regulations;
3 nature of the contract of sale;
4 political situation in the buyer's country and any mandatory arrangements;
5 financial arrangements;
6 relationship between buyer and seller.

Overall there are three principal methods of payment: Open account, Bill of Exchange and Documentary Letter of Credit.

In the documentary collection method of payment for goods, the exporter uses the banking system to send the importer a Bill of Exchange together with the shipping documents, including an original Bill of Lading, which serves as document of title to the goods. On payment or acceptance of the Bill of Exchange by the importer the bank then releases the documents to the importer to claim/collect the cargo.

To empower the banks to implement the documentary collection method of payment, the importer completes a Customer Lodgement Form for the Foreign Bill and/or Documents for Collection, and submits it to the bank.

Non-documentary payment for goods exported is effected either by International Money Transfer (the most common method) or by Express International Money Transfer. In both cases the overseas buyer completes the relevant Customer Lodgement Form, which is essentially a request to a bank to make an international money transfer, or an express international money transfer, to an exporter on the buyer's behalf.

A Documentary Letter of Credit is opened by the importer's bank when the importer requests the bank to authorize the exporter to draw a certain sum by a specified date for a particular consignment on condition that the required documents are presented.

To authorize a bank to open a Letter of Credit the importer completes a Customer Lodgement Form for a Documentary Credit.

5.2 CUSTOMER LODGEMENT FORM FOR THE FOREIGN BILL AND/OR DOCUMENTS FOR COLLECTION

Description

A Customer Lodgement Form for the Foreign Bill and/or Documents for Collection is a document that accompanies the Bill of Exchange (section 5.3) and shipping documents through the banking system when an exporter wishes to make provision for a buyer to use the documentary collection method of payment for goods.

Source of document

An international bank, e.g. Midland International Bank plc.

Purpose/use/function

The Customer Lodgement Form empowers a bank to implement the documentary collection method of payment on the exporter's behalf. In the documentary collection method of payment an exporter sends the Bill of Exchange to the buyer through the banking system with the shipping documents including the document of title to the goods, i.e. an original Bill of Lading. The bank then releases the documents on payment or acceptance of the Bill of Exchange by the overseas buyer.

Other aspects

The financial mechanism under which the documentary credit is operated internationally is contained in the Uniform Customs and Practice for Documentary Letters of Credits (1983 Revision) International Chamber of Commerce Publication, No. 400.

Foreign Bill and/or Documents for Collection

TO **Midland Bank plc**

Date ______________________

Branch ____ Branch reference No. ______________

Please collect on our account the undermentioned Bill/documents (our reference number______________)
which is/are to be forwarded to

If left blank,
the Bank will use its own agents ____

Bills of Exchange __________ Tenor __________ Amount __________ Place drawn on ______________
Insert sole, 2/2, etc

Documents	Statement	Invoices Commercial	Certified	Consular	Certificate of origin	Insurance policy or cert etc	Bill of lading	Air Consignment note	Parcel post receipt			
Number of copies												
For Bank use 1st Mail												
2nd Mail												

Air consignment note/parcel post receipt addressed to ____
If goods are addressed to a bank, see instructions below marked ⁂

Please follow instructions which we have marked X below.
Where alternatives are listed, the alternative not applicable is to be deleted

☐ Release documents against **acceptance**.

☐ Release goods against **acceptance**. ⁂

☐ Acceptance/payment may be deferred pending arrival of the goods.

☐ If unaccepted/unpaid protest.

☐ If unaccepted/unpaid do not protest.
Specific instructions must be given regarding protest

☐ Collect all charges from drawees. these may not be/may be waived if refused.

☐ If documents are not duly taken up on arrival of goods, store goods (if possible in customs or bonded warehouse) and insure against:
a. fire only* b. all available risks*
Claim from drawees, all expenses thus incurred; if refused by them, they are for our account.

** Delete as appropriate*

☐ Release documents against **payment**.

☐ Release goods against **payment**. ⁂

☐ Advise acceptance and due date by airmail/cable.

☐ Remit proceeds by airmail/cable.

☐ Advise non-acceptance by airmail/cable.

☐ Advise non-payment by airmail/cable.

In case of need refer to

____

____

____

☐ Follow their instructions without reserve.

☐ For assistance only

Other instructions

We undertake to reimburse you for all charges, whether or not the collection is paid.

It is understood that the collection is undertaken by you only on the terms set forth on the back hereof.

Note

Original documents will be despatched by registered post, and, if to countries outside Europe, by airmail at the customer's expense, unless otherwise instructed. Duplicate documents will be despatched after the originals by a similar category of mail.

Signed ______________________________

1524-9

5.3 BILL OF EXCHANGE

Description

A Bill of Exchange is legally defined as an 'unconditional order in writing addressed by one person to another, signed by the person giving it, requiring the person to whom it is addressed to pay on demand or at a fixed or determinable future time a certain sum in money to or to the order of a specified person, or bearer'. The Bill of Exchange looks something like a cheque and is prepared by the exporter and drawn on an overseas buyer, or even a third party, as designated in the export contract for the sum agreed as settlement.

Source of document

A bank, e.g. National Westminster Bank plc.

Purpose/use/function

By using a Bill of Exchange with other shipping documents through the banking system, an exporter can ensure greater control of the goods, because until the Bill of Exchange is paid or accepted by the overseas buyer the goods cannot be released. Conversely, the buyer does not have to pay or agree to pay by some agreed date until delivery of the goods from the exporter.

Other aspects

The Bill of Exchange Act 1882 defines further a foreign bill as one which is either drawn by a person who is not resident in the British Islands or is drawn by a person resident in the British Islands or a person resident abroad and is payable abroad.

There are two methods in which Bills of Exchange are used to permit an exporter to be paid for the goods or to establish a commitment to pay on a certain date.

The first one termed clean collection requires established confidence between the two parties, buyer and seller. It involves the exporter to forward all shipping documentation to the importer to allow him to take control of the goods and draws a Bill of Exchange on the buyer which is sent to the exporter's bank and its correspondent in the buyer's country to the buyer for collection. In such a situation the buyer accepts the bill by endorsement which permits him to pay immediately (at sight) or at 60 or 90 days from the date on the bill.

The alternative method requires the exporter to exercise control over the goods and to obtain the buyer's acceptance of the Bill of Exchange before he is allowed to take control of them. This is realized by attaching the shipping documentation to the Bill of Exchange which is released to the buyer when he has accepted the endorsement. This can be undertaken in two ways: documents against payment involving the shipping documents being released against acceptance of a sight draft involving payment being made when the documents are passed to the buyer. The other technique is documents against acceptance which requires the documents to be released against a 'term' or 'usance' bill instead of the sight bill allowing the buyer to pay at a certain date from the date on the Bill of Exchange.

The Bill of Exchange is prepared by the exporter. In the documentary collection method of payment an exporter sends the Bill of Exchange to the buyer through the banking system with the shipping documents including the document of title to the goods, i.e. an original Bill of Lading. The Bank then releases the documents on payment of acceptance of the Bill of Exchange by the overseas buyer. The bank is empowered to implement the documentary collection method of payment on the exporter's behalf by the Customer Lodgement Form of the Foreign Bill and/or Documents for Collection (section 5.2), which is completed and submitted by the exporter to the bank.

Bill of Exchange

No. 1234

Drawn under Credit Number 01/765/NWB/2A
of Traders Bank of Japan, Tokyo, Japan, dated 1 May 1987

14 May 1987 For £100,000

At SIGHT Pay this SOLE of Exchange to the Order

of OURSELVES

THE SUM OF ONE HUNDRED THOUSAND POUNDS STERLING

Value RECEIVED which place to Account

[1] UNITED KINGDOM SELLER LIMITED

To [2] NATIONAL WESTMINSTER BANK PLC

25,OLD BROAD STREET
LONDON EC12

1 Drawer
2 Drawee

5.4 CUSTOMER LODGEMENT FORM FOR INTERNATIONAL MONEY TRANSFER

Description

An International Money Transfer is the most common form of non-documenting payment for export and is effected by mail transfers. The remitter (e.g. an overseas buyer) completes a Customer Lodgement Form for International Money Transfer, which is essentially a request to a bank to make an international money transfer on the remitter's behalf.

Source of document

A bank, e.g. Midland International Bank plc.

Purpose/use/function

For example, an overseas buyer instructs a bank in the buyer's country to transfer an account of money to an exporter's bank by airmail and in due course the exporter receives payment.

Other aspects

The International Money Transfer System is quicker when the Express International Money Transfer process is used. The form must be completed in block capitals or typed and bear an authorized signature. It tends to be used for the small financial transaction often of a personal nature.

Midland International Payment Service

MAIL PAYMENT

TO **Midland Bank plc**

1

_____

_____Branch

Date_____

PLEASE TYPE, OR PRINT IN CAPITALS, ALL ENTRIES   *Please read the terms overleaf*

Method of Payment	
Please tick (√) appropriate box to indicate the method you wish payment to be made by the paying bank. *(If box 1 or 3 is ticked (√) the full name of the bank must be quoted below †)*	☐ 1. Advise and credit the account of the beneficiary ☐ 2. Advise and pay to the beneficiary ☐ 3. Pay to the beneficiary on personal application and identification ☐ 4. Open a new account in the name of beneficiary. (Please attach specimen signature(s))

Amount of Payment	
Please tick (√) & complete appropriate box	☐ 1. Remit in Sterling the sum of £ [●] ☐ 2. Remit in _____ (name of currency) the sum of [●] ☐ 3. Remit the equivalent of Sterling £ [●] in_____(name of currency)

Amount in Words	

Please complete if applicable	Forward Contract No (if any) [ ] [ ] [ ] [ ] [ ]	Exchange Rate	

Beneficiary's Bankers †	
Complete only if 1 or 3 under Method of Payment above has been ticked (√)	

Beneficiary's Account No. (if any)	

Beneficiary's Full Name	

Beneficiary's Full Address	

Message to Beneficiary	

Sender's Name	

Charges	
Please tick (√) 1 or 2 or 3 as appropriate	☐ 1. Debit *me/us with your charges, correspondent's charges to be paid by the beneficiary ☐ 2. All charges to be paid by the beneficiary ☐ 3. Debit *me/us with all charges

Please make the above Mail Payment.   1595-6

Please debit *my / our Sterling Account No. or *receive herewith *cheque / cash [ ][ ][ ][ ][ ][ ] or Foreign Currency Account No. [ ][ ][ ][ ][ ][ ][ ]

I/we* have read and agreed the terms overleaf.

Account Name_____   Signature(s)_____

Address_____

*Delete as appropriate   To be signed in accordance with Bank Mandate.

FROM **Midland Bank plc**

Midland International Payment Service
XX MAIL PAYMENT

2

_____DX   TO: INTERNATIONAL SERVICES BRANCH

_____Branch

PO Date_____

REFERENCE NO:	BRANCH	RX	GLOBAL BANKING SECTOR	RF

TO BE COMPLETED BY GLOBAL BANKING SECTOR ONLY	
Method of Payment	☐ 1. Advise and credit the account of the beneficiary
RC	☐ 2. Advise and pay to the beneficiary
CX	☐ 3. Pay to the beneficiary on personal application and identification
PA	☐ 4. Open a new account in the name of beneficiary. (Please attach specimen signature(s))

Amount of Payment	
CU	☐ 1. Remit in Sterling the sum of £ |_|_|_|_| ● |_| ££
Dealers Initial	☐ 2. Remit in $$ (name of currency) the sum of |_|_|_|_| ● |_|
Conversion Check	☐ 3. Remit the equivalent of Sterling £ |_|_|_|_| ● |_| ££
No. 1 / No. 2	in_____$$ (name of currency)

Amount in Words

Please complete if applicable	Forward Contract No (if any) |_|_|_|_|_|	Exchange Rate **XR**	Value Date

Beneficiary's Bankers †	**PN**	
CB		
CT	**AW**	
CO		

Beneficiary's Account No.   **AC**

Beneficiary's Full Name   **AO**

Beneficiary's Full Address
BM

Message to Beneficiary
VA   **RE**
FC

Sender's Name   **OO**

Charges	☐ 1. Debit *me/us with your charges, correspondent's charges to be paid by the beneficiary	TO BE COMPLETED BY BRANCH:
CH		**Charges**
CC	☐ 2. All charges to be paid by the beneficiary	*Amount_____ taken from Sterling/Foreign Currency account by branch
Signature verified	☐ 3. Debit *me/us with all charges	*Amount_____ enclosed for Global Banking Sector
		*Amount_____ to be taken and retained by Global Banking Sector

Please make the above Mail Payment and either:-   1595·6

(DT) *Receive herewith Branch Advice

or debit
Foreign Currency Account No. |_|_|_|_|_|_|_|

Account Name_____   Account Type_____

Currency_____ Notice given on (if applicable)_____   Authorised Signature_____

*Delete as appropriate   Signature No:_____

TO **Midland Bank plc**

MAIL PAYMENT

_____

_____Branch

Date_____

PLEASE TYPE, OR PRINT IN CAPITALS, ALL ENTRIES   *Please read the terms overleaf*

Method of Payment *Please tick (√) appropriate box to indicate the method you wish payment to be made by the paying bank.* *(If box 1 or 3 is ticked (√) the full name of the bank must be quoted below †)*	☐ 1. Advise and credit the account of the beneficiary ☐ 2. Advise and pay to the beneficiary ☐ 3. Pay to the beneficiary on personal application and identification ☐ 4. Open a new account in the name of beneficiary. (Please attach specimen signature(s))
Amount of Payment *Please tick (√) & complete appropriate box*	☐ 1. Remit in Sterling the sum of £ | | | | • | | ☐ 2. Remit in (name of currency) the sum of | | | | | • | | ☐ 3. Remit the equivalent of Sterling £ | | | | • | | in_____(name of currency)
Amount in Words	_____ _____
Please complete if applicable	Forward Contract No (if any) | | | | | Exchange Rate
Beneficiary's Bankers † *Complete only if 1 or 3 under Method of Payment above has been ticked (√)*	_____ _____ _____
Beneficiary's Account No. (if any)	_____
Beneficiary's Full Name	_____
Beneficiary's Full Address	_____ _____
Message to Beneficiary	_____ _____
Sender's Name	_____
Charges *Please tick (√) 1 or 2 or 3 as appropriate*	☐ 1. Debit *me/us with your charges, correspondent's charges to be paid by the beneficiary ☐ 2. All charges to be paid by the beneficiary ☐ 3. Debit *me/us with all charges

Please make the above Mail Payment.   1595-6

Please debit *my / our Sterling Account No. \| \| \| \| \| \| \| \| or Foreign Currency Account No. \| \| \| \| \| \| \| \|
or *receive herewith *cheque / cash

I/we* have read and agreed the terms overleaf.

Account Name_____   Signature(s)_____

Address_____

To be signed in accordance with Bank Mandate.

*Delete as appropriate

5.5 CUSTOMER LODGEMENT FORM (ORDER) FOR EXPRESS INTERNATIONAL MONEY TRANSFER

Description

An Express International Money Transfer is a system of telegraphic transfer or bank cable and is a more speedy form of non-documentary payment for export than the International Money Transfer (section 5.4). The remitter (e.g. an overseas buyer) completes a Customer Lodgement Form for Express International Money Transfer, which is essentially a request to a bank to make an express international money transfer, either literally or in cypher, on the remitter's behalf.

Source of document

A bank, e.g. Midland International Bank plc.

Purpose/use/function

Money is transferred by coded inter-bank telex, and provided that the exporter makes it clear to the overseas buyer exactly to which bank and account the remittance should be made, the exporter should receive a very speedy payment through the system.

Other aspects

This payment method is used when circumstances warrant early payment and is widely used internationally in a variety of circumstances. It must be completed in a typed form or block capitals and needs an authorized signature.

Midland International Payment Service
PRIORITY PAYMENT

TO **Midland Bank plc**

_____

_____Branch

Date_____

PLEASE TYPE, OR PRINT IN CAPITALS, ALL ENTRIES   _Please read the terms overleaf_

Method of Payment	
Please tick (√) appropriate box to indicate the method you wish payment to be made by the paying bank.	☐ 1. Advise and credit the account of the beneficiary
	☐ 2. Advise and pay to the beneficiary
(If box 1 or 3 is ticked (√) the full name of the bank must be quoted below †)	☐ 3. Pay to the beneficiary on personal application and identification

Amount of Payment	
Please tick (√) & complete appropriate box	☐ 1. Remit in Sterling the sum of £ ⎸ ⎸ ⎸ ⎸ ⎸ ● ⎸ ⎸
	☐ 2. Remit in (name of currency) the sum of ⎸ ⎸ ⎸ ⎸ ⎸ ● ⎸
	☐ 3. Remit the equivalent of Sterling £ ⎸ ⎸ ⎸ ⎸ ⎸ ● ⎸
	in_____(name of currency)

Amount in Words	
	_____

Please complete if applicable	Forward Contract No (if any) ⎸ ⎸ ⎸ ⎸ ⎸	Exchange Rate

Beneficiary's Bankers †	
Complete only if 1 or 3 under Method of Payment above has been ticked (√)	_____
	_____

Beneficiary's Account No. (if any)	
Beneficiary's Full Name	
Beneficiary's Full Address	

Message to Beneficiary	

Sender's Name	

Charges	
Please tick (√) 1 or 2 or 3 as appropriate	☐ 1. Debit *me/us with your charges, correspondent's charges to be paid by the beneficiary
	☐ 2. All charges to be paid by the beneficiary
	☐ 3. Debit *me/us with all charges

Please make the above Priority Payment.   1596-4

Please debit *my / our Sterling Account No. ⎸ ⎸ ⎸ ⎸ ⎸ ⎸ ⎸ or Foreign Currency Account No. ⎸ ⎸ ⎸ ⎸ ⎸ ⎸ ⎸ ⎸
or *receive herewith *cheque / cash

I/we* have read and agreed the terms overleaf.

Account Name_____ _____   Signature(s)_____

Address_____

*Delete as appropriate   **To be signed in accordance with Bank Mandate.**

5.6 CUSTOMER LODGEMENT FORM FOR A DOCUMENTARY CREDIT (REQUEST TO OPEN A DOCUMENTARY CREDIT)

Description

A Customer Lodgement Form for a Documentary Credit is the form used by the buyer to request his or her bank to open a Documentary Credit (also known as a Documentary Letter of Credit) in favour of the seller.

Source of document

A bank, e.g. Midland International Bank plc.

Purpose/use/function

To authorize a bank to open a Letter of Credit (section 5.7).

Other aspects

See pages 52–9 relative to Letter of Credit.

TO **Midland Bank plc** Request to open **1**
Documentary Credit

Branch _____ Date _____

Please open for my/our account a Documentary Credit, in accordance with the undermentioned particulars. I/We agree that, except so far as otherwise expressly stated, this Credit will be subject to the Uniform Customs and Practice for Documentary Credits (1983 Revision), International Chamber of Commerce Publication No. 400. I/We undertake to execute (if not already executed) the Bank's usual Form of Indemnity.

Signed _____

Entries must not be made in this margin   **When completing this form please follow carefully the general instructions overleaf.**

Method of advice	*airmail/cable *full advice/pre-advice (See note overleaf)
Type of credit	*__Irrevocable__ i.e. cannot be cancelled without beneficiaries' agreement **Revocable** i.e. subject to cancellation
Date of expiry	Enter date _____
Place of expiry	Enter place _____
Applicant	_____
Beneficiary Name and Address	_____
Advising Bank	*As far as possible this should be left to Midland Bank plc.*
Amount	_____ say _____
Amount variation	_____
Available with	*To be completed by Midland Bank plc International Division*
Available by	*Payment / Acceptance / Negotiation / Deferred Payment with drafts drawn at _____ and drawn on _____ *To be completed by Midland Bank plc International Division*
Partshipments	*Allowed / Prohibited _____
Transhipment	*Allowed / Prohibited _____
Shipment/Despatch/ Taking in charge	From/at _____ For transportation to _____
Latest date for shipment	Enter date if applicable _____

1016-8   *Delete as appropriate

General instructions for opening Documentary Credit

Responsibility of Bank

It should be clearly understood that the Bank is not directly concerned with the proper fulfilment of the contract between the seller and the buyer. Its duty is simply to receive documents on behalf of the customer which purport to comply with the conditions stated when opening the credit.

The Bank has the right to realise the goods or to take any steps, at its discretion, with a view to safeguarding its position.

Method of Advice

The Bank may use S.W.I.F.T. (Society for Worldwide Interbank Financial Telecommunications) according to circumstances. The instructions of the customer will be regarded as including the use of this method.

Type of Credit

Irrevocable or Revocable: It is essential that definite instructions on this point are given on all occasions. An Irrevocable Credit becomes an engagement on the Bank itself, incapable of cancellation or modification except by consent of the beneficiary. A Revocable Credit may be cancelled without the beneficiary's consent by the customer at any time, subject, however, to the customer remaining liable in respect of any negotiation, acceptance, deferred payment or payment made by the Bank through which the Credit is advised, prior to receipt of notice of cancellation by that Bank.

Availability

Date of expiry: This must always be given. The date of expiry can, of course, be extended on instructions from the customer. When credits are to be opened/advised through a bank abroad, dates of expiry are understood to apply to the latest date for presentation of documents for negotiation, or acceptance, or payment, or deferred payment (as the case may be) in the place abroad at which the negotiation, or acceptance, or payment or deferred payment is to take place, and not to the date of arrival of documents or advices in London. Credits with a London date of expiry can be opened in favour of beneficiaries abroad but it is not customary to advise such credits through a foreign bank.

"Negotiation": This instruction should be used where drafts drawn by the beneficiary on Midland Bank plc are to be honoured if negotiated at the place and within the period of validity of the credit.

"Acceptance": This instruction should be used where the currency of the credit is that of the country of the beneficiary who is to draw drafts for acceptance on a bank abroad. It is also appropriate where credits are to be opened in sterling with a London date of expiry in favour of beneficiaries abroad or in favour of beneficiaries in the United Kingdom.

"Payment/Deferred Payment": These instructions are appropriate where the currency of the credit is that of the country of the beneficiary who is to claim payment or deferred payment from a bank abroad. They are also appropriate where credits are to be opened in sterling with a London date of expiry in favour of beneficiaries abroad or in favour of beneficiaries in the United Kingdom.

Documents Required

It is not sufficient to state "usual documents". The documents should be mentioned in detail. "On board" (i.e. Shipped) Marine Bills of Lading are normally required but if "Received for Shipment" Marine Bills of Lading are acceptable, this should be indicated.

Short Form Bills of Lading and Bills of Lading evidencing shipment in containers will be accepted unless the credit specifically prohibits either or both of them.

General

Unless the credit provides otherwise, transport documents bearing reference to extra charges in addition to the freight charges will be accepted. These charges include for example, "Free In/Out" and other costs and charges incurred in container transport. Should additional charges not be acceptable the specific charges prohibited must be stated.

Unless instructions are given to the contrary, banks will take up documents presented to them up to 21 days from the date of the transport document, even for a short sea voyage. It is essential, therefore, for customers to calculate the maximum period they would wish to accept for presentation of documents to our correspondents abroad bearing in mind the normal airmail time required for the documents to reach us, and to stipulate the maximum number of days permitted between date of issue of the transport document and the date of presentation, even if a latest shipment date is stipulated.

Entries must not be made in this margin

When completing this form please follow carefully the general instructions on the reverse of the first page.

3

Terms: *C.I.F. / C. & F. / C.I.P. / F.O.B. / F.A.S. / F.O.R. etc. _____
This information is required in all cases

Goods
Quantity and
Description

Price per unit _____ (if applicable)

Documents required

Invoice

*Full set "on board" Marine Bills of Lading to order and blank endorsed marked
*freight paid/freight payable at destination.

*OR Air Waybill issued by _____

    evidencing goods addressed to _____
    marked *freight paid/freight payable at destination.

*OR Combined Transport Document issued by _____

    evidencing goods addressed to _____
    marked *freight paid/freight payable at destination

*Insurance *Policy / Certificate for invoice amount plus _____ % covering Marine and War
Risks and including other conditions as follows:

_____

*Insurance effected by _____ where no Insurance is called for.
Other documents: (e.g. Packing List / Weight List / Certificate of Origin)

Additional conditions
(if any) _____
_____

Charges _____
Unless otherwise specified Midland and foreign bank charges will be for account of the applicant

Period for
presentation
Documents to be presented within _____ days of the date of issue of the transport document
but in any event within the validity of the credit.

Reimbursement instructions:

Upon receipt of documents in order:

*Debit my/our Sterling account number _____ *utilising Forward Contract _____

*Debit my/our _____ Customer Currency Account number _____

Signed _____

*Delete as appropriate

5.7 LETTER OF CREDIT (IRREVOCABLE)

Description

A Documentary Letter of Credit is the means whereby at the buyer's request the importer's bank authorizes the exporter to draw a financial amount by a specified date for a particular shipment subject to the detailed documents being forthcoming. It may be revocable or irrevocable. A draft is drawn by the seller on the buyer accompanied by shipping documents. Accordingly the buyer requests his or her bank to open a documentary Credit.

A revocable Credit can be cancelled or amended by the buyer without the supplier's prior knowledge any time before the seller presents the documents for payment. Once the documents complying with the terms of the Credit have been presented to the bank nominated in the Credit, payment is guaranteed, but because of the possibility of cancellation prior to this, revocable credits are seldom used.

Conversely, the irrevocable Credit cannot be altered or cancelled without the agreement of the importer or exporter. It provides a high degree of security.

There are various types of irrevocable Letter of Credit as given below:

1 **Confirmed**. A confirmed irrevocable Letter of Credit is an irrevocable Credit to which the advising bank (at the request of the issuing bank) has added its confirmation that payment will be made. The advising bank thus confirms that it will honour drawings which conform to the terms of the Credit.
2 **Unconfirmed**. If the irrevocable Letter of Credit is unconfirmed the advising bank merely informs the exporter of the terms and conditions of the Credit without adding its own undertaking to pay or accept under the terms of the Credit.
3 **Transferable**. A transferable Letter of Credit is one under which the exporter has the right to instructions to the paying bank (or to the negotiating bank) or to make the Credit available in whole or in part to one or more third parties provided partial shipments are not prohibited.
4 Others. There are other forms of Credit – e.g. **Back to Back**, **Red clause**, and **Revolving**, but they are not widely used.

A specimen of an irrevocable Letter of Credit (Specimen Documentary Credit) is shown.

Source of document

A bank, e.g. National Westminster Bank plc.

Purpose/use/function

The Letter of Credit authorizes credit or cash to a certain sum to be given to the bearer.

Other aspects

The Letter of Credit is very prone to discrepancies and on receiving a Letter of Credit, check the following carefully:

1 Are you as seller, exporter and beneficiary satisfied as to the authenticity of

the Credit? If the Credit has not been advised to you through the intermediary of a bank in the UK, have the signatures checked by your bankers before taking action. An advising bank is required to take reasonable care to check the apparent authenticity of the Credit which it advises.

2 Is the Credit irrevocable on the part of the issuing bank? If it is revocable, the Credit can be cancelled or amended without notice to you and in consequence you have no security.

3 Is the Credit payable in the UK or is it only available for negotiation? In the latter case, the advising bank may only be prepared to handle the documents on a collection basis, which will inevitably delay payment. Should the advising bank be prepared to negotiate, this will be effected with recourse unless that bank has added its confirmation to the Credit.

4 Are the terms of the Credit of a deferred payment nature? You should understand that you will not be in receipt of a bank accepted draft which you can discount in order to obtain immediate finance.

If the Credit is unconfirmed by the advising bank you will receive, against presentation of documents in order, a statement that on a date which is determinable from the terms of the Credit, you may claim the sum due to you. The statement will be given without any responsibility or engagement on the part of the advising bank. Should such a Credit be confirmed by the advising bank, then in place of a formal undertaking to pay on the determinable date, that bank may be prepared to afford some means by which you can obtain immediate finance.

5 If you have stated in your Contract of Sale that the Credit must be confirmed by the advising bank, has this been done? At the same time, examine the terms of the confirmation to satisfy yourself that it provides the additional security that you require – i.e. as a UK exporter you will receive, without recourse, payment or acceptance for your documents or drafts which are presented in good order at the counters of a bank in the UK. If in any doubt, check with your own bankers.

6 Do the terms and conditions of the Letter of Credit conflict with your Contract of Sale? (For example, settlement by means of an accepted draft, whereas you require payment at sight.) Should there by any differences between your Contract of Sale and the Credit terms, you should immediately contact the opener to have the Credit suitably amended.

Having satisfied yourself on the above points (1–6), examine the terms of the Credit for the following:

1 Are the names and addresses of both the opener and yourself complete and correct?

2 Are the terms contradictory? – for example, does the Credit call for the presentation of documents covering dispatch by air, whereas shipment is to be by sea?

3 Are the quantity and the amount sufficient? If the value is prefaced by 'about' or 'circa' etc., a tolerance of plus or minus 10 % is permitted on the amount. However, should the Credit value be a fixed amount – and provided the Credit does not stipulate the quantity of goods in terms of a stated number of packing units or individual items – then a 5 % tolerance in either direction in the quantity of the goods is permissible, even if partial shipment is not permitted, always provided the Credit amount is not exceeded.

4 Are the time limits for shipment and presentation of documents sufficient for your needs?

5 If you require partial shipments and/or transhipment to be permitted does the Credit prohibit either or both?

6 Does the dispatch/shipment or do the places of delivery/discharge conform to your Sales Contract?

7 Do you need to charter a vessel? If so, does the Letter of Credit specifically authorize presentation of Charter Party Bills of Lading?

8 Do you need to ship 'On Deck'? If so, does the Letter of Credit specifically authorize this?

9 Are the descriptions of the goods, quantity and price basis in accordance with your contract terms?

10 Can you obtain the insurance cover required?

11 Can you obtain all the documents required within the time limits permitted?

The following guidelines have been devised for checking documents before presentation.

If the Credit requires the presentation of a draft or drafts (Bills of Exchange), ensure that:

1 it is correctly dated;
2 it is signed and endorsed;
3 it is claused as required;
4 it is drawn upon the correct party, for example:
   (a) the buyer
   (b) the opening bank
   (c) the advising bank
   (d) a third party;
5 the words and figures do not differ;
6 the value accords with the invoice value, unless the Credit states otherwise;
7 it is drawn at sight or at usance as required;
8 the correct period of usance stated;
9 it is drawn for a usance period from or after sight or from or after the 'On Board' Bill of Lading date as stipulated in the terms of the Credit;
10 if specifically required, the drawer's signatures are identified and their signing capacity is shown;
11 it is marked with the Credit reference number.

If an insurance document is required, check that:

1 it incorporates risk cover exactly as stipulated within the Credit;
2 it has been issued and/or signed by an insurance company or underwriter or an agent on their behalf;
3 it is not a broker's certificate or cover note, whose presentation has not been specifically authorized;
4 it is not dated later than the date of shipment, dispatch or taking in charge or, if it is, that the cover includes the 'Warehouse-to-Warehouse' clause;
5 it is issued in the currency of the Credit or, if cover in a different currency is required, that it is presented in that currency;
6 it provides a sufficiency of cover and contains the same details in respect of special risks as are stated in the Credit terms; unless otherwise stipulated cover must be 10 % above the CIF or CIP value;
7 it has been issued in a transferable form or endorsed to the order of a specified party if required, or endorsed by the insured, if it has been issued in his or her name;
8 it shows marks, numbers, weights and quantities and a description of goods which accord with the Bill of Lading and other documents;
9 it does not show alterations which have not been authenticated;
10 it indicates method of carriage of the goods, point of loading on board,

dispatch or taking in charge, name of the carrying vessel if appropriate and port of discharge or place of delivery;

11 it specifically covers transhipment when the transport document indicates that this will be effected;

12 it states a named place where claims are payable when this is required;

13 it covers 'Loaded on Deck' when this is permitted within the Credit terms or when dispatch is effected in containers which may be loaded on deck.

In regard to commercial invoices check that:

1 the invoice is addressed to the buyer unless the Credit specifically stipulates otherwise;

2 the value of the invoice does not exceed that available under the Credit;

3 the description of the goods does not differ from that stipulated in the Credit – the description must be exactly as stated;

4 Import Licence numbers, proforma invoice numbers or any other references required have not been omitted;

5 the invoice does not specify additional goods, possibly without charge – i.e. samples or advertising materials – which are not authorized;

6 the price basis for the goods does not differ from – and the pricing agrees with – any proforma attaching to the terms of the Credit;

7 the calculations do not differ from those in any other document and there are no obvious errors in additions etc.;

8 extra charges and/or commissions are not levied, when they are not authorized with the Credit terms;

9 invoices show your names as the seller;

10 invoices are certified, signed, notarized or legalized as required;

11 marks, weights, number of cases/packages, name of vessel etc. agree with the Bill of Lading and all other documents;

12 packing details accord with other documents and that packing indicated does not differ from that stipulated;

13 the correct number of invoices is submitted;

14 when combined Certificates of Value and Origin (CVO) are required, the Certificate of Origin portion has been completed and signed;

15 when the Document of Movement – e.g. Bill of Lading, Air Waybill, etc. – is required to indicate the amount of freight paid, the invoice does not show an amount in excess of, or less than, this sum; similarly, when an insurance premium has to be stated, either separately or on the insurance document itself, check that the invoice does not reflect an amount in excess of, or less than, this figure.

Unless any Letter of Credit states otherwise, when you are required to present a Marine Bill of Lading, check that:

1 it has been issued by a named Carrier and signed by the Carrier, or on behalf of the named Carrier by the Carrier's Agent;

2 it has not been issued by a Freight Forwarder unless it indicates that such a Freight Forwarder is acting as the actual Carrier or as the Agent for a named Carrier;

3 it indicates that the goods have been 'Loaded' or 'Shipped on Board' a named vessel;

4 the presentation comprises a full set of originals, plus – if required by the Credit terms – a set number of non-negotiable copies;

5 if the credit terms stipulate that the Bill of Lading should evidence that the goods are available to the 'Order of a Named Party' (or parties), it does not

evidence that the goods are straight 'Consigned' to that party; regarding the former, transfer of title may be accomplished by endorsement, but with the latter, the Bill of Lading cannot theoretically be endorsed in favour of third parties unless it specifically states otherwise;

6 if the Credit terms stipulate that the Bill of Lading is to be issued to your order, it is endorsed by you in blank;

7 the 'On-Board' date of the Bill of Lading is not later than the latest date of shipment stated in the Credit terms;

8 the Bill of Lading is not 'Received for Shipment', when this is not specifically authorized by the Credit terms; such Bills of Lading are acceptable provided that they bear an 'On Board' notation duly signed or initialled by the Carrier or the Carrier's agent which must be dated;

9 the Bill of Lading does not indicate any detrimental clauses as to defective goods or packing;

10 it does not indicate marks or numbers which differ from any other documents;

11 it does not show alterations which have not been authenticated by the Carrier or the Carrier's Agent;

12 it does not show shipment of goods other than, or in addition to, those required;

13 it does indicate the port of loading and the port of discharge stipulated within the Credit (the Bill of Lading may indicate a place of 'Taking in Charge' different from the port of loading, provided that the Bill of Lading is annotated to the effect that the goods have been loaded 'On Board' at the stipulated port of shipment);

14 the vessel's name and/or port of loading and/or port of discharge are not prefaced with the word 'Intended'; regarding this point, it should be noted that:

(a) if the word 'Intended' prefaces the name of the vessel, the Bill of Lading must bear a notation stipulating that the goods have been loaded on a named vessel; such a notation must be authenticated by the Carrier or the Carrier's Agent;

(b) if the word 'Intended' prefaces the port of loading, a notation similar to that in (a) above will be acceptable provided it specifically states the port of loading as stipulated in the Credit;

(c) if the word 'Intended' prefaces the port of discharge this will be acceptable provided the place of final destination indicated on the document is other than the port of discharge as stipulated in the Credit;

15 the goods have not been loaded 'On Deck' without the Credit terms authorizing such a shipment;

16 it does not bear a clause re 'Part Container Load' which further stipulates that goods will not be released until all Bills of Lading, issued for the container load, are presented;

17 it does not omit 'Notify Parties' if these are required to be shown;

18 it is marked 'Freight Paid' if the shipment terms are C&F or CIF;

19 if the terms of the Credit require the Bill of Lading to show the freight charges, these are shown.

In regard to the Air Waybill and Air Consignment Notes unless otherwise stated in the Credit terms one must ensure the following:

1 the Air Waybill is issued and signed by a named Carrier or has been signed on behalf of a named Carrier by the Carrier's Agent;

2 if a 'House Airway Bill' is presented, it is signed for and on behalf of a named Carrier;

3 the correct copy is submitted, signed by the Carrier or on behalf of a named Carrier or by the Carrier's Agent;

4 the 'Freight Collect' or 'Freight Pre-paid' columns are completed;

5 dispatch has been effected from the nominated airport of dispatch to the nominated airport of destination;

6 the goods have been consigned to the correct party;

7 'Notify Parties' are shown if required;

8 transhipment has not been effected when this is prohibited;

9 the dispatch date is not later than the latest date permitted in the Credit terms.

If presenting Parcel Post Receipts, ensure that:

1 dispatch has been effected from a Post Office in the place nominated;

2 the date stamp indicates dispatch within the period permitted;

3 the amount of postage paid is not omitted when this is required to be shown;

4 dispatch has not been effected to anyone other than the nominated consignee.

Prior to presentation of such a transport document, check that:

1 it appears, on its face, to have been issued by a named Carrier and signed by the Carrier or on the Carrier's behalf by the Carrier's Agent;

2 if it has been issued by a Freight Forwarder, it is a FIATA Bill of Lading;

3 it consists of a full set of originals if issued in more than one original;

4 it is accompanied by such non-negotiable copies as are required;

5 it indicates, as appropriate, that the goods have been 'Dispatched', 'Taken in Charge', 'Loaded' or 'Shipped On Board';

6 in respect of shipment by sea, it is not subject to Charter Party;

7 in respect of shipment by sea, if the Credit terms stipulate that the transport document should evidence that the goods are to be available to the order of a named party, this stipulation has been complied with;

8 the transport documents do not indicate any detrimental clauses as to defective goods or packing;

9 the transport document does not indicate marks, numbers or descriptions of goods which differ from any other documents; the description of goods on the transport document may be in general terms provided that it does not conflict with other documents;

10 any alterations have been authenticated by the Carrier or the Agent for the named Carrier;

11 it does not show dispatch, taking in charge, or shipment of goods in addition to those required by the Credit terms;

12 if 'Notify Party or Parties' are to be shown, these have not been omitted;

13 if shipment is by sea, the document does not state that the goods have or will be 'Loaded on Deck' unless the Credit specifically permits such a method of shipment;

14 it does not bear a clause re 'Part Container Load' which further stipulates that goods will not be released until all Bills of Lading, issued for that container load, are presented;

15 it is marked 'Freight Paid' if the shipment dispatch terms are C&F, CIF or DCP/CIP respectively;

16 if the terms of the Credit require the transport document to show the freight charges, these are shown.

When Certificates of Origin are required, one must ensure that:

1 details conform with other documents;
2 the Certificate of Origin indicates as consignee, the applicant for the Credit (unless otherwise stipulated);
3 it is issued by a Chamber of Commerce (if required);
4 it is legalized or countersigned by some other party or parties (if required);
5 any alterations have been duly authenticated;
6 marks, case numbers, weights, etc. agree with all other documents.

In regard to packing lists one must ensure the following:

1 that packing lists show the contents of each individual package;
2 that marks, case numbers, weights etc., do not differ from other documents.

In regard to weight notes one must check the following:

1 that they show both net and gross weights;
2 that they quote weights which do not differ from those stated on other documents;
3 that they can be specifically identified with other documents.

Likewise one must check the following in regard to weight lists:

1 that they do not differ from other documents;
2 that they state the individual weights of packages;
3 that they show weights which do add up to the stated total;
4 that they can be specifically identified with other documents.

The majority of discrepancies can be overcome by returning the documents to the seller for the necessary corrections to be made.

Unfortunately, there are occasions when discrepancies cannot be rectified – for example, when late shipment is effected or documents are presented after the expiry of the Credit, etc.

In these circumstances, there are various options open to the exporter as follows:

1 The exporter can request the advising bank to send a telex message to the issuing bank seeking permission for settlement to be made albeit that discrepancies have occurred in the documents, these being spelled out clearly by the advising bank to the issuing bank.
2 Provided the advising bank is in agreement, the seller can obtain immediate settlement by giving an Indemnity – issued either by the seller or the seller's bankers – to the advising bank covering the discrepancies, provided the Credit itself does not specifically prohibit payment against an indemnity. The advising bank will inform the issuing bank of the manner in which it has acted, i.e. paid against an Indemnity covering the discrepancies. Such indemnities only concern the relationship between the party giving them and the advising bank. However, should the documents be refused by the buyer due to any of the discrepancies, then the indemnifying party will be required to repay the advising bank immediately in the currency of the Credit, together with interest.
3 The exporter can request the advising bank to forward the documents to the issuing bank 'In Trust' under the terms of the Documentary Letter of Credit. The advising bank will comply with the exporter's request by dispatching the

documents to the issuing bank advising it of the discrepancies. It will include instructions to the effect that the issuing bank may only release the documents to the buyer, provided that the issuing bank authorizes the advising bank to make payment to the shipper under the terms of the Letter of Credit.

It can be seen from these three options that the advising bank is endeavouring to protect the seller – and the seller's control of the goods – whilst at the same time seeking an amended mandate to pay under the Letter of Credit within the terms of 'Uniform Customs and Practice for Documentary Credits'.

With the above objective in mind– the retention of control of the exporter's goods by the exporter – we would suggest that exporters should consider most carefully the consequences which could occur in respect of documents which do not conform to the terms of the Documentary Letter of Credit:

1 where the Documentary Credit terms instruct the seller to send one negotiable original Bill of Lading direct to the buyer, as this would enable the importer to obtain possession of the goods without making payment;
2 where the Documentary Credit terms call for Air, Road and Rail Waybills and Parcel Post Receipts – none of which are documents of title – evidencing that goods are consigned direct to the buyer.

One cannot stress too strongly the need to ensure that the Letter of Credit terms are complied with and strict observance is made of the Uniform Customs and Practice for Documentary Letters of Credit (ICC Publications No 400).

Documentary Credit

4 United Kingdom Seller Limited
Baltic House
27 Leadenhall Street
London EC3

Dear Sirs

We have been requested by 2 Traders Bank of Japan, Tokyo, Japan to advise the
issue of their irrevocable Credit Number 01/765 in your favour for account
1 of JAPAN BUYER CORPORATION c/o NYK Line 3-2 Marunouchi 2-Chome, Chiyoda-ku,
Tokyo 100, Japan for £100,000 (SAY ONE HUNDRED THOUSAND POUNDS STERLING).

5 available by your drafts on us at..XXXX.. sight accompanied by the
following documents namely:

5 1. Signed Invoices in triplicate certifying goods are in accordance with
     Contract No. 1234 dated 10 April 1987 between Japan Buyer Corporation
     and United Kingdom Seller Limited.

5 2. Marine and War Risk Insurance Certificate covering "all risks" warehouse to
     warehouse, for 10% above the CIF value, evidencing that claims are payable in Japan.

5 3. Complete set 3/3 Shipping Company's clean "on board" ocean Bills of Lading
     made out to order of the shippers and endorsed to order of "Traders Bank
     of Japan", marked "Freight Paid" and "Notify Japan Buyer Corporation c/o
     NYK Line 3-2 Marunouchi 2-Chome, Chiyoda-ku, Tokyo 100, Japan".

Covering: Mechanical Spare Parts CIF Tokyo, Japan.

Shipped from UK Port to Tokyo, Japan.

Partshipment prohibited   Transhipment prohibited

Documents must be presented for payment within 15 days from the date of shipment.

We are requested to add our confirmation to this Credit and we hereby undertake
to pay you the face amount of your drafts drawn within its terms provided such
drafts bear the number and date of the Credit and that the Letter of Credit and
all amendments thereto are attached.

The Credit is subject to Uniform Customs and Practice for Documentary Credits
(1983 Revision), International Chamber of Commerce Publication No. 400

Drafts drawn under this   [X] Payment
Credit must be presented to us for [ ] Negotiation } not later than 14 May 1987
                                 [ ] Acceptance

and marked "Drawn under Credit Number 01/765/NWB/?A of Traders Bank of Japan,
2 Tokyo, Japan   Dated 1 May 1987

Note: On the grounds of security the above Credit, whilst accurate in content, is used for illustrative purposes only.

1 Buyer/Applicant   4 Seller/Beneficiary
2 Issuing/Opening Bank   5 Documents Required
3 Advising/Paying/Confirming Bank

6 Insurance: marine and cargo

6.1 INTRODUCTION

Insurance cover against possible loss or damage to specified merchandise during shipment is of paramount importance. Responsibility for cargo insurance provision is the buyer's or the seller's according to the details of the particular export sales contract. A Certificate of Insurance will provide cover.

In the London insurance market – which undertakes a very large volume of marine insurance and reinsurance – a new Marine Policy Form (MAR) and new Institute cargo clauses were introduced on 1 January 1982. Lloyd's Marine Policy, for example, serves as a contract of insurance for cargo insurance.

6.2 CERTIFICATE OF INSURANCE

Description

A typical Cargo Insurance Certificate includes the following data:

1 name and address of the insurer;
2 name of the assured;
3 the endorsement of the assured where applicable so that the rights to claim may be transferred;
4 a description of the risks covered;
5 a description of the consignment;
6 the sum or sums insured;
7 the place where claims are payable together with the name of the agent to whom claims may be directed.

Source of document

An insurance company or Insurance Broker, Freight Forwarder, e.g. Phoenix Assurance plc.

Purpose/use/function

The Certificate of Insurance is of paramount importance in providing insurance cover against possible loss or damage to the specified merchandise during shipment. The export sales contract detailing the cargo delivery terms/INCO terms 1980 will specify who is responsible for the insurance provision: seller or buyer. For example, under CIF the seller takes care of all the insurance provision to the named destination, whilst under C&F the buyer is responsible for all the insurance when the goods pass the 'ship's rail' at the port of shipment.

Insurance cover for the goods should embrace the following:

1 transportation of merchandise to the seaport or airport;
2 period during which the goods are stored awaiting shipment or loading;
3 the time whilst on board the ship, aircraft, or other conveyance such as the international road haulage operation;
4 the 'off loading' and storage on arrival at destination airport, seaport or other specified place;
5 transportation to the buyer's premises/address.

An insurance certificate should normally indicate that the goods are covered/insured from the seller's warehouse to the buyer's warehouse. In situations where the Insurance Certificate is to be included in a presentation under a Documentary Letter of Credit, the Certificate must be dated before the date of the document evidencing dispatch such as found on the Bill of Lading/Sea Waybill/Air Waybill/CMR Note etc. and must be completely and precisely compatible with such data contained in such accompanying documents.

Other aspects

The cargo description and valuation must conform to the data found on the Bill of Lading/Air Waybill or other carrier's documentation. This includes the valuation of the cargo and details of the consignor and consignee and details of shipment such as date, time of flight/sailing and name of vessel.

Insurance Certificate

PHOENIX ASSURANCE PUBLIC LIMITED COMPANY
Regional Marine Office Freshford House Redcliffe Way
Bristol BS1 6LX

This Certificate requires endorsement

Exporter's Reference **91011**

Certificate of Insurance No. **045826**

This is to Certify that the PHOENIX ASSURANCE PUBLIC LIMITED COMPANY has insured under Policy

No. **20035A** issued to National Westminster Insurance Services Limited

for account of **United Kingdom Sellers Ltd &/or subsidiary &/or Associated Companies**

who hereby declare for Insurance under the said Open Policy Interest as specified below so valued subject to the terms and conditions of the said Open Policy and to the special conditions stated below and on the back hereof.

2 Conveyance **Nippon Maru** From **Southampton**		INSURED VALUE: **One Hundred and Ten** (in words): **Thousand Pounds**	
Via/To	2 To **Tokyo**	1 Figs: **£110,000** Currency: **Sterling**	

Marks and Numbers	Interest
2 JAPAN BUYER CORPORATION ⟨ J.B.C. ⟩ TOKYO I-9	Mechanical Spare Parts in 9 P'kgs

Institute Cargo Clauses (A)
Institute War Clauses (Cargo)
Institute Strike Clauses (Cargo)
Institute Classification Clause

The holder of this certificate is entitled to the above-mentioned insurance by virtue of a policy effected for and on behalf of the holders of this and other certificates, and this certificate (subject to the special terms and conditions printed or written thereon) will, for the purpose of collecting any loss or claims, be accepted as showing that the holder is entitled to the benefit of such policy to the extent herein set forth.
In the event of loss or damage for which the Company is presumed to be liable (see also overleaf), immediate notice must be given to –

Claims payable by:– **British Insurance Group (Japan)**
PO Box 357
Kokusai Building
No. I - I Marunouchi 3 - Chome
Chiyoda-Ku
Tokyo
PHOENIX ASSURANCE PUBLIC LIMITED COMPANY

Consignees are reminded that cover under this Certificate expires in accordance with the Transit Clause in the Institute Cargo Clauses.

Group Marine Manager & Underwriter

Dated at **8 May 1987**

Signed

PU 188/82   This insurance is subject to English jurisdiction

---

1 Insured value is 110% of the CIF value of the shipment.

2 Shipping details, marks and description of the goods should be consistent with the other documents.

6.3 COMPANIES MARINE POLICY

Description

A Companies Marine Policy is an insurance policy subscribed to insurance companies which are Members of the Institute of London Underwriters.

Source of document

The Institute of London Underwriters, 40 Lime Street, London, EC3M 5DA.

Purpose/use/function

A Companies Marine Policy serves as a contract of insurance for cargo. The specimen shown excludes A, B or C clauses. The A clause provides comprehensive insurance for goods on an all-risk basis subject to certain exclusions, on the other hand, the B and C clauses are based on a warned perils approach and the cover is much more limited. Overall the clauses exist to cater for total loss of the goods.

Other aspects

The Companies Marine Policy is not valid unless it bears the embossment of the Policy Department of the Institute of London Underwriters. It is subject to English law and must contain an identical description of the cargo as found on the Bill of Lading, Air Waybill and feature the valuation and transportation details.

The Institute of London Underwriters

Companies Marine Policy

WE, THE COMPANIES, hereby agree, in consideration of the payment to us by or on behalf of the Assured of the premium specified in the Schedule, to insure against loss damage liability or expense in the proportions and manner hereinafter provided. Each Company shall be liable only for its own respective proportion.

IN WITNESS whereof the General Manager and Secretary of The Institute of London Underwriters has subscribed his name on behalf of each Company.

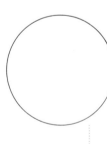

....

General Manager and Secretary
The Institute of London Underwriters

This Policy is not valid unless it bears the embossment of the Policy Department of The Institute of London Underwriters.

This insurance is subject to English jurisdiction.

SCHEDULE

POLICY NUMBER

_____

NAME OF ASSURED

_____

VESSEL

_____

VOYAGE OR PERIOD OF INSURANCE

_____

SUBJECT-MATTER INSURED

_____

AGREED VALUE
(if any)

_____

AMOUNT INSURED HEREUNDER

_____

PREMIUM

_____

CLAUSES, ENDORSEMENTS, SPECIAL CONDITIONS AND WARRANTIES

The Institute of London Underwriters

Companies Marine Policy

This Policy is subscribed by Insurance Companies
Members of The Institute of London Underwriters
40, Lime Street,
London, EC3M 5DA

For use by the Policy Department

of

The Institute of London Underwriters

COMPANIES' PROPORTIONS

Witherby & Co. Ltd., London

PRINTED IN ENGLAND

6.4 LLOYD'S MARINE POLICY

Description

A Lloyd's Marine Policy is an insurance policy subscribed to Underwriting Members of Lloyd's as listed in the policy.

Source of document

Lloyd's (The Association of Underwriters) of London.

Purpose/use/function

A Lloyd's Marine Policy serves as a contract of cargo insurance. The specimen shown excludes clauses and endorsements to the policy since these will vary with individual circumstances. It also covers hull insurance.

Lloyd's Marine Policy

POLICY NUMBER

NAME OF ASSURED

VESSEL

VOYAGE OR PERIOD OF INSURANCE

SUBJECT-MATTER INSURED

AGREED VALUE
(if any)

AMOUNT INSURED HEREUNDER

PREMIUM

CLAUSES, ENDORSEMENTS, SPECIAL CONDITIONS AND WARRANTIES

We, The Underwriters, hereby agree, in consideration of the payment to us by or on behalf of the Assured of the premium specified in the Schedule, to insure against loss damage liability or expense in the proportions and manner hereinafter provided. Each Underwriting Member of a Syndicate whose definitive number and proportion is set out in the following Table shall be liable only for his own share of his respective Syndicate's proportion.

In Witness whereof the General Manager of Lloyd's Policy Signing Office has subscribed his Name on behalf of each of Us.

FOR EMBOSSMENT BY LLOYD'S POLICY SIGNING OFFICE

LLOYD'S POLICY SIGNING OFFICE
General Manager

This insurance is subject to English jurisdiction.

MAR
LPO 82A (1.1.82) Printed by The Carlton Berry Co. Ltd.

THE ATTACHED CLAUSES AND ENDORSEMENTS FORM PART OF THIS POLICY

Lloyd's Marine Policy

The Assured is requested to read this Policy and, if it is incorrect, return it immediately for alteration to:

FOR CARGO INSURANCES ONLY
In the event of loss or damage which may result in a claim under this insurance, immediate notice must be given to the Lloyd's Agent at the port or place where the loss or damage is discovered in order that he may examine the goods and issue a survey report.

Definitive numbers of the Syndicates and proportions

The List of Underwriting Members of Lloyd's mentioned in the above Table shows their respective Syndicates and Shares therein and is deemed to be incorporated in and to form part of this Policy: It is available for inspection at Lloyd's Policy Signing Office by the Assured or his or their representatives and a true copy of the material parts of it certified by the General Manager of Lloyd's Policy Signing Office will be furnished to the Assured on application.

7 Liner conferences

7.1 INTRODUCTION

A Liner Conference is an organization comprising a number of shipowners who offer their services in a given sea route on conditions agreed by their members. Conferences are semi-monopolistic associations of shipping lines formed for the purpose of restricting competition between their members and protecting them from outside competition. Some 360 Liner Conferences are on existence today.

A feature of the Liner Conference system is the General Cargo Contract between the shipper (as principal, not as agent) and the Conference, which restricts the shipper to conducting business only with vessels inside the Conference. For this loyal support on the part of the shipper, a discount (rebate) is offered on the freight rate.

General Cargo Contracts are drawn up under two rebate schemes: the immediate rebate system and the deferred rebate system. To claim rebate the shipper submits a Rebate Claim Form to the shipowner, usually at six-monthly intervals for deferred rebate. Immediate rebate is given at the time the invoice is submitted to the shipper by the shipowner.

7.2 PHILIPPINES/EUROPE CONFERENCE: GENERAL CARGO CONTRACT (EUROPE TO THE PHILIPPINES)

Description

The Philippines/Europe Conference General Cargo Contract – Europe to the Philippines – is a general cargo contract or agreement between the shipper, as principal and not as agent, and the Conference.

Source of document

The Philippines/Europe Conference organization.

Purpose/use/function

The contract broadly reflects the terms under which cargo is accepted for shipment under the Conference. In particular it stresses the loyalty aspect, by requiring the shipper to ship continuously with the Conference and not to permit cargoes to be conveyed on vessels outside the Conference when rates of freight are low. For this loyalty a discounted rate (9½ %) of freight is offered under the immediate rebate system.

Other aspects

The terms of the General Cargo Contract will vary by Liner Conference and likewise the level of the immediate or deferred rebate. Each shipper has identical terms within the Conference and there is no discrimination between the larger and smaller shipper. The consequences of shipping outside the Conference are severe and result in a loss of rebate. Moreover, any shipowner within the Conference offering more favourable rates to one shipper in preference to another is likely to suffer a heavy fine by the Liner Conference Secretariat.

Philippines/Europe Conference

GENERAL CARGO CONTRACT—EUROPE TO THE PHILIPPINES

This Agreement is for signature by Principals only and not by firms acting as Forwarding Agents.

WHEREAS:—

(A)

Belgian Far Eastern Line	Lauro Lines
Ben Line Steamers Ltd.	Lloyd Triestino di Navigazione S.p.A.
Blue Funnel Line Ltd.	Maersk Line
(Ocean Transport & Trading Ltd.)	(Joint Service of Aktieselskabet Dampskibsselskabet
The China Mutual Steam Navigation Co. Ltd.)	Svendborg and Dampskibsselskabet af 1912 Aktieselskab)
Bröstroms Rederi AB	Maritime Company of the Philippines
(Brostrom Shipping Company Limited)	Mitsui O.S.K. Lines Ltd.
Compagnie Generale Maritime	Nedlloyd Lijnen B.V. (Nedlloyd Lines)
Cie Maritime des Chargeurs Reunis	Nippon Yusen Kaisha
Ellerman & Bucknall Steamship Co. Ltd.	A/S Det Østasiatiske Kompagni (The East Asiatic Co. Ltd.)
Glen Line Ltd. (Glen & Shire Joint Service)	Peninsular & Oriental Steam Navigation Co.
Hapag-Lloyd Aktiengesellschaft	Wilh. Wilhelmsen
Jugolinija-East	

(members of the Philippines/Europe Conference) and

Ben Line Containers Ltd.
Ben Ocean
Franco Belgian Services (C.M.C.R. & B.F.E.L. Joint Services)
Overseas Containers Ltd.
Rickmers-Linie K.G.
ScanDutch (E.A.Co., Nedlloyd, C.GM., Brostrom & W.W. Joint Service)

all of which Lines are hereinafter together called "the Carriers", together provide services sufficient for the ordinary requirements of the trade from the U.K., Eire, Norway, Sweden, Finland, Denmark, Germany, Holland, Belgium and French ports from Dunkirk to St. Nazaire both inclusive, also Italian and Jugoslav ports ("Conference Shipment Areas") to ports in the Philippines ("Conference Destinations") and seek to maintain stable rates of freight for such services,

(B)   The Carriers offer a discount to all shippers who agree to give their entire support to the Carriers, and

(C)

NAME AND FULL ADDRESS OF THE SHIPPERS TO BE INSERTED

("the Shippers") wish to benefit from such discount and to give their entire support to the Carriers,

IT IS AGREED between the Carriers and the Shippers as follows:—

1.   The Shippers agree that during the currency of this Agreement they will give the Carriers their entire support (in the sense defined in Clause 3 hereof) in respect of Conference Cargo (as defined in Clause 5(a) hereof).

2.   The Carriers agree to accept Conference Cargo for carriage:—

(a)   by vessels operated by the Carriers, subject only to their ability to carry the cargo and to agreement between the Shippers and the carrying Line concerned as to the quantity to be carried in each vessel;

(b)   at the Conference Tariff rates ruling at the time of shipment, or at such special rates as may be quoted by the Carriers in the case of large parcels of cargo not being ordinary berth cargo, less a discount of 9½% on the amount of freight so calculated except in so far as such rates are nett; and

(c)   subject to the provisions of the Conference Tariff Conditions and to the terms and conditions of business of the carrying Line.

3.   For the purposes of this Agreement, unless otherwise agreed by a Conference Representative, (as defined in Clause 5(c) hereof), the Shippers are deemed to give their entire support to the Carriers in respect of Conference Cargo if, but only if, the Shippers:—

(a)   ensure that all contracts for the carriage of Conference Cargo made by the Shippers, whether as principals or as agents, or by others as agents for the Shippers, are made with one or more of the Carriers;

(b)   refrain from participating directly or indirectly in any arrangements relating to the carriage of Conference Cargo by any vessel not operated by one of the Carriers;

(c)   procure that each Associate (as defined in Clause 5(b) hereof) of the Shippers conducts its business as if it were bound by this form of Agreement and, if and when a Conference Representative so requires, signs this form of Agreement with the Carriers;

(d)   refrain from any action which would enable persons who are neither parties to an Agreement in this form nor their Associates nor consignees of goods sold by such parties or their associates to obtain like benefits as are conferred upon the Shippers hereunder; and

(e)   refrain from acting as agents for competitors of the Carriers in respect of the carriage of Conference Cargo.

4.   Should any of the carriers cease to be, or should any other Line become, a member of the Conference or associated with it in the carriage of Conference Cargo, a Conference Representative shall give to the Shippers such notice as the Carriers consider to be fair and reasonable in all the circumstances of the amendments to the list of Lines at (A) above resulting therefrom. Upon and from the date specified in such notice this Agreement shall have effect as an Agreement between the Shippers and the Lines included in such amended list and, save that Clause 12 hereof shall remain in force, this Agreement shall cease to have effect as an Agreement binding upon or referring to any Line which is not included in such amended list and the expression "the Carriers" shall be construed accordingly. In the event of the Shippers being seriously prejudiced by a Line ceasing on the date specified in such notice to be a member of the Conference or associated with it in the carriage of Conference Cargo, a Conference Representative may, on application by the Shippers in advance of each shipment, agree to the shipment of Conference Cargo by the Shippers in vessels operated by such Line during a limited period after such date.

5.   (a)   "Conference Cargo" means all goods carried or intended to be carried by sea, with or without transshipment, from Conference Shipment Areas for delivery at Conference Destinations other than (i) coal, (ii) commodities listed in the Conference Tariff Conditions ruling at the time of shipment as exceptions either generally or in relation to a particular Conference Destination and (iii) Bulk liquid cargoes shipped in vessels operated by Panocean-Anco Ltd.

      (b)   "Associate" in relation to any shippers means any person, firm or company which is controlled or managed by such shippers or in respect of which such shippers have a sufficient interest to enable them to determine the method of shipment.

      (c)   "Conference Representative" means the Secretary for the time being of the Philippines/Europe Conference or such other person as shall be authorised to represent the Conference.

6.   (a)   In the event of a Conference Representative having grounds for believing that the Shippers have committed a breach or breaches of this Agreement in failing to give the Carriers their entire support in accordance with Clauses 1 and 3 hereof, he shall be entitled on behalf of the Carriers:—

          (i)   to request the Shippers for an explanation; and

          (ii)   if a satisfactory explanation is not received within 30 days of such request, to suspend the entitlement of the Shippers to the discount hereinbefore mentioned and/or to appoint a Trustee for the purposes set out in sub-clause (b) hereof, provided that the Shippers shall be entitled to request the appointment of another person as Trustee in place of the person originally appointed if they have reasonable cause for believing that the disclosure of the information referred to in sub-clause (b) hereof to the person originally appointed would be damaging or prejudicial to their interests and in the event of such objection being sustained by the Carriers the Conference Representative shall appoint another person as Trustee.

      (b)   The Trustee shall investigate the alleged breach or breaches at the office or offices of the Shippers or such other place as the Trustee may consider convenient. The Shippers agree to furnish the Trustee with all such information, explanations, correspondence, books of account and/or other papers as the Trustee may consider relevant to the alleged breach or breaches. The Trustee shall consider the same together with any other material or explanation provided by the Shippers and the Conference Representative who appointed him. The Trustee shall thereafter report in writing to the Shippers and to the Conference Representative who appointed him whether he considers that the Shippers have committed any breach or breaches of this Agreement and, if in his opinion they have done so, shall give details of the same.

      (c)   If neither the Shippers nor the Carriers shall refer the matter to arbitration under Clause 12 hereof within 30 days of receipt of the Trustee's report, both shall be deemed to have accepted the conclusions stated therein and shall not thereafter seek to challenge the same. In such event, if the Trustee reports that in his opinion the Shippers have not committed any breach or breaches of this Agreement, the expenses of the Trustee shall be paid by the Carriers and an amount equivalent to any discount to which the Shippers would have been entitled but for the suspension of their entitlement pending the investigation shall be paid to the Shippers. In all other cases the expenses of the Trustee shall be paid by the Shippers. If the dispute is referred to arbitration the expenses of the Trustee shall be paid or borne as may be directed in any arbitration award.

7.   If the Shippers admit, or accept or are deemed to have accepted a report by a Trustee, that the Shippers have committed any breach or breaches of this Agreement, or if in an arbitration it is so determined:—

      (a)   the Carriers may suspend or continue to suspend the entitlement of the Shippers to the discount hereinbefore mentioned, provided that the suspension of entitlement to discount shall not exceed a total period of six months or continue after the discharge by the Shippers of all liability to the Carriers consequent upon such breach or breaches, and

      (b)   if the breach or breaches consists of or includes a failure by the Shippers to give their entire support in accordance with Clause 3(a), (b) or (c), the Shippers shall pay to the Conference Representative who appointed the Trustee, as agent for the Carriers, agreed liquidated damages in accordance with Clause 8 hereof and, upon payment of such liquidated damages and the discharge by the Shippers of all other liability to the Carriers, an amount equivalent to any discount to which the Shippers would have been entitled but for the suspension of their entitlement shall be promptly paid to the Shippers.

8.   Both the Shippers and the Carriers accept that it is impossible to calculate the precise loss suffered by the Carriers in the event of a failure by the Shippers to give the Carriers their entire support in accordance with Clause 3(a), (b) or (c) but are agreed that the best estimate which can be made is that such loss will amount to two thirds of the freight (excluding transhipment additionals) which would have been payable to one or more of the Carriers if the goods concerned had been carried by them and have further agreed that a sum so calculated shall be payable as liquidated damages in the event of any such failure.

9.   In the event of the Shippers making any false declaration as to the nature, weight, measurement or value of any Conference Cargo, the Carriers may suspend the entitlement of the Shippers to the discount hereinbefore mentioned for such period not exceeding six months as the Carriers think fit and a Conference Representative shall forthwith notify the Shippers of any such suspension.

10.   In the event of the Carriers ceasing together to provide services sufficient for the ordinary requirements of the trade from all or some of the Conference Shipment Areas to all or some of the Conference Destinations, either in consequence of the threat or occurrence of war, warlike action, actions of any government or authority, revolution, riot, civil commotion, strike, lockout, labour dispute or any action or event whatsoever beyond the Carriers' control or following upon the issue of amendments to the list of Lines in accordance with Clause 4 of this Agreement, the Carriers may by notice to the Shippers suspend the operation of this Agreement generally or modify its scope by amendments to the definitions of Conference Cargo, Conference Shipment Areas and Conference Destinations and this Agreement shall thenceforth be suspended or, as the case may be, take effect subject to such modification until such time as the Carriers by further notice restore its full operation. Notices hereunder will be given by a Conference Representative by press announcement or by such other means as may be available at the time. Both the Shippers and the Carriers will be relieved of their obligations under this Agreement to the extent of and during the period of any such suspension or modification.

11.   This Agreement is terminable by either the Carriers or the Shippers by not less than six months' written notice expiring on the 30th June or 31st December in any year.

12.   Any dispute arising out of, under or in connection with this Agreement shall, failing an amicable settlement between the parties concerned, be referred to arbitration in London for final decision by two arbitrators, one to be appointed by a Conference Representative on behalf of the Carriers and one by the Shippers, and otherwise in accordance with the Arbitration Act, 1950, and any statutory modification thereof for the time being in force.

Shippers' Signature . . . .

    Status of Signatory . . . .

        For the Carriers. . . . .
                            For Conference Secretary
                            Philippines/Europe Conference

Date . . . .   Appr.:—. . . . .

M

7.3 FAR EASTERN FREIGHT CONFERENCE: EASTBOUND CONTINENTAL GENERAL CARGO CONTRACT (ALTERNATIVE TO DEFERRED REBATE SYSTEM)

Description

The Far Eastern Freight Conference Eastbound Continental General Cargo Contract is a general cargo contract or agreement between the shipper, as principal and not as agent, and the Conference.

Source of document

The Far Eastern Freight Conference organization.

Purpose/use/function

The contract broadly reflects the terms under which cargo is accepted for shipment under the Conference. In particular it stresses the loyalty aspect, by requiring the shipper to ship continuously with the Conference and not to permit cargoes to be conveyed on vessels outside the Conference when rates of freight are low. For this loyalty a discounted rate of freight of 9½ % is offered, under the immediate rebate system.

Other aspects

The terms in each Conference vary but the dependence on the rebate system as a loyalty instrument is paramount in the interest of retaining the business to the liner tonnage. In an increasing number of trades, new Conference Line vessels are emerging which provide lower rates and often lower quality service.

The Liner Conference offers regularity of service and stability of rates. It works closely with Trade Associations and usually negotiates with Shipper's Councils to ensure the needs of the shipper are met in the type and framework of the service provided.

Far Eastern Freight Conference

EASTBOUND CONTINENTAL GENERAL CARGO CONTRACT
(Alternative to Deferred Rebate System)

This Agreement is for signature by Principals only and not by firms acting as Forwarding Agents.

WHEREAS:—

(A)

Belgian Far Eastern Line	Lloyd Triestino di Navigazione S.p.A.
Ben Line Steamers Ltd.	Maersk Line
Blue Funnel Line Ltd.	(Joint Service of Aktieselskabet Dampskibsselskabet
(Ocean Transport & Trading Ltd.	Svendborg and Dampskibsselskabet af 1912 Aktieselskab)
The China Mutual Steam Navigation Co. Ltd.)	Malaysian International Shipping Corpn. Berhad
Bröstroms Rederi AB	Maritime Company of the Philippines
(Brostrom Shipping Company Limited)	Mitsui O.S.K. Lines Ltd.
Cho Yang Shipping Co. Ltd.	Nedlloyd Lijnen B.V. (Nedlloyd Lines)
Compagnie Generale Maritime	Neptune Orient Lines Ltd.
Cie. Maritime des Chargeurs Reunis	Nippon Yusen Kaisha
VEB Deutfracht/Seereederei Rostock (D.S.R.)	Orient Overseas Container Line
Ellerman & Bucknall Steamship Co. Ltd.	(Chinese Maritime Transport Ltd./
Glen Line Ltd. (Glen & Shire Joint Service)	Orient Overseas Container Line Ltd.)
Hapag-Lloyd Aktiengesellschaft	A/S Det Østasiatiske Kompagni (The East Asiatic Co. Ltd.)
Jugolinija-East	Peninsular & Oriental Steam Navigation Co.
Kawasaki Kisen Kaisha Limited ("K" Line)	Polskie Linie Oceaniczne (Polish Ocean Lines)
Korea Shipping Corporation	The United Thai Shipping Corporation Ltd. (Unithai)
Lauro Lines	Wilh. Wilhelmsen

(members of the Far Eastern Freight Conference) and

Ben Line Containers Ltd.
Ben Ocean
Franco Belgian Services (C.M.C.R. & B.F.E.L. Joint Services)
Overseas Containers Ltd.
Rickmers-Linie K.G.
ScanDutch (E.A.Co., Nedlloyd, C.G.M., Brostrom & W.W. Joint Service)

all of which Lines are hereinafter together called "the Carriers", together provide services sufficient for the ordinary requirements of the trade from Norway, Sweden, Finland, Denmark, Germany, Holland, Belgium and French ports from Dunkirk to St. Nazaire both inclusive, also Italian and Jugoslav ports ("Conference Shipment Areas") to the States of Malaya and Singapore, Thailand, Hong Kong, Taiwan and Korea ("Conference Destinations") and seek to maintain stable rates of freight for such services,

(B)　The Carriers offer a discount to all shippers who agree to give their entire support to the Carriers, and

(C)

NAME AND FULL ADDRESS OF THE SHIPPERS TO BE INSERTED

("the Shippers") wish to benefit from such discount and to give their entire support to the Carriers,

IT IS AGREED between the Carriers and the Shippers as follows:—

1.　The Shippers agree that during the currency of this Agreement they will give the Carriers their entire support (in the sense defined in Clause 3 hereof) in respect of Conference Cargo (as defined in Clause 5(a) hereof).

2.　The Carriers agree to accept Conference Cargo for carriage:—

(a)　by vessels operated by the Carriers, subject only to their ability to carry the cargo and to agreement between the Shippers and the carrying Line concerned as to the quantity to be carried in each vessel;

(b)　at the Conference Tariff rates ruling at the time of shipment, or at such special rates as may be quoted by the Carriers in the case of large parcels of cargo not being ordinary berth cargo, less a discount of 9½% on the amount of freight so calculated except in so far as such rates are nett; and

(c)　subject to the provisions of the Conference Tariff Conditions and to the terms and conditions of business of the carrying Line.

3.　For the purposes of this Agreement, unless otherwise agreed by a Conference Representative, the Shippers are deemed to give their entire support to the Carriers in respect of Conference Cargo if, but only if, the Shippers:—

(a)　ensure that all contracts for the carriage of Conference Cargo made by the Shippers, whether as principals or as agents, or by others as agents for the Shippers, are made with one or more of the Carriers;

(b)　refrain from participating directly or indirectly in any arrangements relating to the carriage of Conference Cargo by any vessel not operated by one of the Carriers;

(c)　procure that each Associate (as defined in Clause 5(b) hereof) of the Shippers conducts its business as if it were bound by this form of Agreement and, if and when a Conference Representative (as defined in Clause 5(c) hereof) so requires, signs this form of Agreement with the Carriers;

(d)　refrain from any action which would enable persons who are neither parties to an Agreement in this form nor their Associates nor consignees of goods sold by such parties or their associates to obtain like benefits as are conferred upon the Shippers hereunder; and

(e)　refrain from acting as agents for competitors of the Carriers in respect of the carriage of Conference Cargo.

4.　Should any of the carriers cease to be, or should any other Line become, a member of the Conference or associated with it in the carriage of Conference Cargo, a Conference Representative shall give to the Shippers such notice as the Carriers consider to be fair and reasonable in all the circumstances of the amendments to the list of Lines at (A) above resulting therefrom. Upon and from the date specified in such notice this Agreement shall have effect as an Agreement between the Shippers and the Lines included in such amended list and, save that Clause 12 hereof shall remain in force, this Agreement shall cease to have effect as an Agreement binding upon or referring to any Line which is not included in such amended list and the expression "the Carriers" shall be construed accordingly. In the event of the Shippers being seriously prejudiced by a Line ceasing on the date specified in such notice to be a member of the Conference or associated with it in the carriage of Conference Cargo, a Conference Representative may, on application by the Shippers in advance of each shipment, agree to the shipment of Conference Cargo by the Shippers in vessels operated by such Line during a limited period after such date.

5. (a) "Conference Cargo" means all goods carried or intended to be carried by sea, with or without transshipment, from Conference Shipment Areas for delivery at Conference Destinations other than (i) coal, gypsum stone in bulk and nitrate of ammonia to all Conference Destinations, (ii) sulphate of potash and muriate of potash to Taiwan and Korea, (iii) commodities listed in the Conference Tariff Conditions ruling at the time of shipment as exceptions either generally or in relation to a particular Conference Destination and (iv) Bulk liquid cargoes shipped in vessels operated by Panocean-Anco Ltd.

   (b) "Associate" in relation to any shippers means any person, firm or company which is controlled or managed by such shippers or in respect of which such shippers have a sufficient interest to enable them to determine the method of shipment.

   (c) "Conference Representative" means the Secretary for the time being of the Far Eastern Freight Conference or such other person as shall be authorised to represent the Conference.

6. (a) In the event of a Conference Representative having grounds for believing that the Shippers have committed a breach or breaches of this Agreement in failing to give the Carriers their entire support in accordance with Clauses 1 and 3 hereof, he shall be entitled on behalf of the Carriers:—

   (i) to request the Shippers for an explanation; and

   (ii) if a satisfactory explanation is not received within 30 days of such request, to suspend the entitlement of the Shippers to the discount hereinbefore mentioned and/or to appoint a Trustee for the purposes set out in sub-clause (b) hereof, provided that the Shippers shall be entitled to request the appointment of another person as Trustee in place of the person originally appointed if they have reasonable cause for believing that the disclosure of the information referred to in sub-clause (b) hereof to the person originally appointed would be damaging or prejudicial to their interests and in the event of such objection being sustained by the Carriers the Conference Representative shall appoint another person as Trustee.

   (b) The Trustee shall investigate the alleged breach or breaches at the office or offices of the Shippers or such other place as the Trustee may consider convenient. The Shippers agree to furnish the Trustee with all such information, explanations, correspondence, books of account and/or other papers as the Trustee may consider relevant to the alleged breach or breaches. The Trustee shall consider the same together with any other material or explanations provided by the Shippers and the Conference Representative who appointed him. The Trustee shall thereafter report in writing to the Shippers and to the Conference Representative who appointed him whether he considers that the Shippers have committed any breach or breaches of this Agreement and, if in his opinion they have done so, shall give details of the same.

   (c) If neither the Shippers nor the Carriers shall refer the matter to arbitration under Clause 12 hereof within 30 days of receipt of the Trustee's report, both shall be deemed to have accepted the conclusions stated therein and shall not thereafter seek to challenge the same. In such event, if the Trustee reports that in his opinion the Shippers have not committed any breach or breaches of this Agreement, the expenses of the Trustee shall be paid by the Carriers and an amount equivalent to any discount to which the Shippers would have been entitled but for the suspension of their entitlement pending the investigation shall be paid to the Shippers. In all other cases the expenses of the Trustee shall be paid by the Shippers. If the dispute is referred to arbitration the expenses of the Trustee shall be paid or borne as may be directed in any arbitration award.

7. If the Shippers admit, or accept or are deemed to have accepted a report by a Trustee, that the Shippers have committed any breach or breaches of this Agreement, or if in an arbitration it is so determined:—

   (a) the Carriers may suspend or continue to suspend the entitlement of the Shippers to the discount hereinbefore mentioned, provided that the suspension of entitlement to discount shall not exceed a total period of six months or continue after the discharge by the Shippers of all liability to the Carriers consequent upon such breach or breaches, and

   (b) if the breach or breaches consists of or includes a failure by the Shippers to give their entire support in accordance with Clause 3(a), (b) or (c), the Shippers shall pay to the Conference Representative who appointed the Trustee, as agent for the Carriers, agreed liquidated damages in accordance with Clause 8 hereof and, upon payment of such liquidated damages and the discharge by the Shippers of all other liability to the Carriers, an amount equivalent to any discount to which the Shippers would have been entitled but for the suspension of their entitlement shall be promptly paid to the Shippers.

8. Both the Shippers and the Carriers accept that it is impossible to calculate the precise loss suffered by the Carriers in the event of a failure by the Shippers to give the Carriers their entire support in accordance with Clause 3(a), (b) or (c) but are agreed that the best estimate which can be made is that such loss will amount to two thirds of the freight (excluding transhipment additionals) which would have been payable to one or more of the Carriers if the goods concerned had been carried by them and have further agreed that a sum so calculated shall be payable as liquidated damages in the event of any such failure.

9. In the event of the Shippers making any false declaration as to the nature, weight, measurement or value of any Conference Cargo, the Carriers may suspend the entitlement of the Shippers to the discount hereinbefore mentioned for such period not exceeding six months as the Carriers think fit and a Conference Representative shall forthwith notify the Shippers of any such suspension.

10. In the event of the Carriers ceasing together to provide services sufficient for the ordinary requirements of the trade from all or some of the Conference Shipment Areas to all or some of the Conference Destinations, either in consequence of the threat or occurrence of war, warlike action, actions of any government or authority, revolution, riot, civil commotion, strike, lockout, labour dispute or any action or event whatsoever beyond the Carriers' control or following upon the issue of amendments to the list of Lines in accordance with Clause 4 of this Agreement, the Carriers may by notice to the Shippers suspend the operation of this Agreement generally or modify its scope by amendments to the definitions of Conference Cargo, Conference Shipment Areas and Conference Destinations and this Agreement shall thenceforth be suspended or, as the case may be, take effect subject to such modification until such time as the Carriers by further notice restore its full operation. Notices hereunder will be given by a Conference Representative by press announcement or by such other means as may be available at the time. Both the Shippers and the Carriers will be relieved of their obligations under this Agreement to the extent of and during the period of any such suspension or modification.

11. This Agreement is terminable by either the Carriers or the Shippers by not less than six months' written notice expiring on the 30th June or 31st December in any year.

12. Any dispute arising out of, under or in connection with this Agreement shall, failing an amicable settlement between the parties concerned, be referred to arbitration in London for final decision by two arbitrators, one to be appointed by a Conference Representative on behalf of the Carriers and one by the Shippers, and otherwise in accordance with the Arbitration Act, 1950, and any statutory modification thereof for the time being in force.

Shippers' Signature . . . .

Status of Signatory . . . .

For the Carriers. . . . .
For Conference Secretary
Far Eastern Freight Conference

Date . . . .   Appr.:—. . . . .

M

7.4 (DEFERRED) REBATE (FREIGHT) CLAIM FORM

Description

A Rebate Claim Form is a declaration and statement concerning shipments, which is completed and submitted by the shipper wishing to claim rebate from the shipowner. It supplies a list of shipments carried during a specified (usually six-monthly) period and arises under the deferred rebate scheme.

Source of document

A Liner Conference, for example the Europe/Japan Freight Conference Secretariat.

Purpose/use/function

Under the contractual terms of a General Cargo Contract (section 7.2) the Rebate Claim Form is used by the shipper to claim rebate from the shipowner, usually under the deferred rebate system, at a rebate level fixed by the shipowners forming the Liner Conference.

Legal context

A condition of payment of rebate is that the shipper has not used other shipowners' services outside the Liner Conference network during the period specified. It is not legally enforceable.

Other aspects

The form is completed by the shipper and the Company who has billed the freight invoice. Only the owners of rebate cargo are entitled to claim the rebate and therefore the form must be signed by them even if the name of another firm or person appears as shippers in the Bill of Lading relating to the rebate cargo. The signatory must be a partner of the firm claiming the rebate or someone holding the firm's procuration.

The deferred rebate scheme is an area of controversy in the industry as the shipowner retains the rebate for six months at zero interest thereby obtaining monies at a zero-rated loan level. The shipowner has an expense to retain staff to administer the system thereby raising the Liner Conference organization cost. A solution practised in many Conferences is to offer an immediate rebate which is slightly lower and rebated at the time the freight invoice is raised by the shipowner to the shipper.

The deferred rebate scheme is practised in many Liner Conferences and has greatly contributed to the continuing loyalty of its members despite the intrusion of new Liner Conference tonnage to poach the business in peak periods.

Rebate Claim Form

DECLARATION AND STATEMENT CONCERNING SHIPMENTS

DURING $\frac{\text{FIRST}}{\text{SECOND}}$ HALF OF 19

To be signed by the Merchant Owning the Goods.

1st $\frac{\text{July}}{\text{January}}$ 19

To: MITSUI O.S.K. LINES LTD.

Dear Sirs,

We refer to your Rebate Circular reading:—

Shipments   from:— United Kingdom, Eire, Norway, Sweden, Finland, Denmark, Germany, Holland, Belgium and French ports from Dunkirk to St. Nazaire both inclusive, also Italian and Jugoslav ports

               to:— Japan.

1.   To all Shippers who give to the following Lines:—

BELGIAN FAR EASTERN LINE
BEN LINE STEAMERS LTD.
BLUE FUNNEL LINE LTD.
   (Ocean Transport & Trading Ltd.
   The China Mutual Steam Navigation Co. Ltd.)
BROSTRÖMS REDERI AB
   (Broström Shipping Company Limited)
CHO YANG SHIPPING CO. LTD.
COMPAGNIE GENERALE MARITIME
CIE. MARITIME DES CHARGEURS RÉUNIS
VEB DEUTFRACHT/SEEREEDEREI ROSTOCK (D.S.R.)
ELLERMAN & BUCKNALL STEAMSHIP CO. LTD.
GLEN LINE LTD. (GLEN & SHIRE JOINT SERVICE)
HAPAG-LLOYD AKTIENGESELLSCHAFT
JUGOLINIJA-EAST
KAWASAKI KISEN KAISHA LIMITED ("K" LINE)
KOREA SHIPPING CORPORATION
LAURO LINE

LLOYD TRIESTINO DI NAVIGAZIONE S.P.A.
MAERSK LINE
   (Joint Service of
   Aktieselskabet Dampskibsselskabet Svendborg
   Dampskibsselskabet af 1912 Aktieselskab
   A. P. Moller
   as one party only)
MALAYSIAN INTERNATIONAL SHIPPING CORPN. BERHAD
MITSUI O.S.K. LINES LTD.
NEDLLOYD LIJNEN B.V. (NEDLLOYD LINES)
NEPTUNE ORIENT LINES (SINGAPORE) LTD.
NIPPON YUSEN KAISHA
ORIENT OVERSEAS CONTAINER LINE/ORIENT OVERSEAS LINE
   (CHINESE MARITIME TRANSPORT LIMITED, TAIPEI)
A/S DET OSTASIATISKE KOMPAGNI (THE EAST ASIATIC CO. LTD.)
PENINSULAR & ORIENTAL STEAM NAVIGATION CO.
POLSKIE LINIE OCEANICZNE (POLISH OCEAN LINES)
WILH. WILHELMSEN

(members of the Europe/Japan Freight Conference) and

BEN LINE CONTAINERS LTD.
BEN OCEAN
FRANCO BELGIAN SERVICES (C.M.C.R. & B.F.E.L. JOINT SERVICES)
OVERSEAS CONTAINERS LTD.
RICKMERS-LINIE
SCANDUTCH (E.A.Co., NEDLLOYD, C.G.M., BROSTROM & W.W. JOINT SERVICE)

(hereinafter called "the Lines") their entire support (as defined in paragraph 2 below), we, the undersigned, will allow until further notice, and subject to the terms and conditions set out below, a deferred rebate of 10% on the amount and in the currency of the freight actually paid on all shipments of Rebate Cargo (as defined in paragraph 7 below) made by such Shippers in vessels operated by us, except in so far as:—
   (a) a discount has already been allowed by us in respect of such freight under the alternative Contract System or would have been so allowed if the Shippers' entitlement to such a discount had not been under suspension; or
   (b) the rates of freight are nett.

2.   For the purposes of this Circular, Shippers are deemed to give to the Lines their entire support if, but only if, such Shippers:—
   (a) ensure that all contracts for the carriage of Rebate Cargo made by such Shippers, whether as principals or agents, or by others as agents for such Shippers, are made with one or more of the Lines;
   (b) refrain from participating directly or indirectly in any arrangements relating to the carriage of Rebate Cargo by any vessel not operated by one of the Lines;
   (c) procure that any person, firm or company which is controlled or managed by such Shippers, or in respect of which such Shippers have a sufficient interest to enable them to determine the method of shipment, complies with the terms and conditions of this Circular;
   (d) refrain from any action which would enable Shippers who have not complied with the terms and conditions of this Circular to obtain the said rebate; and
   (e) refrain from acting as agents for the competitors of the Lines in respect of Rebate Cargo.

3.   We reserve the right to amend the list of Lines in paragraph 1 above and, upon our notifying Shippers of any such amendment, this Circular shall take effect as if the expression "the Lines" meant the Lines included in such list as amended. We also reserve the right at the end of any Shipment Period (as hereinafter defined) to amend or withdraw this Circular.

4.   We will pay the said rebate in respect of any period of six months ending on the 30th June or the 31st December in any year (hereinafter called "a Shipment Period") to all Shippers who have given their entire support to the Lines during such and the following Shipment Period. For this purpose "entire support" means entire support as defined in the Rebate Circular applicable to the Shipment Period during which the entire support is to be given. Shippers wishing to claim such rebate in respect of any Shipment Period must complete and sign the appropriate claim form and lodge it with us or our Agents within three months after the end of such Shipment Period. If correctness of the declarations on this claim form and on the claim form for the following Shipment Period is accepted by us, we will pay the said rebate as soon as possible after the latter form is lodged. Claim forms will be available on application immediately after the end of each Shipment Period.

5.   In the event of Shippers making any false declaration as to the nature, weight, measurement or value of any Rebate Cargo to any of the Lines during a Shipment Period, we reserve the right to withhold payment of the said rebate on all Rebate Cargo shipped by such Shippers during such Shipment Period.

6.   Only the owners of Rebate Cargo are entitled to claim the said rebate and therefore the claim form must be signed by them even if the name of another firm or person appears as Shippers in the Bill of Lading relating to such Rebate Cargo. We are willing, however, to pay the said rebate to another firm or person if so requested by the owners of the Rebate Cargo in completing the claim form.

7.   For the purposes of this circular, "Rebate Cargo" means all goods carried or intended to be carried by sea, with or without transhipment, from United Kingdom, Eire, Norway, Sweden, Finland, Denmark, Germany, Holland, Belgium and French ports from Dunkirk to St. Nazaire both inclusive, also Italian and Jugoslav ports to Japan other than (i) coal, gypsum stone in bulk and nitrate of ammonia, (ii) sulphate of potash and muriate of potash, (iii) commodities listed in the Tariff Conditions ruling at the time of shipment as exceptions, either generally or in relation to a particular destination, and (iv) bulk liquid cargoes shipped in vessels operated by Panocean-Anco Ltd.

8.   Any dispute arising out of, under or in connection with this Circular or any claim thereunder shall, failing an amicable settlement between the parties concerned be referred to arbitration in London for final decision by two arbitrators, one to be appointed by each party and otherwise in accordance with the Arbitration Act 1950, and any statutory modification thereof for the time being in force.

We hereby declare that we have complied with the terms and conditions of this Circular during the period of six months ended 30th June/31st December last.

Overleaf is a list of our shipments by the vessels you have loaded during this period. Provided we fulfil the terms and conditions of your Rebate Circular during the six months ending 31st December/30th June next please pay rebates on these shipments in due course to:—

Name ....

Address...

....

....

                     This space should be completed if the Merchant wishes the Rebate to be paid to a third party

                  Yours faithfully,

             Signature (in full) ....

This declaration must be signed by a Partner of the firm claiming the Rebate or by someone holding the firms procuration.

             Address (in full) ....

             ....

             ....

                     (Owner of the Goods)

NOTE.—To facilitate checking these Accounts, it is essential that the Bill of
Lading Number be inserted in the column for this purpose.

Vessel	Date of Shipment	Port of Shipment	Port of Destination	No. of B/L	Marks	Shipping Agents	Amount of Freight Paid		Amount of Rebate	

| Vessel | Date of Shipment | Port of Shipment | Port of Destination | No. of B/L | Marks | Shipping Agents | Amount of Freight Paid | | Amount of Rebate | |

8 Miscellaneous documents

8.1 INTRODUCTION

Shipowners or agents requiring a berth at a seaport may submit their request to the Port Authority on an official Port Authority form, the Application for Berth. However, such requests are not frequent as shipowners using the port regularly on scheduled services, such as under Liner Conference conditions, tend to have pre-arranged berthing schedules covering a 3–12 month cycle. Port Authorities tend to issue a weekly berth allocation.

The very specialized activity implicit in the sale and purchase of vessels is undertaken by a sale and purchase broker. The broker normally acts either for the buyer or seller of a ship, but occasionally a broker acts between the buyer's broker and the seller's broker, each of whom may be operating from different countries and dealing with a foreign ship. The market is international and the ship may be sold for scrap or operational purposes. In the latter case the new owner must change the ship's name and is usually forbidden to operate in trades competitive with those of the ship's former owner.

On conclusion of the customary haggling over the price and conditions of sale, the seller's broker draws up a Memorandum of Agreement, which is confirmed in due course by the execution and delivery of a Bill of Sale of the vessel.

8.2 APPLICATION FOR BERTH

Description

An Application for Berth is the official form used to request a berth at a seaport. It gives vessel details, cargo details and passenger details, and includes such information as the names of the vessel and shipowner, whether cargo is to be discharged or loaded, cargo-handling needs, the numbers of passengers embarking or disembarking, the estimated times of arrival and departure, and so on.

Source of document

A port authority, for example the Port of Singapore Authority.

Purpose/use/function

The Application for Berth is submitted to a port authority by a shipowner or ship's agent when requesting a berth at a seaport.

Other aspects

The Berth Application tends to arise through the ship's agent representing chartered tonnage. It requires a specialized berth and equipment. The document forms the basis on which all the requirements of the shipowner are specified and details are dispatched to Customs, stevedoring company, Police, Customs Clearance Agents, victualling personnel and so on. The role of the document will vary by port. It is important that details are accurate, especially the draught, beam and overall length of vessel and whether any pilotage/tug assistance is required.

APPLICATION FOR BERTH

Vessel Details:	Name																				Type		
Account No.		Agent							Time of Advice														
Berth Date/ Time required			Estimated Date/Time of unberthing											Length overall								
Draft alongside		Height-highest point alongside at any one time						Last Port of call				Appropriated Berth Indicator										
Advance Loader Scheme:	Yes/No		Service Charge Scheme:	Yes/No			China Cargo Ship?	Yes/No				Dangerous Cargo on board?				Yes/No							
Priority Class		Gateway		Shipping Line Code				Stevedore Name															

Cargo Details:																						Tonnage	
General Cargo																							
Drums																							
Timber																							
Palletised																							
Containers																							
Steel works																							
Heavy-lifts																							
Miscellaneous																							
Calcium Carbide																							

Passenger Details:	Embarking								Disembarking				
Equipment Requirement:	Crane		—		T	Heavy Forktrucks		—		T	Vulcan		
Bulk Services:	Bunker			—		Diesel			—		Water		
Remarks / Special Requirement													
Berth Requested											Bulk Cargo		

Bulk Cargo Details:			Date/Time Loading/Discharging			Tonnage		Distance of Tanks/Hatches From Stern	From Bow

I/We hereby declare and certify on behalf of the owner of the vessel/barge as follows :
(1) The vessel/barge is not permitted to have GROUP 1 Dangerous Goods whilst alongside the Authority's Wharves.
(2) The vessel/barge is carrying Dangerous Goods as cargo, the details of which are declared on the appropriated forms and submitted on application for berth.

....
Agent/Owner

....
Signature

8.3 MEMORANDUM OF AGREEMENT (FOR SALE AND PURCHASE OF SHIPS)

Description

A Memorandum of Agreement for sale and purchase of ships, an example of which is the Norwegian Shipbrokers' Association's Memorandum of Agreement, code-named Saleform 1983, is a contract between a seller to sell and a buyer to buy a particular vessel at an agreed price, subject to certain conditions of sale. It can be amended to reflect the agreed terms of sale including the provision of any clauses.

Source of document

A shipbrokers' association, e.g. The Norwegian Shipbrokers' Association, Oslo.

Purpose/use/function

The Memorandum of Agreement serves as a preliminary to the execution and delivery of the Bill of Sale of the vessel, since it is a condition of the Agreement that, in exchange for currency purchase in accord with the terms of sale, the seller agrees to furnish the buyer with a legal Bill of Sale (section 8.4).

Legal context

Under the conditions of the Agreement, any disputes are to be decided by arbitration in a place specified in the Agreement. The Agreement is subject to the law of the country agreed as place of arbitration.

Ratifying organizations/countries

The Memorandum of Agreement has been adopted by the Baltic and International Maritime Conference (BIMCO), Copenhagen.

Procedure

Instructions for completing the form

The Memorandum of Agreement is drawn up by the seller's broker.

Other aspects

The Memorandum of Agreement is an established document and its terms have been proven in litigation and custom of the trade over a period of years. It is important that the ship's classification papers are available for inspection including latest survey documentation, ship classification and registration. Copies are required by the buyer and seller, the Banks, and other organizations including Registration and Classification Societies/Organizations.

MEMORANDUM OF AGREEMENT

Dated:

Norwegian Shipbrokers' Association's Memorandum of Agreement for sale and purchase of ships. Adopted by The Baltic and International Maritime Council (BIMCO) in 1956.

Code-name

SALEFORM 1987

Revised 1966, 1983 and 1986

hereinafter called the Sellers, have today sold, and   1

hereinafter called the Buyers, have today bought   2

Classification: 3
Built: by: 4
Flag: Place of Registration: 5
Call sign: Register tonnage: 6
Register number: ⁻7
on the following conditions: 8

1. Price   9
   Price: 10

2. Deposit   11
   As a security for the correct fulfillment of this contract, the Buyers shall pay a deposit of 10 % —   12
ten per cent — of the Purchase Money within   banking days from the date of this 13
agreement. This amount shall be deposited with   14

and held by them in a joint account for the Sellers and the Buyers. Interest, if any, to be credited the   15
Buyers. Any fee charged for holding said deposit shall be borne equally by the Sellers and the Buyers.   16

3. Payment   17
   The said Purchase Money shall be paid free of bank charges to   18

on delivery of the vessel, but not later than three banking days after the vessel is ready for delivery   19
and written or telexed notice thereof has been given to the Buyers by the Sellers.   20

4. Inspections   21
   The Buyers shall have the right to inspect the vessel's classification records and declare whether   22
same are accepted or not within   23
   The Sellers shall provide for inspection of the vessel at/in   24

   The Buyers shall undertake the inspection without undue delay to the vessel. Should the Buyers   25
cause such delay, they shall compensate the Sellers for the losses thereby incurred.   26
   The Buyers shall inspect the vessel afloat without opening up and without cost to the Sellers. During the inspection, the vessel's log books for engine and deck shall be made available for the Buyers'   27
examination. If the vessel is accepted after such afloat inspection, the purchase shall become definite   28
— except for other possible subjects in this contract — provided the Sellers receive written or telexed   29
notice from the Buyers within 48 hours after completion of such afloat inspection. Should notice of   30
acceptance of the vessel's classification records and of the vessel not be received by the Sellers as   31
                                                                                                  32

aforesaid, the deposit shall immediately be released, whereafter this contract shall be considered null   33
and void.   34

5. Place and time of delivery   35

The vessel shall be delivered and taken over at/in   36

Expected time of delivery: 37

Date of cancelling (see clause 14):   38

The Sellers shall keep the Buyers well posted about the vessel's itinerary and estimated time and   39
place of drydocking.   40

Should the vessel become a total or constructive total loss before delivery the deposit shall immedi-   41
ately be released to the Buyers and the contract thereafter considered null and void.   42

6. Drydocking   43

In connection with the delivery the Sellers shall place the vessel in drydock at the port of delivery   44
for inspection by the Classification Society of the bottom and other underwater parts below the Sum-   45
mer Load Line. If the rudder, propeller, bottom or other underwater parts below the Summer Load   46
Line be found broken, damaged or defective, so as to affect the vessel's clean certificate of class, such   47
defects shall be made good at the Sellers' expense to [1)]   48

satisfaction without qualification on such underwater parts. [2)]   49

Whilst the vessel is in drydock, and if required by the Buyers or the representative of the Classifi-   50
cation Society, the Sellers shall arrange to have the tail-end shaft drawn. Should same be condemned   51
or found defective so as to affect the vessel's clean certificate of class, it shall be renewed or made   52
good at the Sellers' expense to the Classification Society's satisfaction without qualification.   53

The expenses of drawing and replacing the tail-end shaft shall be borne by the Buyers unless the   54
Classification Society requires the tail-end shaft to be drawn (whether damaged or not), renewed or   55
made good in which event the Sellers shall pay these expenses.   56

The expenses in connection with putting the vessel in and taking her out of drydock, including dry-   57
dock dues and the Classification Surveyor's fees shall be paid by the Sellers if the rudder, propeller,   58
bottom, other underwater parts below the Summer Load Line or the tail-end shaft be found broken,   59
damaged or defective as aforesaid or if the Classification Society requires the tail-end shaft to be   60
drawn (whether damaged or not). In all other cases the Buyers shall pay the aforesaid expenses, dues   61
and fees.   62

During the above mentioned inspections by the Classification Society the Buyers' representative   63
shall have the right to be present in the drydock but without interfering with the Classification Surve-   64
yor's decisions.   65

The Sellers shall bring the vessel to the drydock and from the drydock to the place of delivery at   66
their own expense.   67

7. Spares/bunkers etc.   68

The Sellers shall deliver the vessel to the Buyers with everything belonging to her on board and on   69
shore. All spare parts and spare equipment including spare tail-end shaft(s) and/or spare propeller(s),   70
if any, belonging to the vessel at the time of inspection, used or unused, whether on board or not shall   71
become the Buyers' property, but spares on order to be excluded. Forwarding charges, if any, shall be   72
for the Buyers' account. The Sellers are not required to replace spare parts including spare tail-end   73
shaft(s) and spare propeller(s) which are taken out of spare and used as replacement prior to delivery,   74
but the replaced items shall be the property of the Buyers. The radio installation and navigational   75
equipment shall be included in the sale without extra payment, if same is the property of the Sellers.   76

The Sellers have the right to take ashore crockery, plate, cutlery, linen and other articles bearing   77
the Sellers' flag or name, provided they replace same with similar unmarked items. Library, forms,   78
etc., exclusively for use in the Sellers' vessels, shall be excluded without compensation. Captain's,   79
Officers' and Crew's personal belongings including slop chest to be excluded from the sale, as well as   80
the following additional items: 81

The Buyers shall take over remaining bunkers, unused lubricating oils and unused stores and pro-   82
visions and pay the current market price at the port and date of delivery of the vessel.   83

Payment under this clause shall be made at the same time and place and in the same currency as   84
the Purchase Money.   85

8. Documentation   86

In exchange for payment of the Purchase Money the Sellers shall furnish the Buyers with legal Bill   87
of Sale of the said vessel free from all encumbrances and maritime liens or any other debts whatsoe-   88
ver, duly notarially attested and legalised by the   consul toget-   89
her with a certificate stating that the vessel is free from registered encumbrances. On delivery of the   90
vessel the Sellers shall provide for the deletion of the vessel from the Registry of Vessels and deliver a   91
certificate of deletion to the Buyers. The deposit shall be placed at the disposal of the Sellers as well as   92
the balance of the Purchase Money, which shall be paid as agreed together with payment for items   93
mentioned in clause 7 above.   94

The Sellers shall, at the time of delivery, hand to the Buyers all classification certificates as well as   95
all plans etc. which are onboard the vessel. Other technical documentation which may be in the Sel-   96
lers' possession shall promptly upon the Buyers' instructions be forwarded to the Buyers. The   97
Sellers may keep the log books, but the Buyers to have the right to take copies of same.   98

9. Encumbrances   99

The Sellers warrant that the vessel, at the time of delivery, is free from all encumbrances and ma-   100
ritime liens or any other debts whatsoever. Should any claims which have been incurred prior to the   101
time of delivery be made against the vessel, the Sellers hereby undertake to indemnify the Buyers   102
against all consequences of such claims.   103

10. Taxes etc.   104

Any taxes, fees and expenses connected with the purchase and registration under the Buyers' flag   105
shall be for the Buyers' account, whereas similar charges connected with the closing of the Sellers' re-   106
gister shall be for the Sellers' account.   107

11. Condition on delivery   108

The vessel with everything belonging to her shall be at the Sellers' risk and expense until she is de-   109
livered to the Buyers, but subject to the conditions of this contract, she shall be delivered and taken   110
over as she is at the time of inspection, fair wear and tear excepted.   111

However, the vessel shall be delivered with present class free of recommendations. The Sellers   112
shall notify the Classification Society of any matters coming to their knowledge prior to delivery   113
which upon being reported to the Classification Society would lead to the withdrawal of the vessel's   114
class or to the imposition of a recommendation relating to her class.   115

12. Name/markings   116

Upon delivery the Buyers undertake to change the name of the vessel and alter funnel markings.   117

13. Buyers' default   118

Should the deposit not be paid as aforesaid, the Sellers have the right to cancel this contract, and   119
they shall be entitled to claim compensation for their losses and for all expenses incurred together   120

with interest at the rate of 12% per annum.   121

Should the Purchase Money not be paid as aforesaid, the Sellers have the right to cancel this con-   122
tract, in which case the amount deposited together with interest earned, if any, shall be forfeited to   123
the Sellers. If the deposit does not cover the Sellers' losses, they shall be entitled to claim further com-   124
pensation for their losses and for all expenses together with interest at the rate of 12% per annum.   125

14. Sellers' default   126

If the Sellers fail to execute a legal transfer or to deliver the vessel with everything belonging to her   127
in the manner and within the time specified in line 38, the Buyers shall have the right to cancel this contract   128
in which case the deposit in full shall be returned to the Buyers together with interest at the rate of 12 % per   129
annum. The Sellers shall make due compensation for the losses caused to the Buyers by failure to execute a   130
legal transfer or to deliver the vessel in the manner and within the time specified in line 38, if such are due to   131
the proven negligence of the Sellers.   132

15. Arbitration   133

If any dispute should arise in connection with the interpretation and fulfilment of this contract,   134
same shall be decided by arbitration in the city of[3]   135
and shall be referred to a single Arbitrator to be appointed by the parties hereto. If the parties cannot   136
agree upon the appointment of the single Arbitrator, the dispute shall be settled by three Arbitrators,   137
each party appointing one Arbitrator, the third being appointed by[4]   138
                                                                                          139

If either of the appointed Arbitrators refuses or is incapable of acting, the party who appointed   140
him, shall appoint a new Arbitrator in his place.   141

If one of the parties fails to appoint an Arbitrator — either originally or by way of substitution —   142
for two weeks after the other party having appointed his Arbitrator has sent the party making default   143
notice by mail, cable or telex to make the appointment, the party appointing the third Arbitrator   144
shall, after application from the party having appointed his Arbitrator, also appoint an Arbitrator on   145
behalf of the party making default.   146

The award rendered by the Arbitration Court shall be final and binding upon the parties and may   147
if necessary be enforced by the Court or any other competent authority in the same manner as a   148
judgement in the Court of Justice.   149

This contract shall be subject to the law of the country agreed as place of arbitration. 150

Copyright: Norwegian Shipbrokers' Association, Oslo.
Sole distributor in England: Messrs. S. Straker & Sons Ltd. London.
Printed and sold by Halvorsen & Larsen A.s. Oslo.

1) *The name of the Classification Society to be inserted.*
2) *Notes, if any, in the Surveyor's report which are accepted by the Classification Society without qualification are not to be taken into account.*
3) *The place of arbitration to be inserted. If this line is not filled in, it is understood that arbitration will take place in London in accordance with English law.*
4) *If this line is not filled in it is understood that the third Arbitrator shall be appointed by the London Maritime Arbitrators' Association in London.*

Appendix to Memorandum of Agreement code-name **SALEFORM 1987** — dated

8.4 BILL OF SALE

Description

A Bill of Sale, an example of which is the standard Bill of Sale code named Bimcosale, is the legal document that confirms the sale of a vessel in accordance with the terms of the associated Memorandum of Agreement (section 8.3).

Source of document

The Baltic and International Maritime Conference (BIMCO), Copenhagen.

Purpose/use/function

The Bill of Sale provides written evidence of the sale and transference of the vessel named in the associated Memorandum of Agreement.

Legal context

The document forms the legal commitment to the sale of the vessel and is bound by the terms of the Memorandum of Agreement.

Ratifying organizations/countries

The Bill of Sale code named Bimcosale is recommended by BIMCO, Copenhagen.

Procedure

Instructions for completing the form

The document is completed by the shipbroker representing the ship vendor in consultation with the buyer's representative.

Necessary authorization

The document must be duly notarized and certified by a Consul.

Other aspects

It is usual for all the data found in the Bill of Sale to be obtained through numerous discussions and telexes between the two parties. The extent of such negotiations will vary by circumstance but much will depend on the buyer's result of an inspection of the vessel and the bid which follows. The document will be required by the buyer and seller representatives, classification and registration societies/organizations, Banks, Customs, and so on.

If the vessel is to be sold for demolition, a Standard Contract for the Sale of Vessels for Demolition (termed Salescrap '87) is to be used. This can also be obtained from BIMCO.

BILL OF SALE

RECOMMENDED STANDARD BILL OF SALE — CODE NAME: "BIMCOSALE"

1. Seller(s) (state full name, description and address)	2. Buyer(s) (state full name, description and address)

3. Name of Vessel	4. Type of Vessel	5. Port of Registry	6. Call Signs

7. Gross Register Tonnage	8. Net Register Tonnage	9. Date of Memorandum of Agreement

10. Purchase Sum (in figures and in letters)

11. Details of subsisting or outstanding Mortgage(s) or other encumbrances, if any; also state other details, if any, relevant to the sale and transfer of the Vessel

The Seller(s), named in Box 1, who is (are) the Owner(s) of the Vessel described in Boxes 3 to 8, both inclusive, hereby confirm(s) having sold and handed over the said Vessel with everything belonging to her to the Buyer(s), named in Box 2, for the Purchase Sum, as stated in Box 10.
Unless otherwise stated in Box 11, the Seller(s) warrant(s) that the Vessel is free from encumbrances, debts and maritime liens of any kind whatsoever and confirm(s) that the sale and transfer of the Vessel is effected in accordance with Memorandum of Agreement dated as indicated in Box 9.
In consideration of the said Purchase Sum, paid to the Seller(s) by the Buyer(s), the Seller(s) hereby transfer(s) the Vessel to the Buyer(s) so that the Vessel shall hereinafter become his (their) legal property.
IN WITNESS whereof this Bill of Sale has been issued and signed at the place and on the date stated in Box 12 in the presence of the Witness(es) as indicated in Box 13 whose signature(s) has (have) been certified (if required) by the person indicated in Box 14.

(* Space for translation of text)

12. Place and date and signature of Seller(s)

13. The undersigned Witness(es) hereby certifies(y) the correctness of the Seller(s)' signature(s) to this Bill of Sale and the date hereof (state full name, title and address of Witness(es))

14. The undersigned Consul (General) hereby certifies the correctness of the Witness(es)' signature(s) as stated in Box 13

Published by The Baltic and International Maritime Conference (BIMCO), Copenhagen

Printed and sold by Fr. G. Knudtzon Ltd., 55, Toldbodgade, Copenhagen, by authority of The Baltic and International Maritime Conference (BIMCO), Copenhagen

89-18

THE BALTIC AND INTERNATIONAL MARITIME COUNCIL (BIMCO)

STANDARD CONTRACT FOR THE SALE OF VESSELS FOR DEMOLITION

CODE NAME: "SALESCRAP 87"

PART I

1. Place and Date of Contract	

2. Sellers/Place of Business (full name, address & telex number)	3. Buyers/Place of Business (full name, address & telex number)

4. Name of Vessel (also state ex. name)	5. Type of Vessel	6. Built (year and builder's name)	7. Flag

8. Class	9. Register Number	10. Place of Registration	11. GRT/NRT

12. Light Displacement Tonnage (Lightweight) (state whether in metric tons or long tons) (Cl.3)	13. Working Propeller(s) (state number and material)	14. Spare Propeller(s) (state number and material)

15. Spare Tail End Shaft (state no.)	16. Main Engine (type and number)	17. Generator(s) (state number and type)

18. Purchase Price (in figures and letters) (state both lump sum price and equivalent price per ton lightweight; also state currency in which purchase price is payable) (Cl. 4)

(a) Lump sum price

(b) Equivalent price per ton lightweight

(c) Currency in which purchase price payable

19. Deposit (state amount, name and place of bank to which the deposit shall be paid) (Cl. 5)

20. Letter of Credit (Cl. 6)

(a) Number of banking days for establishing Letter of Credit (sub-clause 6.1. of Cl. 6)

(b) Opening Bank (name and place) (sub-clause 6.2. of Cl. 6)

(c) Advising Bank (name and place) (sub-clause 6.2. of Cl. 6)

(d) Expiry Date of Letter of Credit (sub-clause 6.5. of Cl. 6)

continued

21. Vessel's present position (if trading state "now trading"; if laid up state "in lay-up" and place where) (Cl. 7)	22. Voyage (state whether under own power or under tow, as agreed) (Cl. 8)

23. Place of Delivery (also state approximate arrival draft fore and aft in metres or feet) (Cl. 9)
 	
  (a) Place of delivery (sub-clause 9.1. of Cl. 9)
 	
  (b) Approximate arrival draft fore and aft in metres or feet (sub-clause 9.1. of Cl. 9)
	24. Time of Delivery/Cancelling Date (Cl. 10)
	
	  (a) Expected to be ready for delivery between (two dates to be given) (sub-cl. 10.1. of Cl. 10)

25. Advance Notices of Arrival and Delivery (state number of days definite notice of delivery) (Cl. 11)	(b) Cancelling date (sub-cl. 10.1. of Cl. 10)

26. Financial Documentation and Payment (Cl. 13)
 	
  (a) state by whom Bill of Sale shall be legalised (sub-cl. 13.1.(i) of Cl. 13)
 	
  (b) state number of Commercial Invoice (sub-cl. 13.1.(iv) of Cl. 13)
	27. Buyers' Representative(s) (state no. of Representative(s)) (Cl. 19)
	
	28. Buyers' Default (state rate of interest per annum) (Cl. 22)
	
	29. Sellers' Default (state rate of interest per annum) (Cl. 23)

30. Law and arbitration (state 24.1., 24.2. or 24.3. of Cl.24, as agreed; if 24.3. agreed also state place of arbitration) (if Box 30 not filled in 24.1. shall apply) (Cl. 24)

31. Names and Addresses for Notices and other Communications to be given by the Sellers (Cl. 25)	32. Names and Addresses for Notices and other Communications to be given by the Buyers (Cl. 25)

33. Numbers of additional clauses covering special provisions, if agreed

It is mutually agreed between the party named in Box 2 (hereinafter referred to as "the Sellers") and the party named in Box 3 (hereinafter referred to as "the Buyers") that on the date of this Contract the Sellers have sold and the Buyers have bought the Vessel described in PART I hereof and as may be further described in Appendix "A" (hereinafter referred to as "the Vessel") on the terms and conditions contained in this Contract consisting of PART I including additional clauses, if any agreed and stated in Box 33, and PART II as well as APPENDIX "A" as annexed hereto. In the event of a conflict of conditions, the provisions of PART I shall prevail over those of PART II and APPENDIX "A" to the extent of such conflict but no further.

Signature (Sellers)	Signature (Buyers)

Printed and sold by Fr. G. Knudtzons Bogtrykkeri A/S, 55 Toldbodgade, DK-1253 Copenhagen K
by authority of The Baltic and International Maritime Council (BIMCO), Copenhagen

PART II
"SALESCRAP 87" Standard Contract

1. Vessel

On the date of this Contract the Vessel shall be of the description set out in PART I and, if required, as further described in Appendix "A".

2. Outright Sale

2.1. The Vessel has been accepted by the Buyers without inspection and the sale is, therefore, outright and definite and not subject to subsequent inspection.

2.2. The Vessel is sold with all materials, tackle, apparel, stores and spare parts belonging to her as on board at the date of this Contract but excluding items listed in Appendix "A" annexed to this Contract.

2.3. Unless otherwise agreed, any remaining bunkers on board at the time of delivery shall become the Buyers' property.

2.4. The Sellers shall, at the time of delivery, hand to the Buyers all plans, specifications and certificates, or photocopies hereof, as available and whether valid or invalid.

2.5. The Sellers shall have the right to take ashore without compensation the following items: crockery, plate, cutlery, linen and other articles bearing the Sellers' flag or name, as well as library, forms, etc., exclusively for use in the Sellers' vessels. Captain's, Officers' and Crew's personal belongings including slop chest to be excluded from the sale.

2.6. The Sellers are not required to replace such material, spare parts or stores including spare propeller(s) (if any) which may be consumed or taken out of spare and used as replacement prior to delivery, but all replaced spares shall be retained on board and shall become the property of the Buyers.

3. Light Displacement Tonnage (Lightweight)

The Vessel's Light Displacement Tonnage (Lightweight) as stated in Box 12 shall be evidenced by the Builder's capacity plan incorporating deadweight scale (or an authenticated copy hereof) or, in the Sellers' option, a letter from the Builders (or an authenticated copy hereof) or, subject to Buyers' approval, any equivalent evidence of present lightweight of the Vessel confirming same. Such proof shall be delivered by the Sellers to the Buyers latest 10 days after the date of this Contract but latest on delivery whichever is the earlier.

4. Purchase Price

The Purchase Price is the lump sum stated in Box 18 (a) payable in the currency indicated in Box 18 (c), based upon a price per ton lightweight as stated in Box 18 (b) calculated on the basis of the Vessel's lightweight as stated in Box 12. In the event the Vessel's lightweight as stated in Box 12 differs from the evidence as delivered by the Sellers according to Clause 3 hereof, the lump sum stated in Box 18 (a) shall be adjusted with the amount as stated in Box 18 (b) so as to reflect the difference.

5. Deposit

5.1. As a security for the correct fulfilment of this Contract, the Buyers shall pay a Deposit of 10 (ten) per cent. of the Purchase Price with the bank stated in Box 19 in the joint names of the Sellers and Buyers.

5.2. Such Deposit shall be made latest within 3 banking days from the date of this Contract.

5.3. Interest, if any, on such Deposit shall be credited the Buyers.

5.4. Any fees or charges for establishing and holding such Deposit shall be borne equally by the Sellers and the Buyers.

6. Letter of Credit

6.1. The Buyers shall establish by a fully detailed cable or telex a Confirmed Irrevocable At Sight Letter of Credit in a form satisfactory to the Sellers for the full amount of the Purchase Price latest within the number of banking days from the date of this Contract as stated in Box 20(a).

6.2. Such Letter of Credit shall be established by the Buyers with a first class Bank as named in Box 20(b) (hereinafter referred to as "the Opening Bank") under advice to the Bank nominated by the Sellers as named in Box 20(c) (hereinafter referred to as "the Advising Bank").

6.3. Such Letter of Credit shall contain a provision that if the Opening Bank has not within 3 banking days confirmed by telex or cable to the Advising Bank that Notice of Readiness for Delivery has been tendered according to Clause 12.1., the full amount of the Letter of Credit shall be released to the Sellers immediately upon the Sellers' presentation to the Advising Bank of a copy of the Notice of Readiness for Delivery together with the documents listed in sub-clause 13.1.

6.4. All bank charges in connection with the Confirmed Irrevocable Letter of Credit shall be for the Buyers' account except for Advising Bank negotiating charges.

6.5. The expiry date of the Letter of Credit shall not be earlier than the date stated in Box 20(d).

7. Vessel's Present Position

The Vessel's present position is as indicated in Box 21.

8. Voyage

8.1. The Vessel shall proceed to the Place of Delivery either under her own power or under tow, as agreed in Box 22.

8.2. The Sellers shall have the right either to let the Vessel proceed in ballast to the Place of Delivery or, in their option, to proceed thereto with cargo on board up to the Vessel's full capacity, via port or ports whether en route or not.

9. Place of Delivery

9.1. The Vessel shall be delivered by the Sellers to the Buyers safely afloat, free of cargo and (except for tank vessels) with hatches closed and with the approximate arrival draft stated in Box 23(b) at the place stated in Box 23(a) (hereinafter referred to as "the Place of Delivery").

9.2. If, on the Vessel's arrival, the Place of Delivery is inaccessible for any reason whatsoever including but not limited to port congestion, the Vessel shall be delivered and taken over by the Buyers as near thereto as she may safely get at a safe and accessible berth or at a safe anchorage which shall be designated by the Buyers always provided that such berth or anchorage shall be subject to the approval of the Sellers and the Master. Such approval shall not be unreasonably withheld. If the Buyers fail to nominate such place within 24 hours of arrival, the place at which it is customary for vessels to wait shall constitute the Place of Delivery.

9.3. The delivery of the Vessel according to the provisions of sub-clause 9.2. shall constitute a full performance of the Sellers' obligations according to sub-clause 9.1. and all other terms and conditions of this Contract shall apply as if delivery had taken place according to sub-clause 9.1.

10. Time of Delivery/Cancelling Date

10.1. The Vessel is expected to be ready for delivery between the dates (both inclusive) stated in Box 24 (a) but latest on the date stated in Box 24 (b) (hereinafter referred to as "the cancelling date").

10.2.(i). Should the Sellers anticipate with reasonable certainty that the Vessel will not be ready for delivery by the cancelling date, they shall notify the Buyers hereof without delay stating the probable date of the Vessel's readiness for delivery. Upon receipt of such notification the Buyers shall have the option either to cancel the Contract according to Clause 23 or to postpone the cancelling date.

10.2.(ii). If the Buyers decide to maintain the Contract and postpone the cancelling date or if the Buyers do not within 4 working days of receipt of the Sellers' notification declare their option to cancel the Contract according to Clause 23, the fourth running day after the new date of readiness for delivery indicated in the Sellers' notification shall be regarded as a new cancelling date and shall be substituted for the cancelling date stipulated in Box 24(b).

10.3. If the Buyers elect to maintain the Contract, all the terms and conditions of this Contract including the notification procedures laid down in Clause 12 shall remain in full force and effect.

11. Advance Notice of Arrival and Delivery

The Sellers shall keep the Buyers fully informed about the Vessel's position and about any alteration in expected time of arrival and shall also give to the Buyers the number of days definite notice of delivery as agreed in Box 25.

12. Notice of Readiness for Delivery

12.1. When the Vessel is ready for delivery, the Sellers or their Agents shall give to the Buyers and to the Opening Bank a written Notice of Readiness for Delivery. Such Notice of Readiness for Delivery shall be countersigned by Lloyd's Agents at the Place of Delivery.

12.2. In the event of the Vessel being a tank vessel, the Notice of Readiness for Delivery shall be accompanied by a valid Certificate issued by a competent authority or person acceptable to the Buyers certifying that all cargo tanks, cofferdams and pump rooms are gas-free, safe for men and fire, and substantially free of residues, slops and sludges and such Certificate shall be deemed to be a full compliance and discharge of the Sellers' obligations with respect to the cargo tanks, cofferdams and pump rooms. Such Certificate shall be provided by the Sellers at their cost.

13. Financial Documentation and Payment

13.1. The Sellers shall furnish the Advising Bank with the following documents:

(i) Legal Bill of Sale stating that the said Vessel is free from all encumbrances and maritime liens or any other debts whatsoever, duly notarially attested and legalised by the Consul or other competent authority stated in Box 26(a);

(ii) Certificate of Ownership issued by the competent authorities of the Flag State of the Vessel;

(iii) Certificate stating that the Vessel is free from registered encumbrances;

(iv) Commercial Invoice in the number stated in Box 26(b) signed by the Sellers, setting out the Vessel's particulars;

(v) Certificate of Deletion of the Vessel from the Vessel's Registry or, in the Sellers' option, a Written Undertaking by the Sellers to promptly, and latest within four weeks after the Purchase Sum has been fully paid and the Vessel has been delivered, to effect deletion from the Vessel's Registry and that a Certificate of Deletion will thereupon be furnished to the Buyers;

(vi) A written authorization from the Sellers to release to the Buyers the Deposit established by the Buyers according to Clause 5;

(vii) A Written Undertaking by the Sellers to instruct the Master or their Agents by cable or telex to release and physically deliver the Vessel to the Buyers.

13.2. Immediately upon the tendering of Notice of Readiness for Delivery according to Clause 12.1., the Opening Bank shall confirm by telex or cable to the Advising Bank that the Notice of Readiness for Delivery has been received whereafter the full amount of the Letter of Credit shall be released to the Sellers provided that the Advising Bank has been furnished with the documents listed in sub-clause 13.1.

If such confirmation by telex or cable has not been given by the Opening Bank to the Advising Bank within 3 banking days after the Sellers' Notice of Readiness of Delivery has been tendered, the full amount of the Letter of Credit shall be released to the Sellers immediately upon the Sellers' presentation to the Advising Bank of a copy of the Notice of Readiness for Delivery and the documents listed in sub-clause 13.1.

14. Condition on Delivery

14.1. The Vessel with everything belonging to her shall be at the Sellers' risk and expense until she is delivered to the Buyers.

14.2. Notwithstanding the provisions of sub-clause 14.1., the Vessel with everything belonging to her shall be delivered and taken over by the Buyers substantially in the same condition as she was on the date of this Contract after which the Sellers shall have no responsibility for possible faults or deficiencies of any description.

15. Funnel Mark, etc. 180

As soon as possible after delivery the Buyers undertake to obliterate the 181
name of the Vessel and funnel mark. 182

16. Encumbrances and Maritime Liens, etc. 183

The Sellers warrant that the Vessel, at the time of delivery, is charter-free 184
and free from all encumbrances and maritime liens or any other debts 185
whatsoever. Should any claims which have been incurred prior to the time 186
of delivery be made against the Vessel, the Sellers hereby undertake to 187
indemnify the Buyers against all consequences of such claims. 188

17. Taxes, Dues and Charges, etc. 189

17.1. All taxes, dues, duties (including import duties) and charges imposed 190
upon the Vessel at the Place of Delivery and notarial and/or consular and/or 191
other charges or expenses connected with the purchase and import of the 192
Vessel at the Place of Delivery shall be borne by the Buyers. 193
17.2. All taxes, dues, duties and charges, including notarial and/or 194
consular and/or other charges, or expenses connected with the closing of 195
the Sellers' Register, shall be for the Sellers' account. 196

18. Deratisation Exemption Certificate 197

The Vessel shall be delivered by the Sellers with a valid Deratisation 198
Exemption Certificate. 199

19. Buyers' Representative(s) 200

The Sellers agree to allow the Buyers to place the number of 201
Representative(s) stated in Box 27 on board the Vessel on her arrival at the 202
Place of Delivery. 203
Whilst on board the Vessel, such Representative(s) shall be at the sole risk, 204
liability and expense of the Buyers and the Buyers shall indemnify the 205
Sellers for any claims and damage in this respect. The Buyers' 206
Representative(s) must not interfere with the operation of the Vessel. 207

20. Purpose of Sale 208

20.1. The Vessel is sold for the purpose of breaking-up only and the Buyers 209
undertake that they will neither trade the Vessel for their own account nor 210
sell the Vessel to a third party for any purpose other than breaking-up. The 211
Buyers shall procure that this obligation is made a term of any and every 212
subsequent agreement for the resale of the Vessel. 213
20.2. Non-compliance with the provisions contained in sub-clause 20.1. 214
shall amount to a breach of the contract and the Buyers shall be liable to pay 215
to the Sellers 20 (twenty) per cent. of the Purchase Price as liquidated 216
damages resulting from such a breach. 217
20.3. The Buyers shall, in due course, furnish the Sellers with a Certificate 218
stating that the Vessel has been totally demolished. 219

21. Exemptions 220

The Sellers shall be under no liability to the Buyers if the Vessel should 221
become an actual, constructive or compromised total loss before delivery, 222
or if delivery of the Vessel by the cancelling date should otherwise be 223
prevented or delayed due to outbreak of war, restraint of Government, 224
Princes, Rulers or People of any Nation or the United Nations, Act of God, or 225
any other cause beyond the Sellers' control. If damage is sustained by the 226
Vessel before delivery for any cause whatsoever or howsoever arising and if 227
the estimated cost of repairs to enable the Vessel to proceed to the Place of 228
Delivery would exceed 10 (ten) per cent. of the Purchase Price stated in Box 229
18, the Sellers shall not be bound to repair the Vessel but shall be entitled to 230
treat delivery as having thereby been prevented and shall similarly be under 231
no liability to the Buyers. Where delivery shall become impossible or 232
prevented as aforesaid the Deposit as well as the Letter of Credit, if 233
established, shall be returned to the Buyers forthwith. 234

22. Buyers' Default 235

22.1. Should the Deposit not be paid in accordance with the provisions of 236
Clause 5, the Sellers shall have the right to cancel this Contract, and they 237
shall be entitled to claim compensation for their losses and for all expenses 238
incurred together with interest at the rate per annum stated in Box 28. 239
22.2. If the Buyers fail to establish the Letter of Credit in accordance with 240
the provisions of Clause 6 or should the Purchase Sum not be paid in the 241
manner provided for in this Contract, the Sellers shall have the right to 242
cancel this Contract, in which case the amount deposited together with 243
interest earned, if any, shall be forfeited to the Sellers. If the Deposit does 244
not cover the Sellers' losses, they shall be entitled to claim further 245
compensation for their losses and for all expenses together with interest at 246
the rate per annum stated in Box 28. 247

23. Sellers' Default 248

If the Sellers fail to execute a legal transfer or to deliver the Vessel with 249
everything belonging to her in the manner and at the latest on the date 250
specified in Box 24(b), the Buyers shall have the right to cancel this 251
Contract, in which case the Deposit in full together with the Letter of Credit, if 252
established, shall be returned to the Buyers together with interest at the rate 253
per annum stated in Box 29. The Sellers shall make due compensation for 254
the losses caused to the Buyers by failure to execute a legal transfer or to 255
deliver the Vessel in the manner and at the latest on the date specified in 256
Box 24(b), if such are due to the proven negligence of the Sellers. 257

24. Law and Arbitration 258

*) 24.1. This Contract shall be governed by English law and any dispute 259
arising out of this Contract shall be referred to arbitration in London, one 260
arbitrator being appointed by each party, in accordance with the Arbitration 261
Acts 1950 and 1979 or any statutory modification or re-enactment thereof 262
for the time being in force. On the receipt by one party of the nomination in 263
writing of the other party's arbitrator, that party shall appoint their arbitrator 264
within fourteen days, failing which the decision of the single Arbitrator 265
appointed shall apply. If two Arbitrators properly appointed shall not agree 266
they shall appoint an umpire whose decision shall be final. 267
*) 24.2. This Contract shall be governed by U.S. Law and all disputes arising 268
out of this Contract shall be arbitrated at New York in the following manner: 269
One arbitrator is to be appointed by each of the parties herein and a third by 270
the two so chosen. Their decision or that of any two of them shall be final, 271
and for the purpose of enforcing any award, this agreement may be made a 272
rule of the court. The Arbitrators shall be commercial men. Such Arbitration 273
is to be conducted in accordance with the rules of the Society of Maritime 274
Arbitrators, Inc., New York, as currently amended. 275
A sole arbitrator may be appointed, if so desired by both parties. 276
Either party may call for arbitration by service of notice upon the other. If the 277
other party does not appoint its arbitrator within fourteen days of such 278
written notice, then the first moving party shall have the right, without further 279
notice, to appoint a second arbitrator, with the same force and effect as if 280
said second arbitrator had been appointed by the other party. 281
*) 24.3. Any dispute arising out of this Contract shall be referred to arbitration 282
at the place indicated in Box 30, subject to the law and procedures 283
applicable there. 284
24.4. If Box 30 in Part I is not filled in, sub-clause 24.1. of this Clause shall 285
apply. 286
*) 24.1., 24.2. and 24.3. are alternatives; indicate alternative agreed in Box 30. 287

25. Names and Addresses for Notices and Other Communications 288

All notices and communications shall be in writing or by cable, telex or 289
telegram and shall, unless otherwise provided for in this Contract, be made 290
by the Sellers, respectively the Buyers, to the addresses stated in Boxes 31 291
and 32. 292

(i) Further description of the Vessel (if required):

(ii) Items excluded from the sale:

9 Road transport: International

9.1 INTRODUCTION

Some 80 % of consumer goods exported to continental Europe from the United Kingdom are conveyed by international road transport, usually under a document known as the CMR Consignment Note. CMR is the international convention concerning the carriage of goods by road that came into force in the United Kingdom in 1967. It is embodied in the Carriage of Goods by Road Act 1965 and amended by the Carriage by Air and Road Act 1979. It is aligned to the UN (ECE) layout key and can be used on aligned documentation systems. It permits the carriage of goods by road under one consignment under a common code of conditions applicable to 26 countries, primarily in Europe. The statutory provisions are embodied in the Carriage of Goods by Road Act 1965.

The worldwide transportation group TNT Ipec have developed an alternative consignment note – the exclusive (TNT Ipec) Consignment Note for the carriage of goods, which combines an air freight/sea freight leg with an overland leg to and from airports/seaports.

It is the practice for road trailer operators to instruct their drivers to complete an Equipment Condition report on each occasion when the trailer is used, so that the condition of the equipment can be monitored. The document enables the condition of the equipment to be monitored on a regular journey basis for insurance and legal purposes. It also places an onus on the driver for accountability in regard to the management of the vehicle in international transits.

The equipment handover agreement enables the operator to hand over the container from one carrier to another, such as road to rail, or road to ship, and thereby to monitor the container's condition throughout its combined transport journey. Any damage would be recorded in the document.

9.2 CMR INTERNATIONAL CONSIGNMENT NOTE

Description

A CMR Consignment Note must be carried on all hire and reward journeys involving international road transit, to comply with statutory requirements.

Source of document

The document is issued by the Agent or International Road Haulier and forms evidence of the terms of contract.

Purpose/use/function

The CMR International Consignment Note is a contract of carriage (of goods). It is not a negotiable nor a transferable document or a document of title, but forms a receipt of the cargo.

Legal context

The Convention on the Contract for the International Carriage of Goods by Road (CMR) came into force in the United Kingdom in 1967. The relevant legislation was enacted in the Carriage of Goods by Road Act 1965 and amended by the Carriage by Air and Road Act 1979. Chapter 7 deals with the substance of this law which governs the responsibilities and liabilities of the parties to a contract for the international carriage of goods by road.

Ratifying organizations/countries

The CMR convention is applicable in 28 (mainly European) countries.

Procedure

Instructions for completing the form

The Consignment Note must contain the following particulars: the date when and the place where it is made out; the names and addresses of the sender; the carrier and the consignee; the place and date of taking over the goods and the place designated for delivery; the ordinary description of the nature of the goods and the method of packing and, in the case of dangerous goods, their generally recognized description; the number of packages and their special marks and numbers; the gross weight of the goods or their quantity otherwise expressed; charges relating to the carriage; the requisite instructions for Customs and other formalities; and a statement that the carriage is subject, notwithstanding any clause to the contrary, to the provisions of the CMR Convention.

Further, the Consignment Note must contain the following particulars where applicable: a statement that transhipment is not allowed; the charges which the sender undertakes to pay; the amount of 'cash on delivery' charges; a declaration of the value of the goods; a declaration of the amount representing any special interest in delivery; the sender's instructions to the carrier regarding insurance of the goods; the agreed time limit for the carriage; a list of the documents handed to the carrier; where the carrier has no reasonable means of checking the accuracy of the statements in the Consignment Note as to the number of packages and their marks and numbers, or as to the apparent condition of the goods and their packaging, the carrier must enter his reservations in the Consignment Note specifying the grounds on which they are based; and where the sender requires the carrier to check the gross weight of the goods or their quantity otherwise expressed on the contents of the packages, the carrier must enter the results of such checks; and for any agreement that open unchecked vehicles may be used for the carriage of the goods involving custom formalities. The parties may enter any other useful particulars in the Consignment Note including successive carriers involving names of hauliers and reference numbers. All weights/volumes to be in metric units.

Necessary authorization

The contract of carriage found in the CMR Consignment Note is established when it is completed by the sender and carrier with the appropriate signatures/stamp recorded on it.

Number and allocation of copies

The senders and the carrier are entitled respectively to the first and third copies of the Consignment Note, and the second copy must accompany the goods.

If the goods have to be loaded in different vehicles, or are of different kinds, or are divided into different lots, either party has the right to require a separate Consignment Note to be made out in respect of such vehicle or each kind or lot of goods.

Checklist of what should accompany each copy

Documents to be attached: commercial invoices, dangerous goods notes, SAD, insurance cover notes, customs documentation, certificates of origin, and so on. The number of documents will vary with country of destination.

Discrepancies (i.e. likely errors) and their consequences

The sender is liable for all expenses, loss and damage sustained by the carrier by reason of the inaccuracy or inadequacy of certain specified particulars which the consignment note must contain, or by reason of the inaccuracy or inadequacy of any other particulars or instructions given by the sender.

The carrier is liable for all expenses, loss and damage sustained by the person entitled to dispose of the goods as a result of the omission of the statement that the contract is subject to the CMR convention.

For the purposes of the CMR convention the carrier is responsible for the acts and omissions of the carrier's agents and servants and any other persons whose services the carrier uses for the performance of the carriage as long as those agents, servants or other persons are acting within the scope of their employment.

There is a duty on the carrier as follows:

1 to check the accuracy of the statements in the Consignment Note as to the number of packages and their marks and numbers, and the apparent condition of the goods and their packaging;

2 if the sender so requires, the carrier is to check the gross weight of the goods or their quantity otherwise expressed on the contents of the packages;
3 to check the statement that the contract is subject to the CMR convention is properly included in the Consignment Note.

The sender is responsible for the accuracy and adequacy of documents and information which the sender must either attach to the Consignment Note or place at the carrier's disposal for the purposes of Customs or other formalities which have to be completed before delivery of the goods.

There is a duty on the sender:

1 to ensure that the goods are properly packed;
2 in the case of dangerous goods, to inform the carrier of the exact nature of the danger and indicate, if necessary, the precautions to be taken;
3 to ensure the accuracy and adequacy of certain specified particulars which the Consignment Note must contain and of any other particulars or instructions given by the sender to the carrier.

Further information

For the great majority of international road transport consignments the method of payment is the open account terms.

A bank will normally only make an advance against goods covered by CMR International Consignment Note if the goods are consigned to a bank in the buyer's country and only to be released under payment by the buyer.

LETTRE DE VOITURE INTERNATIONALE (CMR) INTERNATIONAL CONSIGNMENT NOTE

SF 130269

1 Sender (Name, Address, Country) Expéditeur (Nom, Adresse, Pays)	2 Customs Reference/Status Référence/désignation pour mise en douane
	3 Senders/Agents Reference Référence de l'expéditeur/de l'agent

4 Consignee (Name, Address, Country) Destinataire (Nom, Addresse, Pays)	5 Carrier (Name, Address, Country) Transporteur (Nom, Adresse, Pays)

6 Place & date of taking over the goods (place, country, date) Lieu et date de la prise en charge des marchandises (Lieu, pays, date)	7 Successive Carriers Transporteurs successifs

8 Place designated for delivery of goods (place, country)
Lieu prévu pour la livraison des marchandises (lieu, pays)

This carriage is subject, notwithstanding any clause to the contrary, to the Convention on the Contract for the International Carriage of Goods by Road (CMR)
Ce transport est soumis nonobstant toute clause contraire à la Convention Relative au Contrat de Transport International de Marchandises par Route (CMR)

9 Marks & Nos; No & Kind of Packages; Description of Goods* Marques et Nos, No et nature des colis, Désignation des marchandises*	10 Gross weight (kg) Poids Brut (kg)	11 Volume (m³) Cubage (m³)

12 Carriage Charges Prix de transport	13 Senders Instructions for Customs, etc... Instructions de l'Expéditeur (optional)

14 Reservations Réserves	15 Documents attached Documents Annexés (optional)
	16 Special agreements Conventions particulières (optional)

17 Goods Received/Marchandises Recues	18 Signature of Carrier/Signature du transporteur	19 Company completing this note Société émettrice
		20 Place and Date; Signature Lieu et date; Signature

9.3 TNT IPEC CONSIGNMENT NOTE

Description

A TNT Ipec Consignment Note is a seven-part combined transport document for the carriage of goods and is used exclusively by TNT Ipec. It combines an air freight/sea freight leg with an overland leg to and from airports/seaports as required using TNT transport modes.

Source of document

TNT Ipec transportation group. It is exclusive to their organization.

Purpose/use/function

The TNT Ipec Consignment Note contains all the necessary information for the carriage/clearance/delivery of any specific consignment by TNT Ipec Air Freight European Services from the consignor to the consignee.

Legal context

Carriage under the TNT Ipec Consignment Note is governed by the Uniform Rules for a Combined Transport Document, Publication 298 of the International Chamber of Commerce. Carriage by road is governed by the Convention on the Contract of the International Carriage of Goods by Road (CMR, Geneva, May 1956 and Protocol of 5 July 1978, Geneva). Carriage by sea is governed by the International Convention for the Unification of certain rules of law relating to Bills of Lading as amended by the protocol signed in Brussels on 23 February 1968 (Hague Visby Rules). Carriage by air is governed by the Warsaw Convention of 1929 as amended by the protocol signed in The Hague on 29 September 1955. In the Republic of Ireland international carriage by road is subject to CMR convention only.

Ratifying organizations/countries

Austria, Belgium, Denmark, Finland, France, West Germany, Republic of Ireland, Italy, Luxembourg, the Netherlands, Norway, Sweden, Switzerland and the United Kingdom.

Procedure

Number and allocation of copies

1 The top copy – copy number one – is the exporter's certificate of shipment. It is termed an invoice attachment and the following details are added to this copy and posted to the sender attached to the TNT Ipec invoice to produce to the bank as proof of shipment/exportation:
   (i) vessel – name of ship or flight details
   (ii) date of sailing/flight and schedule
   (iii) Customs documents details;
2 The second copy is the export country invoice work sheet. It is termed the export account copy;

3 The third copy is the import country invoice work sheet. It is termed the import account copy. It is retained by the courier – in common with the second copy – and special note is taken of the sending/receiving depot computer codes and any special arrangements regarding invoicing;

4 The fourth copy is the receiver's administrative copy. It is termed an invoice attachment. This copy will permit the receiver to relate to the consignment within his or her 'goods received' department and accounts again by using the Consignment Note number. It will be attached to either the courier invoice or the Customs document;

5 The fifth copy is the proof of delivery document. It is termed the signature copy on the Consignment Note. At the time the goods are delivered a signature must be obtained from the receiver;

6 The sixth copy is the receiver's copy. It is termed the depot copy;

7 The seventh copy is the sender's copy. It is termed the sender's copy on the Consignment Note. It enables the shipper to relate the consignment to anywhere within the TNT Ipec computerized international distribution network by using the Consignment Note number such as when tracing the routing of the goods and searching for any misdirected consignments.

Other aspects

It must be stressed that the TNT document is exclusive to their organization. It would be accompanied by the requisite documentation depending on destination including commercial invoice, insurance certificate, certificate of origin, SAD, and so on.

Sender address / country Expéditeur adresse / pays Absender Anschrift / Land Atzender adres / land **1**	Receiver address / country Destinataire adresse / pays Empfänger Anschrift / Land Ontvanger adres / land **2**
TNT Ipec Netherlands B.V. Rivierweg 12, 6921 PZ Duiven, Holland. Postal code / Code postal / Postleitzahl / Postkode	Mr Alan E Branch, Dept Of Business and Managment Studies, C/O Basingstoke Technical College, Worting Rd,Basingstoke RG21 1TN. Postal code / Code postal / Postleitzahl / Postkode

8, 6, 3, 4, 7, 0   Tel no

Collection address Adresse d'enlèvement Abholadresse Afhaaladres **3**	Delivery address Adresse de livraison Ablieferadresse Afleveradres **4**
Postal code **As Above** Code postal Postleitzahl Postkode	Postal code **As Above** Code postal Postleitzahl Postkode

Delivery instructions / Conditions de livraison / Leiferbedingungen / Leveringskondities **5**	Service required / Service souhaité / Service gewünscht / Service gewenst **6**	Sending depot
Free domicile cleared / Franco domicile dédouané / Frei Haus verzollt / Franco huis ingeklaard ☐ Ex - works / Départ usine / Ab Werk / Af fabriek ☐	Before 9 a.m. / Avant 09.00 / 09.00 Zustellung / Voor 09.00 ☐ Saturday delivery / Livraison le samedi / Samstag - Zustellung / Aflevering op Zaterdag ☐ Desk to Desk ☐	3 4 1 Receiving depot 6 2 5

Special instructions Instructions spéciales Spezielle Instruktionen Speciale instructies **7**	Do you require TNT Ipec to insure? Souhaitez vous que TNT Ipec assure votre envoi? Transportversicherung gewünscht? Wilt u dat TNT Ipec verzekert? **8**	Receivers VAT / TVA / BTW number No TVA / VAT / BTW du destinataire MwSt / EUST. Nummer des Empfängers BTW / VAT / TVA nummer van de ontvanger **9**
☐ Deliver Before (9 AM)	Yes / Oui / Ja ☐	

	Currency Monnaie Währung Valuta	Value for insurance Valeur à assurer Versicherungswert Verzekerde waarde	Currency Monnaie Währung Valuta	Invoice value Valeur facture Rechnungswert Faktuurwaarde **10**
	DFL	9,000.00	DFL	9,000.00

Statistical No. No. statistique douane Statistiknummer Statistieknummer **11a**	Marks Marques Markierung Merken **b**	Number Nombre col Anzahl Aantal **c**	Packing Emballage Verpackung Verpakking **d**	Description of the goods Nature de la marchandise Inhalt Omschrijving van de goederen **e**	Weight kg Poids kg Gewicht kg Gewicht kg **f**
4901 0010	Addressd	1	ENV	Printed Matter	1 Kilo

Your reference no Votre no de référence Ihre Referenz Uw referentienummer **12**	Cubic m³ Cubage m³	Volume m³	Payweight/Poids taxable/Zahlendes Gewicht Betalend gewicht (kg)
	21 cm x 19 cm x 17 cm = 0.006		1 Kilo

Conditions of carriage in the Republic of Ireland: International carriage by road is subject to CMR-Convention only. The liability stated in article 23-3 is equivalent to 8.33 SDR as defined by the International Monetary Fund and shall never exceed IR£ 7.00 per kilogram.

All signatories hereto have read and understood the conditions on this document governing this contract and agree to be bound by them, including the conditions on the reverse side.
Tous signataires de la présente ont lu et compris les conditions régissant le présent contrat, et ils conviennent de s'y engager, y compris les conditions au verso.
Alle Vertragsunterzeichner haben die für diesen Vertrag verbindlichen Bestimmungen gelesen und verstanden und vereinbaren durch sie gebunden zu sein, einschließlich Konditionen umseitig.
Alle hierin genoemde ondertekenaars hebben de voorwaarden die op dit contract betrekking hebben gelezen en begrepen en zij gaan er mee akkoord hieraan gebonden te zijn, inclusief de voorwaarden op de achterzijde.

MOST IMPORTANT
Follow instructions in relation to DANGEROUS GOODS on reverse side of this consignment note.
EXTREMEMENT IMPORTANT
Les indications au sujet de MARCHANDISES DANGE-REUSES, mentionnées au verso de la lettre de voiture, doivent être observées.
WICHTIG
Bei GEFAHRGÜTERN den Anweisungen auf der Rück-seite dieses Frachtbrieles folgen.
ZEER BELANGRIJK
Bij gevarengoed zie instructies ommezijde.

Print name of signatory **14**
M. JAGGARD
Signature of sender
M. [signature]   16.09.87
Carriers signature / Signature du transporteur
Untershrift des Frachtführers / Handtekening van de vervoerder

[clock image] Date / Datum ...... / ...... /

Full names and addresses of head offices on this page.
Vous trouvez les noms et adresses complets des sièges principaux à cette page.
Anschriften der Zentralverwaltungen auf dieser Seite.
Volledige namen en adressen van de hoofdkantoren op dit blad.

9.4 EQUIPMENT CONDITION FORM

Description

An Equipment Condition Form is a document which many (road) trailer operators require their drivers to complete on each occasion when they use the trailer. It enables the Road hauliers to record/monitor the condition of the equipment on each journey and highlight any malpractices.

Source of document

A road trailer operator, e.g. LEP Transport Ltd.

Purpose/use/function

The completed form enables the condition of the equipment to be carefully monitored, and identifies the situation/driver etc. when the trailer is damaged to enable repairs to be effected quickly together with other necessary measures. Also useful for insurance claim purposes.

Other aspects

This document is becoming more important as a management aid to monitor transit performance, quality of equipment, equipment reliability, insurance claim role, equipment utilization, equipment route analysis and so on. It places on the driver improved accountability of performance and quickly establishes malpractice regarding cargo stowage, overloading, accident-prone drivers and the suitability of the equipment for particular commodities and routes.

LEP TRANSPORT LTD.

EQUIPMENT CONDITION

Trailer Number

Collected from		Dropped at	
Date	Time	Date	Time

NOTE POSITION OF DAMAGE | **NOTE POSITION OF DAMAGE**

Front

Offside (from rear)

Rear

Near Side (from rear)

Front

Offside (from rear)

Rear

Near Side (from rear)

Lights/Lenses		Lights/Lenses	
Couplings		Couplings	
Landing Gear		Landing Gear	
Tyres	Spare Yes / No	Tyres	Spare Yes / No
Tilt Boards (missing)		Tilt Boards (missing)	
Sheets (number and condition)		Sheets (number and condition)	
Comments		Comments	

Driver's Signature ....

9.5 EQUIPMENT HANDOVER AGREEMENT

Description

This document is used by container operators to record the condition of the container throughout its transit and to identify any damage sustained to resolve any subsequent claim made in connection with the container and/or its contents.

Source of document

P&O Containers Ltd (previously OCL). It is available from other container operators.

Purpose/use/function

It is used primarily to ensure when the container transfer takes place from one carrier to another, the condition of the equipment is recorded. This would be required as evidence of the responsible carrier for the damage including its contents and thereby used for any claims purposes.

Legal context

The document would be reasonable evidence of any circumstances/carriers identity for any claim processed by the container operator or the shippers of the contents.

Other aspects

The need for management to record the condition of the container throughout its transit is paramount as a means to ensure the equipment is maintained in good condition. It provides data on the frequency and location of damage and the location and responsible carrier. Also it enables transit tests to be conducted regularly to ensure quality of service is maintained and where damage is incurred remedial measures can be taken quickly to prevent a recurrence. This can extend to using a different type of container, improving transhipment equipment, developing better cargo stowage and finally improving the training of personnel.

P&O Containers

P&O Containers (UK Agencies) Ltd.

EQUIPMENT HANDOVER AGREEMENT
SUBJECT TO THE CONDITIONS STATED OVERLEAF

058446

Between the Company and:	Party to be charged if different:

Handover to: (Customer Representative)	Reg. No:	P&OCL (UK) Office:	Place of Handover:	P&OCL (UK) Signature:

OUT

Container Number	C'Base				For Freightliners			Trailer No.	20'	40'	
	Imp FCL	MT	20'	40'	F'liner Origin	Berth	Gross Weight				

Lift Required YES/NO

Is driver taking Equipment covered by another permit into Containerbase YES/NO

FRONT — REAR / FRONT
LEFT SIDE — RIGHT SIDE
FRONT — REAR / FRONT
ROOF — UNDERSIDE
FRONT — INTERNAL — REAR

DAMAGE: List all details of damage and mark on the appropriate plan. If no damage enter "none"

Date/Time Out

The condition of the Equipment is as indicated above:

For the Company

The Equipment above is received in good order except where noted:

For Customer

Received From:	Reg. No.	Place of Handover:	Freightliner Signature for Equipment

IN

Container (status below) and trailer as above   YES/NO

Container Number	C'Base				For Freightliners						Trailer No.	20'	40'	
	Exp FCL	MT	20'	40'	Voy.	F'liner Dest	Gross Weight	Berth	Dest. Port	Haz/Special				

TO
Remain on Trailer
Be off Loaded to Stack
Be off Loaded to Trailer(s)

FRONT — REAR / FRONT
LEFT SIDE — RIGHT SIDE
FRONT — REAR / FRONT
ROOF — UNDERSIDE
FRONT — INTERNAL — REAR

DAMAGE: List all details of damage and mark on the appropriate plan If no damage enter "none"

Date/Time In

The condition of the Equipment indicated above:

For Customer

The Equipment above is received in good order and condition

UK 140A (4/88) **TO BE RETAINED BY THE CUSTOMER**

For the Company

10 Shipboard certificates

10.1 INTRODUCTION

To comply with statutory obligations the ship's master is required to have full details of cargo conveyed on a particular voyage and this is found in a cargo manifest. It is required by Customs personnel.

To accord with the provisions of the International Convention for the Safety of Life at Sea, 1974, held under the auspices of the International Maritime Organization, a number of statutory ship surveys are undertaken periodically and certificates issued by maritime Government surveyors or on their behalf by a Ship Classification Society, e.g. Lloyd's Register of Shipping. Examples of certificates issued under these provisions are the Cargo Ship Safety Construction Certificate, the Cargo Ship Safety Equipment Certificate, and the Cargo Ship Safety Radiotelegraphy Certificate.

The function of the Ship Classification Societies is to lay down standards for ship construction and maintenance and to survey and classify vessels. The societies are completely independent and are staffed by engineers, naval architects and other professionals. Membership is voluntary. To show that a vessel has been classified the Ship Classification Society issues an appropriate certificate, e.g. Certificate of Class (Special Periodical Survey Motor Tanker Machinery) (Classification; LMC); Certificate of Class (Special Periodical Survey Motor Tanker Hull and Equipment) (Classification: + 100 A1 oil tanker); Certificate of Class (Highest classification: + 100 A1 + LMC oil tanker).

Where confirmation is required that a vessel continues in a class previously assigned by a society, a letter may be issued by the society to serve as a Certificate of Confirmation of Class.

A Declaration of Age (of a ship) certificate may be issued by a society when requested. Ship Classification Societies are usually happy to give such information on vessels registered with them.

In the interests of maintaining adequate safety standards, vessels are subject to statutory specific construction and survey provisions. These are broadly laid down by the International Maritime Organization at various conventions and later ratified by maritime Governments in an attempt to adopt worldwide standard or unified conditions of ship construction, survey or maintenance, and operation, including crew manning levels and their certification. The International Load Line Convention, for example, was held in 1966. Under its provisions the Ship Classification Societies carry out surveys and issue International Load Line Certificates (1966). This is an important measure for sustaining adequate safety standards through the operation of well-maintained and equipped vessels.

10.2 CARGO MANIFEST

Description

For a merchant ship it is obligatory to complete a Cargo Manifest, which is an inventory of cargo on board. The Manifest gives the details of the vessel, the voyage, cargo description, Bill of Lading/Sea Waybill/CMR details, name/ address of shipper and consignee, weight of cargo and any marks and numbers.

Source of document

It is compiled by the shipowner at the commencement of each voyage and required by Customs to clear the cargo through Customs prior to the vessel leaving port.

Purpose/use/function

The document is dispatched to the destination port to notify the consignees of their expected cargo arrival time and to facilitate cargo discharge arrangements thereby enabling the importer's Agent to obtain all the requisite documents for early Customs clearance and onward dispatch to the consignee's address.

Legal context

The document is mandatory as part of ship's papers held on a mercantile vessel and is required to be made available to personnel authorized to see them, such as Customs, Police and so on.

Other aspects

The cargo manifest is often a computerized document in modern ship operation and compiled from all the cargo data found on Bills of Lading and consignment notes including the Sea Waybill and CMR/CIM documents. It also records any cargo regarded as non-commercial including ship's stores etc. The cargo description must accord with that found on the Bill of Lading, consignment data and Sea Waybill. Copies are sent to destination ports, ship's agents and various departments in shipowner's offices and Customs.

Noviero 6-78

Sheet No. ....

M/V .... Voy .... Master ....

Sailed from .... on ....

to ....

CARGO MANIFEST

B/L	SHIPPER	CONSIGNEE	MARKS & NUMBER	PKGS		DESCRIPTION	WEIGHT KOS
				No.	Quality		

10.3 CARGO SHIP SAFETY CONSTRUCTION CERTIFICATE

Description

A Cargo Ship Safety Construction Certificate records the results of a statutory ship survey undertaken every five years by a maritime Government surveyor, or on his/her behalf by a Ship Classification Society, e.g. Lloyd's Register of Shipping.

Source of document

The Cargo Ship Safety Construction Certificate is issued by a Ship Classification Society, e.g. Lloyd's Register of Shipping.

Purpose/use/function

To certify where applicable among other requirements that the condition of the hull, machinery and equipment of the ship surveyed are satisfactory in accord with the classification requirements/rules.

Legal context

The survey is carried out and the Certificate issued in accordance with the provisions of the International Convention for the Safety of Life at Sea, 1974, conducted by the Government surveyor. Similar arrangements apply in regard to other Maritime Government legislation which reflects the relevant International Maritime organization convention. The document is mandatory reflecting the Maritime Government legislation and is part of ship's papers required to be displayed on board the vessel in a prominent position at all times. If the renewal of the document lapses the vessel is unable to leave port on a commercial voyage.

Other aspects

Ship surveys are mandatory and on satisfactory completion the appropriate certificate is issued as found in the Cargo Ship Construction Certificate. It is usual for a Ship Classification Society to undertake such work on behalf of the Maritime Government. The survey is very extensive and detailed and includes the vessel hull, machinery and equipment. The certificate also records the name of vessel, date of build, port of Registry, gross tonnage and so on. The survey is conducted every two years and can be undertaken within six months before and after the due date. The survey is scheduled at five-yearly intervals but 50 % of the survey can be undertaken every two and a half years.

Lloyd's Register of Shipping

CARGO SHIP SAFETY CONSTRUCTION CERTIFICATE

Issued under the provisions of the

INTERNATIONAL CONVENTION FOR THE SAFETY OF LIFE AT SEA, 1974

Name of Ship	Distinctive Number or Letters	Port of Registry	Gross Tonnage	Date on which keel was laid See NOTE below
"SPECIMEN"	9 K B C	KUWAIT	27014	1977

, the undersigned, J.A. Moore   certify

That the above-mentioned ship has been duly surveyed in accordance with the provisions of Regulation 10 of Chapter I of the Convention referred to above, and that the survey showed that the condition of the hull, machinery and equipment, as defined in the above Regulation, was in all respects satisfactory and that the ship complied with the applicable requirements of Chapter II-1 and Chapter II-2 (other than those relating to fire-extinguishing appliances and fire control plans).

This Certificate is issued under the authority of the Government of Kuwait

It will remain in force until   17th August 1988

Issued at   London   on the   25th   day of   February 1985

The undersigned declares that he is duly authorised by the said Government to issue this Certificate

Secretary, Lloyd's Register of Shipping
71 Fenchurch Street, London EC3M 4BS

NOTE : It will be sufficient to indicate the year in which the keel was laid or when the ship was at a similar stage of construction except for 1952, 1965 and 1980, in which cases the actual date should be given.

Form 1325 (05/81)

APPLICABLE ONLY TO SHIPS OF TYPES LISTED BELOW

SUPPLEMENT TO THE CARGO SHIP SAFETY CONSTRUCTION CERTIFICATE

According to the provisions of the

PROTOCOL OF 1978 RELATING TO THE INTERNATIONAL CONVENTION FOR THE SAFETY OF LIFE AT SEA, 1974

Deadweight of ship (metric tons)   32140

Year of build   1978

Type of ship : Tanker engaged in the trade of carrying crude oil *
~~Chemical tanker engaged in the trade of carrying cargoes of such~~
~~Gas carrier engaged in the trade of carrying cargoes of such~~
~~Cargo ship other than a tanker, chemical tanker or gas carrier~~

Date of contract for building or alteration or modification of a major character   –

Date on which keel was laid or ship was at a similar stage of construction or on which an alteration or modification of a major character was commenced   1977

Date of delivery or completion of an alteration or modification of a major character   1978

This is to certify: That the ship has been surveyed in accordance with Regulation 10 of Chapter I of the Protocol of 1978 Relating to the International Convention for the Safety of Life at Sea, 1974; and that the survey showed that the condition of the hull, machinery and equipment as defined in the above Regulation was in all respects satisfactory and that the ship complied with the requirements of that Protocol.

This Certificate is valid until   17th August 1988

Issued at   London   on the   25th   day of   February 1985

Secretary, Lloyd's Register of Shipping
71 Fenchurch Street, London EC3M 4BS

* Delete if not applicable

APPLICABLE TO ALL SHIPS

ATTACHMENT TO THE CARGO SHIP SAFETY CONSTRUCTION CERTIFICATE

According to the provisions of the
PROTOCOL OF 1978 RELATING TO THE INTERNATIONAL CONVENTION FOR THE SAFETY OF LIFE AT SEA, 1974

In implementation of Regulation 6 (b) of Chapter I of the Protocol of 1978 Relating to the International Convention for the Safety of Life at Sea, 1974, the Government of Kuwait.

has instituted :

Mandatory Annual Surveys.*†

Unscheduled Inspections.*

This is to certify that the ship has been surveyed in accordance with Regulation 6(b) of Chapter I of the Protocol of 1978 Relating to the International Convention for the Safety of Life at Sea, 1974, and the appropriate provisions of IMCO Resolution A413 (xi).

Place Bombay   Date 25th September 1984

pro Secretary
25.2.85   A.D. Sargant
                       Surveyor to Lloyd's Register of Shipping

Place............   Date............
                       Surveyor to Lloyd's Register of Shipping

Place............   Date............
                       Surveyor to Lloyd's Register of Shipping

Place............   Date............
                       Surveyor to Lloyd's Register of Shipping

*Delete as appropriate

APPLICABLE ONLY TO TANKERS OF TEN YEARS OF AGE AND OVER

INTERMEDIATE SURVEY

This is to certify that at an Intermediate Survey required by Regulation 10 of Chapter I of the Protocol of 1978 Relating to the International Convention for the Safety of Life at Sea, 1974, the ship was found to comply with the relevant provisions of that Protocol.

Place............   Date............
                       Surveyor to Lloyd's Register of Shipping

Next Intermediate Survey due

NOT APPLICABLE

Place............   Date............
                       Surveyor to Lloyd's Register of Shipping

Next Intermediate Survey due

Place............   Date............
                       Surveyor to Lloyd's Register of Shipping

Next Intermediate Survey due

Place............   Date............
                       Surveyor to Lloyd's Register of Shipping

10.4 CARGO SHIP SAFETY EQUIPMENT CERTIFICATE

Description

A Cargo Ship Safety Equipment Certificate records the result of an inspection undertaken every two years by a maritime Government surveyor, or on his/her behalf by a ship classification surveyor, e.g. a surveyor to Lloyd's Register of Shipping.

Source of document

The Cargo Ship Safety Equipment Certificate, an example of which (for a tanker) is shown, is issued by Lloyd's Register of Shipping.

Purpose/use/function

To certify the vessel conforms to the statutory requirements for safety equipment, including life-saving appliances, lifeboats, motor lifeboats, liferafts, lifebuoys, lifejackets etc.

Legal context

The inspection is carried out and the certificate issued in accordance with the provisions of the International Convention for the Safety of Life at Sea, 1974. It is a mandatory document and must be displayed on mercantile vessels. The survey is undertaken every two years within a time band of three months before and after its due date.

Ratifying organizations/countries

The International Convention for the Safety of Life at Sea, 1974, is recognized worldwide by Maritime Governments who are members of the International Maritime Organisation and is a statutory requirement in all their mercantile fleets. An example is the Cargo Ship Equipment Certificate.

Other aspects of the Cargo Ship Safety Equipment Certificate

The range and quantity of safety equipment on a cargo vessel will depend on the complement of crew and type of ship, including the plying limits of the vessel. Each crew member would have a lifejacket with a residue of lifejackets for pilots and other personnel likely to join the vessel. Each item of safety equipment is examined at the time of ship survey at which stage the certificate is renewed if all the safety equipment is in accord with the statutory obligations. Lifejackets, liferafts and associated life-saving equipment have a limited life and are renewed several times throughout the operational life of the ship to ensure each item of equipment is fully serviceable. Lifeboat drills are regularly conducted to test the equipment and to ensure that all crew members are competent and understand fully their tasks in emergency situations.

A number of ship surveys, varying with the class of the vessel, are performed with the appropriate certification. These include the tailshaft, double bottom, loadline, passenger certificate and auxiliary boiler surveys.

Lloyd's Register of Shipping

CARGO SHIP SAFETY EQUIPMENT CERTIFICATE

Issued under the provisions of the

INTERNATIONAL CONVENTION FOR THE SAFETY OF LIFE AT SEA, 1974

Name of Ship	Distinctive Number or Letters	Port of Registry	Gross Tonnage	Date on which keel was laid See NOTE below
"SPECIMEN"	9 K B C	KUWAIT	27014	1977

I, the undersigned, J.A. Moore **certify**

(I)   That the above-mentioned ship has been duly inspected in accordance with the provisions of the Convention referred to above.

(II) That the inspection showed that the life-saving appliances provided for a total number of 50 persons and no more, viz:

1 lifeboats on port side capable of accommodating 50 persons;

1 lifeboats on starboard side capable of accommodating 50 persons;

1 motor lifeboats (included in the total lifeboats shown above), including — motor lifeboats fitted with radiotelegraph installation and searchlight, and. — motor lifeboats fitted with searchlight only;

— liferafts, for which approved launching devices are required, capable of accommodating persons; and

2 liferafts, for which approved launching devices are not required, capable of accommodating 60 persons; and in addition one 6 person liferaft forward.

8 lifebuoys;

55 life-jackets.

(III) That the lifeboats and liferafts were equipped in accordance with the provisions of the Regulations annexed to the Convention.

(IV) That the ship was provided with a line-throwing appliance and portable radio apparatus for survival craft in accordance with the provisions of the Regulations.

(V) That the inspection showed that the ship complied with the requirements of the said Convention as regards fire-extinguishing appliances and fire control plans, echo-sounding device and gyro-compass and was provided with navigation lights and shapes, pilot ladder, and means of making sound signals and distress signals, in accordance with the provisions of the Regulations and the International Regulations for Preventing Collisions at Sea in force.

(VI) That in all other respects the ship complied with the requirements of the Regulations so far as these requirements apply thereto.

This Certificate is issued under the authority of the Government of Kuwait.

It will remain in force until 20th March 1986

Issued at London on the 15th day of June 1984

The undersigned declares that Lloyd's Register of Shipping is duly authorised by the said Government to issue this Certificate.

Lloyd's Register of Shipping
71 Fenchurch Street, London EC3M 4BS

NOTE: It will be sufficient to indicate the year in which the keel was laid or when the ship was at a similar stage of construction except for 1952, 1965 and 1980, in which cases the actual date should be given.

Form 1260 (02/81)

APPLICABLE ONLY TO SHIPS OF TYPES LISTED BELOW

SUPPLEMENT TO THE CARGO SHIP SAFETY EQUIPMENT CERTIFICATE

According to the provisions of the

PROTOCOL OF 1978 RELATING TO THE INTERNATIONAL CONVENTION FOR THE SAFETY OF LIFE AT SEA, 1974

Deadweight of ship (metric tons) 32140

Year of build 1978

Type of ship: Tanker engaged in the trade of carrying crude oil*

~~Tanker engaged in the trade of carrying oil other than crude oil*~~

~~Tanker engaged in the trade of carrying products*~~

~~Cargo ship other than a tanker of 20,000 tons deadweight and over*~~

Date of contract for building or alteration or modification of a major character. —

Date on which keel was laid or ship was at a similar stage of construction or on which an alteration or modification of a major character was commenced 1977

Date of delivery or completion of an alteration or modification of a major character. 1978

This is to certify: That the ship has been surveyed in accordance with Regulation 8 of Chapter I of the Protocol of 1978 Relating to the International Convention for the Safety of Life at Sea, 1974; and that the survey showed that the condition of the safety equipment as defined in the above Regulation was in all respects satisfactory and that the ship complied with the requirements of that Protocol.

This Certificate is valid until 20th March 1986 Mandatory Annual ~~, Intermediate or Periodical~~ Survey(s) subject to ~~Mandatory~~ ~~Annual~~ Survey(s)* due 21st March 1985.

Issued at London on the 15th day of June 1984

Lloyd's Register of Shipping
71 Fenchurch Street, London EC3M 4BS

* Delete as appropriate

APPLICABLE TO ALL SHIPS

ATTACHMENT TO THE CARGO SHIP SAFETY EQUIPMENT CERTIFICATE

According to the provisions of the

PROTOCOL OF 1978 RELATING TO THE INTERNATIONAL CONVENTION FOR THE SAFETY OF LIFE AT SEA, 1974

In implementation of Regulation 6 (b) of Chapter I of the Protocol of 1978 Relating to the International Convention for the Safety of Life at Sea, 1974, the Government of Kuwait.

has instituted :

Mandatory Annual Surveys.*† due 21st March 1985

~~Intermediate Surveys.*~~

This is to certify that the ship has been surveyed in accordance with Regulation 6(b) of Chapter 1 of the Protocol of 1978 Relating to the International Convention for the Safety of Life at Sea, 1974, and the appropriate provisions of IMCO Resolution A413(XI).

Place................................ Date................................

Surveyor to Lloyd's Register of Shipping

Place................................ Date................................

Surveyor to Lloyd's Register of Shipping

Under the provisions of Regulation 14 of Chapter 1 of the Protocol,

the validity of this certificate is extended until................................

Place................................ Date................................

Surveyor to Lloyd's Register of Shipping

Surveyor to Lloyd's Register of Shipping

*Delete as appropriate

~~†An Intermediate Survey may be held in place of a Mandatory Annual Survey.~~

SPECIMEN

APPLICABLE ONLY TO TANKERS OF TEN YEARS OF AGE AND OVER

INTERMEDIATE SURVEY

This is to certify that at an Intermediate Survey required by Regulation 8 of Chapter I of the Protocol of 1978 Relating to the International Convention for the Safety of Life at Sea, 1974, the ship was found to comply with the relevant provisions of that Protocol.

Place................................ Date................................

Surveyor to Lloyd's Register of Shipping

Next Intermediate Survey due................................

Place................................ Date................................

Surveyor to Lloyd's Register of Shipping

NOT APPLICABLE

Under the provisions of Regulation 14 of Chapter I of the Protocol the validity of this certificate is extended until................................

Place................................ Date................................

Surveyor to Lloyd's Register of Shipping

10.5 CERTIFICATE OF CLASS (OF A SHIP) (SPECIAL PERIODICAL SURVEY MOTOR TANKER MACHINERY) (CLASSIFICATION: LMC)

Description

The Certificate of Class (Special Periodical Survey Motor Tanker Machinery) documents details that include: the Lloyd's Register Number, gross tonnage, date of survey and class assigned in the Lloyd's Register Book for a particular vessel, e.g. a motor tanker with a gross tonnage of 27 014.

Source of document

The certificate is issued by a Ship Classification Society, e.g. Lloyd's Register of Shipping, London.

Purpose/use/function

To show that a particular vessel has been classified by a Ship Classification Society, e.g. Lloyd's Register of Shipping. The document confirms that the vessel has been the subject of a special periodical survey relating to the motor tanker machinery and has been assigned the highest class (LMC) found in the Maltese cross symbol category.

Legal context

The rules for ship construction and maintenance are laid down by the Ship Classification Society, and ships must conform to these rules if they are to be classified, i.e. built and maintained under survey by the society.

Other aspects of Certificate of Class (of a ship) (Special Periodical Survey Motor Tanker Machinery) (Classification: LMC)

These three ship classification documents are issued by the ship classification society to which the vessel is assigned. Overall, they confirm the ship has maintained her class with the Classification Society following the surveys undertaken by the society surveyor. In the event of the vessel failing to reach the standard required or if the vessel is involved in an accident and repairs are not adequately undertaken; the vessel is expunged from the society. In consequence, the ship is likely to find it difficult to obtain competitively priced insurance-cover premiums. A vessel classified with a Ship Classification Society will sustain her price in the market place. There are over ten ship classification societies, membership of these is voluntary.

Lloyd's Register of Shipping

CERTIFICATE OF CLASS

This is to certify that the Motor Tanker
"SPECIMEN"

Lloyd's Register No 7701583
Built by Hitachi Zosen

at   Innoshima
Date July 1978

REGISTERED TONNAGES

Gross   27014
Net   17301
MOULDED DIMENSIONS

Length   108.00m
Breadth 20.00m
Depth   10.00m

---

having been built in accordance with the Rules and Regulations under the Special Survey of the Society's Surveyors and reported by them on 23rd July 1978 to be in a fit and efficient condition, has been assigned the class of +100A1 "OIL TANKER".

in the Register Book subject to continued compliance with the requirements of the Society's Rules and Regulations.

Chairman   H.R. Macleod

Secretary   J.P. Cashman

Date of issue 25th February 1985
71 Fenchurch Street, London, EC3M 4BS

Form 1000 (03/81)

10.6 CERTIFICATE OF CLASS (OF A SHIP) (SPECIAL PERIODICAL SURVEY MOTOR TANKER HULL AND EQUIPMENT) (CLASSIFICATION: + 100 A1 OIL TANKER)

Description

The Certificate of Class (Special Periodical Survey Motor Tanker Hull and Equipment) is a document bearing details that include the Lloyd's Register Number, shipbuilder's name, shipyard registered tonnages, moulded dimensions, date of survey and class assigned in the Lloyd's Register Book for a particular vessel, e.g. a motor tanker with a gross tonnage of 27 014.

Source of document

The certificate is issued by a Ship Classification Society, e.g. Lloyd's Register of Shipping, London.

Purpose/use/function

To show that a particular vessel has been classified by a Ship Classification Society, e.g. Lloyd's Register of Shipping. The document confirms that the vessel has been the subject of a special periodical survey relating to the motor tanker hull and equipment and that it has been assigned the highest class: + 100 A1 oil tanker.

Legal context

The rules for ship construction and maintenance are laid down by the Ship Classification Society, and ships must conform to these rules if they are to be classified, i.e. built and maintained under survey by the society. The regulations vary by ship type, plying limits and vessel tonnage. They have no statutory enforcement. All membership is voluntary.

Other aspects

This Certificate of Class indicates the vessel was surveyed and subsequently maintained her classification and assigned the highest class expressed in the Maltese cross symbol. Accordingly, this data will be recorded in Lloyd's Register Book, which is available for inspection or enquiry by Companies/personnel who have an interest in the vessel, such as a marine underwriter.

Lloyd's Register of Shipping

CERTIFICATE OF CLASS

This is to certify that the machinery of Motor Tanker
"SPECIMEN"

Lloyd's Register No. 7701583   Gross Tonnage   27014   having been

constructed in accordance with the Rules and Regulations under the Special Survey

of the Society's Surveyors and reported by them on 23rd July 1984

to be in good working condition, has been assigned the Class ⚓LMC in the Register

Book subject to continued compliance with the requirements of the Society's Rules

and Regulations.

Approved total power	9540	kW at	230	rev/min of Engine
			230	rev/min of Propeller

Chairman   H.R. Macleod

Secretary   J.P. Cashman

Date of issue 25th February 1985

71 Fenchurch Street, London, EC3M 4BS

Form 1001 (09/78)

10.7 CERTIFICATE OF CLASS (OF A SHIP) (HIGHEST CLASSIFICATION: + 100 A1 + LMC OIL TANKER)

Description

The Certificate of Class is a document bearing details that include the Lloyd's Register Number, the dates of surveys cited on associated certificates issued earlier (sections 10.5 and 10.6) and the class continued with for a particular vessel, e.g. a motor tanker with a gross tonnage of 27 014.

Source of document

The certificate is issued by a Ship Classification Society, e.g. Lloyd's Register of Shipping, London.

Purpose/use/function

This certificate is displayed on the vessel. It confirms the motor tanker surveys cited on earlier certificates (sections 10.5 and 10.6). It also confirms that the vessel continues in the highest classification: + 100 A1 + LMC oil tanker.

Legal context

The rules for ship construction and maintenance are laid down by the Ship Classification Society, and ships must conform to these rules if they are to be classified, i.e. built and maintained under survey by the society. The regulations vary by ship type, plying limits and vessel tonnage.

Other aspects

This document confirms surveys were conducted on 15th June and 19th and 28th August 1983. The results were satisfactory and the motor tanker accorded the highest classification expressed in the Maltese cross symbol.

Lloyd's Register of Shipping

CERTIFICATE OF CLASS

Certificate No. 000½

This is to certify that the Motor Tanker
"SPECIMEN"

Lloyd's Register No. 7701583 , having been surveyed by the Society's

Surveyors and reported by them on   15/6/83, 18/8/83 and 19/8/83

to be in a fit and efficient condition and in accordance with the Rules and Regulations,

continues with the class   +100A1 "OIL TANKER".
                               +LMC

in the Register Book subject to continued compliance with the requirements of the
Society's Rules and Regulations.

The undermentioned notations have been made in the Society's Records:

```
D.S.    6.83
S.S.    8.83
C.S.M.  8.83
```

Secretary J.P. Cashman

*(For and on behalf of the
Committee of Lloyd's Register of Shipping)*

Date of issue 25th February 1985

71 Fenchurch Street, London, EC3M 4BS

Form 1004 (11/81)

10.8 CERTIFICATE OF CLASS (OF A SHIP) (CONFIRMATION OF CLASS)

Description

The document is merely a letter of confirmation bearing details that include the Lloyd's Register Number, gross tonnage, date built and the class status for a particular vessel.

Source of document

The letter is issued by a Ship Classification Society, e.g. Lloyd's Register of Shipping.

Purpose/use/function

The letter confirms that the oil tanker continues in the class assigned to it by the Ship Classification Society.

Legal context

The rules for ship construction and maintenance are laid down by the Ship Classification Society, and ships must conform to these rules if they are to be classified, i.e. built and maintained under survey by the society. The regulations vary by ship type, plying limits and vessel tonnage.

Other aspects

This document is merely a confirmation of class of a ship from the Classification Society and could be in response to the sale of the ship enquiries, a claim regarding her hull, machinery, cargo or renewal of insurance cover.

Lloyd's Register of Shipping

71 Fenchurch Street, London, EC3M 4BS

Telephone 01-709 9166   Telex 888379   Cables Committee, London EC3

Please address further communications to The Secretary, and quote

Our Ref   CLASS / CONF.-

Your Ref

Date   25th February 1985

CONFIRMATION OF CLASS

TO WHOM IT MAY CONCERN;

This is to certify that according to current information available in this office, the Class Status of the undermentioned ship/unit is as follows:

L.R. Number	7701583
Name of Ship/Unit	"SPECIMEN"
Gross Tonnage	27014
Date of Build	June, 1978
Class Status	+100A1 "OIL TANKER" +LMC

Issuing Office   London

for the Secretary, Lloyd's Register of Shipping

Form 1437 (Revised) (02/82) GAD168

10.9 DECLARATION OF AGE (OF A SHIP)

Description

A Declaration of Age is a certificate bearing details of a vessel's Lloyd's Register Number, gross tonnage and date built.

Source of document

The certificate is issued by a Ship Classification Society, e.g. Lloyd's Register of Shipping, London.

Purpose/use/function

The Declaration of Age confirms the age of a vessel for ship sale or charter purposes.

Other aspects

This document is used as supporting evidence in the build-up of data for a particular ship thereby providing a ship profile.

Lloyd's Register of Shipping

71 Fenchurch Street, London, EC3M 4BS

Telephone 01-709 9166   Telex 888379   Cables Committee, London EC3

Please address further communications to The Secretary, and quote

Our Ref SIS/INF/   JH/2475

Your Ref   —

Date   13 February 1985

DECLARATION OF AGE

TO WHOM IT MAY CONCERN;

This is to certify that according to the most up-to-date information available in this office, the ship(s) listed below was/were built in the year(s) stated:

L.R. Number	Name of Ship		Gross Tonnage	Date of Build
7806788	'SUCEVITA'	***********SPECIMEN ONLY*************	2473/3531	1978

Issuing Office   LONDON

for the Secretary, Lloyd's Register of Shipping

Form 1436 (02/82)

10.10 INTERNATIONAL LOAD LINE CERTIFICATE (1966)

Description

An International Load Line Certificate (1966) records the results of a statutory cargo ship survey undertaken every 5 years by a Ship Classification and Survey Society, such as Lloyd's Register of Shipping, on behalf of a maritime Government.

Source of document

The certificate is issued by a Ship Classification Society, e.g. Lloyd's Register of Shipping, London.

Purpose/use/function

To certify where applicable that a ship has been surveyed; that the freeboards have been assigned; and that load lines shown in the certificate have been marked in accordance with statutory requirements.

Legal context

The surveys are carried out and the certificate issued in accordance with the provisions of the International Convention on Load Lines, 1966, conducted by the International Maritime Organization. It is part of the ship's papers.

Ratifying organizations/countries

It is adopted by all countries which are members of the International Maritime Organization and have ratified the International Load Line Convention of 1966.

Other aspects

The survey is legally required to be undertaken every five years, but to spread the work load and cost to the shipowner; many vessels have a supplementary survey conducted annually. This results in about 20 % of the survey commitment being undertaken annually. It is called the harmonization of surveys as other survey commitments are done at the same time. This subject is fully discussed in the companion volume *Elements of Shipping*, 6th edition (pages 25–6).

Lloyd's Register of Shipping

No. 000¾

INTERNATIONAL LOAD LINE CERTIFICATE (1966)

Issued under the provisions of the International Convention
on Load Lines, 1966, under the authority of the

GOVERNMENT OF KUWAIT

by Lloyd's Register of Shipping

Name of Ship	Distinctive number or letters	Port of Registry	Length (L) as defined in Art. 2 (8)
"SPECIMEN"	9 K B C	KUWAIT	108.00m

Freeboard assigned as: *A new ship ~~AX NNNNX NXX~~

Type of Ship: *Type A ~~XXXXXXXX XXXXXX XXXXXXX XXXXXX~~ } *Delete as applicable

Freeboard from Deck Line

Tropical 1923 mm (T)

Summer 2127 mm (S)

Winter 2331 mm (W)

Winter North Atlantic NOT REQUIRED mm (WNA)

Timber Tropical mm (LT)

Timber Summer mm (LS)

Timber Winter mm (LW)

Timber Winter North Atlantic mm (LWNA)

Load Line

204 mm above (S)

Upper edge of line through centre of ring

204 mm below (S)

NOT REQUIRED mm below (S)

mm above (LS)

mm above (S)

mm below (LS)

mm below (LS)

Note: Freeboards and Load Lines which are not applicable need not be entered in the certificate.

Allowance for Fresh Water for all freeboards other than timber 208 mm

Allowance for Fresh Water for timber freeboards mm

The upper edge of the deck line from which these freeboards are measured is 1000 mm

below top of steel upper deck at side.

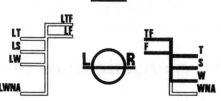

Date of initial or periodical survey 18th August 1983

This is to certify that this ship has been surveyed and that the freeboards have been assigned and load lines shown above have been marked in accordance with the International Convention on Load Lines, 1966.

This certificate is valid until 17th August 1988 , subject to periodical inspections in accordance with Article 14(1)(c) of the Convention.

Issued at London on 25th February 1985

The undersigned declares that Lloyd's Register of Shipping is duly authorised by the said Government to issue this certificate.

Form 1241 9/70

Lloyd's Register of Shipping,
71, Fenchurch Street, London, EC3M 4BS

This is to certify that at a periodical inspection required by Article 14(1)(c) of the Convention, this ship was found to comply with the relevant provisions of the Convention.

Place _Bombay_   Date _25th September 1984_

pro Secretary   A.D. Sargant
25th February 1985   Surveyor to Lloyd's Register of Shipping

Place.................................   Date.................................

Surveyor to Lloyd's Register of Shipping

Place.................................   Date.................................

Surveyor to Lloyd's Register of Shipping

Place.................................   Date.................................

Surveyor to Lloyd's Register of Shipping

The provisions of the Convention being fully complied with by this ship, the validity of this certificate is, in accordance with Article 19 (2) of the Convention,

extended until.................................

Place.................................   Date.................................

Lloyd's Register of Shipping

Notes:

1. When a ship departs from a port situated on a river or inland waters, deeper loading shall be permitted corresponding to the weight of fuel and all other materials required for consumption between the point of departure and the sea.

2. When a ship is in fresh water of unit density the appropriate load line may be submerged by the amount of the fresh water allowance shown above. Where the density is other than unity, an allowance shall be made proportional to the difference between 1·025 and the actual density.

3. This certificate is to be framed and posted up in some conspicuous place on board the ship, so long as the certificate remains in force and the ship is in use.

4. Article 14(1)(c):

   A periodical inspection within three months either way of each annual anniversary date of the certificate, to ensure that alterations have not been made to the hull or superstructure which would affect the calculations determining the position of the load line and so as to ensure the maintenance in an effective condition of fittings and appliances for:

   (i)   protection of openings;
   (ii)   guard rails;
   (iii) freeing ports; and
   (iv)   means of access to crew's quarters.

11 Shipping: commercial documents

11.1 INTRODUCTION

A variety of transportation methods exist in exportation, which include containers, road haulage with ferry, conventional general cargo, shipping, rail and air. With the growth of trade with Europe roll-on roll-off road haulage now accounts for 80 % of UK exports which are conveyed by road transport. In other markets most sea freight other than bulk cargo shipments is containerized. This has revolutionized transport documentation.

Nevertheless, the maritime Bill of Lading is still the most common transport document for exporting from UK to Africa, Asia, the Americas and the Far and Middle East when arranging payment through the banking system for goods delivered. Moreover, in world trade terms, some 70 % of world trade is transported under the Bill of Lading, predominantly in the liner cargo markets. Hence its importance. The role of the Bill of Lading is paramount both as a transportation document and when arranging payment through the world banking system for the delivery of goods in a mercantile condition.

With the growth of container transport and inland collection depots, the received for shipment Bill of Lading has been more widely used. This confirms that the shipping company has the goods in custody for shipment. Exporters now load their goods at the factory into a container provided by the transport operator. If their shipment is less than a full container load; it is sent to a groupage or inland clearance depot to be packed into a container with other goods for the same destination. The container is transported by road or rail to the port for shipment. The received for shipment Bill of Lading can be converted to a shipped bill by an endorsement from a carrier when the goods have been loaded aboard ship.

However, consequent to the modernization of deep sea liner cargo services that result in quicker transit times in both port to port and the through transport service – usually containerized – the non-negotiable Sea Waybill has been introduced in preference to the traditional Bill of Lading used for such goods. Its introduction has been tempered by the experience in some trades that consignments could, on occasions, be subject to delay at the place of delivery because cargo arrived before the documents necessary for clearing and releasing the goods were received by the consignee or the consignee's agent. The main reason for this is the traditional arrangement whereby the shipper/forwarder waits for the return of the original shipped clean Bill of Lading before sending the rest of the shipping documents to the consignee.

For accurate completion of the Bill of Lading by the shipowner; the shipper submits a Shipping Instruction (General Cargo) form when dispatching the goods, to confirm information he or she has given earlier on the telephone to the shipowner.

When an export consignment is offered for shipment the shipper completes a standard Shipping Note to serve as a delivery or receipt note for the receiving port authority.

To confirm to the exporter that goods have been shipped on a specified vessel or aircraft the freight forwarder issues a Certificate of Shipment.

In circumstances where an original Bill of Lading has been lost or delayed in transit, to enable the cargo to be released to the consignee the shipping company will accept a Letter of Indemnity.

When advising a consignee or agent of the impending arrival of a container/ consignment a freight carrier completes an Arrival Notification form requiring the consignee to submit the appropriate documents for Customs clearance purposes.

It is the practice in many countries for goods for export to be collected at the shipper's premises by the agent or freight forwarder for imported cargo after Customs clearance is delivered to the consignee's address with a Delivery Note. A dual-purpose Collection/Delivery Note can serve either function.

To serve as a delivery note for imported cargo a port authority may complete a Delivery/Shipment Note Bill giving details of goods to be delivered to a consignee.

To provide a list of the contents of a package or consignment a Packing List form is completed by the shipper.

To enable a carrier to release a container to a consignee a Release Note is signed by the accepting consignee.

When a container arrives at the destination container base an Unpacking Note is completed giving details of merchandise unpacked and any cargo damage.

11.2 BILL OF LADING

Description

Two main types of Bills of Lading exist which are the long form Bill of Lading with its attendant clauses found on the reverse of the document, and the common short form Bill of Lading. Under the latter, instead of the mass of small print/clauses on the reverse side, there is an approved 'short form' clause on the face which incorporates the carrier's standard condition with full legal effect.

The common short form Bill of Lading has the following salient features:

1 It is fully negotiable and the normal Bill of Lading lodgement and presentation procedures remain unchanged compared with the long form Bill of Lading;
2 It may be used by shippers and freight forwarders and presented for signature to the carrier or the carrier's authorized agents, after a perusal and acceptance of the carrier's standard terms and conditions to which the incorporation clause in the short form Bill of Lading refers;
3 It is suitable for outward shipments from the UK involving through transit or port to port carriage of cargo for both breakbulk and unit loads of all types traditionally covered by long form Bills of Lading;
4 It is based upon an internationally accepted layout adopted by the United Nations. Such widespread acceptance of its format facilitates fast and accurate recording, processing, transmission and receipt of data relating to the movement of cargo;
5 As confirmed by the International Chamber of Commerce (ICC) it is acceptable within the 'uniform customs and practice for documentary credits' (ICC brochure No. 400 refers);
6 It is a document recommended by the General Council of British Shipping (GCBS) for use of all outward shipments from the UK and particularly all UK shippers/carriers and their conference associates;
7 It is a document of title under which the contracting carrier undertakes to deliver the subject goods against surrender of an original document;
8 It is a 'received for carriage shipment' bill with provision for endorsement evidencing goods shipped on board when so required;
9 It is suitable for conventional and through liner services irrespective of whether the vessel is chartered or owned by the contracting carrier. It is not available for goods carried by combined transport operation;
10 It is described as a short form document because of the use of an abridged standard clause on the face of the document which incorporates the conditions of carriage of the contracting carrier. The change eliminates the mass of small print on the reverse side of the Bills of Lading without affecting the status of the documents or rights and obligations of any interested party;
11 It is a document fully aligned to the SITPRO Master Document with the opportunity to complete the Bill of Lading from such a document without any additional typing;
12 It economizes on stationery cost through (i) a reduced need to hold a variety of stocks of long form Bills of Lading with individual carrier's name and conditions plus (ii) the elimination of the risk of using obsolescent forms together with attendant complications.

A common short form Bill of Lading is that shown for P&O Containers Ltd. Brief descriptions are given below for a selection of Bills of Lading: the

Combined Transport; Port to Port Bill of Lading; the Container Bill of Lading; Transhipment Bill of Lading; the Liner Bill of Lading; the Original Bill of Lading; the Through Bill of Lading, and for a Clean Bill of Lading.

Combined Transport Bill of Lading is a document issued by a Combined Transport Bill of Lading operator for the carriage of goods by at least two modes of transport, such as road/sea/road or rail/sea/road. It is used especially in container shipments.

Transhipment Bill of Lading permits cargo to be transhipped from one vessel to another en route to reach the final destination, such as Felixstowe/Singapore – Singapore/Bangkok – under one document and through freight rate.

Liner Bill of Lading is a negotiable document which embodies the Hague-Visby rules and is found in the liner cargo trades.

Original Bill of Lading is the top copy of the Bill of Lading document containing the shipowner's signature/stamp and is the copy required by banks for financial settlement purposes.

Through Bill of Lading is a document acknowledging cargo has been shipped between two specified ports (loading and discharge) plus inland portion of the transit.

Clean Bill of Lading is a document which has no superimposed clause(s) expressly declaring a defective condition of the cargo packaging or missing goods. A document acceptable to banks for financial settlement purposes.

Combined Transport of the Port to Port Bill of Lading, e.g. P&O Containers

With the development worldwide of containerized services, the need to provide a Bill of Lading embracing not only the maritime voyage(s) portion of the transit, but also the overland distribution to the port of departure and from the port of destination involving road, rail, or canal has been paramount. This is contained in the Combined Transport Bill of Lading, which may also be used for port to port shipments.

Under the terms of the Combined Transport Bill of Lading, the carrier as principal accepts 'through liability' for the contracts that he or she makes with sub-contractors. Hence the carrier is liable as soon as his or her sub-contractor has received the goods from the merchant/shipper. Accordingly the Combined Transport Bill of Lading provides for the carrier/shipowner to accept responsibility from the place of the goods acceptance to the place of the merchandise destination after discharge of the goods from the carrying vessel. This may involve a road/rail/canal transit to the departure port: the actual voyage(s) which may involve a transhipment; and finally the journey from the final destination port embracing road, rail or canal. A through rate may be quoted for the transit throughout.

Container Bill of Lading, e.g. Borchard Lines Ltd

With the substantial volume of liner cargo now being conveyed in containers offering shippers a door-to-door service with no transhipment en route, the Container Bill of Lading is proving very popular.

This document is regarded as a through Bill of Lading whereby the shipowner accepts responsibility as an agent from the place of the goods acceptance to the point of loading on board the vessel, and subsequently after discharge of the merchandise from the carrying vessel. The responsibility for the

Bill of Lading for Combined Transport shipment or Port to Port shipment

Shipper

B L No.

Booking Ref.:

Shipper's Ref.:

Consignee

P&O
Containers

Notify Party Address (It is agreed that no responsibility shall attach to the Carrier or his Agents for failure to notify of the arrival of the goods (see clause 20 on reverse))

Place of Receipt (Applicable only when this document is used as a Combined Transport Bill of Lading)

Vessel and Voy. No.

Place of Delivery (Applicable only when this document is used as a Combined Transport Bill of Lading)

Port of Loading

Port of Discharge

Marks and Nos; Container Nos;	Number and kind of Packages; description of Goods	Gross Weight (kg)	Measurement (cbm)

Above particulars as declared by Shipper, but not acknowledged by the Carrier (see clause 11)

*Total No. of Containers/Packages Received by the Carrier

Movement

Freight and Charges (indicate whether prepaid or collect):

Origin Inland Haulage Charge ...   .

Origin Terminal Handling/LCL Service Charge ...

Ocean Freight ...   .

Destination Terminal Handling/LCL Service Charge

Destination Inland Haulage Charge ...   .

ICS
CT B/L
April 78

Received by the Carrier from the Shipper in apparent good order and condition (unless otherwise noted herein) the total number or quantity of Containers or other packages or units indicated in the box opposite entitled "*Total No. of Containers/Packages Received by the Carrier" for Carriage subject to all the terms hereof (INCLUDING THE TERMS ON THE REVERSE HEREOF AND THE TERMS OF THE CARRIER'S APPLICABLE TARIFF) from the Place of Receipt or the Port of Loading, whichever is applicable, to the Port of Discharge or the Place of Delivery, whichever is applicable. One original Bill of Lading must be surrendered, duly endorsed, in exchange for the Goods. In accepting this Bill of Lading the Merchant expressly accepts and agrees to all its terms and conditions whether printed, stamped or written, or otherwise incorporated, notwithstanding the non-signing of this Bill of Lading by the Merchant.

Number of Original Bills of Lading

Place and Date of Issue

IN WITNESS of the contract herein contained the number of originals stated opposite has been issued, one of which being accomplished the other(s) to be void.

For the Carrier: COPY NON-NEGOTIABLE

As Agent(s) only.

P&OCL BL 3 2/88

CONTAINER

Shipper

Consignee (if order state Notify Party)

Notify address

Local vessel	*from (local Port of loading)
Ocean vessel	Port of loading
Port of discharge	*Final destination (if on carriage)

Bill of Lading number ....

BORCHARD LINES
LIMITED

Bill of Lading

DURRANT HOUSE, CHISWELL STREET, LONDON,   EC1Y 4XY

Telephone: 01-628 6961/6
Telex: LONDON 88-69-00
Telegrams: BORLINES, LONDON, E.C.1.

| Freight payable at | Number of original Bs/L |

Marks and Numbers	Number and kind of packages: description of goods	Gross Weight	Measurement

Particulars Furnished by Shippers under Articles 111 & 1V of the Rules Scheduled
to the Carriage of Goods by Sea Act 1924

Said to be loaded in the undermentioned containers

Containers Serial number(s)	Type & size	Gross weight (kilos)	Tare weight (kilos)	Seal reference

The terms, conditions and exceptions of this contract (upon which the rate of freight is based) and which are hereby mutually agreed upon, are as follows:—

Received in apparent good order and condition, subject to all the terms and conditions of this Bill of Lading, the merchandise stated in this Bill of Lading to be conveyed via any port or ports (or as near thereto as she can without detention or delay, safely get and always afloat) for loading or discharging or for any other purpose, and as otherwise provided herein.

1. GENERAL PARAMOUNT CLAUSE. 'This Bill of Lading shall have effect subject to the provisions of any legislation relating to the carriage of goods by sea which incorporates the rules relating to Bills of Lading contained in the International Convention, dated Brussels, 25th August, 1924, and which is compulsorily applicable to the contract of carriage herein contained. Such legislation shall be deemed to be incorporated herein, but nothing herein contained shall be deemed a surrender by the carrier of any of its rights or immunities or an increase of any of its responsibilities or liabilities thereunder. If any term of this Bill of Lading be repugnant to any extent to any legislation by this clause incorporated, such term shall be void to that extent but no further. Nothing in this Bill of Lading shall operate to limit or deprive the Carrier of any statutory protection or exemption from, or limitation of, liability.

2. Freight and/or charges shall be deemed to have been earned on shipment, ship and/or goods lost or not lost. Parcels for different consignees collected and made up in a single package addressed to one consignee, shall pay full freight at the rate applicable to the highest rated parcel in the package.

3. Weight, Measures, Dimensions, Brand, Quality, Contents, Specifications and Value unknown. In accepting this Bill of Lading the shipper or other agent of the owner of the property carried, expressly accepts and agrees to all its stipulations, exceptions and conditions whether written, printed, stamped or pasted on the front or back hereof.

CONTAINER AND VEHICLE DEMURRAGE. Attention is drawn to the Carrier's Terms and Conditions for Container and Vehicle Demurrage which apply to this Contract and which may be obtained from the Carrier or their Agents.

Container demurrage and Pier/Quay rent to be based on charges published by the terminal Operator and/or Carrier, and are payable by the Consignee. If the latter has not taken delivery of, stripped the container and re-delivered same to Ship's Agents, the Carrier or his Agent shall be at liberty to break the seal, strip the container, and stow the cargo contents according to the instructions of the Port/Terminal Management at the sole risk and expense of the owners of the goods.

*Applicable only when document used as Through Bill of Lading

IN WITNESS whereof the Agents of the said ship have signed the said number of Bills of Lading all of this tenor and date, one of which being accomplished the others to be void.

Number of Packages (in words)

ORIGINAL

Conditions continued overleaf

For the master....................... .,,.......................on the...19............

voyage(s) rests with the shipowner in accord with the Maritime Statute law of the ship's country of registry.

Direct or with Transhipment Bill of Lading, e.g. China Ocean Shipping Company

A significant volume of liner cargoes are subjected to transhipment during the transit to enable them to reach the specified destination port. Hence the goods may be conveyed from port A to B and subsequently be feeder service from port B to port C. The Transhipment Bill of Lading enables the goods to be conveyed from port A to port C with a transhipment at port B under one document and one freight rate throughout, incorporating the transhipment charges at port B. Additionally, the shipowner's liability remains the same throughout the transit.

This Bill of Lading may also be used for direct voyage, such as port A to port B with no intermediate transhipment en route.

An increasing number of Letters of Credit indicate that 'transhipment not permitted' in which situation the shipper/exporter must establish the service to be used is not a transhipment service, or alternatively the Letter of Credit permits the use of a transhipment service at an early stage in order to avoid payment problems.

Liner Bill of Lading, e.g. Africa Ocean Lines Ltd

A typical Liner Bill of Lading is used in liner cargo trades. It contains the Africa Ocean Lines Ltd logo. The document is negotiable and is a through Bill of Lading. It is interesting to compare the differing layout of the six Bills of Lading.

Original Bill of Lading, e.g. Islamic Republic of Iran Shipping Lines

A typical original Bill of Lading is a shipped on board Bill of Lading and the example contains the Islamic Republic or Iran Shipping Lines logo.

The original Bill of Lading – the top copy is signed by the shipowner as a receipt for the cargo and dispatched to the exporter. Subsequently the seller dispatches the Bill of Lading with supporting documents to the bank to obtain payment of the goods in accord with the export sales contract.

Through Bill of Lading, e.g. Leopold Walford Shipping Ltd

In many situations it is necessary to employ two or more carriers to get the goods to their final destination. The on-carriage may be either by a second vessel or by a different form of transport, such as road, rail or canal. In such cases it would be very complicated and more expensive if the shipper had to arrange on-carriage by employing an agent at the place of transhipment. Shipping companies therefore issue Bills of Lading which cover the whole transit and the shipper deals only with the first carrier. This type of bill enables a through rate to be quoted and is very popular with containerized shipments.

託運人
Shipper

收貨人
Consignee

或讓受人
or assigns.

通知
Notify

中 國
遠洋運輸公司
CHINA OCEAN SHIPPING COMPANY

總公司 HEAD OFFICE: 北京 PEKING
分公司 BRANCH OFFICE: 廣州 CANTON 上海 SHANGHAI 天津 TIENTSIN
電報掛號 CABLE ADDRESS. "COSCO"

提 單
BILL OF LADING
直運或轉船
DIRECT OR WITH TRANSHIPMENT

正 本
ORIGINAL

船 名 Vessel	航次 Voy.	裝貨單號 S/O No.	提單號 B/L No.
裝 貨 港 Port of Loading		卸 貨 港 Port of Discharge	
國 籍 Nationality THE PEOPLE'S REPUBLIC OF CHINA		運 費 在 Freight payable at	支付

託運人所提供的詳細情況
Particulars furnished by the Shipper

標誌和號數 Marks and Numbers	件 數 No. of Packages	貨 名 Description of Goods	毛 重 Gross Weight	尺 碼 Measurement

合 計 件 數 （大 寫）
Total Packages (in words)

上列外表情況良好的貨物(另有說明者除外)已裝在上列船上並應在上列卸貨港或該船所能安全到達並保持浮泊的附近地點卸貨。
Shipped on board the vessel named above in apparent good order and condition (unless otherwise indicated) the goods or packages specified herein and to be discharged at the above mentioned port of discharge or as near thereto as the vessel may safely get and be always afloat.

重量、尺碼、標誌、號數、品質、內容和價值是託運人所提供的, 承運人在裝船時並未核對。
The weight, measure, marks, numbers, quality, contents and value, being particulars furnished by the Shipper, are not checked by the Carrier on loading.

託運人、收貨人和本提單的持有人茲明白表示接受並同意本提單和它背面所載的一切印刷、書寫或打印的規定、免責事項和條件。
The Shipper, Consignee and the Holder of this Bill of Lading hereby expressly accept and agree to all printed, written or stamped provisions, exceptions and conditions of this Bill of Lading, including those on the back hereof.

運費和其他費用
Freight and Charges:

為證明以上各節, 承運人或其代理人已簽署本提單一式 份, 其中一份經
完成提貨手續後, 其餘各份失效。
In witness whereof, the Carrier or his Agents has signed Bills of Lading all of this tenor and date, one of which being accomplished, the others to stand void.

請託運人特別注意本提單內與該貨保險效力有關的免責事項和條件。
Shippers are requested to note particularly the exceptions and conditions of this Bill of Lading with reference to the validity of the insurance upon their goods.

簽單日期 在
Dated...at...........

船 長
..............................For the Master

請 閱 背 面 條 款　See Clauses on the Back.

Shipper

LINER BILL OF LADING

B / L No

Consignee

A L

AFRICA OCEAN LINES LTD

Head Office: 30-32 CREEK ROAD, APAPA, LAGOS, NIGERIA, PMB 1240 APAPA

Notify address

Shipped on board in apparent good order and condition, weight measure, marks, numbers, quality, contents and value unknown, for carriage to the Port of Discharge or so near thereunto as the Vessel may safely get and lie always afloat, to be delivered in the like good order and condition at the aforesaid Port unto Consignees or their Assigns, they paying freight as indicated to the left plus other charges incurred in accordance with the provisions contained in this Bill of Lading.

In accepting this Bill of Lading the Merchant expressly accepts and agrees to all its stipulations, whether written, typed, printed stamped or otherwise incorporated, as fully as if they were all signed by the Merchant.

One original Bill of Lading must be surrendered duly endorsed in exchange for the goods or delivery order.

IN WITNESS whereof the Master of the said Vessel has signed the number of original Bills of Lading stated below, all of this tenor and date, one of which being accomplished, the others to stand void.

Pre-carriage by *	Place of receipt by pre-carrier *
Vessel	Port of loading
Port of discharge	Place of delivery by on-carrier *

Marks and Nos	Number and kind of packages; description of goods	Gross weight	Measurement

ISSUE No. 3 OCTOBER 1984

Particulars furnished by the Merchant

Freight details, charges etc.

In accepting this Bill of Lading the Merchant expressly accepts and agrees to all its stipulations, whether written, typed, printed stamped or otherwise incorporated, as fully as if they were all signed by the Merchant.

Daily demurrage rate

Applicable only when document used as a Through Bill of Lading	Freight payable at	Place and date of issue
	Number of original Bs/L	Signature

Shipper:

Consignee:

Notify address: (carrier not to be responsible for failure to notify)

*Local vessel: *from:

(Ocean) vessel: Port of loading:

Port of discharge: *Final destination (if on-carriage):   Freight payable at: Number of original Bs/L:

BILL OF LADING   B/L No.:

Islamic Republic of Iran Shipping Lines

Marks & Nos.:	Number and kind of packages; description of goods:	Gross weight kg

PARTICULARS FURNISHED BY SHIPPER OF GOODS

Original

Shipper's Ref.:

Freight and charges:

SHIPPED in apparent good order and condition unless otherwise specified on board the aforementioned vessel the goods described above (the particulars given being supplied by the Shipper and the measurement, weight, quantity, brand, contents, marks, numbers, quality and value being unknown to the carrier) for the carriage to the port of discharge or so near thereunto as she may safely go subject to the terms, conditions and exemptions of this Bill of Lading.

In accepting this Bill of Lading the Owners of the goods expressly accept and agree to all its stipulations on both pages, whether written, printed, stamped or otherwise incorporated, as fully as if they were all signed by the Owners of the Goods.

In WITNESS whereof the Master, Purser or Agent of the said vessel has signed the number of original Bills of Lading stated above, all of this tenor and date, one of which being accomplished, the others, stand void. One of the Bills of Lading must be given up, fully endorsed in exchange for the goods.

Place and date of issue:

for the Master:

*) Applicable only when document used as a Through Bill of Lading

Shipper TATE AND LYLE TECHNICAL SERVICES ENTERPRISE HOUSE 45 HOMESDALE ROAD BROMLEY KENT	B/L No. CD/1854

Consignee (If 'Order' state notifying party)
THE ZAMBIA SUGAR CO LTD
NAKAMBALA ESTATE
P.O. BOX 240
MAZABUKA
ZAMBIA

Notify (No liability is accepted by the carrier for failure to notify).
B S BWALYA
ZAMBIA SUGAR CO LTD
P.O. BOX 30489
LUSAKA ZAMBIA

Place of Receipt

LEOPOLD WALFORD SHIPPING LIMITED

PRUDENTIAL BUILDINGS, 103 CRANBROOK ROAD,
ILFORD, ESSEX 1G1 4QA

Agents for

WALFORD CONTAINER SERVICES

THROUGH BILL OF LADING

Intended Port of Loading CRANACH	Intended Vessel FELIXSTOWE		
Intended Port of Discharge DAR ES SALAAM	Intended Place of Delivery MAZABUKA	Freight Payable at	Number of Original Bs/L THREE

Marks and Numbers	Number and kind of Packages: Description of Goods
AJCU0691253 ZAMBIA SUGAR CO LTD NAKAMBALA EASTERN EXTENSION MAZABUKA ZAMBIA VIA DAR ES SALAAM ZSC ORDER NO 13746 104-120	2 x 20ft CONTAINERS OCLU 4164388 S.T.C 2 PIECES FOR PUMPING STATION AJCU 0691253 S.T.C. 15 PACKAGES FOR PUMPING STATION

SEA FREIGHT AND DAR ES SALAAM CLEARANCE
CHARGES PREPAID. ONCARRIAGE TO CONTAINER
TERMINAL ZAMBIA PREPAID. TERMINAL HANDLING
AND RE-DELIVERY COSTS FOR CONSIGNEES ACCOUNT.

PARTICULARS OF GOODS ARE THOSE DECLARED BY SHIPPER

TO OBTAIN DELIVERY THIS THROUGH BILL OF LADING, DULY ENDORSED, MUST BE DELIVERED TO:—
LEOPOLD WALFORD (ZAMBIA) LTD P.O. BOX 31280 LUSAKA ZAMBIA

SHIPPED in apparent good order and condition (except as otherwise noted hereon) on board the vessel named herein the packages of merchandise described herein (the particulars given being supplied by the Shipper the contents and condition of contents, the measurement, weight, quantity, brand, gauge, marks, numbers, quality and value being unknown) for carriage by that vessel and/or any ship or ships substituted therefor or to which transhipment may be made once or oftener in the course of the voyage via Panama Canal, Suez Canal or Cape of Good Hope or otherwise howsoever subject to the terms, conditions and exceptions of this Bill of Lading as set out on this page and overleaf to the intended place of delivery.

In accepting this Bill of Lading the Merchant expressly accepts and agrees to all its stipulations exceptions limitations conditions and liberties whether written stamped or printed.

IN WITNESS whereof there have been signed the number of original Bills of Lading stated above all of this tenor and date one of which being accomplished the others to stand void.

Dated..

Number of packages (in words)

TWO

COPY NOT NEGOTIABLE

TERMS AND CONDITIONS CONTINUE ON REVERSE.

As Agents

JMB216TT Jan 1984

The specimen of a Through Bill of Lading features two 20 ft containers shipped between two specified ports, plus the on-carriage to the container terminal. All the sea freight, including Customs clearance charges in Dar es Salaam, together with the on-carriage to the container terminal have been prepaid by the shipper. The delivery costs from the container terminal are borne by the consignee.

Under the Through Bill of Lading the shipowner accepts responsibility as an agent from the place of acceptance of the goods to the point of loading on board the vessel, and subsequently after discharge of the merchandise from the carrying vessel. The responsibility for the voyage(s) rests with the shipowner in accord with the Maritime Statute Law of the ship's country of registry.

Clean Bill of Lading, e.g. NYK Line

The Clean Bill of Lading, sometimes termed unclaused bill of Lading, contains no endorsements. It confirms the cargo has been accepted by the shipowner in accord with the description of the goods and the goods are undamaged, not soiled, adequately packed and none missing. Such a document is acceptable to banks for financial settlement payment of the goods by the buyer purposes.

Source of document

A shipping company, e.g. P&O Containers Ltd.

Purpose/use/function

Overall, the Bill of Lading has four functions. It is a receipt for the goods shipped and provides certain details as to their condition when placed on board the ship. In the event of the goods being damaged, missing, stained, inadequately packed, the Bill of Lading is endorsed accordingly. The document is therefore regarded as unclean, foul or dirty. Conversely, goods which are placed on board without defect are regarded as a clean shipped Bill of Lading. Secondly, it is evidence of the terms of the contract of affreightment between either the exporter or importer and a shipping company to transport the goods by sea. Thirdly, it is a document of title. This empowers the company named on the Bill of Lading to the right to possess the goods. A transfer of title on the Bill of Lading acts as a transfer of ownership of the goods. Finally, the Bill of Lading is regarded as a quasi negotiable instrument.

Legal context

The conditions of carriage are found in a series of international conventions which include the following:

1 Hague rules: Agreed at an international convention at Brussels in 1924 and govern liability for loss or damage to goods carried by sea. They are officially known as 'the International Convention for the unification of certain rules relating to Bills of Lading', signed in Brussels on 25 August 1924, and were given effect in the United Kingdom by the Carriage of Goods by Sea Act, 1924.
2 Hague Visby rules: In 1968 an international conference adopted some revisions to the Hague rules, officially known as the Brussels Protocol, signed on 23 February 1968. They were called the Hague Visby rules and were given effect in the United Kingdom by the Carriage of Goods by Sea Act, 1971.

Some 18 countries have ratified the rules, of which 11 were European.
3 Hamburg rules: In March 1978 an international conference in Hamburg adopted a new set of rules called the Hamburg rules which were to radically alter the liability which shipowners had to bear for loss or damage to goods. The rules were to come into effect one year after ratification or accession by twenty nations. By 1988 eight nations had ratified.

Number and allocation of copies

Bills of Lading are made out in sets usually of two or three originals, any one of which gives title to the goods. When the shipper has sold the goods on Letter of Credit terms established through a bank, or when the shipper wishes to obtain payment of his or her invoice before the consignee obtains the goods, the shipper will pass the full set of original bills to his or her bank who will in due course arrange presentation to the consignee against payment.

Checklist of what should accompany each copy

The Bill of Lading will be sent by the seller to the bank and accompanied by the commercial invoice, packing list, insurance certificate, and so on.

Discrepancies (i.e. likely errors) and their consequences

The following items are common discrepancies found in Bills of Lading when being processed and should be avoided:

1 document not presented in full sets when requested;
2 alterations not authenticated by an official of the shipping company or its agents;
3 the Bill of Lading is not clean when presented, such as, when it is endorsed regarding damaged condition of the specified cargo or inadequate packing thereby making it unacceptable to a bank for financial settlement purposes;
4 the document is not endorsed 'on board' when so required;
5 the 'on board' endorsement is not signed or initialled by the carrier or agent and likewise not dated;
6 the Bill of Lading is not 'blank' endorsed if drawn to order;
7 the document fails to indicate whether 'freight paid' as stipulated in the credit arrangements, namely C&F or CIF contracts;
8 the Bill of Lading is made out 'to order' when the Letter of Credit stipulates 'direct to consignee' or vice versa;
9 the Bill of Lading is not marked 'freight prepaid' when freight charges are included in the invoice;
10 the document is dated later than the latest shipping date specified in the Credit;
11 it is not presented within twenty-one days after date of shipment or such lesser time as prescribed in the Letter of Credit;
12 the Bill of Lading details merchandise other than that prescribed;
13 the rate at which freight is calculated, and the total amount, are not shown when Credit requires such data to be given;
14 cargo has been shipped 'on deck' and not placed in the ship's hold; basically, 'on deck' claused Bills of Lading are not acceptable when clean on-board Bills of Lading are required;
15 shipment made from a port or to a destination contrary to that stipulated;
16 other types of Bills of Lading presented, although not specifically authorized; for example, Bills of Lading issued under a Charter Party, or

forwarding agents' Bills of Lading are not accepted unless specially authorized in the Letter of Credit.

Further information

The Bill of Lading is an important document. It is completed by the agent or shipowner and the cargo description must conform to the details found on the commercial invoice and Letter of Credit. The subject is fully examined in Chapter 12 of *Elements of Shipping* (6th edn, A. Branch, Chapman and Hall).

Bill of Lading

This is a 'Clean' Bill of Lading, there being no superimposed clause indicating a defective condition of the goods or packing.

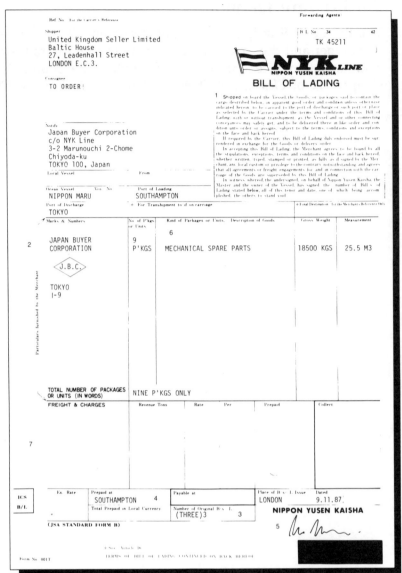

Ref. No. For the Carrier's Reference

Shipper
United Kingdom Seller Limited
Baltic House
27, Leadenhall Street
LONDON E.C.3.

Consignee
TO ORDER

Notify
Japan Buyer Corporation
c/o NYK Line
3-2 Marunouchi 2-Chome
Chiyoda-ku
TOKYO 100, Japan

Local Vessel   From

Ocean Vessel   Voy. No.   Port of Loading
NIPPON MARU   SOUTHAMPTON

Port of Discharge   + For Transhipment to if on carriage   + Final Destination (for the Merchant's Reference Only)
TOKYO

Forwarding Agents

B.L. No   34   42
TK 45211

NYK LINE
NIPPON YUSEN KAISHA

BILL OF LADING

1 Shipped on board the Vessel, the Goods, or packages said to contain the cargo described below, in apparent good order and condition unless otherwise indicated herein to be carried to the port of discharge or such port or place as selected by the Carrier under the terms and conditions of this Bill of Lading, with or without transhipment, as the Vessel and or other connecting conveyances may safely get, and to be delivered there in like order and condition unto order or assigns, subject to the terms, conditions and exceptions on the face and back hereof.

If required by the Carrier, this Bill of Lading duly endorsed must be surrendered in exchange for the Goods or delivery order.

In accepting this Bill of Lading, the Merchant agrees to be bound by all the stipulations, exceptions, terms and conditions on the face and back hereof, whether written, typed, stamped or printed, as fully as if signed by the Merchant, any local custom or privilege to the contrary notwithstanding, and agrees that all agreements or freight engagements for and in connection with the carriage of the Goods are superseded by this Bill of Lading.

In witness whereof, the undersigned, on behalf of Nippon Yusen Kaisha, the Master and the owner of the Vessel, has signed the number of Bill's of Lading stated below, all of this tenor and date, one of which being accomplished, the others to stand void.

Marks & Numbers	No. of P'kgs or Units	Kind of Packages or Units. Description of Goods	Gross Weight	Measurement
2 JAPAN BUYER CORPORATION ⟨J.B.C.⟩ TOKYO 1-9	9 P'KGS	6 MECHANICAL SPARE PARTS	18500 KGS	25.5 M3

Particulars furnished by the Merchant

TOTAL NUMBER OF PACKAGES OR UNITS (IN WORDS)	NINE P'KGS ONLY

FREIGHT & CHARGES	Revenue Tons	Rate	Per	Prepaid	Collect
7					

ICS B/L	Ex. Rate	Prepaid at SOUTHAMPTON 4	Payable at	Place of B.'s L. Issue LONDON	Dated 9.11.87
		Total Prepaid in Local Currency	Number of Original B's. L. (THREE) 3 3	NIPPON YUSEN KAISHA 5	

(JSA STANDARD FORM B)

+ See Article 16
Form No. 001T   TERMS OF BILL OF LADING CONTINUED ON BACK HEREOF

1 'Shipped on Board.'
2 Shipping marks.
3 Number of bills of lading in the set.
4 Transportation charges have been prepaid in line with the sale contract terms which are CIF.
5 Signed by, or by an Agent on behalf of, NYK.
6 Description of Goods should be consistent with the other documents.
7 Freight charges as calculated by the shipping company.

11.3 SEA WAYBILL

Description

Basically a Sea Waybill is a receipt for cargo which incorporates the contract or carriage between the shipper and the shipowner but is non-negotiable and is therefore not a document of title. Hence, provided the person applying to take delivery of the goods can identify himself or herself as the consignee nominated on the Sea Waybill, a document of title will not be necessary, and the goods will be delivered to the specified consignee.

Source of document

A shipping company, e.g. Maersk Line.

Purpose/use/function

In preference to the traditional Bill of Lading (section 11.2) the Sea Waybill is ideal in four basic situations relative to deep sea cargo liner services as given below:

1 for shipments by multi-national companies which ship from a plant in one country to a plant in another;
2 for open account sales or wherever finance is not advanced in exchange for the documents;
3 for cargo which could arrive before the relevant documents;
4 in any situation where companies have been trading with each other for some time and trust each other, and therefore do not require a document of title to protect individual interest in the matter of payment.

Legal context

The Hague Visby rules feature in the Sea Waybill with a few exceptions such as it is not negotiable and therefore not usable as a means of transferring title to the goods.

Ratifying organizations/countries

It is used worldwide but not on the same scale as the Bill of Lading, possibly up to 20 % of cargo liner trade.

Procedure
Instructions for completing the form

When using a Sea Waybill it is essential that the shipper consigns the cargo to a specific consignee. Cargo cannot be consigned 'to order'. However, delivery can be effected to anyone in accordance with the consignee's specific written instruction.

Further information

Banks are unlikely to finance transactions on the strength of a non-negotiable Sea Waybill without suitable alternative security arrangements.
  However, numerous benefits accrue to the shipper/consignee through using

a Sea Waybill; these are as follows:

1 The commercial documents (invoice, Certificates of Origin etc) can be sent to consignees immediately they are ready – there is no waiting for the issuance of the Sea Waybill;

2 Waybills do not have to be sent to the consignee and postal charges are saved;

3 It is a received for shipment document with the option for use as a shipped document;

4 Clerical work in checking that the Bill of Lading has been received and the detailed checking associated with a document of title is obviated;

5 The shipper can provide an easier and faster service to customers (consignees);

6 The whole documentary process is improved and as a result market potential can be improved;

7 The Waybill shipment can be converted to a Bill of Lading (or vice versa) provided the cargo has not already been released. A Waybill can be assigned by the shipper to a new consignee provided the cargo is still under the shipowner's control;

8 Delays to cargo clearance or delivery due to non-receipt of documents are avoided which greatly benefits the consignee;

9 Costly demurrage/warehouse rent should no longer be incurred;

10 No clerical effort is required in checking for Bills of Lading that may be delayed or lost in transit;

11 Bank guarantees are no longer necessary – if a Bill of Lading is delayed or mislaid in the post, the consignee will have to arrange for a bank guarantee so that delivery of cargo can be effected;

12 The Waybill system allows quicker cargo distribution; faster turnover; less capital tied up in transit, and improved profitability;

13 It is based upon an internationally accepted layout adopted by United Nations;

14 It is suitable for a 'through' transit or port to port carriage of cargo for both breakbulk and unit loads of all types. Additionally, it is acceptable for conventional and through liner services irrespective of whether the vessel is chartered or owned by the carrier.

Shipper

SEA WAYBILL

Contract No.

Consignee

Notify party

Pre-Carriage by *   Place of receipt *

MAERSK LINE

Ocean Vessel   Voy. No.   Port of loading

Managed by A.P. Møller, Copenhagen

Port of discharge   Place of delivery *   Final Destination for information only

Container No.	Seal No. Marks and Numbers	No. of Containers or pkgs	Kind of packages; description of goods	Gross weight	Measurement

PARTICULARS FURNISHED BY SHIPPER

Freight and Charges	Prepaid	Collect

Received for carriage as above in apparent good order and condition, unless otherwise stated hereon, the goods described on the above particulars.

Delivery of the goods will be made to the consignee or his authorised representative upon proper proof of identity and authorization without the need of producing or surrendering a copy of this waybill.

Ex. Rate	Total prepaid	
	Total collect	

W/B No.:

By _____

Agents

Month   Day   Year

* Applicable only when document
  Used as a through Sea Waybill

NON NEGOTIABLE SEA WAYBILL

11.4 SHIPPING INSTRUCTION (GENERAL CARGO)

Description

The Shipping Instruction (General Cargo) is a three-part document that serves as confirmation of the information regarding the goods to be shipped provided earlier on the telephone by the shipper to the shipowner/agent. It is aligned to the SITPRO Master Document.

Source of document

Freight carrier, e.g. Ben Line Containers Ltd.

Purpose/use/function

The document is intended to facilitate accurate completion of the Bill of Lading. It can only be used for general cargo shipment and not for dangerous goods, obnoxious cargo or merchandise requiring controlled temperature (refrigerated cargo). In some companies where the carrier ships goods under both the Bill of Lading and the non-negotiable Sea Waybill, a dual purpose Shipping Instruction (General Cargo) is used.

Legal context

It has no legal role other than through misrepresentation of the data.

Ratifying organizations/countries

It is used in many trades worldwide but the layout may differ. It has no mandatory requirement.

Procedure

Instructions for completing the form

The Shipping Instruction (General Cargo) is completed by the shipper and submitted to the shipowner.

Necessary authorization

It must be signed by an Executive in the Shipping Company.

Number and allocation of copies

Original/top copy for the shipowner (Ben Line Containers Ltd); a copy for cargo control (Ben Line Containers Ltd); and a copy for the shipper. The document is handed to the driver at the time the goods are collected for dispatch and the top copy duly signed and returned to the shipper.

Checklist of what should accompany each copy

The packing list should accompany the document.

Discrepancies (i.e. likely errors) and their consequences

The cargo description must conform to that found on the commercial invoice and Letter of Credit.

Further information

The document is a means of speeding up the Bill of Lading completion and reducing the risk of errors. It also enables the shipowner to pre-plan the shipments and ship stowage/distribution arrangements having regard to cargo quantity, mode of transport, i.e. container, destination port and location of consignee.

Shipping Instruction General Cargo

This form should not be used for DANGEROUS GOODS, OBNOXIOUS or CONTROLLED TEMPERATURE CARGO, which require the presentation of a Shipping Application (Special Cargo)

(A) (B) (C) (D)

Shipper's name and address (in whose name Bill of Lading to be drawn)

BLC BEN LINE CONTAINERS LTD

CAN/Pre-Entry No.	
Shipper's reference (if any)	
Agent's reference	Booking reference

Consignee's name and address (if Bill of Lading to be drawn to 'order' state Order and give Notify Party's name and address)

(E) Notify Party's name and address

Forwarding Agent

Place of Acceptance of cargo by BLC (please state full name and address) or Container Freight Station/Container Yard

Other Party's name and address

Place of delivery of cargo in country of destination (please state full name and address) or Container Freight Station/Container Yard

Required vessel (Sailing number)	Port of Loading	Cargo Insurance
		If you require insurance arranged please state type of cover required and insured value:
Port of Discharge		

Marks and numbers	Number and kind of packages: description of goods	HMC Tariff/Trade code number*	Gross weight Kilos	Measurement cbm
		Quantity*	Nett weight*	FOB value

*Please complete only if BLC are required to attend to Customs Entry

Customs Status	Free	CUSTOMS REQUIREMENTS please indicate with (X)	OTHER INSTRUCTIONS
	Mandatory Pre-entry	BLC Agent to prepare and lodge Customs Entry	
	Under Bond	BLC Agent to lodge prepared Customs Entry	
	Under Drawback	I/We will attend to preparation and lodgement of Customs Entry	

Freight and Charges please indicate party to pay by inserting:

Type of service required please indicate with (X) in boxes below:

(A) (B) (C) (D) (E)

UK Inland/ Delivered in Charge	
UK LCL Service Charge	
Ocean Freight	
FE LCL Service Charge	
FE Inland	
Customs Entry	
Insurance	
Extra B/L†	

Container Packed by	BLC (LCL Cargo)	
	Shipper/Supplier (FCL Cargo)	
Container Unpacked by	BLC (LCL Cargo)	
	Consignee (FCL Cargo)	

Quantity and type of Containers required (FCL)

BILL OF LADING REQUIREMENTS:
Number of Bills of Lading required?

_____ Original _____ Copy

(A full set of 2 originals and 2 copies is provided free)
Do you require shipped on board endorsements? YES/NO

Post Bill of Lading to (A) (B) (C) (D) (E)
or to be collected at the following BLC Agent's office:

SHIPPER'S DECLARATION
We require Ben Line Containers Ltd to arrange through transport of the cargo detailed above between the place of acceptance and the place of delivery shown. We warrant that the details of the cargo declared above are correct as known to us and undertake to advise the BLC Agent of any subsequent alterations. We undertake to comply with the provisions of Customs Notice 275

Signatory's Company and Telephone Number

Name of Authorised Signatory

Place and Date of Issue

Signature

All goods are accepted for transportation on the terms and conditions of the Carrier's current Bill of Lading and applicable Tariffs

COPY FOR BLC

11.5 SHIPPING NOTE

Description

A Shipping Note gives information about a particular export consignment when offered for shipment. To accord with local port practice it either accompanies the goods or is lodged at the receiving authority's designated office before arrival of the goods for shipment. It can be SITPRO unaligned (e.g. the Port of Singapore Authority form) or SITPRO aligned (section 11.6).

Source of document

A port authority, e.g. Port of Singapore Authority, Forwarding Agent.

Purpose/use/function

The completed Shipping Note serves the receiving berth operator/port authority/shipping company as a delivery or receipt note for particular consignment(s).

Other aspects of Shipping Note

It is often called a Mate's Receipt and its role in various ports and trades differ worldwide. The cargo description should conform to that found on the commercial invoice.

Name of Agent

Endorsed by Agent ....
Signature & Stamp

Shipper

Consignee

Notify Party

Port of Loading		
Vessel's Name		Voyage No.

Port Code	Port(s) of Discharge	Final Destination

SHIPPING NOTE

Booking Ref.

FOR PSA USE ONLY		Operator Code	
Godown No.			
Loading Index No.		Shipper's PSA A/C No.	

STATEMENT UNDER SECT.106 OF THE PSA ACT (CAP.173)
I hereby state that the particulars given by me in this Shipping Note are true and correct.

Shipper's Name   NRIC No.   Signature   Date

For Shipping Lines' use only

SPECIMEN

Cargo Marks & No. or Container & Seal No.	Quantity and Description of Packages and Goods	Gross Weight (Kg)	Measurement (Cubic Metre)

Commodity Code		Total No.of Pkgs/Containers								

FOR CONTAINERS ONLY

Status/Size- Type Code		Gross Container Weight		Remarks		Accepted by Shipper
Special Details(Temp.Setting/Hazard Class/Others)						

SPECIMEN

Date   Name & Signature of Shipper

(a) At the point of receipt, no survey is carried out except in (b) below.

(b) The condition of container shipped through the Tanjong Pagar Container Terminal will be noted in the Equipment Interchange Receipt at the point of receipt.

FOR PSA USE ONLY

Status		Stored In		Packing Indicator		Special Cargo Type	G.C.V No. & Date	
Ex-Vessel						Ex-Godown	G.C.V. Amount (Store-Rent)	
1.Date/Time Cargo/ Ctr, rec'd or COD				3.Date 1st lot of local cargo received for stuffing			AMOUNT RECEIVED IN CASH	
2.Date/Time Completed Unstuffing				4.Date/Time Completed Stuffing				

Removals within same Gateway	From Gdn	To Gdn	No. of Pkgs/ctrs	From Gdn	To Gdn	No. of Pkgs/ctrs

No. of pkgs/ctrs removed Intergateway		No. of pkgs/ctrs Shut-out	

Description of miscellaneous charges	Tariff Code	Billable units

11.6 STANDARD SHIPPING NOTE

Description

A Standard Shipping Note (SSN) gives information about a particular export consignment. It is used when delivering cargo to any British port, container base, or other freight terminal. It must accompany the goods to the receiving berth/dock or container base etc. or be lodged at the receiving authority's designated office before arrival of the goods for shipment according to local port practice.

It is not a document of title to the goods. All the merchandise data is transferred to the Bill of Lading at the time of shipment on the specified vessel. It is a six-part aligned document pioneered by SITPRO and may be used only for one consignment to one port of discharge on one sailing on one Bill of Lading.

Purpose/use/function

The Standard Shipping Note serves the receiving authority as a delivery or receipt note for a particular consignment. It is for use with all export consignments delivered to container reception points as well as to conventional dock receiving areas.

Legal context

It has no legal role other than being a cargo receipt at the departure port but is not acceptable to banks for financial settlement purposes.

Ratifying organizations/countries

The Standard Shipping Note was introduced in the United Kingdom in 1975.

Procedure

Instructions for completing the form

The Standard Shipping Note is completed by the shipper or agent.

Number and allocation of copies

The Standard Shipping Note is a six-part document. Copies are retained by those parties handling the goods until they are finally placed on board the vessel, at which stage a shipped Bill of Lading is issued using the SSN data.

Other aspects of the Standard Shipping Note

The Standard Shipping Note is a six-part document and the following points are relevant:

1 When a haulier takes goods (or a container) into his charge, the haulier should sign for receipt of the goods with the exporter or his agent retaining the back copy of the Standard Shipping Note as a receipt.
2 On delivery of the cargo to the docks, the haulier should ensure that the

STANDARD SHIPPING NOTE

Exporter | 1

Veh. Bkg. Ref. | 2

Customs Reference/Status | 3

Exporter's Reference | 4

Exporter
Freight
Forwarder
Other (Name and Address)

Port Charges
Payable by * | 5

Forwarder's Ref. | 6

SS Co. Bkg. No. | 7

Name of Shipping Line or CTO | 8

Port Account No.

Freight Forwarder | 9

For use of Receiving Authority Only

Receiving Date(s) | Berth/Dock/Containerbase etc. | 10

The Company preparing this note declares that the goods have been accurately described, their quantities, weights and measurements are correct and at the time of despatch they were in good order and condition; that the goods are not classified as dangerous in any UK, IMCO, ADR, RID or IATA/ICAO regulation applicable to the intended modes of transport. | 10A

Vessel | Port of Loading | 11

TO THE RECEIVING AUTHORITY — Please receive for shipment the goods described below subject to your published regulations and conditions (including those as to liability).

Port of Discharge | Destination | 12

Name of Receiving Authority | 13

Marks and Numbers; Number and Kind of Packages; Description of goods | 14

Receiving Authority Use

Gross Wt (kg) of goods | 15

Cube (m³)of goods | 16

SYSTEMFORMS LTD 01 505 6125

SPECIAL STOWAGE * | 17

For use of shipping company only

Total Gross weight of goods

Total Cube of goods

PREFIX and Container/Trailer Number(s) | 18 | Seal Number(s) | 18A

Container Trailer Size(s) and Type(s) | 18B

Tare wt (kg) as marked on container | 18C

Weight of container and goods (kg) | 18D

Received the above number of packages/containers/trailers in apparent good order and condition unless stated hereon.
RECEIVING AUTHORITY REMARKS

Name of Company preparing this Note | 19

Haulier's Name

Vehicle Reg. No.

DRIVER'S SIGNATURE | SIGNATURE AND DATE

Date

(Indicate name and telephone number of contact)

630 *Mark X as appropriate. If box 5 is not completed the company preparing this note may be held liable for payment of port charges

receiving authority signs and stamps the Standard Shipping Note, returning one copy to the driver to acknowledge receipt.

3 When goods are delivered in several vehicles, a Standard Shipping Note must be completed for each load with the Standard Shipping Note being cross-referenced.

4 Continuation sheets may be attached where there is insufficient space on the Standard Shipping Note for details.

5 Where local practice requires an additional copy of the Standard Shipping Note being required, such as HM Customs, these can be obtained by photocopying to ensure clarity.

In some trades the Standard Shipping Note is referred to as the Mate's Receipt.

11.7 CERTIFICATE OF SHIPMENT

Description

A Certificate of Shipment is merely a document confirming for the exporter that goods have been shipped on a specified vessel/aircraft and date. It is often associated with groupage or consolidated container shipments, and is also known as the 'in house' Bill of Lading/Air Waybill under groupage arrangements. It contains details of the exporter, consignee, vessel/flight, port/airport of loading, port/airport of discharge, place of delivery, and details of the merchandise, including a description of goods and their gross weight and volume.

Source of document

The Certificate of Shipment is issued by the freight forwarder.

Purpose/use/function

The document confirms that a specific consignment has been shipped in accordance with the shipping instructions.

CERTIFICATE OF SHIPMENT

Exporter

TO ▶

| Customs reference status |
| Exporter s reference |
| Forwarder s reference |

Consignee

SITPRO®
Simpler International Trade

Simplification of International Trade Procedures Board (SITPRO)
Almack House, 26/28 King Street, London SW1Y 6QW
Tel: 01-930 0532   Fax: 01-930 5779
Telex: 919130 SITPRO G.   Prestel 20468
VAT Reg. No. 241 8235 77
SITPRO is a BOTB activity

Other UK transport details

| Vessel/flight no. and date | Port/airport of loading |
| Port/airport of discharge | Place of delivery |

Shipping marks; container number	Number and kind of packages; description of goods	Gross weight (kg)	Cube (m³)

Dear Sirs,
We hereby certify that this consignment has been shipped in accordance with the above mentioned details.

Yours faithfully,

11.8 LETTER OF INDEMNITY

Description

A Letter of Indemnity may be submitted to a shipping company by a consignee in circumstances where an original Bill of Lading has been lost or delayed in transit. It is an undertaking by the consignee to guarantee the shipping company exemption from liability where the shipping company releases the goods to the consignee without production of the Bill of Lading. The Letter of Indemnity is usually countersigned by a bank, except when submitted on behalf of a national Government, in which case a banker's counter-signature is not required.

Source of document

A shipping company, e.g. Mitsui OSK Lines Ltd.

Purpose/use/function

The acceptance of the Letter of Indemnity by the shipping company empowers the release of the cargo to the consignee on production of a duplicate set of documents.

The Letter of Indemnity relieves the shipping company of any liability should another person eventually come along with the original Bill of Lading.

Issuance of the Letter of Indemnity obviates problems emerging through possession of the goods by the carrier before payment, and precludes a dispute occurring between the seller and buyer, with the carrier in the centre of the dispute.

Other aspects

This document is long established and is completed by the consignee. It is basically an indemnity and should be used with discretion. It needs to be signed by an executive of the consignee company and only used when all reasonable efforts have been taken to obtain the absent original Bill of Lading.

LETTER OF INDEMNITY

To The Mitsui O.S.K. Lines, Ltd.

Stamp

Gentlemen,

In consideration of your granting delivery to _____ of the undermentioned goods without production of Bill(s) of Lading due to the non-arrival or loss thereof, we hereby represent and warrant, with the knowledge and intention that such delivery be made in reliance thereon, that we are entitled to delivery of the goods and no other person, firm or corporation is so entitled and that we have full power and authority to make and issue this Letter of Indemnity.

Further, to induce you to deliver the said goods and in consideration thereof, we hereby undertake and agree as follows:

(1) To use our best efforts to locate and produce the said Bill(s) of Lading and thereupon promptly to deliver and surrender the same to you, properly endorsed ; and

(2) To pay you on demand all freight, salvage, general average and/or other charges or expenses whatsoever in respect of the said goods; and

(3) To indemnify and hold you, the vessel, her owners, charterers, operators, master and agents harmless from all demands, claims, liabilities, actions and expenses, including legal expenses and attorneys fees, and consequences of whatever nature which may arise out of or be connected with such delivery ; and

(4) Promptly on your demand, to settle directly by us any claim or to enter our general apperance in any proceedings instituted against you or any party protected by this undertaking in respect of the said goods, whether by a holder of the said Bill(s) of Lading or otherwise and/or to provide you with sufficient funds to defend the same and to meet any proved claims.

Executed this _____ day of _____, 19 _____, at _____

_____
(Name of Consignees)

By _____
(Signature)

_____
(Signer's Name and His Title)

We join in the above guarantee:

_____
(Name of Bankers)

By _____
(Signature)

_____
(Signer's Name and His Title)

Ship ; _____ Voy. _____ B/L No.; _____
Shipper; _____
Port of Loading ; _____ Port of Discharge; _____
Place of Delivery; _____
Consignee ; _____

Marks & Numbers	Number of Packages	Description of Goods

11.9 ARRIVAL NOTIFICATION

Description

An Arrival Notification is a document advising the consignee or agent of the impending arrival of container(s)/consignment(s) and requesting the appropriate documents to be submitted to enable the consignment(s) to be cleared through Customs and subsequently dispatched to the consignee or assignee.

Source of document

A shipowner or agent, e.g. P&O Containers Ltd (previously OCL).

Purpose/use/function

The Arrival Notification gives notice to the consignee or other party (known as the 'notify party'), such as the agent, of the impending arrival of container(s)/consignment(s). It also requires the consignee/agent to submit to the place of Customs clearance, such as seaport/inland clearance depot/inland freight station the original Bill of Lading, the requisite Customs clearance documents, details of delivery arrangements, any freight and other charges, and finally details of any change of ownership of the goods.

Legal context

To avoid rent or demurrage charges, dispatch of the appropriate documents to the specified enquiry office is required at least six days prior to the arrival of the vessel.

Other aspects

This document has an important role inasmuch to ensure the consignee is given prompt notice of the anticipated arrival date of the goods. It enables the consignee to assemble all the requisite Customs clearance documents. This aids prompt clearance of the goods at the terminal and thereby avoids congestion. Details of the ship's arrival is usually transmitted by telex. Information of the consignment/consignee found on the cargo manifest is dispatched by airmail from the previous seaport.

ARRIVAL NOTIFICATION

P&OCL
P&O Containers (UK Agencies) Ltd

FIRST | FOLD BACK

CONSIGNMENT REF. No.

ENQUIRIES TO

VOYAGE NUMBER
VESSEL
EST. ARRIVAL DATE

EXIT PORT
ENTRY PORT
C/BASE
TRADE

BILL OF LADING
PRINCIPAL CARRIER

CONTAINER No./TYPE SERVICE SEAL No.	MARKS AND NUMBERS	NUMBER OF PACKAGES	CARGO DESCRIPTION	WEIGHT KGS.	MSMT CB. MTS.

ADDITIONAL INFORMATION

PLACE OF DELIVERY (AS PER B/LADING)

REPLY INSTRUCTIONS

This is a notice of impending arrival of containers/consignments. According to the Transport Documents issued you are named as the notify party or consignee. To facilitate prompt clearance and delivery and to avoid rent or demurrage charges, it is **IMPORTANT** you act promptly by despatching to the enquiry office shown at least 6 days prior to vessel arrival:-

1. An ORIGINAL BILL OF LADING either blank endorsed or endorsed through to the Party seeking delivery.

2. FREIGHT AND CHARGES (if applicable).

3. Confirmation of DELIVERY requirements.

4. CUSTOMS CLEARANCE DOCUMENTS (If you wish P&OCL(UK) to prepare and lodge customs entries we require at least supplier's invoices, C105, VAT No. Full details can be obtained from above office).

5. Details of any CHANGE of ownership.

NOTES OVERLEAF SHOULD BE READ CAREFULLY.

UK201 1/87

11.10 COLLECTION/DELIVERY NOTE

Description

A Collection/Delivery Note is a dual purpose document used as a collection note for goods for export or a delivery note for imported goods.

Source of document

A freight forwarder, e.g. Lep Transport Ltd.

Purpose/use/function

The Collection/Delivery Note serves:

1 as a collection note complying with the consignor's/shipper's instructions, where goods for export are to be collected at the shipper's premises by the agent/freight forwarder, for consolidation at the inland clearance depot/container base/warehouse/seaport/airport, for subsequent dispatch overseas by air, LCL container or trailer; or

2 as a delivery note complying with the consignee's instructions, where imported cargo after Customs clearance through the inland clearance depot/container base/warehouse/seaport/airport is to be delivered to the consignee's address by the agent or freight forwarder.

Other aspects

This document is widely used in the market where the agent/freight forwarder/haulier arranges to collect the goods or delivers them. The layout of the document varies. The top copy (blue) is retained by the driver; the second copy (green) is held by the shipper/consignee; the third and fourth copies (white) are retained by the haulier for the office file.

INTERNATIONAL FREIGHT FORWARDERS

Lep Transport Limited

117-120 Snargate Street, Dover, Kent CT17 9EB

Telephone: 0304 203186   Telex: 965196

Collection/ Delivery Note

Job Reference:

Haulier:	Vehicle No:	Trailer No:

From: —

To: —

Collection/Delivery Booking in Date and Time:	Consignee's/Shipper's Reference:

	The following goods have been received in good order and condition:

Vehicle/Trailer Arrived
UNSEALED/SEALED NO:

Vehicle/Trailer Departed
UNSEALED/SEALED NO:

Time arrived on site:

Time started
Loading/Unloading:

Time Finished/
Departed:

Special instructions to driver:

Marks	Numbers	Description	Weight	Kg

Delivery is considered effected on tendering the goods on the vehicle at consignee's street door. Consignees asking driver to take goods inside do so at their own risk.

EXTRA CHARGES WILL BE INCURRED AFTER 3 HOURS ON SITE

Signature:

....

Blue sheet = Driver's copy

Green sheet = Shipper's/consignee's copy

White sheet = Office file copy

11.11 DELIVERY/SHIPMENT NOTE BILL

Description

A Delivery/Shipment Note Bill gives details of imported goods that are to be delivered to a consignee/agent by a port authority. It accompanies the goods.

Source of document

A port authority, e.g. Port of Singapore Authority. Also similar document used by haulier/forwarding agent.

Purpose/use/function

The document serves:

1 as a delivery note for imported cargo;
2 where applicable as remittance advice for an account holder to return (the relevant portion) to the port authority with the appropriate payment.

Other aspects

This document in varying layouts is used extensively worldwide. The cargo description must accord with the details found on the Bill of Lading and other shipping/Customs documents. It also features details of the vessel and arrival date. Overall, it is an authority for the goods to leave the port area.

DELIVERY / SHIPMENT NOTE
BILL

STATEMENT UNDER SECTION 106
OF THE PORT OF SINGAPORE AUTHORITY ACT (CAP. 173)

I hereby state that I am authorised to deliver the goods herein and that no goods other than those so stated are loaded on the vehicle(s) stated below.

Cargo Owner ....

Vehicle No. (1) .... (2) .... (3) ....

(4) .... (5) ....

....
Name of person making declaration | NRIC No. | Signature

Released by ....
Signature of Traffic Assistant & Employee No. | Time

FOR PSA POLICE USE	
Signature of I/C	Checker

Cargo Marks & Numbers/Shipper	No. of Packages	Contents
Total		

Godown	Name of Vessel & Voy. No.	Berthing Date & Time	Date & Time Del'd/Bill Date	Delivery Note/Bill No.

Storage Class	Trans. Code	Status Code	M'fested Packages	Manifested Tonnage	Balance to be Del'd as M'fested	Date & Time Completed Discharge*

Reference No.	Description of Charges	Billable Units	Rate	Amount
				$

REMITTANCE ADVICE — Account Holder to tear and return this portion to PSA with payment.

Account No.	Name of Customer	Bill No.	Amount Payable

IF PART PAYMENT, PLEASE INSERT AMOUNT OF PAYMENT HERE $ ....

- Cheques must be crossed to the order of the Port of Singapore Authority and sent to the Treasurer's Dept., P.O. Box 555, Singapore 9011.
- Payment is deemed to be made on the day the cheque is received by the Port of Singapore Authority.
- Interest charge at 1% per month will be levied on any amount outstanding for more than 30 days from Bill Date.

TO AVOID INTEREST FROM BEING INCORRECTLY CHARGED THROUGH UNIDENTIFIED PAYMENT, THIS PORTION MUST ACCOMPANY YOUR PAYMENT

FOR ACCOUNT HOLDERS ONLY

11.12 PACKING LIST

Description

Overall the document provides a list of the contents of a package(s)/consignment(s) and in some trades is termed a packing note.

The document gives details of the invoice, buyer, consignee, country of origin, vessel/flight date, port/airport of loading, port/airport of discharge, place of delivery, shipping marks/container number, weight/volume ('cube') of merchandise, and the fullest details of the goods including packaging information.

Purpose/use/function

The document is provided/completed by the shipper. Its prime purpose is to give an inventory of the goods shipped by all sea containers, or road haulage and is attached to the Bill of Lading, Air Waybill, CMR, CIM consignment notes.

Other aspects

This important document gives a detailed description of the goods and is used extensively. In particular, consignments which are composite and comprise of a number of articles all dispatched as one consignment. The nature of the packaging must be specified and its marks. The document accompanies the Bill of Lading, Air Waybill and is required by Customs for clearance purposes. It accompanies the goods throughout the transit and placed in the container, trailer etc.

ESPECIFICACION DE EMBALAJE
VERSANDLISTE

PACKING LIST

Exporter/Shipper (Name and Address)	UK Customs Reference/ Status		Sheet No.
	Invoice No. and Date (Tax Point)	Exporter's Reference	
	Buyer's Reference	Other Reference(s)	
Consignee	For Official Use		

Marks and Numbers; No. and Kind of Packages; Description of Goods	Quantity	Other details

141 See Principal Sheet for further details of this Consignment

11.13 RELEASE NOTE

Description

A Release Note gives a full description of the cargo, the vessel, container details, and so on.

Source of document

A shipowner, freight forwarder, e.g. P&O Containers Ltd.

Purpose/use/function

The role of the Release Note or receipt is to enable the carrier to have a signed document by the consignee/agent accepting the cargo or container, the contents of which will be discharged by the consignee/agent at the named destination.

Other aspects

This document is a form of receipt to the carrier, container operator etc., relative to the acceptance of the cargo. It must reflect the details of the cargo which must accord with the data on the Bill of Lading. It will give details of the vessel and the arrival date. The layout of the document will vary with shipowner.

RELEASE NOTE

P&O Containers
P&O Containers (UK Agencies) Ltd

RECEIPT (P&OCL(UK) COPY)

CONSIGNMENT REF.

PAGE No.

SPECIAL INSTRUCTIONS/CHARGES TO

2 P&OCL(UK) OFFICE

FOR THE CONSIGNEE TO COMPLETE ▶

	DATE/TIME
NAME CONTACTED	
AT	
DEL./COL. ARRANGED	
RECONFIRMED	
LCL UNPACKED	
RELEASED	

	DATE TIME
ARRIVED	
DEPARTED	
CONTAINER IN BASE	

1 PLACE OF DELIVERY

3 POINT OF DELIVERY (if different from 1)

TEL. No.

VOYAGE	ARRIVAL DATE	
VESSEL	BILL OF LADING	
	EXIT PORT	
	ENTRY PORT	
	TRADE	

CONTR. No., TYPE & SIZE, TYPE OF SVCE. & CELL. POS.	MARKS AND NUMBERS	NUMBER UNPACKED	NUMBER & TYPE OF PACKAGES	CARGO DESCRIPTION	WEIGHT KGS.	MSMT CB. MTS.

All Equipment made temporarily available to Customers, either directly or through the agency of their servants, agents or sub-contractors, is made available subject to the Equipment Handover Agreement terms and conditions of the Carrier, copies of which are available on request from all P&OCL(UK) offices.

HAULIER DETAILS/REMARKS

Release to P&OCL(UK)/CUSTOMER* haulage
*Delete not applicable.

P&OCL(UK) AUTHORISATION

RECEIVED from P&OCL(UK) (in the case of FCL service) the container referred to on this sheet in good condition and sealed with seal no.

OR

(in the case of LCL service) the cargo detailed on this sheet in apparent good order except where stated.

COMPANY STAMP

SIGNED..............................

POSITION..............................

11.14 UNPACKING NOTE

Description

An Unpacking Note gives details of the merchandise unpacked and any cargo damage.

Source of document

A Shipowner, agent, e.g. P&O Containers Ltd (previously OCL).

Purpose/use/function

The role of the Unpacking Note is to give details of the result of unpacking the container on arrival at the destination container base. It is provided for Customs, consignee, agent's information.

Other aspects

The role of this document varies by port but it provides the fullest information on the consignment which has been unpacked/discharged/unloaded from a container. Such a document would prove useful for any subsequent claim on the cargo and to identify responsibility.

P&OCL

P&O Containers (UK Agencies) Ltd

UNPACKING NOTE

CONSIGNMENT REF.		
P&OCL(UK) OFFICE	PAGE No.	

VOYAGE
VESSEL

ARRIVAL DATE
BILL OF LADING

EXIT PORT
ENTRY PORT
TRADE

CONTR. No., SIZE & TYPE, TYPE OF SVCE & CELL. POS.	MARKS AND NUMBERS	NUMBER UNPACKED	NUMBER AND TYPE OF PACKAGES	CARGO DESCRIPTION

DETAILS OF DAMAGES

STORED IN SHED

No. OF PALLET LOADS ....

PALLET LOCATION REFERENCES ....

HAULIER ....

Received, the goods detailed above in apparent good order and condition.

FOR WAREHOUSE COMPANY	No.	FOR CONSIGNEE

VEHICLE No. ....

P&OCL

UNPACKING NOTE

RETURN TO
CONTAINERBASE OPERATIONS

CONSIGNMENT REF.		
	PAGE No.	

VOYAGE
VESSEL

ARRIVAL DATE
BILL OF LADING
EXIT PORT
ENTRY PORT
TRADE

CONTR. No.

IF DISCREPANCY, GIVE DETAILS

WEIGHT KGS.	MSMT. CB. MTS.

UNPACKED DATE ....

FOR CONTAINERBASE
(IF DISCREPANCY)

SUPERVISOR ....

SPECIAL INSTRUCTIONS

UNPACKED DATE ....

FOR CONTAINERBASE ....

UK 123 (1 87)

12 Data folders for processing the export/import consignment

To lessen the errors implicit in processing the export/import consignment folders have been devised which set out the various stages involved in the process so that the person undertaking each requisite task can sign or initial the entry on completion.

Four kinds of folder are shown, all self-explanatory in function. Supplies are available from Formecon Services Ltd, Douglas House, Gateway, Crew, CW1 1YW.

1 Export Data Folder (ref FS4). It is very comprehensive in detail and has an insert – not featured in the specimen – on Letters of Credit guidelines; export terms, shipping abbreviations, country information and Customs data.
2 Export Data Folder (ref FS5). Less comprehensive than FS4 but containing an identical insert.
3 Import Data Folder. Again, very comprehensive in detail and containing a similar insert. Very useful for monitoring progress of the import order and thereby lessening the risk of any delays.
4 Forwarding Operations Control Folder. Ideal for use by the freight forwarder.

Other aspects of Data Folders for processing the export/import consignment

The use of these folders has tended to increase and in so doing it aids the management to execute the international trade contracts. Each constituent progress can be carefully monitored and thereby lessen the risk of any short-coming.

Each contract is given a folder and accredited number. It is retained in a central file in the export/import office and is often linked to a computerized system. Various members of the export/import office staff will use the folder relative to their responsibility of execution of the contract. The folders are used by exporter/importer/freight forwarder/international road hauliers.

EXPORT

FORMECON
DATA FOLDER

CONTACTS	BUYER	CONSIGNEE	FORWARDER	Vehicle Bkg. Ref.				Tariff Heading
Person					CAN			
Telephone				Invoice No. and Date			Exporter's Reference	
Telex				Buyer's Reference			F/Agent's Ref.	S.S. Co. Bkg. No.
Cable								

Consignee (If 'ORDER' State Notify Party and Address)	Buyer (If not consignee)		
	Name of Shipping/Air Line		Port Account No.
Forwarding Agent	Coding for H.M. Customs	Destination ICD	Container	Ro Ro (a) (b)	Flag	Port
	Country of Origin of Goods	Country of Final Destination	

Receiving Date(s)	Dock Container Base Etc.	Terms of Delivery (see INCOTERMS)	
Pre-Carriage By	Place of Receipt by Pre-Carrier		
		PAYMENT TERMS	
Vessel/Aircraft Etc.	Port of Loading	INSURANCE. SELLER/BUYER	Letter of Credit No.
Port of Discharge	Place of Delivery by On-Carrier	Insured Value (State currency)	Name of Receiving Authority

Marks, Nos. and Container No.	ORDER FOR/DESCRIPTION OF GOODS (specify nature of hazard if any)	QUANTITY	PRICE	TOTAL VALUE (State currency)

Customs Free Status	Special	AGI/ATRI/CT	AGI/ATRI/CT	TOTAL INVOICE
Customs Pre-Entry	Stowage	Form type .... lodged-Customs No .... attached to C273	form not required	ORDER VALUE
Customs Office		Telephone No	See back cover for packing details	Total Net Wt (kgs)	Total Gross Wt. (Kgs)	Total Cube (M3)

E. C.	COVER REQUIRED FOR THIS ORDER	ACKNOWLEDGEMENT OF ORDER. Date sent (note amendments)	
G.	VALUE OUTSTANDING FROM PREVIOUS SALES	DELIVERY REQUIRED BY	
D.	TOTAL COVER REQUIRED	LATEST DATE FOR DESPATCH	

See H.M.C. & E. Notice 276 FOB Statistics	Cost of freight	Ocean Freight Payable at	Signatory's Company and Telephone Number
	Cost of Insurance	Number of Bills of Lading	Name of Authorised Signatory
	FOB Value	.... Original .... Copy	
FREE DISPOSAL			

REVIEW THIS FOLDER <u>REGULARLY</u> UNTIL ORDER COMPLETE

ACTION

CHECK CURRENT REGULATIONS FOR EXPORTING TO COUNTRY OF DESTINATION
COMPLETE FIRST SECTION ON DOCUMENTS REQUIRED FOR EXPORTATION AND PAYMENT

Enter number req'd							
Commercial Invoices		Consignment Notes		Customs C273........................	
Certified Invoices		Shipping Instructions...................		Bank Doc. Collection Form............	
Consular Invoices		National Std. Shipping Notes		Bills of Exchange	
Certificate of Origin		Packing Notes		....	
Certificate of Value		Health Certificate		....	
Bill of Lading/A.W.B.		Movement Certs/T. Forms		....	
Certificate of Shipment		Insurance Certificates			

1 SEE FRONT COVER FOR PAYMENT TERMS

2 If letter of Credit being used
a) Does L/C agree with our requirements....... YES/NO (delete)
b) If not quickly notify Buyer requiring him to modify L/C from his
end. Request sent...
Modified Letter of Credit received on...

3 If L/C not in use, check order against antecedent negotiations or
current terms of trading....................... If not OK, quickly acquaint
foreign importer and ask him to reply accepting modified terms.
Requested on......................... Replied on.........................
CREDIT WORTHINESS APPROVED BY......................... Signed

4 EXPORT LICENCE. Is a licence required? YES/NO (delete)
If YES details of application.........................
Licence issued.........................

5 Foreign Regulations. Write here any special requirements
....
....
Import Licence No......................... Expiry Date.........................

6 Issue Works Order or Buying Requisition as required.
See front cover for latest despatch date and
chase progress on................................. again on ....
Notify Customer of any delay if necessary check if this affects Licence
or L/C expiry dates (see also 9)

7 Acknowledge Order (complete box on front cover)

8 Is Freight Forwarder being used? YES/NO (see front cover)

9 If L/C being used note any special requirements here
a) Date of Shipment by..................... b) Documents (see panel above)
c) Is Buyer insuring? If so we must advise him of named ship etc.
in good time.........................
d) Is import inspection scheme or other inspection required?
If so advise in good time.........................
e) Date of expiry of L/C......................... (Shipment must
be earlier if documents are to be presented in time)

10 Obtain Packing Note details (complete back cover)

11 If Freight Forwarder being used, instruct fully
a) Instructed on.........................
b) Copy of L/C sent (if applicable).........................
c) If UK Buying House or Agent has placed the order apply to them
for forwarding instructions, documentation requirements etc
Applied on.........................

12 If Freight Forwarder not being used
a) Book space with Shipping/Air Line ....
b) Ascertain loading details.........................
c) Ascertain E.T.D and E.T.A......................... /
d) Foreign Importer notified of E.T.A ....
e) Check packing details and ensure packing is appropriate and/or
conforms with L/C.........................
f) Check type of stowage.........................
g) If hazardous cargo — double check document requirements and
precaution measures.........................

13 Marine Insurance (see front cover for value)
a) Declare against open policy, if applicable.........................
b) If not, arrange cover through Broker.........................
c) Check Lloyds authorised to settle claims at destination
d) Declare shipment to ECGD if applicable (see front cover)

14 Prepare SITPRO Master Document if appropriate from details on
front cover, check for accuracy in every detail
Assemble documents required for duplication
All documents checked on............................ by.........................
Total number of documents prepared.........................
Check that print quality is adequate on EVERY copy

15 External Validation
Invoice/Cert. of Origin to Cham. of Comm. Date sent.........................
Cost......................... Date returned.........................
Invoices to Consulate (if app) Date sent.........................
Cost......................... Date returned.........................

16 Presentation to Bank — Letter of Credit
a) Ensure Bill of Lading or A.W.B. received in good time
b) Ensure clean Bill of Findings rec'd if import inspection scheme app.
c) Assemble documents exactly in accordance with L/C
d) Present to Bank in good time and in perfect order
Date documents presented .... post/hand
Date payment received ....(see Summary)

17 Presentation to Bank — Docs. against Payment or Acceptance
a) Prepare documents in perfect order
b) Prepare sight draft or term draft for payment or acceptance to
correct value
c) Present to Bank with instructions for collection
Date documents presented... post/hand
Date payment received... or date the
accepted term draft received.........................
Term draft discounted on.........................
Discount House.........................

18 Open Account dealings
a) Send documents to Buyer — date sent.........................
b) If policy, second set sent abroad on.........................
c) Send Bank promissory note to cover loan for value if arranged
against ECGD cover

19 Write or telex Customer advising successful completion — opportunity
to invite further business

20 Final Report. Notes for next time — record here any problems
encountered with this order

CHECK THAT ALL DOCUMENTS ARE ENCLOSED —
COMPLETE SUMMARY ON POCKET FLAP — THEN
RELEASE THIS EXPORT DATA FOLDER FOR FILING

ENCLOSE

Cross each box as document inserted in folder pocket

☐	COSTING RECORD(S)	☐	CERT OF ORIGIN
☐	SALES QUOTE(S)	☐	INSURANCE CERT.
☐	BUYERS ORDER	☐	CUSTOMS C 273
☐	OUR ACCEPTANCE	☐	SHIPPING INSTRUCTIONS
☐	WORKS ORDER	☐	CONSIGNMENT NOTE
☐	PACKING NOTE	☐	BILL OF LADING/AWB
☐	COMMERCIAL INVOICE	☐	CERT OF SHIPMENT
☐	CERTIFIED INVOICE	☐	HEALTH CERTS.
☐	CONSULAR INVOICE	☐	BILL(S) OF EXCHANGE
☐	NAT. STD. SHIPPING NOTE		
☐			
☐			
☐			
☐			
☐			

SUMMARY

Sales and Accounts

ORDER RECEIVED	: : 19
FINAL DESPATCH	: : 19
INVOICE NUMBER(S)	
PAYMENT CLEARED	: : 19

FORMECON SERVICES LTD.
GATEWAY · CREWE · CW1 1YN

Publishers and Suppliers of

1   EXPORT INVOICE $\left(\begin{smallmatrix}\text{Origin}\\\text{Value}\end{smallmatrix}\right)$ FORMS

When ordering please state
*   Form reference number
*   Country for which forms are required
*   Type of paper required
    a) Spirit duplicator two sided
    b) Spirit duplicator one sided
    c) Blue airmail two sided

2   BILLS OF EXCHANGE (Foreign & Inland)
3   HOME MARKET DATA FOLDERS
4   IMPORT DATA FOLDERS
5   EMPLOYEE DATA FOLDERS
6   JOB APPLICATION FORMS etc

TELEPHONE (0270) 587811   TELEX 36550 Eurofs G

PACKING NOTE DETAILS

No's	KIND OF PACKAGES	CONTENTS	NET WT (KGS)	GROSS WT (KGS)	DIMENSIONS (M)			CUBE (M3)
					LENGTH	WIDTH	HEIGHT	
		TOTALS					TOTALS	

(MODIFICATION TO THIS FOLDER MAY BE NECESSARY FOR INDIVIDUAL REQUIREMENTS)

RECORD OF PART SHIPMENT

PACKAGE No's	QUANTITY AND GOODS CONTENT	DESPATCH DATE	PARTICULARS OF CARRIER	ETA

FS.4 FORMECON SERVICES LTD GATEWAY CREWE CW1 1YN Tel (0270) 587811 Telex 36550 © COPYRIGHT

Ref. No.

EXPORT DATA FOLDER

Customer / Buyer - Invoice Address

....
....
....
....

Consignee / Delivery Address (if different from above)

....
....
....

Freight Forwarder

....
....
....

Contact Name	
Tel. No.	Telex No.
Fax No.	Cable
Customer Order No.	Date / /19
Payment Terms	
Letter of Credit No.	Expiry / /19
Contact Name	
Tel. No.	Telex No.
Fax No.	Cable
Date delivery required at destination	/ /19
Latest despatch date ex. warehouse/factory	/ /19
Load at	Unload at
Contact Name	
Tel. No.	Telex No.
Fax No.	ECI
Insurance Value	Cover by
Carrier(s) details	
Terms of Delivery	Incoterms see insert

PACKAGES AND DESCRIPTION OF GOODS	Commodity Code	QUANTITY	UNIT PRICE State Currency	AMOUNT
			TOTAL AMOUNT	

Total Net Wt. (kg)		Total Gross Wt. (kg)		Total Cube (m³)		Total No. of Packages		FOB Value £

			Shipping marks, container/trailer No.	Acknowledgement of Order date / /19	Method of order acknowledgement	Verbal / Written / Telex / Fax
E C G D	Cover required for this shipment	£				
	Value Outstanding from previous sales	£		Remarks		
	Total Cover Required	£		....		

DOCUMENTATION CHECKLIST

List all documents required	Enter Ref. No./Description (number copies required)	Document to be completed by (tick column)		
		Exporter	Freight Forwarder	Other (state)

Form Pdq

EXPORT SOFTWARE

Complete export/shipping documents by computer – accurate and speedy form filling

Telephone 0270-500800 for details/demo disk

ENCLOSURES

Retain all documents relevant to this shipment,
enter each document name when filed in this pocket

ACCOUNTING SUMMARY

	£	p
SALES – AMOUNT PAID INTO BANK A/c		
TOTAL COSTS, CHARGES (see below)		

ANALYSIS OF COSTS & CHARGES

Date, name, details	£	p
TOTAL COSTS, CHARGES		

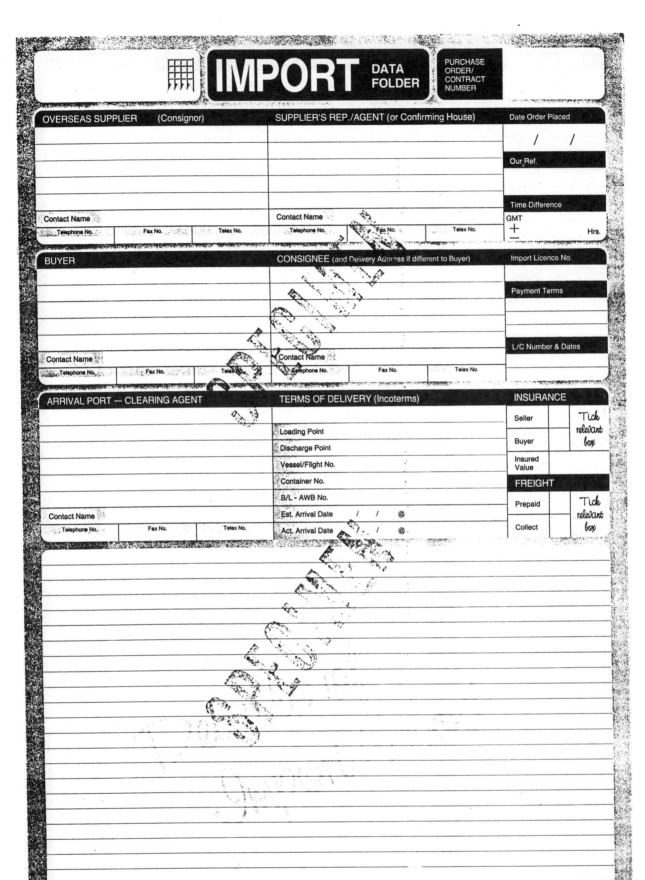

	NOTES	
Date	Record of all actions taken, telephone conversations, etc.	

ENCLOSURES

Retain all relevant documents in Data Folder Note inclusion thus	✓
Supplier's Quotation	
Costing Record	
Official Order to Supplier (Copy)	
Letter of Credit (Details)	
Import Licence (Details)	
Supplier's Order Acknowledgement	
Supplier's Despatch Advice	
Instructions to Import Clearing Agent	
Supplier's Invoice (Copy)	
Bill of Lading / AWB (duplicate)	
Insurance Certificate	
Health Certificate	
Preferential Certificate	
Supplier's Certificate of Origin	
Supplier's Packing Spec. Note	

RECORD OF ORDER COMPRISING MORE THAN ONE IMPORTATION

Number and Contents of Packages	Date	Mode (Name / Number)	Place and Date	Date

DISTRIBUTION / RESALE OF CONSIGNMENT

Date	Delivered to	Item Ref.	Quantity	Price	Balance of Item Remaining	Remarks

RECORD OF CLAIMS

Date	Description of Item(s) Claimed for	Quantity	Value of Claim	Reason for Claim

Insurance Company	U.K. Agents	Appointed Surveyors
Contact Name	Contact Name	Contact Name
Tel. Number	Tel. Number	Tel. Number

FORWARDING OPERATIONS
CONTROL FOLDER

Job Ref. No.	Forwarder's Office of Issue

EXPORTER	FIRST AGENT	E C I	
		Exporter's Ref.	
		F/Agents Ref.	

CONSIGNEE	TRANSIT AGENT	Date (Tax Point)		SS Co. Bkng. No.
		Container	T o T Flag Port	

NOTIFY	FINAL AGENT	
		Country of Final Destination

				Special Instructions
Date of Departure		Dock, Wharf Station etc.		
Unit No.		From Local Port of Loading		
Vessel, Ferry Aircraft, etc.		Port of Loading		
Port of Discharge		Place of Final Delivery		

Marks & Numbers	No. & Kind of Packages	Description of Goods	Tariff/Trade Code No.	Gross Weight (Kg)	Cube (m³)

			Quantity	Net Weight (Kg)	FOB Value (£)

INSURANCE	Value		Currency	Cover Arranged

L/C Shipment Expiry Date		L/C Expiry Date for Presentation/Negotiation	
Letter of Credit Number		Export/Import Licence No.	
Collect From		Deliver To	

CUSTOMS DOCUMENTS REQUIRED	Tick/Complete Relevant Box	C273	MOVEMENT CERT.	
			Type:	
		Pre-Entry	No:	

Invoice To: (if not Exporter)	Freight Payable at	
	No. of Original Bills	

OUTLAYS (excluding VAT)		EXPORT CONSIGNMENT		CHARGES TO BE RENDERED		E/O/S
£	p	Item	ANALYSIS OF CHARGES	£	p	VAT
		1	FOB Ancillaries			
		2	Fixed Consolidation Charge			
		3	Inland Carriage/Haulage			
		4	Terminal handling/Wharfage/Dock Dues			
		5	Customs Entry			
		6	Additional Tariff Heading			
		7	Customs presentation and attendance			
		8	Documentation (inclusive B/L etc.)			
		9	Consular Fees			
		10	Preparation and presentation C/O's — Consular Invoices			
		11	Preparation and presentation of EEC Documentation			
		12	Packing			
		13	Postage, petties, telex, telephone			
		14	Service/Agency Fee			
		15	Freight			
		16	Insurance — Value £ @ £ : % = £ + Policy £			
		17				
		18				
		19				
		20				
			Sub TOTAL			
				Sub TOTAL		

DEDUCT TOTAL OF CREDIT NOTES RECEIVED		C/N		P & L Summary	£	p	C/N		DEDUCT TOTAL OF CREDIT NOTES ISSUED	
		C/N					C/N			
		C/N		TOTAL CHARGE			C/N			
				TOTAL OUTLAY						
£		TOTAL OUTLAY (exc. VAT)		PROFIT/LOSS			TOTAL CHARGE £			(exc. VAT)

ANALYSIS OF CHARGES TO BE INVOICED (see items 1-20 above)						E/O/S
INVOICE TO		Item	INVOICE DESCRIPTION	£	p	VAT
				£		
Invoice No:			Total of charges vatable @ 'S' rate £ VAT %			
Date:				TOTAL £		
				£		
Invoice No:			Total of charges vatable @ 'S' rate £ VAT %			
Date:				TOTAL £		
				£		
Invoice No:			Total of charges vatable @ 'S' rate £ VAT %			
Date:				TOTAL £		

ENCLOSURES	
Retain all relevant documents in the Data Folder. Note inclusion thus	✓
Bill of Lading/Air Waybill	
Copy Bill of Lading	
Certificate of Shipment	
Commercial Invoice*	
Certified Invoice*	
Consular Invoice	
Insurance Certificates	
Certificates of Origin*	
Standard Shipping Note*	
Customs Entry Certificate	
Shipping Instructions	
Consignment Note	
Certificate of Posting*	
Health Certificates	
Movement Certificate / T. Form	
Freight Account	
Analysis of Charges	
F O B Account	
Final Account	
Supplementary Account	

NOTES

*These forms are available from the publishers of this DATA FOLDER

FORMECON SERVICES LIMITED
Douglas House, Gateway,
Crewe, CW1 1YN. England
Telephone Crewe (0270) 587811   Telex: 36550 Eurofs G

FORMECON

DETAILS OF CONTACTS

Representing	Company	Name of Person	Tel. No.	Telex	
Client					
Consignee					
Shipping / Air Line					
Haulier					
Packers					
Others					

TELEPHONE CONVERSATIONS

Date	Time	Person Spoken To	Summary of Conversation

DISPOSAL OF DOCUMENTS

Enter dates in relevant boxes	Shipper	Consignee	Agent	Bank	Customs Export Entry
Original B/L					Form Type
Copy B/L					
C I M / C M R					Customs Office
Air Waybill					
Insurance Cert.					Date Sent / Date Returned
Consular Invoice					
Cert. of Origin					H. M. Customs
Cert. of Shipment					Entry No.
Movement Cert.					
Invoice					Date

LODGING OF DOCUMENTS

Type	Location	Date

Appendix A

Further recommended textbook reading

Branch, A. E. (1989) *Elements of Shipping*. 6th edn. Chapman and Hall, London.

Branch, A. E. (1990) *Elements of Export Marketing and Management*. 2nd edn. Chapman and Hall, London.

Branch, A. E. (1987) *Dictionary of Shipping/International Trade Terms and Abbreviations*. (7000 entries). 3rd edn. Witherby and Co. Ltd., London.

Branch, A. E. (1984) *Dictionary of Commercial Terms and Abbreviations* (6000 entries). 1st edn. Witherby and Co. Ltd., London.

Branch, A. E. (1989) *Multi-lingual Dictionary of Commercial International Trade and Shipping Terms in English/French/Spanish/German* (10 000 entries). 1st edn. Witherby and Co. Ltd., London.

Branch, A. E. (1988) *Dictionary of English-Arabic Commercial, International Trade and Shipping Terms* (2200 terms). 1st edn. Witherby and Co. Ltd., London.

Branch, A. E. (1988) *Economics of Shipping Practice and Management*. 2nd edn. Chapman and Hall, London.

Branch, A. E. (1986) *Elements of Port Operation and Management*. 1st edn. Chapman and Hall, London.

Schmitthoff, C. M. (1980) *The Export Trade*. 8th edn. Sweet and Maxwell, London.

Watson, A. (1985) *Finance of International Trade*. 3rd edn. Institute of Bankers, London.

Appendix B

International trade and shipping terms and abbreviations

AAA — Association of Average Adjusters.

A/C — Account current.

Accepting House — Financial house, often a merchant banker, specializing in financing foreign trade.

Act of God — Any fortuitous act which could not have been prevented by any amount of human care and forethought.

ADR — European agreement on the international carriage of dangerous goods by road.

Ad valorem freight — Freight rate based on percentage value of goods shipped.

Affreightment — A contract for the carriage of goods by sea for shipment expressed in charter party or bill of lading.

Agent — One who represents a principal, or buys or sells for another.

Air waybill — Air freight consignment note.

Aligned Export Documentation System — Method whereby as much information as possible is entered in a 'master document' so that all or part of this information can be reproduced into individual forms of a similar design.

AMT — Air mail transfer – a remittance purchased by the debtor from his banker in international trade.

Arbitration — Method of settling disputes which is usually binding on the parties concerned.

ASP — American selling price. A Customs term for the retail price of a product in the USA.

ATA carnet — International Customs document to cover the temporary export of certain goods (commercial samples and exhibits for international trade fairs abroad and professional equipment) to countries which are parties to the ATA convention. Also covers the re-importation of such goods.

Average bond — Bond in which cargo owners agree to pay their share in the general average losses, each contribution being determined by the average adjuster.

Average deposit — Cash security deposited by the consignee pending

	assessment of general average contribution.
Back freight	Freight (additional) incurred through cargo being returned from destination port, usually because its acceptance was refused.
Balance of trade	Financial statement of balance of a country's visible trade export and imports.
Bilateralism	Trade between two countries.
Bill of exchange	Written request from a creditor to a debtor ordering the debtor to pay a specified sum to a specified person or bearer at a certain date.
Bill of lading	Receipt for goods shipped on board a ship signed by the person (or his agent) who contracts to carry them, and stating the terms on which the goods are carried.
Bill of sight	Customs import form, used when importer cannot make Customs entry complete owing to insufficient information from the shipper.
Bond	Guarantee to Customs of specified amount of duty to be paid.
BOTB	British Overseas Trade Board.
B/P	Bills payable.
Broken stowage	Space wasted in a ship's hold or container by stowage of uneven cargo, that is, irregularly shaped consignments.
Bulk licence	Licence issued to manufacturers and exporters to cover their requirements for certain bulk quantity or period.
Bulk unitization	Means to consolidate multiple packages or items into a single-load-device.
CAD	Cash against documents.
Cargo manifest	Inventory of cargo shipped.
Carr fwd	Carriage forward.
CAP	Common Agricultural Policy.
CB	Container base.
CCC	Customs clearance certificate or Customs Co-operation Council.
CCLN	Consignment note control label number.
C & D	Collected and delivered.
C & F	Cost and freight.
CENSA	Council of European and Japanese National Shipowners' Association.
CI	Consular invoice.
CIF	Cost, insurance and freight.
CIFCI	Cost, insurance, freight, commission and interest.
Clean bill of lading	A bill of lading which has no superimposed clause(s) expressly declaring a defective condition of the packaging or goods.
Closing date	Latest date cargo accepted for shipment by (liner) shipowner for specified sailing.
C/N	Consignment note.
C/O	Certificate of origin or cash with order.
COI	Central Office of Information.
Collectors Office	Customs accommodation where declaration(s) (entries) are scrutinized and amounts payable collected.
Conference	Organization whereby number of shipowners often of different nationality offer their services on a given sea route on conditions agreed by members.

Consignee	Name of agent, company or person receiving consignment.
Consignor	Name of agent, company or person sending consignment (the shipper).
Consul	Commercial representative of one country residing officially in another whose duties are to facilitate business and represent the merchants of his nation.
C/P	Charter party.
CTL	Constructive total loss.
Customs clearance	Process of clearing import/export cargo through Customs examination.
D/A	Deposit account.
DDA	Duty (Customs) deferment account.
Dead freight	Space booked by shipper or charterer on a vessel but not used.
Deferred rebate	System whereby shippers are granted a rebate on freight for consistent exclusive patronage over a given period.
Del credere	Agent/broker guarantee to principal for solvency of person to whom he sells goods.
Dis	Discount.
Discount market	Process of selling and buying bills of exchange and Treasury bills and providing a market for short-bonds.
D/N	Debit note.
D/O	Delivery order.
D/P	Documents against payment.
Dunnage	Wood, mats, etc. used to facilitate stowage of cargo.
Dutiable cargo	Cargo which attracts some form of duty, that is, Customs and Excise, or VAT.
D.W.T.	Dead-weight tonnage.
EC	European Community.
ECGD	Export Credits Guarantee Department.
Exchange rate	Price of one currency in terms of another.
Export house	An export merchant responsible for buying goods outright and selling them on their own account; acting as an export department or agent on behalf of a client; or acting for an overseas buyer.
Exporters acceptance credit	Credit opened by an exporter with his own bank which entitles the exporter to draw bills on his own banker.
Ex-quay	Buyer responsible for charges after delivery on quay at bill of lading specified destination – seller pays landing charges.
Ex-ship	Seller pays freight to port of discharge and the buyer landing and other charges.
Ex-works	A cargo delivery term whereby the seller (exporter) undertakes to make the goods available at the specified premises i.e. factory, warehouse. The buyer (importer) bears the full cost and risk of the goods from the point of acceptance at the specified premises until they reach their destination thereby particularly embracing insurance and freight charges.
Factoring	Company which administers the sales ledger and collects payments on behalf of an exporter once the goods have been shipped.
FAK	Freight all kinds. Term used to show that the freight

	rate charged is not based on the individual commodity but freight of all kinds.
FAS	Free alongside ship.
FCL	Full container load.
FIO	Free in and out. – Cargo is loaded and discharged at no cost to the shipowner.
FIO & stowed	Free in and out. – Cargo is loaded as a charge to the shipper including stowage, and discharging expense borne by the receiver.
FIW	Free into wagon.
Fixture	Conclusion of shipbroker's negotiations to charter a ship.
Floating exchange rates	Currency rate which varies according to world trade distortions and not subject to exchange control
Floating policy	Cargo policy which underwrites series of consignments declared.
FOB	Free on board.
FOR	Free on rail.
Forwarders bill of lading	A bill of lading issued by a freight forwarder.
Forwarders certificate of shipment	A document issued by a freight forwarder certifying that the goods have been shipped on a named vessel or service.
Forwarders delivery order	A document issued by a freight forwarder authorizing the entitled party to deliver the goods to a party other than the consignee shown on the consignment note.
Forwarders receipt	A document issued by a freight forwarder which provides evidence of receipt of the goods.
FOT	Free on truck (rail) – exporter meets all charges until cargo placed on truck from which point importer bears all cost.
FPA	Free of particular average – insurers not responsible for partial loss claims with certain exceptions.
Franco pour (French)	Sender undertakes to pay fixed amount in carriage charges.
G/A	General average.
GIFT	Glasgow International Freight Terminal.
GSP	Generalized system of preferences.
GV	Grande vitesse – fast rail merchandise service.
Heterogeneous cargo	Variety of cargoes.
High stowage factor	Cargo which has a high bulk to low weight relationship, i.e. hay.
IATA	International Air Transport Association.
IBAP	Intervention Board Agricultural Produce.
ICAO	International Civil Aviation Organization.
ICB	International Container Bureau.
ICD	Inland clearance depot.
IMO	International Maritime Organization.
Indemnity	Compensation for loss/damage or injury.
Individual licence	Licence issued for one particular import/export consignment.
Inherent vice	A defect of inherent quality of the goods or their packing which of itself may contribute to their deterioration, injury, wastage and final destruction, without any

	negligence or other contributing causes.
Inland clearance depot	Customs cargo clearance depot.
Invisible exports	Income from exports embracing tourism, net shipping and air receipts, foreign investments, banking and insurance.
IRU	International Road Transport Union. Based in Geneva, its role is to develop national and international transport.
ISO	International Standards Organization.
Jus disponendi (Latin)	Law of disposal.
LASH	Lighter aboard ship.
Letter of hypothecation	Banker's document outlining conditions under which international transactions will be executed on exporter's behalf, the latter having given certain pledges to his banker.
Letter of indemnity	A document indemnifying the shipowner or agent from any consequences, risk or claims which may arise through 'clean' bills of lading being irregularly issued.
LIFT	London International Freight Terminal.
LNG	Liquified natural gas – type of vessel.
Loading broker	Person who acts on behalf of liner company at a port.
Low stowage factor	Cargo which has low bulk to high weight relationship. i.e. steel rails.
Lump sum freight	Remuneration paid to shipowner for charter of a ship, or portion of it, irrespective of quantity of cargo loaded.
Market rate	Rate charged by brokers, discount houses, joint stock banks and other market members for discounting first-class bills.
Mate's receipt	Document issued to the shipper for ship's cargo loaded from lighterage and later exchanged for bill of lading.
MCD	Miscellaneous cash deposit.
M'dise	Merchandise.
MIFT	Manchester International Freight Terminal.
MT	Mail transfer – a remittance purchased by the debtor from his banker in international trade.
Negotiable bill of lading	One capable of being negotiated by transfer or endorsement.
NSSN	National Standard Shipping Note.
OBO	Oil bulk ore carriers – multi-purpose bulk carriers.
O/C	Overcharge.
OECD	Organization for European Co-operation and Development.
Open cover	A cargo insurance agreement covering all shipments of the assured for a period of time, subject to a cancellation clause and a limit to the amount insured in any one ship. Other conditions include a classification clause.
Overvalued currency	Currency whose rate of exchange is persistently below the parity rate.
Per pro	On behalf of.
PIRA	Research Association for the Paper and Board, Printing and Packaging Industries.
P/L	Partial loss.
Pre-entered	Process of lodging with Customs appropriate

	documentation for scrutiny prior to cargo Customs clearance and shipment.
Rebate	An allowance made as discount on an account/rate.
Receiving date	Date from which cargo is accepted for shipment for specified sailing.
RHA	Road Haulage Association.
Ro/Ro	Roll-on/roll-off – a vehicular ferry service.
Shipping invoice	Document giving details of merchandise shipped.
Shut out	Cargo refused shipment because it arrived after closing date.
Sine die (Latin)	Indefinitely – without a day being appointed.
Stale bill of lading	In banking practice, a bill of lading presented so late that consignee could be involved in difficulties.
Subrogation	Process of substituting one person for another in marine insurance matters in which the latter inherits the former's rights and liabilities.
TAN	Transit advice note.
TCM	Draft convention on combined transport.
THE	Technical Help to Exporters – service of the British Standards Institution.
TIR	Transport International Routier. Bond conditions under which containerized/vehicular merchandise is conveyed internationally under the convention.
T/L	Total loss.
Tramp	Vessel engaged in bulk cargo or time chartering business, i.e. not a liner vessel.
Transferable credit	One which may be transferred by the first beneficiary.
Transhipment entry	Customs entry for cargo imported for immediate re-exportation.
TT	Telegraphic transfer. A remittance purchased by the debtor from his banker in international trade.
ULCC	Ultra large crude carrier.
ULD	Unit load device.
Undervalued currency	Currency whose rate of exchange is persistently above the parity.
Unit loads	Containerized or palletized traffic.
VLCC	Very large crude carrier.
WA	With average.
Warranty	An implied condition, express guarantee or negotiation contained in marine insurance policy.
WPA	With particular average.

NB: Readers are also recommended to study the *Dictionary of Shipping/International Trade Terms and Abbreviations*, 3rd edn. 1987 (9000 entries) (see Appendix A).